By Us! For Us!

Activism in Jane-Finch
A Working-Class Community

by Wanda MacNevin

Chapter Ten contributed by Dr. Sam Tecle

 FriesenPress

One Printers Way
Altona, MB, R0G 0B0
Canada

www.friesenpress.com

Copyright © 2022 by Wanda MacNevin
First Edition — 2022

Additional Contributors
Honourable Dr. Jean Augustine
Sam Tecle, PhD

ISBN
978-1-03-912172-0 (Hardcover)
978-1-03-912171-3 (Paperback)
978-1-03-912173-7 (eBook)

1. SOCIAL SCIENCE

Distributed to the trade by The Ingram Book Company

"The book by Wanda MacNevin *(By Us! For Us!)* is a strongly written social history of the development and growth of the Jane-Finch community. In essence, she has a profound understanding of the impact of social development. The story needs to be told."

—Ato Seitu, Activist and Professional Artist

"MacNevin filters her findings through her own sixty-year experience of living and working in the area and creates a huge contribution to understanding the community. She has produced a chronological text, expansive and dense in detail, that informs readers about the mis-design of the community, which fosters serious problems. Most importantly, she documents the tireless and resilient community reactions that spun bureaucratic straw into neighbourhood gold. She does this so that others can learn from it. MacNevin's book shines a light on these efforts that are most overlooked, neglected, and unrecognized in many political circles, the media, and the wider Toronto community."

—B. J. Richmond PhD, University of Toronto

"This book is a wonderful, well-researched history of the challenges and achievements of the people of the Jane-Finch community told by one of its most recognized members. Wanda MacNevin draws on her own long personal and professional history and her extensive interviews of the Jane-Finch leaders and allies to document the hard work and persistence of the community in the face of constant obstruction by every level of government. It is a story of inspiration and hope and should be required reading for all students at neighbouring York University, particularly those in urban planning, politics, geography, and social work."

—Susan McGrath C. M., York University

"The Jane-Finch book gives a comprehensive history of the area, from its being home to various indigenous peoples, to early European settler-farmers, to the current multi-racial population. It documents through stories the determination, creativity, and expertise of residents who created community-based organizations and tapped into nearby resources such as York University to respond to local needs, despite the unwarranted negative picture of the neighbourhood depicted in public media. It highlights the importance of social partnerships, including faith communities, in creating a new future for residents. The book is a testimony to hope in what is usually depicted as a hopeless situation."

—The Honourable Lois M. Wilson, O.C., O. ONT

TABLE OF CONTENTS

Foreword   7

Preface   11

Introduction   15

CHAPTER ONE   19

   Peoples of the First Nations

CHAPTER TWO   29

   European Settlement in Upper Canada

CHAPTER THREE   47

   Creation of an Inner City
   in a Suburban Environment

CHAPTER FOUR   69

   Critical Decade of Growth

CHAPTER FIVE   137

   Community Response and Action

CHAPTER SIX   219

   Struggling Against Austerity

CHAPTER SEVEN   265

   Another Decade of
   Political and Social Action

CHAPTER EIGHT   341

   The Struggle Continues

CHAPTER NINE   377

   The State of the Community

CHAPTER TEN   393

    How Anti-Black Racism
    Underdeveloped Jane-Finch

Acknowledgements   411

Appendix A   415

    Black Creek Living History
    Project (BCLHP) Interviews

Appendix B   417

    Demographics

Appendix C   419

References   421

About the author   437

Dedication

By Us! For Us! is dedicated to the courageous and spirited women of Jane-Finch. Women who struggled tirelessly. Women who supported residents as local community agency staff. Women who volunteered on committees and boards of directors. Women who refused to accept government neglect and built community organizations that were needed. Women who fought private developers. Women who challenged school systems. Women who worked diligently to raise their children, while always striving for the best for their community.

The net proceeds of this book will go to the
Jane Finch Community Hub and Centre for the Arts.

FOREWORD

There is no community in Canada that is more researched, analyzed, and policed, or that has received more media attention and reporting than the Jane-Finch neighbourhood.

Sociologists, planners, and social scientists have all cited the community in their work.

When I was appointed as vice-principal of an elementary school in the area, I had the sympathy of colleagues and friends who were concerned for my safety and wondered whether this was a demotion. Jane-Finch's reputation as an area of high-rise buildings, compact living, scant green spaces, little recreational facilities, high incidence of crime, and daily news appearances were all they knew from their vantage point.

I had friends and colleagues who lived and worked in the community and therefore knew differently. I knew that the reputation of the community discounted the resilient, hardworking families who lived in public housing and loved and cared for their children. Parents worked away from the community, and because of the poor transportation links, spent hours waiting for crowded buses to and from work. They started the day early and returned home late, complicating the need for childcare and dependence on the school to meet the needs.

The children were aware of the reputation of their community and the diverse multicultural nature of their school environment. Teachers in the community's schools were dedicated professionals who went beyond the call of duty to build self-esteem and shelter their students from the marginalization and racism they were wont to encounter.

I found the community of parents caring and expecting the best of educators as all parents everywhere do. Our students, on the whole, were respectful and excelled in many areas of the curriculum. Many are now in positions of responsibility and leadership in Toronto and elsewhere, not forgetting their roots in the Jane-Finch neighbourhood, and some wearing it as a badge of honour to show the character and resilience of those raised in that maligned community.

As the chair of Metro Toronto Housing Authority (MTHA), I witnessed the poor infrastructure that was the result of the lack of planning of the neighbourhood and the poor upkeep of the buildings. Much was accomplished with tenant involvement. They participated in community programs, attended meetings, and volunteered. They were able to express concerns and provide suggestions to the staff of MTHA on issues that could make their situation better.

I was always amazed by the way they tolerated the zillion questionnaires and surveys by community services and social scientists.

The author, Wanda MacNevin, represented the concerns of the area as a director of the Metro Toronto Housing Authority Board. Hers was a strong activist voice for the community as the Board struggled to meet its legal responsibility and support the work of its administration. She was always focussed on making a difference in and to the community. This book, in my view, is a continuation of her leadership to change the negative narrative about Jane-Finch.

This book provides us with a history worthy of note—the land, the early settlers, the planning, and development of the area as we now know it. Wanda brings knowledge as a resident, community advocate, and leader. She conducted interviews, as well as archival and library searches, to give credit to this telling.

With facts and documentation, we can erase the past reputation and, through knowledge of its history, see the strengths, achievements, and resilience of the Jane-Finch community.

It is time for the political decision makers to focus on the errors made in poor planning and make good on transportation links, infrastructure support and provide resource to community organizations especially those that empower youth. Media organizations must move to curtail the portrayals and images that damage.

As I write, the pandemic (COVID-19), conversations around Black Lives Matter, systemic discrimination, and anti-Black racism should converge on the focus on diversity and inclusion, never permitting us to identify people caught in socio-economic situations as marginalized.

It is my hope that this book will be illuminating to many.

Honorable Dr. Jean Augustine, P.C., C. M., O. Ont., C.B.E.

PREFACE

The Jane-Finch community, located in the northwest area of the City of Toronto, is known to many around the world. This vibrant community, with its unwarranted bad reputation, is well-known for the challenges faced by its diverse, multicultural, working-class population, which deals with issues of marginalization, immigration, over-policing, racism, and multiple forms of discrimination. It is not known for its rich cultural mosaic of peoples—people with talents, knowledge, experience, and skills that are largely unknown by the broader public. And, yet there are well-known celebrities who grew up in the area like singer Jully Black, choreographer Luther Brown, actor Lyriq Bent, and CBC correspondent Dwight Drummond. The strengths of this community have largely been hidden or ignored.

This legendary community has had a profound effect on the way I see the world. My values and beliefs come from the many experiences gained, and challenges overcome, while having the privilege of living in this part of the city for more than sixty years. I grew up on the former Downsview military base. Eventually, I moved into 15 Tobermory Drive, a newly built, high-rise public housing complex, as a single mother with three children supported by social assistance ("welfare").

My work life in Jane-Finch started in 1975, when I was hired by the Black Creek Venture Group to work on a short-term project. I was then hired as the first staff person to work at the newly formed Jane/Finch Community and Family Centre in 1976, where I worked for fifteen years. In 1991, I moved to the Black Creek Community Health Centre for twelve years, then I returned to the Jane/Finch Community and Family Centre as a program manager, and I worked there for another thirteen years before retiring as the director of Community Programs.

Throughout those years, I also volunteered in the community, sitting on boards of directors for community service organizations, joining grassroots committees, and participating in community political action. As a result of my paid and volunteer work in the community, and my interest in community development and activism, I accumulated an abundance of reports, letters, and documents about Jane-Finch.

In 2009, I decided to interview a few past residents and workers who were significant to the community and who had moved away, along with two people who grew up on farms in Elia, the area that became Jane-Finch. Their stories had not been told. It was not my intention at that time to write a book; I just wanted to make their stories accessible so that others could learn about the rich history of the Jane-Finch community, the place I spent most of my life and grew to love.

The interviews were intriguing. Over time, I interviewed a total of thirty-nine wonderful people—many of whom had lived or are currently living in the community. I interviewed compassionate people who worked in the community for long periods of time and who have contributed to it substantially.

I reviewed past reports and thought about the multiple involvements and engagements people had in Jane-Finch. This enabled me to better understand how the community came into being and the challenges this community has faced since the early 1960s. I then decided that the story of Jane-Finch must be told.

I spoke with leaders and residents in the community and given my long history living and working in the community, I felt both supported and compelled to write this book. I had written two books in the past, *From the Edge: A Women's Evolution from Abuse to Activism* and *If I Only Knew: Stories of Teen Moms*[1], both based on my own personal and work experiences. Having received an honorary doctor of laws degree from York University (for my decades of work in the community) also gave me the confidence to take on what turned out to be a monumental task.

A Nigerian man once told me that when he was preparing to leave his village in Nigeria, people told him that he must go to Jane-Finch in Toronto. When he landed at the airport and was processed through immigration, a

---

1   Wanda MacNevin, *From the Edge: A Woman's Evolution from Abuse to Activism* (Toronto: Picas & Points Publishing, 1999); *If I Only Knew ... Stories of Teen Moms* (Toronto: Black Creek Community Health Centre, 2008).

Customs and Immigration official asked where he was going to settle. He responded that he was not sure. The officer told him *not* to go to Jane-Finch, so he went elsewhere.

That type of negative stereotyping must stop, and one way to stop it is to share another narrative—one that speaks to the community's richness, resiliency, and response to poor government planning and a lack of social infrastructure. The way governments have envisioned this community created many of the problems that residents must deal with today. Continuing negative media coverage further stigmatized the community, often without looking at the systemic issues that caused the problems in the first place—not the residents. This is a community that has been over-researched, over-analyzed, over-policed, and over-judged. Racism (especially anti-Black racism), xenophobia, and anti-working-class biases are at the root of this negative attention. The people of this community have yet to see their stories of persistence, resilience, experience, knowledge, and talents written.

There are many stories that need to be told—those in this book are just a few. Some residents or workers will recognize these stories but may remember them differently. The stories are how I remember them, informed by my experiences, as well as the interviews and information I obtained. No one perspective can truly speak for all the residents in the community or all the organizations and networks they created or participated in.

It takes a community to create the rich tapestry that is the history of Jane-Finch. This is but one thread. I hope to make a small contribution to that story that inspires others to act.

INTRODUCTION

Jane-Finch is a community like many others but with unique challenges and characteristics. It is a community that was rapidly built, and without the social infrastructure to support a mostly immigrant, racialized, and poor working-class population from all over the world. Residents took collective action to fight for everything they needed, despite the barriers and obstacles placed in their way by government and institutional bureaucracy and the capitalist system.

This story of Jane-Finch is not so much about what politicians and governments have done to this low-income, working-class community through planning (or lack thereof), nor the policies—political, social, and economic—that negatively affected the residents repeatedly for the last seventy years. It is about resiliency and collective action by marginalized and disadvantaged peoples who did not accept their undeserved circumstances. It is about the strong sinews within working-class individuals, groups, neighbourhoods, and community institutions (organizations, agencies, faith communities) that hold them up and often bind them into more effective groupings. Residents continue to transcend adverse circumstances to create community and inspire hope in its members. There are important lessons about the strengths of poor and working-class people resisting oppression and neglect that can be learned from the experiences described in this book.

The voices of Jane-Finch residents and workers are heard throughout the chapters of this book, describing decades of challenge, activism, and development through the struggles of committed people in the community. Multiple themes are woven throughout, including residents' experiences and responses, city planning, the education system, media, government, and institutional responses. The rapid development and lack of social infrastructure created enormous challenges, but by taking personal responsibility, developing leadership, and building community capacity, many have made significant contributions to improving community life.

Chapter One starts with the long and fascinating history of the Indigenous peoples who lived here for thousands of years. Chapter Two describes the early European settler-farmers, with farm families living on the land from the late 1770s into the 1950s. Chapter Three, the 1960s, introduces families who purchased the new houses in this "suburban" community, along with the borough of North York's plans for the area, including employment and the development of the Jane-Finch Mall.

Chapters Four, Five, and Six—covering the 1970s, 1980s, and 1990s—speak to how residents and community workers put their hearts and souls into advocating for essential programs and services and responded collectively to issues that affected the residents who called Jane-Finch home. The community responded to the urban plans, and through diligent work, residents, with the support of key leaders, created community-based organizations in response to local needs. The community was the target of poor urban planning during this time, with social infrastructure development lagging decades behind the rapid population growth.

Research was conducted, and multiple networks and coordinating committees were established. The community fought to keep scant resources in the community and ensure good planning for the empty lots of land. Government pumped small amounts of money into the community, and some organizations sustained themselves while others dissolved. Through it all, the community survived in an environment that was constantly negatively labelled, particularly in the media. The media coined the term "corridor" and it was frequently used when referring to Jane-Finch, but the community determined they did not live in a "corridor", but in a community

Austerity policies continued to confront communities in the 2000s, which I examine in Chapter Seven. This brought several locally run community conferences and initiatives and the establishment of resident-led action groups. It was also the time of the "summer of the gun," leading to both local actions and responses by the city.

The 2010s, Chapter Eight, saw more government action, such as the Toronto Strong Neighbourhood Strategy and Jane-Finch continued to demonstrate that people, regardless of race or class, did not accept the status quo. There are many examples of how the community both responded and acted proactively to create and lead organizations to fight for what their community required.

Chapter Nine brings the reader up to 2020 and gives examples of the community's current situation, including plans for gentrification for this area of the city, along with my concluding thoughts.

Lastly, Chapter Ten provides a significant perspective on anti-Black racism by former long-term resident, Sam Tecle.

By Us! For Us! should be of particular interest to residents, activists, students, city planners, social researchers, community workers, social workers, and others.

CHAPTER ONE

Peoples of the First Nations

The community now known as Jane-Finch has been inhabited for generations beyond our knowing. This book was written on the historical territory of the Huron-Wendat, Petun, Seneca, and most recently, the Mississaugas of the Credit River First Nations. This territory is covered by the Dish with One Spoon Wampum Belt Covenant, an agreement between the Haudenosaunee and the Ojibwe and allied nations to peacefully share and care for the lands and resources around the Great Lakes. Today, this region is home to people from around the world, as well as many Indigenous peoples from across Turtle Island [North America] including survivors and family members impacted by the legacy of the residential school system and other systemic inequities. This calls on us to commit to learning to be better stewards of the land and express solidarity with Indigenous communities across the country.

Historical perspectives

Indigenous peoples lived on and cared for this land for thousands of years. While the Humber River served as a main transportation route for First Nations, Indigenous people lived along the banks of the Black Creek, a tributary of the Humber, on a seven-acre site just north of what is now Finch Avenue, south of today's York University campus. In the last Indigenous settlement in the area, the Huron-Wendat people lived in a village of almost a dozen longhouses.

The longhouses were up to one hundred and twenty feet long and thirty feet wide, with a ten-foot aisle down the centre. Within the longhouse settlement, men and women had separate duties, with women gathering firewood, spinning hemp, preparing animal skins for clothes, making baskets and pottery, and raising beans, corn, and squash crops (the "Three Sisters"). Men traded, fished, hunted, made canoes, nets, and weapons, and defended the village. The village existed from approximately 1400 to 1550.[2]

Susan Gemmell, who grew up in the community, researched what life was like in the Huron-Wendat village: "[Four hundred] years ago, if you had taken a walk along the Black Creek just north of [present day] Finch, you would have found yourself in the middle of a thriving village with an estimated population of over 1,000. The Hurons were farmers, raising crops of corn, squash and beans for their food, supplemented by bear, deer and small game which they hunted. The society was matriarchal, probably because women were so important to farming, and inheritance was passed through the mothers. All cooking and food storage and preparation were done in the longhouses. Eye diseases would have been common, the result of living in such closed smoky quarters. Pollution was a problem in those days too. Life in [this settlement] was hard and probably short. The location, called the Parsons site, is the last of three in North York to remain uncovered."[3] The other two have been built over in modern times.

꩜

The Huron-Wendat village became known as the Parsons site by archaeologists in recognition of the Parsons family who farmed on the land and later sold it to the City of North York and Ontario Hydro in 1958. The Parsons themselves were major landowners and farmers in the area. "The naming of the site as 'Parsons' after a prominent Euro-Canadian land-owning family, a common naming practice throughout the region, constitutes one level of erasure of the area's Indigenous presence."[4] Despite what we know today about the injustices done to the Indigenous peoples—for example, their displacement, residential schools, loss of language and culture—the land is

---

2   *From Longhouse to Highrise: Pioneering in our Corner of North York* (North York: Downsview Weston Action Community, 1986), 3.

3   Susan Gemmell, "Jane-Finch Decades Ago" (North York: *Jane Echo*), June 1982.

4   L. Anders Sandberg, Rene Gualtieri, Jon Johnson, *Re-Connecting with a Historical Site: One Narrative and the Huron-Wendat Ancestral Village at York University* (Toronto: York University), 3.

still referred to as the Parsons site. This site is one of the most significant and best-documented Indigenous archaeological sites in Toronto.

For several years, Tom Peace, a graduate student working on his PhD at York University, led bus tours in the community that included the Indigenous village. During one of the tours, he described the site.

> This was the Parsons site—a 15th century Iroquoian village that has been studied by archaeologists since the 1950s. Although today the site is dominated by a hydro-corridor and large apartment building, in the 15th century the walled village would have been home to at least 10 longhouses and a vibrant community. The village likely only existed for around 10–20 years. Iroquoian villages tended to move their location when agricultural yields declined due to soil exhaustion. It is likely that the people who lived in the village were the ancestors of the Huron-Wendat who lived around Georgian Bay two centuries later.[5]

Excavations of the Parsons site by archaeologists began in 1952, when J. Norman Emerson, who established the Ontario Archaeological Society in 1951, held a series of field schools at the site with students and scholars from the University of Toronto. The site was believed to be one of the best documented ancestral Wendat villages in Toronto. Emerson believed that the site had potential for development as an Indigenous counterpart to the Black Creek Pioneer Village. He also believed that it could be a site for summer archaeological training for students to learn about the history of the site. While Emerson worked to realize his plans, without participation from the Huron-Wendat peoples, his plans did not come to fruition.[6]

There were others who had plans for the site.

> In the late 1980s, faculty members at York University revived Emerson's idea. The project, a joint undertaking with the Metropolitan Toronto and Region Conservation Authority, was headed by Professor Bill Mahaney under the title, "Geology,

---

5   Tom Peace, "Stops Visited Along the Way," Black Creek Living History Project (bus tour narration).

6   Sandberg et al, *Re-Connecting*, 4.

Prehistory, and Re-construction of the Parsons Archaeological Site" and supported as a potential winner in the University's Fund-Raising Campaign for research projects. They planned to have a living village, portraying the lifestyle at the time and demonstrate techniques and methods of archaeology, prehistoric investigation, and site reconstruction. While the intent was also to be profit-making and informative of that period, the proposal was not successful.[7]

John Morrison, an avocational archaeologist who worked with Emerson, gathered a huge collection of items from the site and stored them in his basement. He wrote, "From 1956 to 1971, I had uncovered 230,382 archaeological artefacts, as well as 18,513 bones of animals and fish, 1,117 bones of human skeleton remains, all of which are catalogued and re-stored."[8] It was felt that bringing public school students to the site to dig and collect "souvenirs" meant that artefacts were not properly handled or documented.

Morrison visited many schools and spoke to hundreds of students about the Huron-Wendat village on the Parsons site. While the village was not able to be replicated, Morrison managed to bring artefacts of the village to the people.

Another group came in to excavate the site in 1989–90 and conducted a partial examination of the site. ASI, a team of professionals who work to provide high-quality consulting services in cultural heritage conservation, planning, and management, revealed a considerable amount of the ancient village.

> ASI's investigations took the form of an 18-meter-wide and 175-meter-long corridor running the breadth of the site, with an additional 50-meter trench extending to the Black Creek floodplain. These excavations revealed a considerable amount of the ancient village, with the remains of 10 longhouses, subterranean

7   Sandberg et al, *Re-Connecting*, 6.
8   John Morrison (n.d.) Index. "The Parsons Site" in L. Anders Sandberg, Rene Gualtieri, Jon Johnson, *Re-Connecting with a Historical Site: One Narrative and the Huron-Wendat Ancestral Village at York University* (Toronto: York University), 7.

sweat lodges, the eastern and western portions of a palisade, and the remains of four midden (refuse) areas. Over 6000 artefacts were recovered and subsequently analyzed.[9]

Sadly, there were no consultations or engagement with the Huron-Wendat people.

> The people at the site, the Huron-Wendat, were seen as past rather than present people. The proposed plans for the site were similarly constructed without the presence of the Huron-Wendat who were still living. Instead they focused on engaging students to perform digs at the site as an outdoor exercise to learn more about Canada's Indigenous peoples, and to reconstruct the village as an ancestral site, with local Indigenous peoples being engaged as guides, dressed up in historical clothes and performing traditional activities.[10]

Signs acknowledging Indigenous lands

Finally, on June 15, 2013, after sixty years, the Huron-Wendat ancestral village at Black Creek was publicly acknowledged on the land from Keele Street to Jane Street through the hydro-electricity power line corridor, that includes the Finch Hydro Corridor Recreation Trail. It was named the

---

9   Lanna Crucefix, "The Parsons Site" (Toronto: *Journal of the Ontario Archeological Society*, 1998).

10   Sandberg et al, *Re-Connecting*, 16.

"Huron-Wendat Trail." Wendat representatives from Quebec, including Grand Chief Konrad Sioui, attended. June 15 was officially declared "Huron-Wendat Day" in Toronto. Grand Chief Sioui said, "We must never forget that our ancestors have walked, lived and died in the Greater Toronto area and in the Great Lakes area. The Huron-Wendat Trail is a positive reminder of our past, present and future presence of our unceded ancestral lands."[11]

Interpretive signs are now posted along the trail honouring the historic Indigenous presence and their contribution to Toronto. They contain information about the Indigenous peoples who lived in this area. The signs are posted at Sentinel Road and Pond Road, in Driftwood Park, and on Jane Street, north of Finch Avenue.

Indigenous perspective

There is a great deal to learn from the Indigenous peoples who lived on this land before us, according to Shane McLeod, from the Anishinaabe community in Nipissing. He now lives in Toronto and serves the Indigenous community as a knowledge carrier and traditional teacher. McLeod spends a great deal of his time going into the schools or colleges to teach students about the knowledge, history, language, and, most importantly, the identity of Indigenous people as persons. He shared his thoughts on the importance of identity.

> Identity for me, is how I introduce myself. When I speak in my language, I speak to the Creator. I'm showing that I'm here—confirming that, 'I am here, Creator.' They know me by name, so that's another thing. We have a spirit name from before we're born. That's part of my identity, that's half of it. The other half is knowing who you are and what you do—your clan, the roles they have, tells you your character traits. If you are not doing them [the clan way], you might be doing them in a different way, like doing them the same way as an animal, but you still have those traits.

---

11   City of Toronto news release, "Huron-Wendat Day honours Toronto's First Nation history" (*NationTalk,* June 12, 2013).
https://nationtalk.ca/story/huron-wendat-day-honours-torontos-first-nation-history

An example would be, for me, Crane Clan. A friend mentioned to me about reading and I was like, 'I'm not a good reader.' 'Yes, you are.' 'But I barely read any books.' And, he says, 'You read people very well.'

That's when I realized, the crane sits in the river and watches everything, everybody—people, animals, birds, fish. They just stand there, and they eat food, and they are watching everything. If something moves in the woods, they move, they look, they see, and they watch it. Its like they are studying everything in the woods and the river. That's when I realized that's what he was saying to me. That's what I've been doing since I was a kid, not knowing who I am, what my culture is, what it does and eventually, like I said, when I gravitated to it, I realized what it really means. That's part of knowing who you are. You just can't go out there and say a bird does that and that's it. You have to study what that bird does, how it eats, how it gathers—it's all the same things that we do as a person in this life and as human beings.[12]

Many problems for the Indigenous community came with the European settlers. The government took land away from the Indigenous peoples and gave or sold it to settlers. They also brought diseases and alcohol to the people of this land. Later, they sent children away from their families, their homeland, and their cultures to residential schools. They were trying to force the young people to become European and ignore their identities as Indigenous persons. What the settlers did not understand, nor attempt to understand, was how the Indigenous peoples had lived for thousands of years with rich cultures and languages. McLeod gave an example.

In our long house, we all had different roles. Everybody was on point—everybody was on track. Talking about language, about 'maybe' and 'ifs,' 'would' or 'should'—well, we never had that in our language. So there was nobody saying, 'maybe I'm going to do that' or 'that could be done'—there was nothing like that. It was 'yes, I'm doing that,' 'yes, I will,' because it was an important part of

---

12   Shane McLeod interview (Toronto: York Woods Library, Black Creek Living History Project, February 2020).

responsibility in that community. Its very important for language—what you say and how you say it because its for the spirit.

Discrimination against Indigenous people and oppression continue to be very real for Indigenous people in every mainstream community across the country. "You mentioned the '60s Scoop,' " McLeod continued. "Residential schools and everything. And, I hear some people say, 'My people went through tough times too—why don't you get over it?' I heard that before and I'm sure that everybody else has heard this. Its not about getting over it—it's still happening now."

People don't realize it. It's the institutions, the school system—people just don't know the stories. It's just not done the same way, either, with the hitting or the beatings or whatever. Its just done differently in an institutional way where they keep the separation of language because language classes aren't happening that often.

I've been working fifteen years in the schools. I started in the school as the language teacher with my kids learning. Years go by and I'm teaching my kids more about language, about culture, than they are learning and getting from the educational system. I was one of those advocates that pushed for Indigenous language classes. So, fifteen years goes by and there's maybe two language teachers, to now about eight or maybe ten. But, there's 500 schools and ten language teachers aren't going to do it. I'm sure there are many more French teachers out there than Indigenous [languages] teachers. I'm working with language teachers all over and we still don't have enough—even if you had 100, its still not close to what they have.

Basically, I'm still not seeing the reconciliation. The news says this and that, but its not coming together in my head and I work in that system. Another example would be that those from the residential schools are still being affected right now, including people who weren't even in the schools.

Even though they are not in residential school, fast forward another ten years, it's the drugs, the alcohol, not going to school, not educated, no drive to be educated, not even in their own culture. They don't know what that feeling is of "What is my responsibility?" "What is my purpose?" They don't feel that and what's going to happen to their kids. It's a generational affect from the residential schools.

When we see this time and time again, generation after generation—still the same story, you know that they don't really want to help. We're telling them this is what we really want, and they come to ask us again what we want or need, so we tell them, and they don't do it. For instance, me in the school board, and elders too, are telling them this is what we need to do for our kids—not for you to have a job, not for you to do this and that. Its for the kids to be going on their way, thinking, evolving, learning about their culture, their purpose of themselves, their identity. This is what they need. I see the least amount of that being done. We should have the same amount of Anishinaabe teachers teaching the language to our kids as they do with the French language.[13]

McLeod believes that the concept of giving the land back to the Indigenous peoples is not part of reconciliation. Indigenous people have reservations that they live on, live off of, and protect. They don't own the land, rather they are stewards of the land. The land is sacred, and reserves are more sacred to their ancestors. "For me, when I hear the words, 'left the land' it's not their land in the first place, it's Mother Earth. We're not taking the land back to the spirit world. Everything on this earth is for human beings to share and to survive—that's how I feel and understand it."

For centuries, the Indigenous peoples had lived along the banks of what became knowns as the Black Creek and the Humber River. By the 1700s, Indigenous peoples had left local settlements for many reasons, such as the land becoming exhausted or other pressures. The British Crown took control of the lands and encouraged European settlement in order to protect what the Crown considered their "property." There was an abundance of land in Upper Canada (Ontario).

In the late eighteenth century, what was to eventually become Jane-Finch existed only as wilderness and a few scattered farms north of the township of York.

---

13   McLeod interview.

CHAPTER TWO

European Settlement in Upper Canada

Newcomers to Canada

Following the American Revolution, many settlers moved north and began establishing farms (now northwest Toronto) between 1795 and the late 1800s.[14] The earliest settlers were German-speaking, and they migrated from Pennsylvania after the American Revolution because of political persecution in the United States and for a chance of free land. The British government, under Lieutenant Governor John Graves Simcoe, advertised free lots of two hundred acres to any "law-abiding Christian who was capable of manual labour." To receive the final deed to the property, it was necessary for the settler to build a shingled-frame or log house, clear a certain amount of land for cultivation, and improve the road in front of the property, all within two years.[15]

Other pioneers came to Canada from the United States under one of the British programs for settling farmers on the former Indigenous lands. The settlers arrived with their oxen pulling Conestoga wagons in the late 1790s.

Conestoga wagon

Conestoga wagons were built to carry up to six tons, and they were used extensively during this period to carry all the supplies settlers would need to

---

14   Timothy B. Yip and Lena Pizzardi, *DWAC Statistics: A Student-Community Service Program* (North York: Downsview Weston Action Community, 1975, ii).

15   *Longhouse*, 7.

establish their new homes. Settlers were dependant on their livestock and their wagons.

Isaac Devins and his family were the first to arrive in the area. They built a large cabin on the east side of the Humber River on the path to the Toronto Carrying Place, the old "Indian trail" where the Devins family often met Indigenous travellers. Thick woods covered the Devins farm, and the Humber River provided a good means of transportation.[16]

Crosson House

The Crossons settled in 1799, walking the distance from Pennsylvania carrying all their family possessions on the back of their two-year-old horse. They traded the horse with Isaac Devins for one hundred acres of farmland west of Jane Street. A year later, the Kaisers arrived, building their farm just south of what is now Steeles Avenue, on the property that is now part of York University.[17]

The area where these farms were established was later called Downsview. "The Downsview Lands were part of an extensive land parcel acquired by the British Crown in 1787 from the Mississauga First Nation in what is referred to as the Toronto Purchase. Downsview received its name in the 1830s after a farm on the property called "Downs View," attributed to its commanding vista of Lake Ontario to the south, looking down from the plateau. The

---

16   *Longhouse*, 7.
17   *Longhouse*, 7

area was connected with Toronto in the 1850s when Dufferin Street and the Northern Railway were constructed."[18]

The farm is where the George Jackson house was built in 1827 by newly-wed Irish immigrants William and Jane Jackson and it was them who called it Downs View. In Ireland, when you see a large parcel of land in the country, it's called the "Downs." And, it had quite a view!

The villages of Emery and Elia, located within the Downsview area, intersected at Concession Road 5 (later Jane Street) and the Emery-Elia Side Road (later Finch Avenue), which ran parallel to a few farmhouses. The name "Finch Avenue" was named after John Finch, a proprietor of an Inn at Yonge Street and Finch Avenue. Finch purchased that property in 1847 and developed it into a popular spot with circuses and other events held regularly on the site. Jane Street first appeared on record in Goad's Fire Insurance plan in 1844. The street was named after the wife of Toronto developer John Canavan. "Thus, one could argue that the area became 'Jane Finch' in the way one understands it today."[19] What is less clear is why the area that was known as the village of Elia came to be known for the major intersection of two roads—Jane Street and Finch Avenue West. ["Finch Avenue West" will be referred to as just Finch Avenue from this point on.]

At that time, the lack of permanent roads and the distance between the early farmsteads meant that the farm families were quite isolated from one another. Travelling was easier in the winter when travel by sleigh was possible. However, they needed better ways to send their produce to Toronto and gain access to better mail service. The railway came to this area in 1853 with the York station located just south of Finch Avenue and east of Keele Street.

≫

18   "History of Downsview Air Force Base" *Wikipedia,* website. https://en.wikipedia.org/wiki/Downsview_Airport#:~:text=Downsview%20Airfield%20opened%20in%201929,and%20renamed%20RCAF%20Station%20Downsview.

19   Chris Richardson, *Canada's Toughest Neighbourhood: Surveillance, Myth and Orientalism in Jane Finch* (St. Catharines, Ontario: Brock University, Faculty of Social Sciences, MA thesis, 2008, 74).

Then came a second wave of settlers arriving from England and Scotland.[20] Many of the European-born immigrants were impoverished or persecuted in their original lands, with little chance of improving their lives in Europe. They came to Canada hoping to create a better life for themselves and their children. Like many of the Indigenous peoples before them, the European immigrants were mostly farmers.

The Dalziels, who came from Scotland, bought their farm in 1828 and had a saw- milling business, blacksmith shop, carpenter's shop and a wagon maker's shop that became the centre of industry for the community. In 1954, the barn was converted to a public museum and later became one of the original buildings in the Black Creek Pioneer Village. The farmhouse is still standing on Jane Street north of Steeles Avenue. This later became the home of Jean Agnew, a direct descendent of the original Dalziels.[21]

Agnew was interviewed by York University students for an historical project called "The Community Speaks," published in the *Jane Echo* on July 23, 1982. She was seventy at the time, and it was her grandfather, Dalziel, who built the homestead in the Jane and Steeles area. "The rural communities were made up of the school, the church, the community hall; if there wasn't a community hall, the parties and things took place in private homes, or the church or the school, but in this area, we had a community hall on the east side of the road very close to the school, across the road from the church."[22]

Recognizing that it was important for their children to go to school, and in keeping with the passage of the *Grammar Schools Act* in 1807, the first local school was built in Kaiserville (Jane and Steeles) in 1824 on what is now Black Creek Pioneer Village, and the lessons were taught in German, not English. English did not become the language of instruction until the early 1830s. This small, one-room log schoolhouse, about eighteen by twenty feet, had a fireplace or stove at one end. The students sat in two rows at log

---

20   *Longhouse*, 11.
21   Van J. Newell, "Rural Roots of Old Jane-Finch" [calendar] (North York: Jackson & Cowan, 1983).
22   Jean Agnew, "You Got Good and Bad in the Beef Ring" (*Jane Echo*, July 1982).

desks on log benches without backs, with the girls on one side of the room and the boys on the other. The school had one or two small windows, a slanted writing board along the wall, a few textbooks, a teachers' table and chair, a pointer, a pail and cup for drinking water, and a birch rod used to discipline students. Teachers were often discharged British soldiers. A teaching certificate or formal education was not needed to become a teacher, and school always started and ended with a prayer. Daily lessons included religious instruction and memory work. This school closed fifteen years later, and another school was built further north.[23]

The Elia School was built in 1830 at the corner of Keele Street and Finch Avenue, where lessons were taught in English. This log school was replaced by a frame building in 1851, and a brick schoolhouse was built across the road in 1873, on the east side. Classes were provided in this building until 1956.[24] The original Downsview Public School was built further south on Keele Street in 1850 with a newer school built in 1948 for the growing community.

Elia School

A new community hall was built in 1894, south of John Snider's general store (at Keele and Finch). On the property, which was owned by Abraham Snider and leased for 99 years, or as long as the Foresters retained the

---

23 *Longhouse*, 13.
24 Newell, Rural Roots Calendar.

building, was the sign, "Canadian Order of Foresters, Court Elia, No. 514." The hall served as a gathering place for town meetings and municipal voting, social suppers and dances, Christmas concerts, and minstrel shows. In 1946, the Court was disbanded, and the hall was destroyed in 1956.[25]

～

Jacob Stong was born in the log cabin that now stands in the Black Creek Pioneer Village. Surrounding their home was a dense forest of pine, beech, hard and soft maple, white and red oak, black and white birch, basswood, ironwood, hickory, cedar, elm, ash, cherry, tamarack, and many other varieties of trees.[26] The two houses and most of the farm buildings are still standing in their original locations in Black Creek Pioneer Village. "Jacob, the eldest son of Daniel and Elizabeth Stong became a prominent member of the community in the 19th Century. He was a farmer, sawmill owner, Justice of the Peace and in 1879 was appointed an original director and judge of the Canadian National Exhibition. His house still stands, abandoned, on the southwest corner of Keele and Steeles."[27] The signage in front of the house on Steeles Avenue reads, "Originally the home of Jacob and Sarah Snider Stong, this house was built circa 1857 by Jacob Stong on an 80-acre parcel of farmland purchased from his father. The house of his parents, Daniel and Elizabeth Fisher Stong, from the 100 acres to the west, is preserved at BCPV [Black Creek Pioneer Village]." Several generations of the Stong family occupied these lands, beginning with Daniel and Elizabeth as the first settlers in 1816. Bertha Price was a descendant of the Stong family. She was interviewed by the *Jane Echo* on August 27, 1982.

> Well, it was all bush, apparently, when (our families) arrived. When our cattle went out to that barn, the back barn, and went down through, those were the original Indian paths, we were told. We went to school up about Highway 7, you see, and that was about a mile and a half. Actually, we should have been going across to

---

25 *Longhouse*, 21.
26 Patricia W. Hart, *Pioneering in North York; a History of the Borough* (North York: General Publishing, Canadian First Edition, 1971).
27 Newell, Rural Roots calendar.

Emery, but it was further still. When we went to school there were no snowplows like there is now. The old milk truck would come along with a plow in front of it and us kids, we'd jump in the back among the milk cans, you know, and get a ride up to school. There were no buses.

It was milking in the morning, and we milked by hand then, and then we girls went in and did our housework and tried to get done in the morning. Then we'd do, depending on what was to be done, like if we'd butchered, why there'd be canning of the sausage, or if we had extra work to do that was up to us. We didn't have electric stoves then. We had a summer kitchen and you baked, and you put your wood fire on, if you can imagine how hot it would be. We got a lot of fun out of the hills, you know, like for tobogganing and that in the winter. And then in the summer we dammed up the creek and of course we'd hurry as children to get our work done to go down swimming. There was quite a creek run down through there then. Skating was another thing, but we didn't go to a rink. My uncle had a big pond back of his farm—this was Uncle Ernie—and we'd all, maybe 10, 20 of us, go back there and have a good time all together. In those days' farmers, well, I had some of Dad's old bank books and boy, they just, they had nothing, I mean.[28]

Another early settler was Samuel Snider, who lived in Elia from 1807 until 1876. He moved here with his wife, Mary from Pennsylvania, in 1806 and bought two hundred acres of land on Jane Street, south of Finch. It was heavily wooded with pine, oak, and maple trees; the soil was heavy clay; and there was a good supply of sand and gravel on the banks of the Black Creek.

Percy Snider, a direct descendant of Samuel, married Sylvia in 1930 and farmed on the land now occupied by Sentinel Park south of Finch Avenue, west of Keele Street. Percy farmed there until 1953, when "the city got too close and chased [them] out." They moved to a house at what is now Jane Street and Grandravine Drive, which is now occupied by a high-rise. Percy said the farm was a great place to grow up. When he was growing up, it was

---

28   Berta Price and Ed Price, "Oyster Suppers Were a Big Deal Here" (*Jane Echo*, August 27, 1982).

still possible to skate on Black Creek all winter, swim in it all summer, and ski and toboggan in the surrounding hills.

Snider family reunion

The Sniders had a big family, needing eight boards to extend their table at Christmas time. The church was their social life. Percy was the youngest of twelve brothers and sisters, and their family home was huge. Percy remembers square dancing until 2:00 a.m. and then getting up early to milk cows. The dances were often held in someone's house, and he recalls one where it was so crowded that they had to prop up the kitchen floor, and the fiddler sat in the sink. Because of his large family, and with hired farm and kitchen help, Percy says that it often took two table sittings before the household—which numbered about twenty—all ate dinner. He could not say how many pies his mother would have to make, but the table was covered with them.

At that time, families went to Weston to do their shopping. In 1916, they purchased a generator for their own use that ran on sixteen wet-cell batteries. Hydro came into the area in 1927. The Sniders said that it was hard to sell the family farm to a developer, but they did not feel that they had much choice, although it hurt to see the land lie unused for several years. When they moved from Jane Street in 1953, it was not paved—in fact, it did not get paved until the 1960s. And then the street's increasing traffic and noise forced the Sniders to make another move several miles north.[29]

Two 19th-century buildings remain in this area on the York University campus. The first, known as Hoover House, is located on the south side of Pond Road and atop the eastern edge of the Black Creek Ravine. The house was built in 1848 by Abraham Hoover and his father, Christian. The Hoovers, who were Pennsylvania Mennonites, were distantly related to Herbert Hoover, the thirty-first president of the United States, whose branch of the family remained in the United States. Today fruit trees from the Hoover estate are found along the edges of the ravine.

Hart House is on the north side of Pond Road, across from the Passy Gardens residence. Although it is over 170 years old, this hand-hewn squared timber home was not originally built here. It was moved down to the Hoover property from King Township in the 1930s to serve as the Hart family's summer retreat. It was used by the family until purchased by York University in 1964, where it became a student activity centre.[30]

In 2017, at a ceremony during National Aboriginal Day, Hart House was renamed Skennen'kó:wa Gamig (House of Great Peace), and it is a welcoming, safe, and supportive space for Indigenous students, faculty, and staff to come together in the spirit of Skennen'kó:wa to celebrate and to share knowledge and teachings. The new name, Skennen'kó:wa Gamig, comes from both Mohawk and Anishinaabe languages bringing together two of the confederacies that uphold and engage in the Dish with One Spoon Wampum Covenant to share territory in peace.[31]

29   Patti Tasko, "Christmas Concert Was the Big Deal," (*Jane Echo*, December 17, 1982); *Henry Snider: His Ancestors and Descendants* (Snider Genealogical and Historical Research Group, 1976).

30   Peace, "Stops Visited".

31   Amara McLaughlin, "Cabin Transformed to 'Further Understanding and Reconciliation' for York U Indigenous students" (Toronto: CP24.com, June 21, 2017).

Church in the community

Religion played an important role for the families who settled on farms in Elia. Until the first church was built, services were held in schools or in the farmers' homes. One early church was the Kaiser Chapel, built in 1830, on Jane Street north of Steeles, in the village of Kaiserville, where there is now just a cemetery (present City of Vaughan). The chapel was opened to itinerant preachers of other denominations, and in the 1840s, weekly "spiritualists" meetings attracted large crowds.[32]

The Edgeley Mennonite Church was built in 1824 on Jane Street, north of Highway 7 to serve the Mennonite community that arrived from Pennsylvania and had farms in the area. This church was later moved to Pioneer Village in 1975.

The first church building in the village of Elia was not built until 1851. Prior to this, the services were held in the home of John Boot. In 1851, Conrad Gram donated land for an Episcopal Methodist Church and cemetery on Finch Avenue, east of the railway tracks.[33] The cemetery was there before the church was built, with a Gram headstone dated 1832. The original deed was signed and sealed by Mr. and Mrs. Conrad Gram and five trustees of the church. The indenture was made on March 31, 1851 and recorded in the County of York on October 27, 1851.[34]

It is believed that this first church was built on the land with logs, followed by a frame church. The present brick church was built in 1901 at the cost of $2,700, including all the materials and seating. Electricity was not installed until 1928, and in 1942, an addition was added onto the back of the church for a cost of $1,300.

The Episcopal Methodist Church became the Elia Methodist Church in 1874, and in 1925, it became the Elia United Church, both named after the area of its location. When the post office, located in William Snider's general

---

32 *Longhouse*, 15.
33 Longhouse, 15.
34 Rev. G. W. Lynd and Mrs. Paul Snider, "Elia United Church Centennial—50th Anniversary of the Present Church" (1951).

store at Keele Street and Finch Avenue, was established in 1878, the Postal Department also gave it the name of Elia.

The last regular service was held in December 1956. For two years, the church building remained empty. It was then rented to a Dutch Reform congregation from January 1, 1960, to December 31, 1961. The church was sold to this congregation on January 1, 1962.[35] The church still stands at 1130 Finch Avenue, between Keele Street and Dufferin Avenue, with signage stating, "Dutch Reform Congregation."

The women of Elia were progressive and in 1908 they organized a Women's Institute that met in the local church. The modern women at the time wanted to have the term "housewife," used on legal papers, replaced by "homemaker." It was quite possible that the members of the Elia Women's Institute were the instigators of this movement, for as far back as 1916, the Elia schoolteacher, Miss Moran, delivered a paper at the Women's Institute entitled "Housekeeping as a Profession."[36]

Two historic 19th-century structures are still being utilized. The Downsview United Church on Keele Street was built in 1870 for a cost of $6,500. This was raised by members in the community and from the sale of the old building. The church was first called the York Methodist Church, then changed to the Downsview Methodist Church in the 1880s. The church became known as the Downsview United Church in 1925 and remains active today.

The George Jackson House on Keele Street is located north of the Downsview United Church. The original Jackson house was built in 1827 by newlywed Irish immigrants, William and Jane Jackson, when they purchased two hundred acres for one pound an acre. That is not what land costs today!

Jackson worked the land and eventually served as a justice of the peace and a public-school trustee. Near the end of the 19th century, William's son, George, and his wife, Sarah, inherited the land, and they built the current

---

35   Lynd and Snider, "Elia United Church Centennial".

36   Beth Peteran, "Time Marches On in North York" (photocopy—newspaper source and date unknown).

redbrick home. George also took up public office and became a school trustee and a city alderman. In the 1960s, it became a nursing home, and then later an office building. The history of the Jackson family is mounted on the walls on the ground floor.[37]

The Anderson family

In the early 1900s, the Anderson family bought land on the southeast corner of Jane Street and Finch Avenue and their farm extended down to the Black Creek. Ross Anderson was born in Edgeley Village at Jane Street and Highway 7, and his grandfather also farmed in the Edgeley Village area. The Andersons were familiar with this area of the township. His son, Doug Anderson, was born on the farm in 1927. He grew up on the farm, and he moved only when the family sold it in 1951.

Anderson grew up playing sports, attending church, and participating in local activities such as dances, Junior Farmers, and the 4H Club. He also enjoyed swimming in Black Creek in the summer and skating on the creek during winter months. "Every community sponsored a 4H Club. There would be Calf Clubs, where a child between 12 and 21 would get a calf in April and look after it all summer. He'd train it to lead and show. In the fall, we would have an Achievement Day at Woodbridge Fair, where we would show our calf to see who had the best calf and the best trained calf. This was held on Thanksgiving weekend."[38]

Anderson attended Elia Public School. There were about forty students in one classroom, which accommodated grades one to eight and one teacher. Anderson finished school when he was thirteen to help on the farm, but he remembers his sister going to high school. "I know my sister, when she went to high school, she had to walk about a mile at six in the morning to get a ride with a fellow that worked in Weston to go to high school. The high school was in Weston."[39]

---

37   Michael MacDonald, "The Beauty within Downsview's History" (*Downsview Advocate*, January 2016).
38   Doug Anderson interview, (Black Creek Living History Project, October 10, 2009).
39   Anderson interview.

Their farm was one of four farms on the four corners of the intersection of Jane Street and Finch Avenue. The Andersons sold their farm in 1951 to the Toronto General Burying Grounds. Anderson said, "They couldn't get any more land around it, so they sold it again… Now I don't know where it went from there. Likely sold it to the developers."[40]

They did in fact sell it to developers who built the Jane Finch Mall on the southeast corner of Jane-Finch.

The Snider family

Marion Snider Thompson's father was a Snider and they had been farming on the land that is now at Yorkwoods Gate and Jane Street. "Samuel Snider lived there from 1773 to 1884 and I'm the fifth generation of Sniders who lived on the farm. Samuel, Henry, John C., my dad Vern, and myself. The Sniders moved here in 1773 from Pennsylvania. They came from Germany to Pennsylvania and came up by covered wagon."[41]

Snider farm, circa 1955 Courtesy M.S. Thompson

Marion Snider was born on the farm in 1924 and was married in 1946, at which time she and her new husband moved to Bracebridge for their first year. They came back and built a house at the corner of the farm. While their parents sold their farm in the 1950s, they continued to live in their house

---

40   Anderson interview.
41   Marion Snider Thompson interview, (Black Creek Living History Project, June 9, 2010).

until 1967. The Snider farm was known as the local recreation place in the community. Marion recalls a wonderful and happy life on the farm.

> We never wanted for anything because it was all there, we didn't have to go anywhere. We had aunts, uncles and cousins by the dozens who would come and have Sunday swimming and they'd bring their lunch, and we had a great time.

Marion's father dammed up the creek in the winter so that they could skate, and young people came together to play hockey on the creek. Apparently, Marion was the only girl who played hockey. She was the goalie.

At the south end of the farm, there was a loam pit. Loam is a type of soil that contains sand, silt, and clay and this soil was used to help build the Oakdale Golf and Country Club. The *Toronto Daily Star* (1926) headlines read, "Hebrews Buy Farm—Start Golf Course." The article stated it was for exclusive use for Toronto's Jewish population. At that time, the Jewish community was not welcome at other country clubs, or other institutions, for that matter. As a result, they had to create their own clubs, hospitals, etc. Marion shared how the loam pit helped to build the golf club.

> The pit was all loam, and my dad and Uncle Ivan built this machine where the loam was put on cups, and it went up and into the truck. Dad took it down to the Oakdale Golf and Country Club below Sheppard and on the west side of Jane. Well, he helped to build that. He took all his loam down there when they were building it. When I go down Jane Street now, you can't see the golf course for the trees.[42]

Marion spoke about the maple sugar bush [stand of sugar maple trees] in the community and how people came from the city to purchase maple syrup for $5.00 a gallon.

> Now it's $60.00 or more. That was good money in those days. I remember we had no electricity for a long time, no bathroom—we had to go out to the little house behind the garage and I had my bath in a galvanized tub down by the kitchen stove. For electricity, we had to put in our own poles, buy the poles, dig the hole and put the

---

42   Snider Thompson interview.

poles in and then the hydro came and wired it. I was eleven or twelve maybe when we got electricity. I was coming home from school one day and I got closer to the house, and I heard music and I knew the electricity was in the house because a radio was on. [43]

The health care system was quite different when Marion was growing up. She recalls a time when her appendix ruptured.

I had a serious appendix attack—it broke. We didn't know what it was. At the time, my brother Harold had the flu. He had stomach cramps and I guess mother thought that was what I had but it was so bad—it was horrible, and we had no telephone at the time. So dad had to drive to Weston and told the doctor and the doctor drove up. I remember him kneeling on the side of the bed and pushing on my stomach and it was hard as a rock, and he went out into the hall and told mom and dad that he was sending an ambulance up. It took me down to Wellesley and I was there for about a month because they had to drain it. The doctor said that if I hadn't been a healthy and happy farm girl, I would never have made it. [44]

The doctor at that time came to the farms for homebirths. Marion's mother told her that when she went into labour with Marion, they were doing threshing [the process of separating grain from corn or other crops] on the farm. Marion said that when she was delivered, "I don't know who was helping or doing the work, but I was born in the bedroom right off the kitchen and all the thresher men were at the table having their dinner!"[45]

The city was gradually expanding and getting closer and closer to the village of Elia. Marion and her family were experiencing new things, such as new residents coming into the community. Changing population brought its own challenges.

I had four children and one of my sons got a chicken, I think, from school. He told the teacher that he could look after it. Well, some dogs came in from the new housing and a dog killed the chicken. He

43 Snider Thompson interview.
44 Snider Thompson interview.
45 Snider Thompson interview.

had rabbits and the same thing happened to the rabbits. Just different things like that that we couldn't handle. We had a lovely dog—a Chow. He always roamed loose—never tied up and one day he went across Jane Street and one woman was so frightened and thought it was a bear and called the police and we were told that we either had to keep it tied up or build a six-foot fence that he couldn't jump over. So, we kept him tied but the poor thing died. We had him for years and years. It was things like that and as the city grew closer, things weren't what we were used to.[46]

Jane Street looking north to Finch, 1957.

Marion also talked about the challenges her daughter was having by attending different schools.

I think that Joan, my daughter, went to five different schools. The city was growing so she started way over at Weston Road and Sheppard. Then she went to Stanley Public School and then to on Sheppard, east of Jane Street. As the area grew up, they built more schools closer to where we lived, and so our children had to keep moving closer. She went to Yorkwoods last, before we moved up here (Schomberg) where we bought a farm. The youngest boy would have been in kindergarten when we moved up. There was still a field

---

46   Snider Thompson interview.

around our house when we moved, and that's where Yorkwoods School was built.[47]

Like Doug Anderson, Marion continued to call the area Elia at the time of her interview.

> They must have started to call it Jane and Finch when the townhouses were built (Yorkwoods) and it became known as not a wonderful place to live. That's when we heard the name Jane and Finch; before that it was always Elia. The new people who moved there did not know it as Elia. I don't know where the name Elia came from, but it was just always Elia. We still say Elia today when I talk to people. Edgeley was Jane and Highway 7, and Emery was Weston Road and Finch. Our Mennonite cemetery is north of Highway 7 on the east side of Jane and that's where a lot of my family were buried. We were originally Mennonite. The Edgeley Mennonite Church was built in 1824 on Jane Street, north of Highway 7. I think they moved it into the village [Pioneer Village], maybe twenty years ago.[48]

When the last of the Sniders moved away, the spruce trees on the former Snider property, now well over one hundred years old, still stand in Sentinel Park, north of Elia Junior High School on Sentinel Road.

The farming community of Elia existed for over one hundred years before the land was purchased by the government and developers to build a model suburban community. It remained farmland through the 1950s, and Jane Street and Finch Avenue were dirt roads until the 1960s. With new roads and developments came young families hoping to settle into this new, modern community.

---

47   Snider Thompson interview.
48   Snider Thompson interview.

CHAPTER THREE

Creation of an Inner City in a Suburban Environment

Jane-Finch: a new era

Of all the new homeowners and renters moving into the community in the 1950s and later, nobody referred to the area as "Elia," the name of the settlement that was used by the farmers. Rather, the new people moving in simply referred to it as "Jane and Finch" (or just Jane-Finch) for the intersection of Jane Street and Finch Avenue. The boundaries of this community are not easily identified; it is roughly the area covering the land between Steeles Avenue West to the north, Sheppard Avenue West to the south, Highway 400 to the west, and Keele Street to the east, representing a roughly three-kilometre radius from the Jane-Finch intersection.

There were well-built townhouses put up by private developers along Sheppard Avenue, east of Jane Street, meant for homeowners, but the townhouses on both sides of the street were purchased by Ontario Housing Corporation (OHC) in the 1960s and rented to families on social assistance or those working in low-wage jobs. Moving up Jane Street, single-family homes were built along with high-rises at Jane and Grandravine, and townhouses spilled along Driftwood Avenue.

A community centre was built on Yorkwoods Gate to accommodate the homeowners of the townhouse units. In the early 1960s, people were awestruck at the architecture of the round white building, imagining that only rich people lived in that area. Neither Yorkwoods Public School nor the Yorkwoods/Grandravine social housing townhouse complex existed at that time.

In the 1960s, the De Guerre family bought a home in the Topcliff neighbourhood, which won an award when it was developed. Topcliff was given that name because it overlooked a huge hill at the back of the development. Joan De Guerre fondly remembers that time. "Kids played in the creek. Lots of people went on picnics. There was a rope at the top of the ravine on a tree and kids used to swing out."[49]

Diane Hodge moved into the area with her family in 1966. Originally from northern Ontario, the surrounding parks and ravines were a draw for the Hodge family, who took advantage of the natural beauty of the area by visiting these sites regularly. She recalls happy times with the children playing along the Black Creek and skating at the Black Creek Pioneer Village. The surrounding area was undeveloped, so there were lots of bushes, ponds, and pear trees.

Their next-door neighbour was a history teacher who told them about the Indigenous people who used to live on the land along the Humber and its tributaries. Hodge, with her family, excavated at the northern end of Black Creek and found artefacts—pottery, tools, and rocks that looked like hammers.[50]

Numerous Italian families moved into the new homes in Jane-Finch. Joe Astrella purchased his home on Grandravine Drive in 1967. Astrella, like many other Italian immigrants in that period, moved to Toronto from Italy when he was eighteen years old. He first lived at Oakwood and St. Clair, then moved further north to Lawrence and Keele, before moving to Grandravine. "But it wasn't only Italians who first purchased the homes," Astrella said. "There were people of Jewish descent, there were Europeans, like Germans, Italians, and Austrians, [and] someone from Antigonish [Nova Scotia]—my next-door neighbour—and on the other side was a Canadian family, an Air Force pilot."[51] A synagogue was built on the west side of Keele Street, just south of Sheppard, to accommodate members of the Jewish community who were moving to the suburbs, especially between Bathurst and Keele.

---

49   Joan De Guerre interview (Toronto: York Woods Public Library, Black Creek Living History Project, November 2010).

50   Diane Hodge interview (Toronto: York Woods Public Library, Black Creek Living History Project, November 2010).

51   Joe Astrella interview (Toronto: York Woods Public Library, Black Creek Living History Project, April 10, 2012).

Astrella was a foreman at a company that supplied the windows for the new homes built largely by Greenwin Construction. There were other developers as well, but Greenwin was the main one. Astrella explained, "There were many [workers] that were in the building trades, in the plumbing or electrical supply, but they were here. The houses were custom built to their liking and, for the time, they were very futuristic, you know. They built here, and they stayed here. Eventually, they moved to Woodbridge in Vaughan, but originally, they were here." Astrella himself knew that the houses were well-built, and that was why he moved into the area. Not only were they well-built, but they were reasonably priced for the time.[52]

The Second World War was over, families were growing, and immigrants were moving to Toronto to build new lives. As a result, demand for housing was critical. By the mid-1960s, the federal government de-racialized the immigration policy by introducing a merit-based point system to determine admissibility to the country, meaning that immigrants from previously excluded parts of the world—Africa, the West Indies, Asia, and Latin America—were able to come to Toronto. "Jane-Finch, newly developed with a lot of affordable housing, came to house a proportionately large number of new immigrants, many of whom were people of colour."[53]

Canada was also expanding its social welfare program with the inclusion of private housing and social housing, believing that the integration of different levels of socio-economic housing within a community would lessen the negative effects of the class structure. It was also hoped that if housing had equally high standards in terms of planning and design, neighbours would live together harmoniously.[54] However, there was little regard for

---

52   Astrella interview.

53   Julie-Anne Boudreau, Roger Keil and Douglas Young, "The In-Between City," in *Changing Toronto: Governing Urban Neoliberalism* (Toronto: University of Toronto Press, 2009, 127).

54   Beth Bow, "Community Spirit of the Jane Finch Corridor" (North York: paper for York University, 1984).

communities having open space, schools, and commercial facilities properly integrated with the residential areas according to a study done in 1963.[55]

Employment

Highway 400 (then called the Barrie Highway) had been completed in 1952 and provided the first controlled-access highway in Ontario, a transportation route needed for the growth of industry. With this growth, the demand for housing and the interest of families who wanted to move to the "suburbs" was compelling.

That was also a period when there were lots of jobs. In the 1950s, several large industrial facilities were built. They were still operating in the early 1960s. As well as industry, there was the Ontario Department of Highways, Toronto District Office employing over 3,500 people (Keele/Highway 401). Located next to Highway 400, adjacent to the Oakdale Golf Club, the Workmen's Compensation Board Hospital and Rehabilitation Centre had a staff of 335 to support workers' rehabilitation for the entire province of Ontario.[56] These institutions are no longer in the area.

In terms of industrial lands, 3,600 acres were set aside and anticipated employing 36,000 people, at ten workers per acre. About forty per cent of the ultimate population were expected to be employed locally and, of this figure, about thirty-five per cent would be employed in manufacturing. The Commercial Study indicated that enough industrial land was allocated to serve a population exceeding 257,000.[57]

The area east of Keele Street and north of Finch Avenue contained the oil tank storage facilities, built in the 1940s. In later decades, there were also building products depots, office furniture assembly plants, and transport terminals built nearby.[58] The area adjacent to Highway 400 to the east included a variety of warehousing and small manufacturing plants. This industrial area along Norfinch Drive and Oakdale Road continues to exist, as does

---

55   Macklin L. Hancock, *Jane Finch Commercial Study* (Toronto: Project Planning Associates, for the City of North York Planning Board, February 1963).

56   Hancock, *Commercial Study*, 12

57   Hancock, *Commercial Study*, 21

58   Hancock, *Commercial Study*, 10.

the petroleum tank farm and a large commercial-industrial area developed between Keele and Dufferin.[59] Surrounding the Highway 400 is a broader area of light industrial and commercial facilities, including the large Apotex pharmaceutical plant since 1974.

Initial planning

While Steeles Avenue was still a dirt road into the early 1960s, a federal-provincial partnership purchased approximately 655 acres of land in the northwest portion, bounded by Steeles Avenue to the north and between Jane and Keele Street in 1954. York University was in development from 1959 onward; 476 acres were sold to York University for its new campus. Eighty-eight acres along the Black Creek were sold to the Regional Conservation Authority, and after widening Jane Street to its present 120-foot allowance, ninety-one acres, roughly shaped in a triangle, were left for residential purposes. At the time, it was planned that two kinds of housing (public and private) would be developed with equally high standards of site planning and design, and that the two would develop harmoniously "…without sharp contrasts in architectural style."[60] That was supposed to minimize the identification of one type of accommodation with one particular income group. This describes Edgeley Village on the east side of Jane Street that includes Driftwood and Shoreham and the seniors' building at 35 Shoreham Drive, property of Toronto Community Housing.

In 1960, the planning department determined, "…its situation adjacent to the suggested industrial area and what will probably be the 'noisier' portion of the university campus suggests that low-income housing is particularly appropriate here."[61] It is not clear why the city concluded that the noisier part of the campus would align better with people living in low-income housing. But, one might assume those residents were less valued.

---

59 This area makes up the DUKE [Dufferin-Keele] Heights Business Improvement Area (BIA) today.
60 Beth Bow, Community Spirit, 5.
61 North York Planning Department re: York University Site, Federal-Provincial Housing Lands Jane Street and Steeles Ave. (Reference to ACT for Youth, An Overview of Development in Jane-Finch—1950s to Present), 1960, 13.

The Black Creek, a tributary of the Humber River, is located between Edgeley Village and York University. When Hurricane Hazel swept through the area in 1954, causing great damage in the Humber River basin, Black Creek became protected and was acquired by the Toronto Region Conservation Authority in 1955. Many of the original buildings on the site were repaired, and on June 1, 1960, the Black Creek Pioneer Village was opened.[62]

～

The new single-family homes in the area were quite affordable at that time. For example, Peggy Gemmell and her family bought one of the new houses on Gosford Boulevard in 1963 for $72,000 (the principal, interest and taxes cost them $98.00 each month). New bungalows in the 1950s were in the $13,000 to $16,000 price range, and apartment development was largely of the three-storey walk-up type and located near to the main traffic routes.[63] Today, a single-family detached house would sell for over $800,000.

While some of the neighbourhoods had beautiful parks and conservation land, the impact of rapid growth was felt by the new homeowners. Lolanda Canzana moved into a home in the Blacksmith neighbourhood in 1969, where there were new houses on the west side of Jane Street south of Steeles Avenue. There was a farm on the southwest corner of Jane and Steeles (now an apartment complex), where they took their children on pony rides, and they enjoyed skating on the pond at Hullmar and York Gate Boulevard. Land adjacent to York Gate Boulevard, west of Jane, was open land, and it was where they learned to skate on the pond. At the time, families felt like they were living in the country. St. Augustine Catholic Church was built in 1984, and shortly afterward homeowners found out townhouses were going to be built along Gosford Boulevard and they were not happy. After the town-houses and high-rises were completed, Canzana expressed that they felt they were being closed in.[64]

---

62 *Longhouse*, 25.
63 Hancock, *Commercial Study*, 9.
64 Lolanda Canzana, oral history interview (Toronto: York Woods Public Library, Black Creek Living History Project, November 2010).

Having large sections of social housing development in the community was not the most critical error. Rather, it was the lack of social infrastructure and supports for families moving into the area, especially for new immigrants and other newcomer families. An integrated mix of social housing and private housing made sense, but how do you do that without social infrastructure for all the children, isolated seniors, or stay-at-home parents who would live in the community? What about the impact of rapid population increase? Is the transit system keeping up with the population so that people can get to their jobs? What about daycare? What about social services for those who needed them? Family doctors, dentists, and other health care specialists? Sufficient schools to prevent overcrowding? Community recreation centres? Entertainment? Local jobs? Parks with playgrounds and sports fields? Good, accessible food markets, restaurants, stores?

District 10 plan

In 1962, staff of the Metropolitan Toronto Planning Board, in cooperation with the staff of the North York Planning Board, North York Board of Education and the Metropolitan Separate School Board, submitted a preliminary report called, *District Plan 10,* for this area of the city. This document was prepared as a pilot document "...to illustrate the content of district plans within the context of the overall Metropolitan Official Plan and to indicate the function which district plans will perform after adoption of the Metropolitan Official Plan."[65] The district plan was also the first one of its type prepared in Metropolitan Toronto and was "...thus experimental in nature."[66]

The District 10 area was bounded by Dufferin to the east, Humber River to the west, Highway 401 to the south, and Steeles Avenue to the north. This includes the current neighbourhoods of York University Heights, Glenfield-Jane Heights, Black Creek, Downsview-Roding, Humbermede and Humber Summit. While the official plan was being prepared for land use, road

---

65   "District Plan 10," Prepared by: Metropolitan Toronto Planning Board, North York Planning Board, North York Board of Education and Metropolitan Separate School Board (February 1962, 22).
66   Hancock, *Commercial Study*, 2.

system, residential development (including population densities), elementary schools, local parks, and local commercial requirements, the growth in population and pace of development had outstripped the planning process.

The planning report focused on three main areas: land use, population, and transportation, with no provision for social factors beyond the designation of land for schools and parks. It did recognize that it was difficult to establish apartment sites alongside of single-family homes, especially when the apartments have a low standard of design and construction, inadequate community provisions (such as adequate open park space and facilities for children to play), and an overconcentration of apartment buildings in continuous strips.

The plan was to build a community with a vision of good suburban development, turning existing farms into a modern and balanced community. It was believed that prior to 1969, the neighbourhoods were "developing in a manner people considered appropriate for suburban development. The first homes were for young families, away from the centre of the city, isolated perhaps, with no stores or public transportation, but suitable as bedroom communities for breadwinners, housewives, and growing children."[67]

Although developed in 1962, recommendations from the plan were to be implemented over a twenty-year period. The plan was finally approved in 1969. Yet, barely five years after approval of the plan, nearly eighty per cent of development had already taken place.

According to the *Review of Planning Policies* report by Klein and Sears the plan was outdated at the start. "Although the *District Plan 10* has effectively guided the development of Ward 3 in terms of residential land use, densities and the distribution of population by neighbourhoods, it did not project a rate of development which would see almost 90% of development projected for 1990 realized some 15 years early and merely five years after the *District Plan 10* was approved."[68] By 1975, more than half of the residential units

---

67   Helen Ede, "Neighbourhood Planning—Social Evolution of Jane Finch Area" (June 1978).

68   Jack Klein and Henry Sears, *A Review of Planning Policies re: Lands Bounded by Finch Ave., Hwy 400, the H.E.P.C. right of way and Jane Street* (North York Planning Board, December 1975).

in the neighbourhoods were apartments and the population reached almost 50,000 in the former Ward 3.[69]

In an article by York University professors Boudreau, Keil and Young, "The In-Between City," (in *Changing Toronto: Governing Urban Neoliberalism*) they indicated that the people of Jane-Finch did not cause the problems in the community.

> Rather, the failure is on the part of traditional methods of urban analysis employed by many scholars, planners, politicians, and the press to acknowledge the vision of the progressive urbanism upon which Jane-Finch was founded and the important contribution which that vision—now embodied in the lived modernity of the neighbourhood—could make in the present-day consideration of social problems in Toronto's older suburbs.[70]

The article also spoke about the attraction of allocating social housing in North York, with its open land and the open arms of North York's politicians.

> Ontario Housing Corporation (OHC) was attracted to the green fields of the Jane and Finch area, and the pro-development North York Council welcomed them. By 1975, 22.5% of all dwellings in North York's Ward 3 (Jane-Finch) were public housing units developed by OHC. In contrast, [only] about 10% of all dwellings in the post-amalgamation City of Toronto and only 5% nationwide are social housing.[71]

The *District Plan 10* report, which provided the general direction for development, also focused on a diversified form of housing for the Jane-Finch community.

> To overcome the tendency of establishing a one-sided community in the suburbs consisting largely of young families, it is desirable to introduce a variety of dwellings, which cater to a wide range of community. Second, to achieve higher residential densities, which can support a full range of services and community facilities, multiple

69   *Longhouse*, 27.
70   Boudreau et al, "The In-Between City," 124.
71   Boudreau et al, "The In-Between City," 124.

housing, including apartments, need to be introduced. A subsidiary reason for apartment buildings—architectural effect and relief of the monotony of uniform low housing development is an important aspect from a civic design point of view.[72]

In terms of housing variety, the plan said that housing types needed to be balanced to meet the needs of the whole population, but that is not what occurred in Ward 3.

> Housing policy is based on the need to provide a balanced stock of accommodation capable of satisfying the housing needs of a wide cross-section of the population. The residential lands of Planning District 10 will be virtually surrounded by industrial development. The northwest sector of Metropolitan Toronto will offer the opportunity for a fair balance between workplace and home for the residents within the area. To realize this opportunity, provision is required for rental accommodation as well as home ownership, and the rental units should primarily be for families.[73]

There was a demand for rental accommodation for families across the City of Toronto, and this was provided in the suburbs. Much of what were Toronto's suburbs were burdened with high-density construction.

> The demand for rental accommodation is the economic reason for the introduction of apartments in the suburbs; the other two reasons—variety of housing types and higher densities—are social and planning aims. A misunderstanding of these aims often leads to an unsatisfactory form of rental housing development. Since about 1955 when rental dwellings began to be provided in greater number, there has been an over-emphasis on apartments and more recently an almost exclusive supply of higher density apartment buildings. Nearly all the rental units in the suburbs are in apartment buildings, with only a small number of 'plexes,' maisonettes and garden courts or row houses.[74]

---

72   *District Plan 10.*
73   *District Plan 10.*
74   *District Plan 10.*

A commercial study

The *Jane Finch Commercial Study* was prepared for the North York Planning Board by Project Planning Associates Limited in February 1963. This report examined the existing and future commercial requirements in the broader Jane-Finch area bounded by Highway 400, Steeles Avenue, Keele Street and Sheppard Avenue. The report considered the future building of York University and the possibility of commercial uses being developed on the campus. The original map indicated their thinking about curving Jane Street and Finch Avenue so that the University would be better aligned with and accessible to the Jane-Finch area.

> The introduction of a university in the north-eastern quadrant of the block bounded by Steeles Avenue, Keele Street, Finch Avenue and Jane Street will have far-reaching effects on surrounding areas and conversely the surrounding development must be complementary to an important institution, both in the physical and psychological sense.
>
> It is an acknowledged fact that any university, to a great extent, influences the community of which it forms a part. On the other hand, every effort should be made to create environs which are beneficial to the University as well as to the community. It cannot be expected that the University will influence the character of Metropolitan Toronto as a whole, but certainly it will, and should influence greatly this north-western part of the Metropolitan area. Two points must be considered of major importance. These are: the community concept, i.e. the setting of the University within the community structure, and the transportation pattern.[75]

≈

In terms of social housing built in the 1960s, planning did not incorporate streets that run through the developments, leaving people to walk through mazes. Most housing projects were built that way, from Tandridge in Rexdale (further west), Flemingdon Park in the east, and Regent Park in the south.

---

75   Hancock, *Commercial Study*, 51.

Without through roads, there would be no eyes on the street along with no easy access for emergency services.[76]

Michael A. Amos, an actor and author who grew up in Jane-Finch in the 1980s and 1990s, wrote, *Both Sides of the Fence: Surviving the Trap* describing his housing complex.

> The Trap was a formation of townhouses set up almost like a maze—a trap. Shoreham Court consisted of about 180 housing units, and Driftwood Avenue contained about 100 units. My native Driftwood Court alone comprised approximately 140 housing units. Aside from that stretch of roughly 420 government-owned housing units, those figures didn't include the numerous low-income apartment buildings that spanned our Trap, and other townhouse complexes that were privately owned.[77]

While public open green space was designated along the valleys and ravines of the Black Creek and the Humber River, including Black Creek Pioneer Village, plans also included a replication of an Indigenous village that would be located on the southeast corner of Jane-Finch. The commercial study said, "The remaining corner at the intersection of the now Jane and Finch, lying on the south-east side, would be used as a park or conservation area, and possibly be included as part of the proposed Indian Village site."[78] This did not happen, it became the site of the Jane Finch Mall, which opened in 1969.

The Jane Finch mall

That was not all that was originally planned for the area commercially. According to this report, the community shopping centre would be 100,000 to 300,000 square feet and in addition to the retail function, it would also provide for community activities that may include an arena, a curling rink, a bowling facility, a library, and a police station. After reviewing this report,

---

76   Jane Jacobs, *Death and Life of Great American Cities* (New York: Random House, 1961).
77   Michael A. Amos, *Both Sides of the Fence: Surviving the Trap* (Toronto: Famos Books, 2014).
78   Hancock, *Commercial Study*, 55.

community members were astounded about what should have happened, but did not.

> Within this north-western sector of North York Township, where the land has been laid out in blocks 1 to 1 ¼ miles square, such a centre will normally be located at the intersection of the boundary streets, although the true community centre providing a complete range of retail and other facilities cannot develop successfully at every such intersection, due to the limited population served.[79]

There was also a recommendation to have local shopping centres that would be retail in nature, catering to the day-to-day needs of residents immediately adjacent to these facilities, such as Shoreham Plaza to the north and Yorkwoods Plaza to the south. In the plans above, Jane-Finch did get a library, a police station, and the John Booth Arena, but they are not located within the community shopping centre. Further in this report, it was recommended "that a total estimated requirement of 251,150 square feet be divided between the proposed site at the 'new' intersection of Jane and Finch and the existing site to the south-east of the present intersection." The report went on to say that it must be located at the intersection of Jane Street and Finch Avenue, "making it conveniently accessible from all parts of the community that it is intended to serve."[80]

Community response to planning

Ward 3 was growing in leaps and bounds. Thirteen thousand of the forty-three thousand (thirty per cent) Ontario Housing units in North York were in Ward 3, and approximately thirty-three per cent were in five percent of the Borough's total acreage. Between 1961 and 1971, the North York population doubled, while Ward 3 tripled. By 1971, Ward 3 reached sixty-one per cent of its total population, but only forty-four per cent of its proposed dwellings. It was assumed that there would be "an overall average of about 3.4 persons per dwelling in the district." Yet, in 1971, the average was in fact 4.1 persons

---

79   Hancock, *Commercial Study*, 41.
80   Hancock, *Commercial Study*, 45.

per dwelling. [81] Clearly, the area was growing too fast and had the structure of a suburban setting, with the problems of a deteriorating inner-city core.

A paper was presented by the community at a Primary Prevention Institute Conference outlining the consequences of the *District Plan 10* report in 1980.

> Isolation was a problem. It is a problem for children in high rises, mothers at home and immigrants. The lack of a sense of community is due in part to its newness, to the heterogeneity of the population, making it hard for us to identify common interests, and very likely to the effort many residents have to put in to managing their day-to-day lives, leaving them little time for community involvement. Children grow up in over-taxed families only to move on to an over-taxed school system. There is a lack of adequate day-care for young children and many latch-key arrangements for older ones. For teen-agers, the lack of community contributes to a sense of alienation and a lot of them spend leisure time in shopping plazas and poolhalls for the lack of alternatives.

> The problems are exaggerated by media coverage of the area such as 'Suburbia Gone Sour: The Jane-Finch Tragedy' (*Toronto Star*, August 26, 1979). While their intention is to support change in the situation, too much coverage by the media creates myths, leaving residents feeling inadequate and funders often feeling that the area is hopeless and that funds could do more elsewhere.

> The political route to change was hampered by the fact that ward boundaries are virtually impossible to change with the result that representation for rapid growth suburbs is sometimes half that for older areas. Also, in the two-tier metropolitan Toronto system of government, Borough Councils elect representatives to the Metro Council often with the consequences that the Aldermen from areas like Jane-Finch do not get to Metro Council, and the area's interests are not adequately represented at the Metro level, where social

---

81   Bow, *Community Spirit.*

welfare decisions are made. Other routes to change, besides this particular one, had to be found.[82]

In the 1970s, Helen Ede, a passionate and dedicated activist in the community, shared her frustrations at a local meeting about the city's planning. "Aside from the anticipated demand in the area, which I find difficult to explain why it should be greater than elsewhere in the borough, is the matter of 'over the next decade or two.' I would presume this to include the years 1989–1994."[83] Ede understood that revisions were to be made at approximate five-year intervals, but nearly ten years later, no reviews or revisions had taken place. She was upset that the plan did not project a rate of development that would see almost ninety per cent of growth projected for 1990 realized fifteen years early and merely five years after the Plan was approved.

Pat O'Neill was a resident and another activist with incredible perseverance and determination. She had a strong commitment to the community and was later elected City Alderman for the area. In an interview years later, O'Neill eloquently summed up the district plan.

> I think to some extent, it took them by surprise. It was a twenty-five-year plan from '65–'90, and the fact was that in ten years it was almost complete; I think that shocked them. That was because the federal and provincial government made funding available for social housing and, of course, our community still had space to build it. So we got quite a large influx of social housing without the services. Not that that always solves the problem, as you can tell from some of the downtown projects, but nevertheless, there weren't services. Then there was a huge wave of immigration, and we were fairly close to the airport, so again it was a natural reception place for people to come.[84]

---

82   Helen Ede, Peggy Birnberg and Mary Lewis, "A Case Study of the Child/Parent Centre of the Jane/Finch Community and Family Centre," North York: Primary Prevention Institute, February 1980.

83   Helen Ede, *Workshop Five, "Neighbourhood Planning–Social Evolution of Jane Finch Area,"* June 1978, 9

84   Pat O'Neill interview (Toronto: York Woods Library, Black Creek Living History Project, August 24, 2009).

She felt strongly that the development needed to be community led. "A doctor can't treat a patient without knowing what's wrong. The community knows what the problems are and, in a sense, how to cure them."[85]

Many reports and papers, along with a few books, have been written about the blunders of government planning and the challenges facing Jane-Finch. For example, in 1983, Beth Bow worked for the United Church's Jane-Finch Community Ministry in the Firgrove area. She came to know the community well, and in the time that she worked there, she also came to see the community as "home." As a result of her rich experience, Bow wrote a paper in 1984 called, "Community Spirit of the Jane-Finch Corridor," while studying at York University.

> It has been described as an 'instant city' growing out of farmers' fields in a short decade. A very planned 'instant city' it was designed specifically to avoid the social problems now so overwhelmingly prevalent in it. The results of the planning have turned out to be worse than those of the traditional lower socio-economic areas in the city. In many cases, it has made the same problems it was designed to remove, worse.[86]

> It became obvious to the residents that the considerable and unanticipated rate of growth (an increase of 2,438% in the decade spanning 1961–1971), was responsible for many of their concerns; especially those of public facilities and services, which did not materialize at the same rate as the population increased.[87]

Newcomer families

The new federal immigration policy meant that many more newcomers were settling in Jane-Finch and bringing their own unique social experiences with them. In the early years, new immigrants were often from a non-urban background and political systems that were corrupt, including favouritism, patronage, and paternalism. Many newcomers arrived with strict moral codes

---

85   O'Neill interview.
86   Bow, *Community Spirit*, 1.
87   Bow, *Community Spirit*, 7.

and devout religious beliefs. The values and expectations of leaders such as elected officials, teachers, and police officers were different from those in their home countries. For example, many assumed that the teachers knew what was best for the student, and the parents left that responsibility to the teachers, trusting that the school would prepare their children for a better life.

The extended family in their homelands played a significant role in helping to raise children, along with members from within their cultural communities, but as newcomers, their extended family may have been left behind, and life in a high-rise was not necessarily conducive to community support. For some, there was also an understanding that the father should be the sole support of the family, but this was not always possible given the cost of living requiring both parents to work.[88] Clearly, the government failed to ensure the appropriate development of a community where the needs of those who lived there were secondary concerns.

Planning perspectives

Professors Boudreau, Keil and Young describe the ideas behind the development of Jane-Finch.

> [F]ounded on three modern ideas that were made real in the 1950s, 1960s, and 1970s: the large-scale production of public housing, experimentation in urban planning and urban design, and the de-racialization of Canadian immigration policy. In the post-modern era of the early twenty-first century, these ideas are widely discredited, along with places like Jane-Finch, where they are so strongly evident. In that sense, Jane-Finch is in-between modernity and postmodernity. The plan recommended that more than 50 per cent of all dwellings be provided in high-rise buildings.[89]

Arik C. Day wrote his master's thesis for the University of Amsterdam, and it included a case study of Jane-Finch. The paper was called, "Social Innovation as Community Governance: Critical Success Factors in the Neoliberal City." After

88   Ede, *Workshop Five.*
89   Boudreau et al, "The In-Between City," 125.

interviewing many people in Toronto, including a local worker who lived in Jane-Finch, he shared his perspective on the community.

> Jane-Finch was designed according to the 'neighbourhood plan' concept (created by the North York Department of Planning & Development), which divided the area into six subcentres. Each subcentre developed around a neighbourhood school and park. The housing stock contained a mixture of single-family homes, townhouses, and low- and high-rise apartments. In the 1960s, politicians and policymakers decided to establish several social housing units in Jane-Finch (e.g. Yorkwoods), as they sought to avoid the social problems associated with high-density urban housing.[90]

According to the Metro Toronto Police Force (1987) community profile, "The development of Jane-Finch was prototypical of North American suburban development. However, as the population increased and more social housing was built, adequate services (e.g., immigration, employment) were not provided to keep pace with the growing disadvantaged (and new immigrant) populations. Meanwhile, the media branded Jane-Finch as a Black community with an epidemic of drugs, gangs, guns, and teenage mothers."[91]

Jasmine Ali, a York University student conducting research into the Jane-Finch area for this book, made the following observation about the *District Plan 10* report.

> This shows me that community building was really developer led. From reading these extracted minutes it does not appear that the City took any proactive approach in encouraging a diversified type of development in Ward 3, that it was left to the developers to create ideas of infrastructure that would benefit the community in their proposals. So, here we have an issue. If the community is complaining to the government that they don't have the services they need, and the government is not relaying this information to developers,

---

90   Arik C. Day, *Social Innovation as Community Governance: Critical Success Factors in the Neoliberal City* (Amsterdam: University of Amsterdam, [Master's Thesis in Urban and Regional Planning], August 15, 2016).

91   Jackson, Suzanne, "The Yorkwoods-Grandravine Neighbourhood in the Broader Jane Finch Community" (Toronto: University of Toronto, Report, late 1990s), 10.

rather sitting back and waiting for developers to present ideas to them, how will these needs be met? The community will continue receiving things they don't need, i.e., more apartment buildings.[92]

⤳

In the early 1970s, the provincial government gave twenty-four million dollars to a private developer for a mortgage on 1,114 condominium apartments and townhouses.[93] The complex on Four Winds Drive, between Keele Street and Sentinel Road, along Finch Avenue, was among the first condominium built in the province of Ontario. The condominiums, called University City, consisted of high-rise buildings and townhouses. At the time, when people came to look at the units, it had to be explained that they were for purchase, not rent. In 1972, a letter went out to residents to introduce this new kind of [Cadillac Development Corporation] home at University City. The letter indicated that they would be managed and maintained as carefully as any Cadillac apartment. But they would belong to the purchaser so that they could build equity, rather than giving their money to a landlord in rent. University City was initially described as a model community that included a recreation centre, indoor and outdoor pools, shops, and a professional building.

A *Globe and Mail* newspaper wrote about this new way of living. The units were to accommodate 3,500 people in 195 townhouses and 919 apartments in the six eleven-storey buildings. The units were geared for people with incomes ranging from $7,600 to $10,900 per year [in 1972].[94] When I discussed this with local activists, they thought the $24 million from the Province would have been better spent developing the social infrastructure needed to support the growing community.

⤳

---

92   Jasmine Ali, "Research Findings for Jane-Finch History Project" (North York: York University, 2018 [now titled, *By Us! For Us!*, 2021]).

93   "OHC, Cadillac plan 1,114 units in North York" (Toronto: *Globe and Mail*, January 23, 1971).

94   "OHC, Cadillac plan."

In July 1992, the North York Inter-Agency and Community Council compiled a community profile of the City of North York.[95] The report described the Jane-Finch community in the northwest, covering a three-kilometre radius around the intersection of Jane Street and Finch Avenue. This area had the highest child population aged 0 to 9 years; the highest population with a mother tongue other than English; the highest number of residents over the age of fifteen with less than a Grade 9 education; the highest rates of unemployment; the lowest average household income, below forty thousand dollars. The community had the highest population of teenagers and the lowest population of seniors in North York.

The North York Public Health Department reported that the northwest had the highest number of babies born with a low birth weight, less than 2,500 grams (126 out of 443 for the city), and the highest percentage of teen mothers between the ages of fourteen and nineteen years of age (4.3 per cent). This report also showed how participation in breakfast clubs was growing. Six breakfast clubs across North York showed an increase of participation from 2,952 in January 1990 to 4,294 in March 1991, a forty-five per cent increase. For example, the Edgeley neighbourhood (around Jane Street and Driftwood Avenue) went from 711 to 1,253."[96] Clearly, the City should have known that poor planning and lack of funding to a low-income and high-density population community was having an impact on those who lived there.

Maria Augimeri, a former city councillor, offered her thoughts about the planning of the community.

> I got into some trouble for saying this, but I'll say it again. The way housing was planned here and is perpetuated (I said this when I was extremely angry), is a de facto apartheid, because people of colour are automatically shut into communities where there is no hope of getting out. Drug trafficking is exasperated by nooks and crannies that are architecturally built into the townhouse communities. The

---

95   In 1998, NYIACC officially joined the other five social planning councils in the newly amalgamated City of Toronto forming the Community Social Planning Council of Toronto (now called Social Planning Toronto).

96   North York Inter-Agency and Community Council, "Community Profile of the City of North York" (North York: North York Inter-Agency and Community Council, July 1992).

ideas of 'towers in the park,' which was supposed to be a wonderful idea...works in Don Mills, so why doesn't it work here. It didn't work here, because as I said, no social safety net and not enough programs to provide the backup for struggling families and individual needs.[97]

Despite the poor planning, the lack of social infrastructure and negative reputation of the area, there were progressive leaders and newcomers moving into the Jane-Finch area in the 1970s with a vision and enthusiasm for starting a new life in a new community. The new pioneers decided to organize, mobilize, and begin to address the mounting issues facing the community.

---

97   Maria Augimeri interview (Toronto: York Woods Library, Black Creek Living History Project, June 2, 2019).

CHAPTER FOUR

Critical Decade of Growth

Community action

Pat O'Neill had six children, and she got involved in the community because of them. They were living in the area of Jane Street and Sheppard Avenue West when she began volunteering by leading a pack of Brownies—first becoming a Tawny Owl, then a Brown Owl, a Guide Captain, and then a Commissioner. O'Neill later figured that was a good investment. "When I ran for Alderman in 1976, my Brownies were all at a voting age and I also knew a lot of people in the community because of the work I had done. I think that it surprised everyone that I won, because I took only three weeks holiday from work and used my $1,000 savings!"[98]

While O'Neill loved her neighbourhood, she had eight people living in a three-bedroom home, and they were cramped. When she was offered a larger townhouse within a new social housing complex, she accepted and came to her new neighbourhood at Driftwood Court with volunteer experience, energy, and a commitment to community involvement. The five-bedroom townhouse provided enough for her large family and an opportunity to help build a new and growing community.

Edgeley Village, the area south of Steeles and east of Jane Street, including the neighbourhoods of Shoreham and Driftwood, was initially planned as a mixed community of condominiums and public housing with the condos coming later. For O'Neill, the first order of business was to start a tenants association, along with programs for the children—evening youth programs in the school, soccer, and social activities for families. There were a lot of five-bedroom units built, and as a result, there were a lot of children in the new development.

---

98   O'Neill interview.

"We started the Tenants' Association as a way for people to get involved and to get volunteers to help run the programs."[99]

The Tenants' Association was soon faced with a political issue. The provincial and federal government were in a dispute over money, so the provincial government, who ran housing put a freeze on their rents. O'Neill was worried about this, as it could mean huge increases in their rent when the government dispute over money got resolved.

> We all moved in at a certain rate, and then maybe a year or so after being there, the federal and provincial governments solved their problem and suddenly there were rent hikes of 50% and 75%. Of course, people can't absorb that immediately—you know you plan your budget according to what you've got, and if your rent is a certain rate, and you've got payments on things, that means an increase like that was incredible. You just couldn't manage. It was still geared to income, but people had moved in at the fixed rate and then suddenly, they were hit with this large increase. Some people who moved in were on unemployment insurance. When the economy improved, many got jobs and some of them were making good money so consequently their rent jumped an enormous amount. The tenants organized at that point and organized a rent strike themselves.[100]

The association, where more than fifty per cent of the residents were members, made a lot of noise and as a result, the board of Metro Toronto Housing Authority invited them to a meeting. In the end, it was agreed to stagger the increases so that it made it a little easier on people, so it was a partial victory. They did not get the increase stopped, rather they got incremental increases, which made a difference.[101]

≈

---

99   O'Neill interview.
100 O'Neill interview.
101 O'Neill interview.

When city alderman Katie Hayhurst organized a meeting of area residents in 1973, it made sense to have O'Neill at the table.[102]

Alderman Katie Hayhurst at Firgrove in 1970s

Hayhurst, a young and insightful resident, was elected for two terms with O'Neill following her. She was concerned about the rapid development happening in the community. It was rumoured that "arrangements" had been made between a previous politician and developers for the density of this area and, subsequently, it was difficult to legally overturn future high-density development at Council and/or the Ontario Municipal Board. It was a time when the Ontario government was pushing municipalities to integrate public housing into their communities.

Hayhurst's goal was to help the community become self-sufficient so they could get improved social and public services in the area they desperately needed and get control over further development along Jane Street. "In the beginning, there wasn't much, if any community activism, so those four years on Council were a real beginning to community action in the Jane-Finch area."[103] Hayhurst found that thirteen thousand tenants were living in the ward. "Its not an affluent area. But the rest of North York is, and North York

---

102   The term "alderman" was changed to "councillor" on January 20, 1986, after an eight-year long battle led by Alderman Marie Labatte.
103   Email from Katie Hayhurst to Wanda MacNevin (2018).

makes the policies. Ward 3 got—I worked it out—0.0037 per cent of the borough's $2,000,000 budget for Parks and Recreation this year, although we have about 8 per cent of the people."[104]

By 1975, more than half of all residential units in these neighbourhoods were apartments, including private rentals and social housing.[105]

Downsview Weston Action Community

The work of the Downsview Weston Action Community (DWAC) was the first community-wide response to the rapid development and growing population, where people were struggling with poverty, discrimination, and social isolation. DWAC was established in 1975 with support from a group of local leaders who were residents and from key workers in the area. The idea was to identify the needs and concerns of people living in the area, and to look for ways of improving the quality of life in the community. As a result of that early work came many more opportunities for residents to come together to respond to issues that were impacting their lives, to become engaged in the community and to fight for change. However, it was a challenge for residents to become engaged.

Many saw the move to Jane-Finch as "temporary," so they felt no need to get involved. For those in social housing, plans were to secure a job and make enough money to leave because people wanted their kids to go to a better school outside the community; people wanted more programs for their children and better access to services. Perhaps residents were simply too busy to be engaged, trying to navigate oppressive systems, working in unsafe environments for low salaries, and simply trying to survive from one day to the next.

Workers from social agencies who began to work with the DWAC leadership understood the importance of listening to the community and responding to the community's agenda. One agency was the Children's Aid Society (CAS), and its first community worker was Audrey McLaughlin, who subsequently became the first woman to lead the national New Democratic Party.

---

104 Penney Kome, "A High-Rise Isn't a Home for Families and Children" (Toronto: *Globe and Mail*, November 7, 1973).
105 *Longhouse*, 27

A philosophy and goal statement were established, and the committee held elections for an interim Council of Representatives from the community. It was the first community-based planning entity in Jane-Finch, and it had the goal of "uniting, giving leadership to, and encouraging the development of efforts to improve the quality of life in District 10." Their work included sharing information, assisting community groups, encouraging the development of new groups, researching and determining community needs, and negotiating with other organizations and agencies. The initial priority tasks were to compile data and information about Ward 3, assess and define needs, and establish priority guidelines regarding needs and resources of the greater Ward 3 community.

DWAC applied for incorporation, and this was granted in 1976. The membership of DWAC at the time of incorporation included residents from neighbourhood-based organizations and ratepayer groups, not mainstream agencies and institutions. They were strong and resilient, including residents who started the first local newspaper and others who organized programs for seniors, youth, and young single mothers. Residents understood that the Jane-Finch community needed programs and services and that those programs and services also needed to respond to the immigrant and newcomer families who lived in the neighbourhoods.

≈≥

Representatives from some agencies attended the meetings as a resource but Mary Lewis played a different role. Lewis, a respectful and engaging worker who strongly believed in building capacity, replaced Audrey McLaughlin and became the new CAS community worker. She played that role over a five-year period with a strong belief in building resident capacity. The only requirement from CAS was that her work have a preventive aspect regarding child welfare.

Lewis saw her role as being available to community groups or residents and to assist them in organizing a response to the needs they identified. After spending time familiarizing herself with the community and getting to know what was going on in the community, she started to provide much needed staff support to DWAC.

At the same time, Lewis was also engaged with parents with young children in the community. The YWCA was completing a Life Skills program at 15 Tobermory. Next, they moved the program to 415 Driftwood and then to the Firgrove neighbourhood, all social housing apartment buildings and townhouse complexes in the community. The Life Skills program was over a six-month period. Lewis contacted some of the graduates from the program and together they figured out how to provide support for the continuation of the programs. Instead of being a resource to each group separately, she brought the leaders of the groups together and, in 1974, formed a network that called itself the Tiny Toddlers Club, where leaders supported and encouraged each other, shared ideas and skills, and found resources to maintain their groups in their local neighbourhoods. By 1976, there were seven Tiny Toddler programs running in the community. This also served as a contact point and the base for recruiting potential community leaders to become engaged in broader issues in the community. Wendy Brazier is one example of this concept. Wendy became a board member for the Jane/Finch Community and Family Centre and an activist in her community.

≈

Over time, through the efforts of DWAC and resident leaders, the community became known for its social engagement, resilience, activism, and self-determination. O'Neill was the alderman for three terms after Hayhurst moved out west. She shared local concerns regarding the overpopulation in the schools (too many portables), the hospital overcrowding, the library was overwhelmed, and there were too few services for the community. O'Neill believed that, "It was a time when there was a freeze on funding because of another downturn in the economy, so there was no money to do anything. No services, nothing for seniors, nothing at all!"[106]

Some people chose to live in this growing, culturally diverse community. Helen Ede became involved with DWAC from its inception. Initially, Helen and her husband Gary had dreamed of living in Africa with their two young children to experience life in a third-world country. Helen was a nurse and

---

106 O'Neill interview.

Gary was a teacher, so their jobs were portable. They felt confident in securing employment until their daughter Meghan developed a health problem that would put her at risk in an underdeveloped country. Determined to bring up their children where there was cultural diversity and not in their current area on Bayview Avenue, they began their search for a new neighbourhood.

Helen grew up in a poor area of Thunder Bay, Ontario, and valued low-income and working-class people. When they went for a drive through the Jane-Finch community and walked through the Jane Finch Mall, they noticed people from around the world speaking different languages and some women wearing saris with choli tops. They were eager to bring their children up within a diverse community, so they purchased a new townhome in 1967, south of Finch and across the street from the newly built Yorkwoods Community Centre.

It didn't take long for them to settle in with their children, Andy and Meghan. The children loved the Black Creek ravine, spending countless hours exploring the woods and the creek. The Edes didn't give too much thought to them playing in the ravine—it was safe and without traffic.

Helen and Gary became increasingly disturbed by what they were reading about Jane-Finch in the newspapers. It was the early 1970s, and they thought the news was horrendous. How could the planning department locate a large number of low-income housing units in one area and not even look at the potential impact? Helen already knew that many of the area schools had portables to accommodate the growing number of children in the area. She also knew that there was a great need for public and affordable housing in response to the rapid urban growth in Toronto. Newcomer families were arriving by the hundreds and families in downtown Toronto wanted to move to the suburbs where the houses were affordable. With the growing population of children and youth and the lack of safe spaces for them, where were they going to gather after school or on the weekends? Helen was thinking that bad publicity, poverty, and isolation, especially in high-rise buildings, would inevitably cause people to be distrustful and anxious about their neighbourhoods.

In the summer of 1976, DWAC undertook an inventory of human services in the area. The inventory was compiled by Bev Varney, a resident and York University student, with a grant from the Ministry of Culture and Recreation.

> On the basis of this inventory, DWAC contends that the indiscriminate growth of Jane Finch 'Instant City' through poor planning, both physical and social, has resulted in an unreasonable lack of human services and service planning in the area. Furthermore, the community need not apologize for its depressed outlook, but rather, the blame must fall on elected governments and social welfare agencies for not fulfilling responsibilities to this and other 'instant' communities where human needs are assessed secondly to the rate of physical development.[107]

This inventory was contrasted with Parkdale "on the basis that both communities were similar in economic, social, and population characteristics at the time of the 1971 census." The inventory indicated that less than sixty per cent of both populations were born in Canada, determining that both areas had a high immigrant population. The intention of the inventory was not to suggest that services in Parkdale were enough or that identical services should be available.

Varney showed that residents in Jane-Finch had eight places to go for information and counselling, whereas Parkdale had nineteen; that there were three social and recreation centres in Jane-Finch, whereas Parkdale had ten; that Jane-Finch had one immigrant service to go to, whereas Parkdale had eighteen. While Jane-Finch had more daycare centres (still not enough), they had fewer daycare subsidy spaces for families.

Over a two-year period, DWAC formed sub-committees around specific concerns, such as transportation, daycare, statistics, communication, social services, youth issues, and urban planning that yielded some success. Beyond the committee work, they held a series of Neighbourhood Action Hearings in various neighbourhoods, both north and south of Jane-Finch to evaluate the

---

107   Helen Ede, "Inventory of Human Services in the Jane Finch Area" (North York: Jane Corridor News, January 1976).

neighbourhoods, find out what people wanted to see happen in their neighbourhoods and to take steps to attain them. While some of the meetings were still being held, actions identified at the meetings were taking place.[108]

≫

During the 1950s, North York's population grew by almost 20,000 a year, and by 1960, the population of North York reached almost 250,000. In the Jane-Finch community, the Jane Heights neighbourhood [now called Glenfield-Jane Heights], from Finch to Sheppard and from Highway 400 to the Black Creek, and the Black Creek neighbourhood, from Steeles to Finch and Highway 400 to the Black Creek, experienced an increase of population from 1,301 in 1961 to 33,030 in 1971. These two neighbourhoods continued to grow rapidly in the 1970s with the construction of many high-rise buildings. By 1975, more than half of all residential units in these neighbourhoods were apartments, including private rentals and social housing.[109]

With an increase of young families moving into the area, daycare was needed so that parents could work. DWAC's Day Care Committee successfully lobbied for four new daycare centres and DWAC's Urban Planning Committee held a series of public meetings on this issue. While DWAC was successful in securing more daycare spaces and more subsidized spaces than any other ward in North York, all the needs were still not met.

O'Neill reported on the issue of daycare in the local newspaper.

> A study completed last fall by the Metro Toronto Day Care Planning Task Force shows that our area still falls into the high need category. In our planning area, there are 16,807 children between the ages of 0–9 years. Almost 40% of mothers with children under five are working. Almost 60% of women 15–24 have low incomes and almost 50% of women 25–54 have low incomes. The study concluded that we would need an additional 118 subsidized day spaces

---

108 Cynthia Green, "Neighbourhood Action Hearings" (North York: *Jane Corridor News*, May 1976; June 1976).

109 *Longhouse*, 23–27.

just to bring us to 672 or the 4% of 16,807 which is the "equitable" figure for a high-need area.[110]

The Social Services Committee of DWAC developed a proposal and received funding to begin the Jane/Finch Community and Family Centre, an organization that continues to thrive today. Support was given to the York Youth Connection (YYC), an initiative between York University and the community, to operate a four-week summer camp on the York campus for Jane-Finch children and youth. That led to a formal agreement for mutual cooperation between the university and the community during that period.

～◦

DWAC received funding from the Student-Community Service Program of the Secretary of State in 1975 to collect statistics primarily for Ward 3, but also from wards 1 and 5, which together comprised planning District

	Number of Units	% of District 10	% of North York
Ward 1	142	5.4	2.2
Ward 3	2,286	86.2	35.6
Ward 5	223	8.4	3.5
Disctrict 10	2651		41.3

10. The report, titled "DWAC Statistics," came to be known as the "Blue Book," giving detailed demographic information on the community. It was intended for use in future planning from a community perspective, with a focus on the population—who lived there, incomes, housing, public spaces, industrial areas, and schools.

The Blue Book indicated that 86% of all the Ontario Housing units in District 10 were in Ward 3, the area known as Jane-Finch.[111]

At that time, Downsview included Steeles Avenue West to the north, 401 Highway to the south, Dufferin Street to the east, and Highway 400 to the

110   Pat O'Neill, "I know why daycare is needed" (*Jane Echo*, April 15, 1981).
111   Yip and Pizzardi, *DWAC Statistics*, 40.

west. West North York would be the area from Highway 400, west to the Humber River, from Steeles to Wilson Avenue or Ward Five.

From 1961–1966, the West North York population doubled from 11,000 to 21,000, and the Downsview population doubled from 36,000 to 68,000. From 1966—1971, the population almost tripled from 1961. By 1971, West North York had 29,000 and Downsview had 96,000. The report also stated that there was a relatively high proportion of young adults, and children under 14, and a relatively low proportion of people over 45.[112]

Transportation was also a concern noted in the DWAC statistics given the population growth. The Blue Book explained that in terms of travel demand of all workers who lived in Downsview, an estimated fifteen per cent worked locally in north Downsview and north Dufferin industrial area; an estimated twenty per cent went south of Highway 401 to work in the area between Dufferin, Keele and CNR tracks; thirteen per cent travelled to the Rexdale-Malton area; nine per cent travelled to the Highways 400 and 401 industrial area west of the 400 in West North York; and only five per cent worked downtown or midtown.

Services for youth

While Downsview Weston Action Community was being established in the early 1970s, attention was being given to the needs of youth in the community. The first two community-based youth organizations were established to support them—Youth Clinical Services and Black Creek Venture Group.

The number of young people utilizing the emergency department at the former York Finch General Hospital (which became Humber River Regional Hospital and is now the Reactivation Care Centre) was a growing concern for both the hospital and for the community given the increased drug use, addictions, and sexually transmitted diseases. Lenore Suddes shared those concerns, having raised five sons herself. Suddes, who cared deeply for young people, moved into the community in 1970. While she managed to raise her sons well, she was concerned about the high number of youth in the area without programs or services.

---

112   Yip and Pizzardi, *DWAC Statistics.*

Suddes had a conversation with Hayhurst, who had been speaking to representatives at the hospital about emergency department issues. She then jumped on board to help establish the Youth Clinical Services, becoming one of the founding board members. She lobbied the hospital to provide space so they could have a facility that would move traffic away from the hospital emergency department and yet would be accessible to high school students attending Westview Centennial Secondary School. With some funding, they bought two portables, and the hospital generously agreed to have them located behind the hospital. Honey Kerr-Went was hired as the first executive director, and they opened their doors for services in early 1970s.

Kerr-Went was both community-minded and passionate about ensuring the clinic provided well-rounded programs and services. Experienced, youth-focused, clinical counsellors were hired, and one of the hospital's doctors worked out of the clinic on a part-time basis to deal with medical issues. Working closely with the emergency, pediatrics, and psychiatry departments, they provided services to youth from twelve to twenty-two years old, focusing on family, peer issues, school, drugs, and mental health.

⁓

While Lenore Suddes was an active volunteer at the Youth Clinical Services, she figured out that there were few places for young people to safely socialize, so she started a drop-in one evening a week that ran for two years at Driftwood Public School. She also initiated the Black Creek Venture Group (BCVG) in 1973, an organization that focused on prevention. Initially, they were considered an Advisory Board to Parks and Recreation at Driftwood Community Centre until their incorporation in 1975.

They did research to figure out how this new organization could be best utilized, leading to a proposal to the North York Parks and Recreation department for funding to run more programs. BCVG was successful with their proposal and the drop-in program was extended to five nights a week in four local schools. After-school programs were started at Driftwood and Shoreham schools, along with a baseball league and lunch programs.[113]

---

113 BCVG Proposal to North York Parks and Recreation Youth Services Division (1980).

Black Creek Venture Group moved into a small office adjacent to the kitchen in the newly built Driftwood Community Centre in 1977, shortly after it opened. Suddes, affectionately known as "Ma" at the Centre, could be found most evenings during the week working in the snack bar, providing informal counselling, and generally being available to young people who came to the drop-in.

The part-time staff for the after-four and drop-in programs were young people from the community who participated in Parks and Recreation training and who did some volunteer work. The youth had a great deal of respect for Suddes. "She's a second mother to the kids at the centre," said Sean Grimes. "She's the most fantastic person I have ever worked for," said Brian Stevens. "She has more love for the kids of the drop-in than many of their own parents."[114]

Suddes had a strong opinion about the media. When they organized a talent night with over three-hundred people attending and featuring the Dynamite Five, a talented group of young musicians and forty other contestants, she later told a reporter who came looking for stories what she thought. "Why aren't you screwy reporters ever around when something like that happens? Do you know what it means to this community to get 300 people out for something like that? All we ever get is bad publicity and we get studied to death by these so-called experts and every time we get studied, we get clobbered."[115]

Having a local community organization located in the Driftwood Community Centre that was operated by the North York Parks and Recreation department would not have happened without the support of its director, Bill Traynor. Traynor was exceptional, with a background in social work, early childhood education, and in working with youth. When he came to the Centre, people saw dramatic changes—it was always in use and

---

114   Lorna Van Amelsfort, "Raised 5 Sons, Now 'Ma' to Hundreds" (*Jane Echo*, May 28, 1983).
115   Lawrence Goldstein, "The Corridor—Pain, Anger…Hope" (*The Mirror*, May 17, 1978).

buzzing with activities. He opened the doors—not just for recreation, but for community programming. Traynor and Suddes made an excellent team.

The sky was the limit in terms of what local staff did with the youth. Brian Whitehead, who spent his teenage years living in the newly built Driftwood townhouses and who as an adult became a lawyer, was hired by BCVG as a youth. Whitehead's family was also there before the Driftwood Community Centre was built.

> There was a forest and we used to play in there—games like hide and seek, that kind of thing—kick the can. The Driftwood Plaza was there, and we used to hang around there as young teenagers and, if I remember 1970–1971, it was the start of the drug culture, and the drug culture was already starting to filter down to younger teenagers. So, there was stuff going on in the community back then and we were all starting to experiment with things. It was all new. We didn't know much about it. Our parents wouldn't have known anything about it—it's hard to know where that leads.[116]

The lack of safe spaces for youth to hang out was, and continues to be, a problem for the community. There was a high incidence of youth-related crime, and there were few resources, services, or even safe spaces for youth to gather. O'Neill pointed out that in 1976, there were twenty thousand young people under the age of twenty, but one pool and one arena.

> The kids in this area have lived a long time with nothing to do— they've grown up here that way. Kids are angry and frustrated because they are probably ripped off more than anyone else.[117]

The management of the Jane-Finch Mall was concerned that youth were hanging out in the mall. Given the lack of youth-friendly space in the community, it was a logical place for them to gather. However, from the store owners' and security guards perspective, they felt that youth in the mall were

---

116 Brian Whitehead interview (Toronto: York Woods Library, Black Creek Living History Project, August 2010).

117 O'Neill interview.

creating problems. The community responded through the Youth Committee of DWAC, exploring options and working with the Youth Services Network, a group of service providers. They collectively submitted a proposal to the Solicitor General of Canada and the Ministry of Corrections for a five-year Youth Crime Prevention Program for the area. The proposal, called the Youth Action Project (YAP), was developed because youth crime had increased by sixty-five per cent in District 10 between 1971—1973. In Patrol Area 3103 (31 Division), which covers the Jane-Finch community, the increase in the juvenile crime rate was 145 per cent from 1972 to 1973.[118]

The five-year proposal was successful and in the mid-1970s a trailer, located in the parking lot behind the Jane Finch Mall, was set up to reduce the number of youths engaged in crime. The staff were to reach out to the youth population and engage them. The trailer was staffed by four full-time workers, and community volunteers, and open seven days per week for twelve hours each day.

It became an effective, supportive, and safe space for youth. Malcolm Shookner, who later became involved in Jane-Finch, explained,

> I was working with the Youth Services Network at that time, and we were trying to work with youth across Metropolitan Toronto. The Youth Services Network had grown out of downtown youth issues, and we were trying to be Metro-wide, so Jane-Finch was a community we wanted to connect with, especially with the high number of youth in that community. There was also the Clinic [Youth Clinical Services] that had been set up in a portable beside York Finch Hospital and we thought, 'Okay, let's work with the clinic and residents up there to figure out a way to develop some kind of youth programs that were responsive to youth needs in that community.' That trailer behind the mall was the Yorkville trailer model that had been done in the sixties and early seventies downtown and taking it to the suburbs. So, that was my first connection to Jane and Finch.[119]

---

118   Klein and Sears, *Review of Planning Policies*, 35.
119   Malcolm Shookner interview (Toronto: York Woods Library, Black Creek Living History Project, February 7, 2010).

Whitehead, who grew into a responsible young man, described his memory of the trailer.

> Barb Dorrie, John Parker, Irene Shapiro, and Tom Hartman worked out of a trailer behind the Jane Finch Mall. They had a trailer, and it was supposed to be a meeting place and they were doing street work; they were youth workers. I'm not even sure how, but I remember wandering into the trailer myself and meeting them. We were doing things in the community and so were they. We were sort of older youth, Stefan and me (nineteen). We were sort of a Mutt and Jeff partnership, the two of us. We had been personal friends before that, and we were both hired as youth workers, and we linked up with them. John Parker was already doing street-work at the time, meeting with families and kids who had been identified, I guess by the schools, who had been in trouble with the law and trying to work with them and trying to give them some positive direction. Great, great program! They were probably there from I think about '74 to '78. I don't think it lasted very long. Tom Hartman was one of the street workers and he was a musician when he wasn't doing that and, eventually, he taught guitar lessons at the Driftwood Community Centre. They bought a bunch of guitars for kids who couldn't buy their own guitars and they would run music lessons.[120]

The trailer was an immediate success. It also identified the effectiveness of supervised youth programs and supported the view that eight- to eighteen-year-old children and youth in the area needed more recreational opportunities than existed at that time.[121]

≈

While YAP, Youth Clinic Services and Black Creek Venture Group were addressing some of the needs of youth, there continued to be insufficient support for youth in the neighbourhoods further north of the mall and in neighbourhoods south of the mall. On May 24, 1978, the Children's Aid

---

120   Whitehead interview.
121   Klein and Sears, *Review of Planning Policies*, 34.

Society convened a meeting of representatives from community groups and agencies to talk about issues related to youth in the area. At that meeting, it was suggested that there might be community residents who were working with young people on an informal basis. It was agreed to identify those people, find out what resources were needed, and find a way to support their efforts.

The objectives of representatives at the meeting included developing an overview of program needs for youth in the area, identifying resources needed to support current and future programs and the people working with youth, identifying actual and potential resources available, and developing a plan to provide ongoing support, both financial and practical to residents working with youth. At the end of the meeting, it was proposed that DWAC sponsor the project and be responsible for the funds, hire a community resident to do the job and publish recommendations that would emerge from the study.

Irene Pengelly, a local resident activist who had worked with YAP, was hired to conduct the study and compile a list of residents working with youth, or residents who were interested in working with youth. Irene spoke with three residents: Mrs. O'Brien was teaching some young girls how to knit, crochet, and cook. Bev Folkes was operating a drop-in at Yorkwoods Community Centre for the Caribbean Youth Connection. Mustafa Yusuf was working in the Firgrove community with the Firgrove United Sports and Cultural Club. These programs were not adequately funded, and volunteers played a big role in keeping them going.

The study spoke about the lack of parental guidance, a lack of adult role-models for youth to emulate, and family breakdown as contributing factors. Children were being left unsupervised, especially after school, as parents had to work. Youth who have been long-time residents of Ontario Housing seemed to have especially poor self-images and a lack of confidence in their ability to achieve. That feeling was often reinforced by attitudes of non-Ontario Housing residents, personnel of agencies and institutions, and the media.

Many residents moving into the community at that time, believing the media stereotypes, did not plan to stay in Jane-Finch and, as a result, did not get involved in community activities. At the same time, it was felt that if parents were involved, whether with the school system or within their neighbourhood, youth would have role models and be more inclined to become engaged in community activities.

Those interviewed also spoke about how youth were discouraged in the school system and dropping out. That meant they were not getting the skills necessary to secure or maintain jobs. Extracurricular activities were limited, making school less interesting. Peer group pressure played a strong role in determining the future of youth in the community. The report indicated that programs should be geared towards improving self-worth and in developing life skills, so youth would not be diverted by peer pressure.

The report generated a list of program needs that were not met due to the lack of funding. "Workers get quite frustrated because a considerable amount of their time and energy is consumed in 'selling' program ideas to funding agencies, when they could otherwise be giving attention to program planning development."[122]

Funding is sought to respond to an issue, a project is implemented, and successes and challenges are then shared with the funding body. For example, YAP was hugely successful, but unfortunately, as with most program grants, the funding ended after five years, and no further funding was given to continue the program. A secondary problem was that the trailer was located at the back of the mall. While the trailer attracted youth in the community to that site, the perception of youth hanging around the parking lot was seen to be not conducive to business, according to the storeowners.

According to police sources at the time, the highest percentage of crimes occurred between 3:00 p.m. and 8:00 p.m. The youth involved were usually between the ages of fifteen to seventeen years, and they were committing offences such as breaking and entering into homes. Those in the younger age groups tended to be involved in lesser offenses, for example, breaking into cars. Other issues identified by key residents who worked with youth indicated that there was a lack of motivation, lack of ambition, lack of discipline, poor self-image, low levels of moral standards, lack of participation, and high drop-out rates.[123] Today, those characteristics might be categorized as being

122   Irene Pengelly, *Jane Finch Youth Study* (North York, September 1978).
123   Pengelly, *Jane Finch Youth Study*.

the result of depression and/or anxiety, but it was not recognized as such in those years.

What was needed was an understanding of how mental health issues affected people. For example, what we now know as post-traumatic stress disorder was being experienced by newcomer families because of the experiences in their countries of origin, where war, poverty, and deprivation were occurring. The parents who came to Canada may have been suffering and did not get the professional help they needed for a variety of reasons, including a lack of understanding or stigma against mental illness in their culture. Most concerning was that there was a lack of doctors or health care professionals who spoke their languages or understood their cultures. When combined with the pressures of racism and poverty, there was a "perfect storm" of conditions challenging newcomers and racialized populations. The impact on children would have been symptoms of depression and as a result, drug misuse, and abuse.[124]

York University stepped up in the late 1970s in support of youth programming, but not without being pushed by the community. Pat O'Neill, while living in the Driftwood neighbourhood and prior to being elected as a city alderman, secured a job at York University. "I started to work at the university and saw all the facilities they had. It seemed to me that the University had the resources to be able to provide that, so I started working with Denise Brown at the university and, over a period of time we developed a program called the York Youth Connection (YYC)."[125]

The YYC, a summer camp for children and youth, was one of the first initiatives with York University. DWAC was concerned about youth in the community and through O'Neill's position as an employee of the university, worked with senior officials to start the camp for children and youth in the Jane-Finch community and for children and youth of staff working at the university. That led to a formal agreement for mutual cooperation between

---

124   Discussion with social workers.
125   O'Neill interview.

the university and the community during that period. O'Neill herself needed to find a place for her children during the summer and became an active board member of the York Youth Connection.

The July camp was for younger children, and August was for older children—all between the ages of ten and seventeen. The staff hired were York students. Later, youth who had attended the camp became counsellors-in-training. After much work and securing some funds (with DWAC acting as the trustee for the funds), the camp started with one hundred children and youth in each month-long session on the campus. Children were exposed to the university and participated in activities including theatre, music, making musical instruments, crafts, sports, overnight camping, photography, wood etching, and totem-pole carving. This was a great early example of cooperation between the community and the university. York Youth Connection started in the late 1970s and continued for many years to offer the camp with funds donated by the Toronto Star Fresh Air fund and money from private donors, including faculty members and students of York. Over the years, the camp changed from one month to offering a two-week day camp experience on campus, with no overnights. YYC ran for many years, though solely by York in later years, and ended in 2016 due to lack of enrollment and increased cost of running the camp.

This was not the only experience the community had with York University students. O'Neill described one other.

> In the early days of Edgeley, we had a group of students from York called the Monday Group. You know who was part of that? The young man who ran for the Liberal leadership, Gerrard Kennedy, a nice young man. They were trying to develop some programs to help take kids out of the community to do other activities. For a lot of youth, it was the only time they left Jane-Finch. It was quite fascinating. It really worked with the kids to try to get them out and do things. I think they took them on a couple of camping trips and so forth. They were a nice group of youngsters, but when they

graduated, it never continued. There were a couple of involvements at the university, but the YYC was a good start.[126]

Another initiative that started at the same time was the York-Community Connection. The purpose was to bring community organizations together with York University representatives to build bridges between the university and the community. The monthly meetings took place for several years and was supported by York's community relations officer.

Community services grow

While youth programs and other services were starting, the residents in the community were having difficulty finding out about programs and services, hence the formation of the Downsview Weston Information Post (DWIP). It was founded by DWAC members who wanted to give residents better access to information in the early 1970s. Two streams were created: the information post and a community newspaper.

Members of DWAC wanted information to be accessible, so they approached the Jane Finch Mall management, who agreed to provide the floor space, but not the booth that would be used as an information post. The students at Westview Centennial Secondary School built the first booth. Later, a kiosk was provided that gave more space for the volunteers and information materials. The kiosk opened in 1976 with financial support from the Jane Finch Mall, Bank of Montreal, Metro Toronto Community Services, Westview Community Venture, and Metro Children's Aid Society. The next challenge was to identify people who would staff the booth. After conversations with workers, service providers, and DWAC, a schedule was set up to include workers and volunteers from the community. Katie Hayhurst utilized that space one evening a week so that residents could access her for help with municipal issues and information, and Fred Young, the member of provincial parliament for the riding, also took one evening a week to be there for constituents.

The Information Post was a hit, and in its first month it had 1,444 inquiries. Most were about citizenship, followed by recreation, adult education,

---

126   O'Neill interview.

and government income programs. Funding was eventually secured for a coordinator through a Local Initiative Project (LIP) grant, but ongoing funding was difficult to secure. With more businesses coming to the community, the mall decided that they wanted the kiosk for a vendor who could pay rent, so Hayhurst secured space for the Information Post in the newly purchased Yorkwoods Community Centre. The Yorkwoods Community Centre was originally built as a private community centre for the townhouses and condominium on Driftwood Avenue and London Green Court. The City purchased it for the whole community to use.

With Downsview Weston Information Post located at the community centre in a residential neighbourhood, it was difficult to recruit volunteers. The space was not visible to the broader community as it was in the mall, but they continued to receive a lot of telephone inquires, and they managed to produce a directory of community services that they gave to residents. They expanded their services to include credit/debt counselling services—utilizing bank employees who volunteered their time—but they were unable to secure ongoing funding. The Information Post closed its doors a couple of years after it opened.

⁓

Information was critical to the community. During this time, the mainstream media coverage was negative, depicting Jane-Finch as a place of poverty, crime, and social dysfunction. Positive information about the community, and for the community, started when Peggy Gemmell got involved in the community through the DWAC. She worked for the National Institute for Mental Retardation (now G. Allan Roeher Institute), where she worked in the print shop preparing newsletters and flyers. With her skills and infectious enthusiasm, and with support from DWAC, Gemmell started the first newspaper called the *Jane Corridor* in 1975 with Katie Hayhurst and Pat O'Neill. The *Jane Corridor* ran into financial trouble in 1979, but those who put out the paper felt strongly that the Jane-Finch community still needed a newspaper, so she established the *Jane Echo*. Having left the Institute, she started a local typesetting business that she ran from her basement and where she published the newspaper.

The *Jane Echo's* first edition came out on May 15, 1980, with Gemmell at the helm along with Tom Kear and Lorna van Amelsfort, two other local community activists. They worked with the publishing firm, Town Crier, Inc., to produce the monthly paper. While Kear secured a job teaching in a local school, he felt strongly that good news was just not getting out to the community, only negative stories about a shooting or a drug bust.

Local newspapers struggled in this community without adequate support. Gemmell said, "We are not the first newspaper to attempt to operate out here; and no newspaper ever received regular advertising from the City. The City has a policy passed by council that states that City advertising will be placed only in the *North York Mirror* (owned by the Toronto Star Corporation*)*, and the *Toronto Star's* North York edition (that carried mostly York Region news), and *Corriere Canadese* in the west end." [127] She went on to say that they had been struggling financially because ads were hard to sell in the community. However, local community newspapers continued to exist for many years.

∽

There was another population in the community that was being neglected. In 1974, Inger Holmes, a local resident who was also a member of DWAC, applied for a small grant and started Downsview Services to Seniors (DSS). Holmes was working as a local nurse and wanted a meals-on-wheels program in the Downsview area.

In a May 1976 article, the *Jane Corridor* reported on this mobile meals initiative.

> Two years ago, seven ladies together started a service called 'Downsview Meals-on-Wheels.' They began to deliver hot meals at noontime to elderly persons who, for some reason or other, could not shop or cook for themselves. They called on volunteers, steadily expanding their service through Downsview and, today, seventy volunteers deliver between 50–55 meals 3 times a week in Downsview to senior citizens or to other persons who are ill or convalescing. [128]

---

127 Peggy Gemmell, in telephone conversation with author.
128 "Meals On Wheels" (*Jane Corridor*, May 1976).

An office was secured at 35 Shoreham Drive, a Toronto Housing building for seniors in Jane-Finch. In 1978, services were expanded, and it became a multi-service home support agency with Holmes at the helm as the executive director. Downsview Services for Seniors incorporated in 1982. What started as a three-day-a-week Meals-on-Wheels program has blossomed into an agency of two hundred staff who served over three thousand older adults annually, now called Lumacare.

᚜᚛

There is a long history in the Jane-Finch community of residents becoming leaders. For example, Donna Wilson was a woman who had a "head start" in adult life responsibilities. She met her husband when she was twelve years old (he was a neighbour), she dropped out of school at thirteen for a job in a mailing department, married at sixteen, had four children, and became a grandmother at forty-one. While she regretted not completing her education, she felt that life was good.

Wilson had an infectious laugh and always looked at life optimistically. She got involved in the community in 1967 when she moved into the newly built Yorkwoods social housing development. She attributes her dedicated volunteer work to her fear that her children would be burned by firecrackers. As the story goes, the neighbourhood kids would light firecrackers wherever and whenever they wanted, so she got the community to organize a display on Victoria Day. It did so well that she organized another one for Canada Day. She then helped to organize a tenants' association and became known as a local organizer. But, she said, "All I knew was that from a proposal, you got married." However, living in social housing gave her the experience of prejudice. "I was no longer seen as a reasonable, articulate, intelligent woman; I was one of 'those'!"[129]

Helen Ede, who lived up the street from Wilson, met her in a local park. She quickly saw that while Wilson was quiet, she had a booming personality, along with huge enthusiasm for living and a remarkable sense of humour. "What a wonderful person to have at the DWAC table," thought Ede, so she

---

129   "C&$!%! What a Way to Live Happily" (North York: *Jane Echo*, May 15, 1980).

invited her to the next meeting.[130] Wilson did not know if she would have anything to contribute, but she liked Ede and, while it did not seem like they had much in common, with Ede being an educated professional, they both had children. Wilson attended the next meeting with Ede and never looked back.

Donna Wilson soon figured out that the neighbourhood needed a training program for mothers with limited working skills, considering herself to be one of them. While participating in DWAC, she felt supported in her dream and utilized every resource available to her to open Mothers on the Move in 1978. Mothers on the Move was a low-priced grocery/convenience store, where women worked for the minimum wage. At their new jobs, they developed new life skills and had employment possibilities opened for them in the retail sector. She wrote a proposal and secured a small grant that helped her to get the store opened by working with Ontario Housing along with all three levels of governments. This new asset in the community was located within the Toronto Housing recreation centre in the Yorkwoods neighbourhood. With additional funding secured from a federally funded grant called Local Employment Assistance Program (LEAP), women continued to build their skills and were able to secure employment.

Mothers on the Move successfully operated at that location until the board of directors decided to relocate to the Jane Eglinton area, because Toronto Housing wanted the space back for recreational use. [Mothers on the Move no longer exists]. Meanwhile, Wilson did not stop with setting up the store. She was then hired to run the newly opened Jane Finch Red Cross office in Yorkwoods Public School. Volunteer work did not stop for Wilson either. She sat on the York Youth Connection committee representing DWAC, joined the board of the Jane/Finch Community and Family Centre, was a member of the Pilot Committee on Law Enforcement and Race Relations, and became a member of Downsview-Weston Information Post.[131]

Most of the leaders in the community, at the time, were women who worked hard to improve the community for themselves and for their children.

---

130   Helen Ede interview (Toronto: York Woods Library, Black Creek Living History Project, August 21, 2009).

131   "C&$!%!".

At a meeting paying tribute to women, Donna Wilson joked, "We're called Jane Finch. If men were at the table, they can call it John Finch!"

~

The 1970s was a busy decade. DWAC was playing a significant role in developing community-based organizations with passionate and committed leaders to address the lack of social infrastructure neglected by the city planners and elected officials. One priority for DWAC was to meet the needs of families with young children, a group assumed to be frequently isolated.

Ede also had an interest in this area and agreed to chair a committee with a mix of residents and professionals to explore the idea of a multi-service centre. When asked about her volunteer work in this area, she said,

> I joined a committee to put their work on a stronger footing. Community input was scant because most people were simply confused, as I was, about what we were attempting. We could only look to the past for models. Hull House (Chicago), and settlement houses and similar agencies provided models we could modify to suit a suburban situation. A location for a centre like downtown centres was out of the question.[132]

As part of that exploration, Ede researched models that existed in the United States, England, and Australia. As a result of her research, the group began to think about a place that would have three components of service: a centre for parents and children, a community office, and community outreach. Those recommendations were informed by the committee members' visits to existing sites in Toronto—the Children's Storefront (for the Child/Parent Centre), Don Vale Secretariat (for the Community Office) and St. Christopher House (for Community Outreach). While these were the initial services to be delivered, other services and programs were also investigated.

Ede said, "Some other components were set aside due to lack of expertise, time, and cost. These included a music component (the schools provided music) and a community credit union. The practicalities took much time and energy. These included drawing up a constitution, applying for Letters

---

132 Ede interview.

Patent and incorporation, getting a non-profit status, organizing an interim board of directors, and the time-consuming process of applying for grants and looking for space."[133]

Recognizing that such a centre needed to expand its support base, a letter was sent to the Social Planning Council of Metro Toronto (SPC) to ask for assistance to help formulate an approach to developing the centre.

The SPC executive director gave the letter to two of the planners and asked that one respond. Marvyn Novick, who later played a significant role in exposing the depth of poverty in the suburbs, tells this story of how they decided who should check out this organization.[134]

> I was working at the Social Planning Council and in a staff meeting we were advised that a request had come from a group in the Jane-Finch community for somebody from the professional staff to come out to do some consulting with the community. I was chair of the social development group. I had people working with me. The guy who was doing a lot of the consulting was a guy named Doug Barr, who became a trustee and chair of the Toronto School Board and head of the Canadian Cancer Society. But at that time, he was in my unit, and we were confirmed parochials [sic]—provincials from downtown Toronto. The whole debate was about who was going to respond to this request because neither of us wanted to. The agreement between Doug Barr and me was that we would flip a coin and whoever 'lost' would go up to Jane-Finch and consult. I lost the coin toss, and I was the one who went out to Jane-Finch. It was one of the best losses in my life. Had I won the coin toss, my whole professional life would have changed. Doug Barr would have gone to Jane-Finch.

He went on to say, "Downtown Toronto was where all the exciting things were happening with wise young people who were into new ways of living.

---

133 Ede interview.
134 Marvyn Novick was a visionary policy thinker/social activist who worked tirelessly to end child poverty, a co-founder of Campaign 2000, professor of social work, and dean of social work at Ryerson University. He died in 2016.

We were on the cutting edge of urban life. [...] Why would anybody want to go up to Jane-Finch?"[135]

Mary Lewis used to do some work with SPC and given that she was already connected to Jane-Finch and knew Marvyn, she followed up with a phone call. "Marvyn, you really have to come and see what's happening in Jane-Finch—could I pick you up one morning and take you there, and we'll do a tour?"[136] Lewis took him on a tour around all the different neighbourhoods and emphasised that there was a role for Social Planning Council to play. Marvyn agreed and so the DWAC sub-committee met with Novick to discuss what was needed in terms of a resource centre and to ask for his advice and suggestions.

Novick remembered his first impressions.

> As soon as I came into the community, it dawned on me that there was a world of people in the Jane-Finch community who were basically forgotten. Nobody knew about them. But they were quite committed to their area and they were every bit as committed as people in the Annex, people in the Beach, people in Regent Park. We didn't know about them though; nobody knew about them at all. They were just 'up there' and forgotten. There was a lot of learning.[137]

Meetings followed to discuss the formation of a board of directors, a community self-study, going to the Province of Ontario for a coordinator, and seeking sources of funding. The SPC agreed to have Novick attend one meeting a month to provide some support.

The committee also met with Dr. Wilson Head, a professor at York University who was a sociologist and community planner known for his work in race relations and human rights. Dr. Head [former senior researcher and planner at SPC] spoke about two topics: a community centre that would offer programs based on resident needs, and the importance of

---

135   Marvyn Novick interview (Toronto: York Woods Library, Black Creek Living History Project, June 2012).
136   Mary Lewis interview (Toronto: York Woods Library, Black Creek Living History Project, January 14, 2009).
137   Novick interview.

community development. At that time, Dr. Head sat on the Innovative Services Committee of the United Way, a funding source the Centre would later approach.

Based on the information gathered through consultations, discussions between residents, and visits to other sites, further thought was given to developing a community resource centre. This centre would encourage and expand participation in the community, provide family support, secretarial support to individuals and groups, act as a catalyst for residents to respond to community needs, and play an active role in resolving problems. The committee felt that it was important for community members to realize their strengths and ability to make their lives better. They wanted members to understand that the community could be different, that needs could be met, that each resident had a contribution to make, and that each contribution was necessary for community and social change to occur.[138]

Mary Lewis summed up the investigation into developing a community resource centre in the Jane-Finch community.

> The community people who had worked on the sub-committee identified the importance of developing the initiatives of the community, building on its strengths, and responding to the everyday needs of its residents. This proposal represented a significant shift from a multi-service centre approach, which they perceived would perpetuate the problem focus that had dominated the initiatives of social service agencies. The development of this preliminary document served several important purposes. It provided a vehicle for reporting back to the community, and it provided a basis for further development and refinement.
>
> The SPC consultant introduced the committee to further alternative models, helped to articulate the specific strategies for the centre, and provided a link to additional outside resources. The next steps included a series of meetings with agencies in the community to outline the proposed plan, the development of initial funding

---

138 Wanda MacNevin, "The Historical Highlights of the Jane/Finch Community and Family Centre" (North York: Jane/Finch Community and Family Centre, 2016).

applications, and the technical steps of forming a board of directors and applying for incorporation.[139]

The initial four purposes were: to study, review, and coordinate programs and services for residents of Planning District 10, North York, with emphasis on the Jane-Finch area; to provide a central location for community groups and local service organizations; to offer services to individuals and community groups for the purpose of improving the social well-being of residents; and to sponsor and promote educational, cultural, and recreational programs. From the beginning, the Centre had a strong community base and worked closely with community leaders and other community organizations.

The Centre's name, the Jane/Finch Community and Family Centre came about at one of the early board meetings at Ede's house. After a thorough discussion it was determined that the location was Jane-Finch, the programs and services were to align with the community, and the space was for families—hence the Jane/Finch Community and Family Centre [I will refer to it as the Jane/Finch Centre or Centre for brevity, and in fact that change was later formalized]. The Centre was founded through a community-development process and continues to utilize this strategy to this day. It is an organization that employed a positive approach, aiming to build on the strengths of the community.

From its inception, the Jane/Finch Centre committed itself to planning according to a responsive process rather than to delivering specific programs. It was the Centre's philosophy that confidence is built within individuals and the community when those people come to value their own judgment. This did not occur through having programs designed and done for them, but by having an organization respond to the community identifying what was needed. As such, there were nine community residents who formed the board of directors. The board was responsible for the management and operation of the Centre.

The Jane/Finch Centre did not have the funding to hire people with the necessary skills and expertise required to assist in program development, fundraising, staff development and general administration. Mary Lewis, who

---

139   Lewis interview.

was assigned to the community, could provide some support, but this would not be sufficient in the long-term. Until additional funding could be secured, Mona Robinson, branch director of the Children's Aid Society, was most supportive to this endeavour and agreed to loan Lewis out to the Centre in the capacity of interim coordinator for two-thirds of her time.

> The next two years represented a period of building up the new organization, helping the board of directors—who were all community residents—to become familiar with their responsibilities and increase their confidence to assume those responsibilities. Applying for and receiving a variety of alternative funding to enable the centre to carry out some of its objectives. Working with community residents to hire staff for these projects and working with the staff to develop them into a comprehensive unit. Continuing to work on program development to ensure that the resources of the centre were really the most effective ones to respond to the wide range of needs of this large community. Out of the process emerged a new organization operated by community residents, responding effectively to a variety of community needs, and fulfilling an important preventive function in relation to the welfare of mothers and children.[140]

In the spring of 1976, after a little more than two years of research and investigation, the Jane/Finch Centre officially opened, and I was hired as their first employee to provide administrative support with funding from the United Way. The United Way gave the Centre three thousand dollars a month every three months, at which time they reviewed the work. One early task was to find suitable office space for the Centre, a difficult job due to the lack of public and commercial space and zoning restrictions at that time. This was a long-term problem for not-for-profit community organizations in all the former suburbs of pre-amalgamation Toronto.

After exploring multiple options, the Jane/Finch Centre landed in a small office in Driftwood Public School for a few months. When speaking with the local social housing Community Relations Worker, Terry Skelton, I stated that we were looking for a larger space that would accommodate a few staff,

---

140   Lewis interview.

office furniture, and space for programming. Six months later—thanks to Skelton, a community-minded worker who deeply cared about the Jane-Finch community—the Jane/Finch Centre moved into two recreation rooms at 4400 Jane Street, an Ontario Housing apartment building, with a plan to stay for only one year. It would be from there that the Community Office, Community Development and the Child/Parent Centre operated.

The first of the two rooms became the location of the Child/Parent Centre, and the second room had a desk for reception that made up the Community Office, along with a large table for staff to work. Sheena Suttaby, an enthusiastic local resident, was hired to work in the community office providing secretarial and bookkeeping services to individuals and other community groups along with administrative support to staff. I became the program worker for the Child/Parent Centre.

The Child/Parent Centre offered programs for parents and their preschool children three mornings a week. With no door between the Community Office and the Child/Parent centre, staff and volunteers were able to focus on their tasks despite the rambunctious noise coming from the room next door. I was committed to providing preschool programs in an environment where those who felt shy and vulnerable would feel comfortable and accepted. We wanted the programming to enable women to receive support from one another and develop their own personal support networks through the contacts they made at the Centre. If the Centre provided these opportunities, supportive role models, and consistent encouragement, participants would get involved in the community and help to identify what was needed to improve their lives. Participants emerged as new community leaders.

Affordable space could not be found elsewhere, so over time the Centre grew along the hallway at 4400 Jane Street to include four apartment units. The Jane/Finch Centre remains in that location as of this writing.

The Jane/Finch Centre received its first federal grant to hire six staff for six months to work in five local organizations and to do outreach. They were from regions around the world—Africa, Sri Lanka, South Asia, and the Caribbean—with a goal to assist local groups in one or two short-term initiatives. Their role was to reach out into the community to share and solicit information that would be helpful in addressing issues in the community.

To support and work with the team, the Jane/Finch Centre decided to find a university social work student in need of a practicum. Shortly after the start of this project, Marvyn Novick introduced the Centre to Peggy Edwards, a remarkable young woman with a great passion for social justice and equity. Edwards was in her final year as a student at Wilfrid Laurier University, working on her master's degree in social work with a focus on community development and social planning. She was from Guyana on a leadership scholarship and was seeking a field placement in an environment where there would be diverse immigrants and people trying to settle into a new community.

Her faculty advisor in Waterloo told her that she would not find such a placement in Kitchener-Waterloo (this was in 1977), so she was referred to Dr. Wilson Head, who understood what she wanted to learn and how she wanted to contribute, since she was supposed to go back to Guyana.

> After I met with Wilson Head, he said, 'I know the person who you should talk to—you should talk to Marvyn Novick.' He sent me to speak with Novick and when I met with him, he was intrigued with what my interests were, and he said, 'I know where you should go.' He told me about this project he was involved in developing in the Jane-Finch area—the Jane/Finch Community and Family Centre. So, Marvyn sent me to the Centre. From there, I met with Mary Lewis. When I came to the meeting, I think Helen Ede, who was the president of the Jane/Finch Centre at the time, may also have been involved. After my meeting at the Jane/Finch Centre, I immediately decided that the Jane/Finch Centre was the place that I would like to do my student placement.[141]

Edwards was to be supervised by someone with a master's degree. The Jane/Finch Centre negotiated with the Children's Aid Society that Lewis, who had a master's degree, would supervise Edwards in her placement. Edwards was assigned to support and work with the federal project team. After she completed her placement and graduated, the Jane/Finch Centre

---

141 Peggy Edwards interview (Toronto: York Woods Library, Black Creek Living History Project, June 2, 2010).

applied for a work permit for her to stay and gain experience as a professional community worker.

She went back to Guyana in 1978 and returned to Canada in October 1979. The Centre offered her a full-time job while she was in Guyana, thanks to the commitment of funding from the United Way.

Edwards, proven to be highly skilled and committed to both the work and to the community, was hired as the community development coordinator, and for many years, she was the only full-time permanent staff person doing this work. "The Centre was unique in having a philosophy of service," she said. "Key principles of that philosophy were to work with the residents where they were at, and that everyone had strengths and something to contribute. I have carried that philosophy throughout my professional life." Edwards ensured that whoever she worked with at the Jane/Finch Centre understood that philosophy.[142]

She also clarified the important role the Community Office played in supporting the development of new services, making office services available to community organizations that could not afford them.

> The Community Office was set up to be like a place where fledging organizations or individual residents or small groups of residents could come and talk about needs or get support around self-help initiatives that they had in mind, or they wanted to undertake. When my position came into being, that whole infrastructure of support between the Community Office and the Community Development Component is what enabled the emergence of the groups and services that led to what we have today.[143]

The office served as an information hub and as a place where people could link up with other services and service providers.

When microcomputers emerged, the Jane/Finch Centre's board of directors responded favourably to a proposal from Edwards to take a lead in automating the Centre and promoted the idea to organizations supported by the Community Office and Community Development components. Edwards

---

142 Peggy Edwards interview.
143 Peggy Edwards interview.

did the research to determine which computers to buy and to purchase them in bulk (ten) for a reduced price. Five were distributed to local organizations, at the same reduced price, and the Centre kept five computers. The Centre was also the first community group to establish an extended benefits plan for staff, including a health plan and pension contributions. The Centre leadership encouraged other community-based organizations to follow suit.

Edwards also provided staff time to the DWAC Executive Committee to carry out the various tasks of community organizing, coordination, development, and planning with respect to the local community groups. This included establishing new groups, board and staff training, program planning, long-term planning, preparation of funding submissions, and leadership training. DWAC was not able to secure funding for its social action work because it was not a direct service provider, leaving the Executive Committee to continue to carry out its mandate as volunteers with the support of Edwards.

On April 19, 1979, Mona Robinson, the executive director for the Children's Aid Society who supported Mary Lewis's involvement in Jane-Finch, wrote a letter to the president of the United Way encouraging it to accept the Jane/Finch Centre as a member agency, thus securing more permanent funding. Robinson, who was a strong advocate for the Centre, fully understood the importance of supporting communities so that children might stay in their homes.[144]

There were also many factors that influenced the Jane/Finch Centre's early work. The Centre made a commitment to have a community board of directors made up of residents who participated in the community. Outreach was extensive to community groups for their input and door knocking was the norm at that time to reach new residents.

The Jane/Finch Centre prided itself in not saying "no." No one would leave feeling hopeless, and a positive approach was always given, including to those who made telephone inquires, and to people who had an idea for a community program. The Jane/Finch Centre recognized that it could not take on everything, so it played a role in supporting other groups to respond

---

144 Mona Robinson, letter to the United Community Fund (April 19, 1979).

to issues or helped to establish new services. The founding board made a commitment to hire a combination of community residents and people with special skills from within and outside the community. The residents who became staff members reinforced the message that the community had strengths, and this helped participants identify with the staff and see them as role models.

Two employees of the Jane/Finch Centre were good examples of this philosophy in action, Nesta Blake and Mary Crabbe.

Nesta Blake lived in Jane-Finch along with other members of her family. She was a strong and determined single mother from Jamaica who while raising four children, succeeded in obtaining an early childhood education diploma. She also volunteered on the Jane/Finch Centre's board of directors. In 1987 she was hired as a childcare worker, and in 1989 became the team leader for the Child/Parent Component. Given the Jane/Finch Centre's philosophy to build on strengths and recognizing Blake's growth in her work with children and parents, she was the ideal candidate for the position of team leader. She believed throughout her thirty years at the Centre that parents should be equal partners in determining the programs and services offered through the Child/Parent component.

Blake recalled a time when she was observing Janine Bielskis reading a story to children in the drop-in centre. Not only was Bielskis engaging her own son, but other children in the drop-in were listening to the story. As Blake got to know Bielskis, she encouraged her to become a leader in the community. Over time, Bielskis volunteered on the Child/Parent Committee and eventually joined the Jane/Finch Centre's board of directors, where she played a leadership role in helping the directors to develop it into a policy governance board.

The other resident-employee, Mary Crabbe, was from the East Coast and lived in Jane-Finch for forty-nine years. After she was hired as the office assistant for the Community Office in 1989, she became a key figure of that component. When she retired in 2016, Crabbe was the executive assistant, but she had played multiple roles in her twenty-eight years at the Centre. As well, she lived two blocks away from the office, so she was the one who, when needed, stayed late or came in early and checked on the offices if the alarm company called.

Her office was next to the reception area, and she had acute hearing. If office staff were having difficulty or needed information, she would make an appearance to help out. Throughout the years, she was well-known for giving hugs to people she knew or to those just needing one, always making people feel welcomed and cared about. She would often sit with a program participant to offer support or was a backup to other office staff.

Mary Crabbe did so much at the Centre, yet she also found time to volunteer. She sat on local boards of directors and volunteered on committees. Every Christmas, Crabbe dressed as Santa's helper and attended various children's Christmas parties. After retiring, Mary Crabbe moved back to New Brunswick and became active in her local community.

Post-secondary engagement

One of the early community engagement initiatives in partnership with York University was called "training through experience," which hosted a class for first-year social work students at the Driftwood Community Centre for an introduction to the community. Elspeth Heyworth, a dynamic professor who taught the class, started the session by introducing two Jane/Finch Centre staff and Fay Cole, a resident. Together they introduced the community and the Centre. Following this, students were given an assignment to go out in pairs to designated apartment buildings throughout the community to do outreach—armed with flyers and information to share. They were hesitant and nervous about going out to knock on doors and speak with strangers.

The professor and presenters stayed back in the Driftwood Community Centre. They questioned whether they were doing the right thing by sending students into reputedly tough Ontario Housing neighbourhoods, who were not familiar with the community. This was a new initiative by the university and by the community.

When the students returned from their outreach, they were genuinely excited and enthusiastic. When residents had opened their doors, they were pleased to receive the information, and some of the students engaged with residents to the point of agreeing to do some follow-up work for them, such as finding a local food bank or agreeing to advocate for them on an issue of concern. While this was a successful initiative, it was unfortunately not repeated due to potential liability issues.

The Jane/Finch Centre heard from residents that they had an interest in taking courses on various topics. The first course was Community Service Training, offered in the fall of 1977 by the Centre. This course helped community residents identify skills and talents that could be used in community services and identified some agencies and programs in which people could serve the community. After discussions with Tony Flynn, a young man employed by Seneca College and who was looking beyond the walls of Seneca, agreed to run a series of courses through a program called, "Seneca College without Walls," in various locations throughout the community. The courses ran for one session a week for two to nine weeks and the fees ranged from free to fifteen dollars per course. Some courses included: Issues in Our Community, Working with Teenagers, How to Make Life more Livable, Women's Slim and Trim, and Understanding our Canadian Cultures.[145]

Seneca saw that there was a need and desire for people in the west end of the city to learn and to take courses. Seneca then proceeded to build a satellite campus at Jane and Wilson. The Centre was also able to work with the North York Board of Education, through Continuing Education to offer courses such as cake decorating, typing, and bookkeeping.

Neighbourhood planning

While Helen Ede was busy working on the development of the Jane/Finch Centre, she was being invited to speak at conferences and events. In 1978, Ede presented a paper that she called "Neighbourhood Planning—The Social Evolution of the Jane-Finch Area." She said, "The area is involved in two crises: the first, rapid and poorly planned growth, the second, becoming an immigrant reception area without the structures necessary to aid newcomers

---

145 "Register Now for Jane/Finch Community and Family Centre Seneca College Courses" (*Jane Echo,* January 1977).

and without planning to provide for numbers or cultures, so that a healthy adjustment to a new way of life could be attained."[146]

Ede explained that the area was designed to have seven neighbourhoods that would be similar in physical design. Those neighbourhoods formed Ward 3 in the former borough of North York. Generally, the core of the neighbourhoods would have an inner park, usually abutted by school property and semi-detached housing, and a few single unit dwellings to surround the core. The periphery would have high density, high-rise apartment buildings with an occasional small neighbourhood plaza. At the time, there were more children per family in Ward 3 than average for North York. By 1978, the population had already doubled, growing at a rate that was forty per cent faster than projected. At that time, 21,000 of the 56,000 residents were children.[147]

According to Ede, throughout most neighbourhoods in Jane-Finch, they built Ontario Housing Corporation developments (twenty-three in all), ranging from fifty units to 579 units. By 1967, 22.5 per cent of all residential dwellings in the Jane-Finch community was public housing. Meanwhile, three per cent of North York was designated as having public housing at the time. Also, at that time, some of the privately owned buildings offered rent supplements and there were more than twenty condominium complexes developed in Jane-Finch.

At the Neighbourhood Planning event, Ede pointed out that family income in the community was lower than the Metro average, even though historically men in Jane-Finch had a greater participation rate in the labour force (sixty per cent) than elsewhere (Metro forty-seven per cent). She also pointed out that more than half the women aged twenty-five to forty-four (fifty-three per cent) were also part of the workforce, indicating that there was little time for community involvement, or indeed, even for their children.

Ede ended her presentation with a definition of community, "A community is defined in terms of the solidarity shared by the members, which forms the basis of their mutual orientation to social action" and a plea to ensure that poor planning that happened in Jane-Finch does not happen again, quoting

---

146   Helen Ede, "Neighbourhood Planning—Social Evolution of Jane Finch Area" (North York: June 8, 1978).
147   Ede, "Neighbourhood Planning".

Wallace Clement's *Continental Corporate Power*, "Poverty in Canada may not be the poverty of other parts of the world, but can we accept this planned type of poverty? Can we continue to 'blame the victim' for the results of this type of planning?"[148]

Ede then said, "May this planned blunder that is Jane-Finch never be repeated elsewhere! None of us, Canadians, old or new, can afford what this has done or may do to our lives or the lives of 20,000 kids."[149]

Neighbourhood design perspectives

Numerous people were concerned about the number of young families moving into the community. Lewis was working with local parents through the Tiny Toddlers Club, and she went into some of the neighbourhoods to meet with parents. She was astounded by some of the designs of the neighbourhoods. For example, Yorkwoods, an area south of Finch Avenue developed in the 1960s, consisted of 306 Ontario Housing townhouse units, five privately owned high-rise apartment buildings, Yorkwoods Community Centre, Yorkwoods Public School, Oakdale Middle School, and a small park. She found that it was also a culturally diverse neighbourhood with high rates of poverty and many single mothers.

The Yorkwoods area faced inward, without local streets going through the development. While children could be considered safe from traffic, she realized that this model created other safety risks by impeding access for emergency services and delivery persons. There were narrow concrete pedestrian pathways with blind spots throughout. It was obvious that some residents walked great distances to deposit garbage in bins and others lived right next to the smelly bins. Ontario Housing did not build basements as part of the units and the yards were small.

When Mary Lewis visited a family in their home, she found the units did not provide adequate living space for the large extended families that lived there. "I'd been overwhelmed when I came to Jane-Finch. I mean the

---

148   Wallace Clement, *Continental Corporate Power* (Toronto: McClelland and Stewart, 1977).
149   Ede, "Neighbourhood Planning."

Yorkwoods public housing has the same site plan as Alexander Park. And I thought, 'My God, they've taken the site plan and just rebuilt it here without any consideration about how this environment is different from downtown Toronto'." Another Ontario Housing building in Jane-Finch was located at 15 Tobermory Drive that Lewis visited. "Tobermory overwhelmed me because it felt like the elevators were freight elevators instead of human elevators. And, what...? How many floors? Twenty-five! It just seemed vast for this downtown person. It was a new experience."[150]

Fifteen Tobermory was built to be a condo or a private rental building. As such, there was an outdoor swimming pool and community recreation space in the building. Ontario was looking for more affordable housing, so when the developer filed for bankruptcy, Ontario Housing purchased the building and turned this twenty-five-storey building, with sixteen units per floor, into a social housing building to accommodate close to twelve hundred people in the early 1970s.

Edgeley Village, consisting of the Driftwood and Shoreham neighbourhoods north of Finch Avenue, was also poorly planned and faced issues similar to Yorkwoods. It consists of a twelve-storey apartment building and a series of connected townhouses that are maze-like. The numbering system is confusing to visitors, delivery drivers, and emergency vehicles.

Developments such as these are not easily patrolled by the police. Past Sergeant Rob Swann of 31 Division puts it, "We're in the top echelons of weapons-related offences for Toronto, and for all of Canada. With the tunnels and courtyards and blind alleys, there are too many places for people to stand back and watch and not be watched. It makes it very difficult to police and patrol. The inward facing streets are isolated from the public streets."[151]

The Firgrove neighbourhood was the last large Toronto Community Housing development to be built in the community [and the first to be demolished]. The architect who designed the complex won an award. Again, there were no streets running through it, most of the townhomes faced inwards and the townhouses were stacked to four levels without an elevator

---

150 Lewis interview.
151 Lisa Rochon, "Designs for Urban Fear" (Toronto: *Globe and Mail*, February 2000).

for families to get to the fourth floor. The other error they made was to build above-ground parking with no gates or doors, leaving those with cars feeling unsafe, as anyone would have access to what would normally be "underground" parking.

If someone were viewing the community from a helicopter, you would see about seven areas and central to those areas are the schools. Around the schools are the parks and houses where families live. Children have access to the schools and parks. Along the main arterial roads are the apartment buildings that were planned for young couples who were starting out and may or may not have had children. A lot of the children ended up in the apartment buildings without good access to outside play space and as the neighbourhood population aged, seniors continued to live in their homes, without children, but with good access to the parks.

Another problem with the design was that it separated neighbourhoods, and over time, the neighbourhoods became identified as territories (turf), particularly among youth in the community. The Driftwood neighbourhood has a different vibe than Firgrove or Yorkwoods. While the intent may have been to create neighbourhoods within a larger community, the plan simply did not work.

Many of the social housing apartment buildings were built on or just off the main roads. If you lived at 2999 Jane Street, for example, you had to walk some distance just so your children could play in a park. While most social housing buildings had a small playground on their property, they did not have what a local park had to offer. The lack of social infrastructure meant that there were few opportunities to attend programs and services that would support low-income families on social assistance and others who were isolated. There are only two community recreation centres along Jane Street between Steeles and Grandravine, one north of Finch and one south of Finch and most people take a bus to get to these centres. It is not a "walkable" community, amenities are not easily accessible and there were no central meeting places where information could be found or for people to engage with others.

Equitable representation

Another issue brought to DWAC's attention was the ward boundaries. The ward boundaries were not equitable, and North York was attempting to equalize the population in each of the fourteen wards for the 1980 municipal elections. Wards 3, 5 and 14 had one alderman representing 53,000 people each, yet in Wards 6 and 11, the alderman spoke for only 24,000 and 29,000 people. [152] Clearly, Ward 3 (Jane-Finch) did not have equal representation.

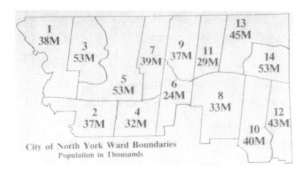

City of North York Ward Boundaries
Population in Thousands

Alderman O'Neill reported monthly in the local newspaper about what she was doing in response to the issues facing the community and how she fought on these issues with the support of DWAC. DWAC joined with rate-payers' associations across the city and the two boards of education to oppose the plan for realigning ward boundaries sent by the North York City Council to the Ontario Municipal Board (OMB) for approval. DWAC said that the changes did not end the disparities in ward population. Council's plan would put the population of the new Ward 3 at 41,900.

Tom Kear, chairman of the DWAC subcommittee on realignment of ward boundaries, stated, "The plan proposed by council is still inequitable. If you divide North York's population by 14 you should have about 40,000 people in each ward." [153] The North York Board of Education also agreed the changes were unacceptable.

---

152 Pat O'Neill, "Rally for Just Representation" (North York: *Jane Corridor*, January 19, 1980).

153 Benjamin N. Muego, "O'Neill Talks About Ward Problems, Prospects" (*Jane Echo*, February 9, 1979).

In the January 19, 1980, issue of the *Jane Corridor*, it gave further details of the representational inequity.

> This disproportionate representation is carried further by the way in which aldermen [councillors] in North York are elected to the Metro Toronto Council which spends more of our tax dollar than the North York Council. In North York, we have indirect election to the Metro Council. This indirect election to Metro in North York has led, in this present term of office, to the whole section of the city north of 401 and west of Dufferin having no alderman representing it on Metro Council.[154]

In the end, O'Neill voted for Council's map because, "Some plan had to go to the OMB or the new ward boundaries would never be in effect before the next municipal election." She agreed on the plan where residents west of Jane Street and south of Eddystone Avenue would be part of Ward 1 and those south of Sheppard Avenue would be part of Ward 5. Several years later, the area north of Eddystone, south of Finch and west of Jane, also became part of Ward 5.[155] This eventually caused problems when the Ward was divided into three, having three Councillors with different points of view and not necessarily working together for the community.

Jane-Finch corners

It was during this time that DWAC took on the two remaining vacant corners at the Jane and Finch intersection, the northeast and the northwest corners. The northeast corner was a concern for the previous alderman, Katie Hayhurst, who prepared a bylaw for North York Council to stop the development there as she was concerned about density issues. Unfortunately, a bylaw passed in 1969 allowing development of the northeast corner and the ratepayers' association at that time preferred apartment towers to townhouses.

As the Greenwin development was getting closer to building on the northeast corner, the University Village Ratepayers Association petitioned North York Council with respect to zoning amendment applications for

---

154 Pat O'Neill, "Rally for Just Representation".
155 Muego, "O'Neill Talks"

lands north of Finch Avenue and Jane Street. Council minutes indicated that residents voiced their concerns to the Planning Board on March 27, 1974, and the board acknowledged their distress about the serious lack of social infrastructure. The Planning Board unanimously voted to recommend that Council conduct an immediate reassessment of all vacant lands in Ward 3, north of Finch Avenue, and to appoint independent consultants to conduct the study. They also recommended that no applications for development be processed until the study was completed.

A motion was moved [at North York Council] to the effect that the matter above be deferred to a special council meeting at which time the appropriate staff reports would be provided by the borough Solicitor and the building commissioner.[156] Unfortunately, the attempt to reduce density issues was defeated, as was any attempt to stop further development until a report was completed.

By 1975, the population had almost doubled reaching 60,000, with 59 high-rise apartment buildings with four more such buildings under construction. An assessment of the population in Ward 3 in 1976 showed that it had the highest population density in Canada at 24.3 persons per acre and the most Ontario Housing Corporation subsidized housing units (33%). The concentration of housing was made even more scandalous by the fact that ward occupied only 5% of the total acreage of the borough of North York. Thus by 1975, and despite the protestations of local residents, City Council and developers had managed to produce the most ripe of conditions for concentrated urban poverty to develop.

Population census taken during the mid 1970s attests to the fact that the population became more diversified and most of the residents in the community were immigrants, notably West Indians, Italians, and Spanish-speaking people. By 1976, the ratio of foreign born to Canadian born residents had drastically changed. People of British

---

156   George S. Rigakos, Francis Kwashie and Stephen E. Bosanac, "The San Romanoway Community Revitalization Project: Interim Report" (North York: San Romanoway Revitalization Association, March 2004).

origin had dropped to 30% of the population from 98% in 1960. 35% were Italian and 15% were West Indian.[157]

❦

O'Neill, with support from DWAC, was fighting against the developers with regards to density issues and, as a result, she was threatened with a lawsuit because of her opposition to high-rise development. The North York Council received a report from the Ontario Municipal Board (OMB) ordering the North York Council to pass bylaws that allowed higher density development than permitted. Alderman Michael Foster wanted Council to ask the OMB for a rehearing, stating, "I'm concerned that we have a precedent where a member of council is under legal advice not to represent the interest of the community because she would not support a high-rise application." Mayor Mel Lastman ruled Foster's motion out of order saying, "We can only deal with bylaws before us." Council could not stop the trend of high-density developments despite evidence pointing to its undesirability.[158]

❦

The northwest corner, known as the Yorkgate lands, or as the "Commons," was a different fight that carried on for many years. Initially, the 1969 Official Plan designated the north-west corner of Jane-Finch for high density residential and commercial uses. In 1974, the community, through DWAC, requested a study be done as the population had grown from thirty thousand in 1969 to 46,438 in 1973.

The Board of Control of the borough turned down the request for a study on the grounds that it would cost too much. The developer presented his proposal for this fifty-acre site to build three thirty-two-storey buildings and three twenty-three-storey buildings for a total of 1690 units, adding six thousand people to the area. To do this, the builder had to get support from North York Council to rezone the area. Pressure from Alderman Hayhurst

---

157 Rigakos et al.
158 *"Alderman faces suit over high-rise stand" (Toronto Star*, December 16, 1980: A13), quoted in "Interim Report" (North York: San Romanoway Revitalization Association, March 2004). 19.

33333332333

and DWAC continued and, as a result, Council agreed with the Klein and Sears study in 1975. The traffic issue was sited as a real concern in the report.

> It was found that the actual traffic conditions on the arterials justify the concern expressed by the residents. A severe overloading of traffic is already occurring at the intersection of Norfinch Drive and Finch Avenue. By 1980, if no local street improvements are introduced and all or most of 1600 dwelling units now under construction or permitted north of Finch Avenue (excluding the lands in question) are completed and occupied, the situation at the Norfinch-Finch intersection will become seriously overburdened as well. With localized street improvements, such as additional turning lanes, all three intersections could be marginally improved to acceptable or near acceptable standards.
>
> Most of the residents are in the low-income brackets, the exception being a distinct concentration of homeowners, mainly of Italian origin, who have above average incomes. The problems are many and varied due to the socio-economic setting of the area. Some of these problems may be related to an alleged shortage, and in some instances, a lack of public and private recreational facilities. [...] In the northwest section of the borough known as District 10, population has increased so rapidly that the construction of recreational facilities has not been able to keep pace. The faster than expected population increase has put a burden on the many social services normally offered in the community.[159]

DWAC was genuinely concerned about the rapid rate of growth that was already heavily overtaxing the limited facilities and social services. In November 1975, a community meeting was held with over two hundred people who adamantly expressed that no development should occur until steps have been taken to ease some of the existing problems. The consultant, Henry Sears of Klein and Sears, validated residents' concerns. The overcrowded schools were evident with forty-four portables in use. There was a shortage of active recreational space and an upsurge of minor juvenile crime.

---

159   Klein and Sears, *Review of Planning Policies*, 32, 40.

Mr. Sears suggested that a smaller commercial development would be appropriate and that the rest of the site should be left at its present designation of semi-detached housing and low apartments not to exceed thirty-seven feet.[160]

Murphy Hull originally owned this last piece of land for development under Elderbook development, but it was the DelZotto Real Estate Developer who wanted to change the zoning to build high rises. "The area was zoned for 550 units. DelZotto proposed 1300 more—if he doesn't agree he'll simply have to wait for rezoning."[161]

By the end of the 1970s, "a decade during which our population exploded and our reputation as a 'troubled' community came to be, residents had grown weary of the high-rise suburb development model that had come to dominate our landscape."[162]

The Klein and Sears report recommended the density of the proposal be lowered and staged over several years. Over a thousand people attended the Planning Board hearing at Westview Centennial Secondary School in 1975 to oppose the plan, and students collected over three thousand signatures to protest the development. O'Neill said, "The community hired a lawyer to represent us, and I ran for councillor to continue the fight against development."

O'Neill explained that Katie Hayhurst, alderman at the time, organized opposition to development as the community, "…was suffering extreme overcrowding in our schools, we had few public recreation facilities and almost no support services to meet the needs of the fifty thousand people in Ward 3." She elaborated that the development in the area, anticipated by area planners, would take twenty or twenty-five years, but had reached its peak in only five years. No more development was needed at that time.[163]

160   Pat O'Neill, "Consultants Meet the People" (*Jane Corridor,* December 1975).
161   Alana Hardy Smith, "Pat O'Neill Interviewed" (*Jane Corridor,* New Year's 1976).
162   Mark Kear, "A maker of history in the York West community" (*York West Advocate,* September 2008).
163   Pat O'Neill, "Accusations Are Ironic" (*Jane Echo,* October 1982).

Government response

The report was submitted to Council in February 1977, but no action was taken. On March 17, 1977, at a five-hour public hearing, Council voted 11–8 against a motion to approve the necessary rezoning to accommodate the proposed development. O'Neill had convinced North York Council not to approve the plan. The developer appealed Council's decision to the Ontario Municipal Board (OMB) and the OMB hearings were held in the summer of 1978.[164]

The City of North York offered a swap—Hull's land at Yorkgate for a comparable site at the North York corner of Finch and Dufferin for a "… badly needed park for the growing number of low-income residents" that would be run by Toronto Regional Conservation Authority (TRCA). The offer fell through as Hull was not willing to cede his property to the City. The TRCA, which controlled the Finch and Dufferin parcel, was reluctant as well, explaining that it was "…not in the business of providing parks for local municipalities."[165]

The whole development was to have six luxury apartment towers of over 1,200 units on the land between Norfinch Drive and York Gate Boulevard at Finch Avenue, a shopping plaza on the land between York Gate and Jane Street, and a commercial site—probably a hotel or motel and/or restaurants—between Norfinch and Highway 400. There were also two schools to be built on both sites, of which the Metro Separate School Board held options. One would be for a secondary school and the other an elementary school. The new plans would increase the floor area in the apartments and recreation section but would not change the number of units.

Hull wanted community approval for his plans before getting final approval for changes from North York, which had turned down the original plans in 1977. However, the OMB approved plans in July 1978 for two towers and the shopping plaza that would include a theatre and bowling

---

164   Mark Kear, "A Maker of History."
165   O'Neill, "Accusations Are Ironic."

alley, not the six towers he wanted. The towers would be twenty-nine storeys and twenty-six storeys high with a total of 436 units. Prices were to be from $65,000 to $110,000, with an estimated monthly maintenance fee of $170 to $200. One criterion set down by the OMB was for no subsidized housing, so they enlarged the rooms to make the apartments more luxurious and included amenities such as indoor and outdoor pools.

Hull met with members of DWAC and proposed the changes. "The OMB told us we could build two buildings and a plaza. We have to put a bowling alley and theatre into the plaza, and if everything turns out the way we say it will, we can have approval for the rest of the development."[166] The plaza was being planned in stages because the two key necessary tenants had not been found. The two high-rises were not built.

The first section was to include the Loblaw's store. The second section, which would have the recreation facilities requested by the community and ordered by the OMB, would proceed as soon as the second key tenant is signed up. The OMB said that this could be six months after the first section is completed or it could be simultaneous. A thirty-two-lane bowling alley and two theatres were planned, but "such tenants are hard to find," according to Hull.[167] He did not proceed with the construction at the time.

Education system

While the mall would benefit the community, building condominiums would bring added pressure on the school system. The Klein and Sears report indicated that the North York Board of Education operated ten elementary schools, two junior high schools, and one secondary school in Ward 3, while the Metropolitan Separate School Board operates five elementary schools (junior kindergarten to Grade 8) in the area. At that time, there was only one secondary school in Ward 3 (Westview), and it had a capacity of 2,004 students, but the enrollment was 2,270, requiring them to have fifteen portable classrooms. The two public junior high schools in the Ward were also operating above capacity, with Oakdale rated for 883 students, yet in 1975, they

---

166 Peggy Gemmell, "Hull Back with Plaza Plans" (North York: *Jane Echo,* January 1981).
167 Gemmell, "Hull Back".

had 986 students and eight portables. Jane Junior High [now Brookview], considered an inner-city school, required ten portables to accommodate special program requirements, such as English as a second language courses, putting it beyond its rated capacity.

In the Klein and Sears report, they reported, "Overcrowding in schools was identified by residents as a major problem in Ward 3 and a significant example of how the provision of services and facilities in the Ward has not kept pace with development."[168]

The Board of Education tried to accommodate the overpopulation at Westview Centennial, one of the local high schools, by having students attend their school on a shift system. Pat O'Neill, whose children attended Westview, explained how that worked.

> Half would go to school in the morning and half in the afternoon. They went to Westview and Westview was so crowded. I don't think that many of our children went to C. W. Jefferies Collegiate Institute at that time and there wasn't a Catholic High School in the neighbourhood. The shifts went on at Westview for at least two years and then they expanded Westview. There were about 4,000 youth in the area then. I mean it was huge, absolutely huge. At that time, the province was expected to deal with problems of school over-crowding and traffic congestion. They didn't. Now, at a time of cutbacks, there is no reason to believe they will be more co-operative.[169]

The feeder school for Westview was Jane Junior High. When Brian Whitehead moved to the Driftwood area in the early 70s, he went to Grade 9 at Jane Junior High. His family was the first to live in the newly built Ontario Housing Corporation townhouses on Driftwood Avenue, having moved from the Parkdale neighbourhood. Attending Jane Junior High was a very new experience due to its "open school" concept, with no classroom walls and huge areas filled with hundreds of children and youth. Whitehead described his experience as being an unproductive year.

---

168   Klein and Sears, *Review of Planning Policies*, 23.
169   O'Neill interview.

I had never seen anything like it in my life. They had, instead of teachers like a home-room teacher, you had a "Star-Master." That is what they called the teacher. Instead of a homeroom, it was a "star cluster." In other words, this was very Star-Trekky. Because I had come from this really strict Catholic school-regimented system and I had done relatively well as a student academically, they immediately made me what was called a "self-orbiter." A "self-orbiter" was someone who just did whatever they wanted—going from class to class—and I thought this was amazing! I didn't even have to come to school if I didn't want to. They would trust me to make decisions as to whether I should be at school to learn something that day or not. Needless to say, I had a very unproductive year!"[170]

Perhaps the school administration was heavily influenced by the Summerhill School model from Britain that was popular in North America in the 1960s.[171] When Whitehead attended Westview Centennial Secondary School in 1971 to 1972, he found himself back in a traditional classroom.

The kids from Jane Junior didn't have any structure, they didn't have a sense of how to organize themselves, write essays, study, do homework. It was too loose, too open, and they were being streamed into general and basic courses. It was really working against them, and the kids apparently from Oakdale Junior High were much more academically inclined. So, we were almost labelled and stigmatized for coming from Jane. But I had only been there for a year, so I only 'played' for one year—basically, I had still learned enough to pick up the pieces in Grade 10 and get back on track. Grade 10, of course, was the classic classroom with desks and a teacher at the front.[172]

Whitehead completed Grade 13 at Westview, and he found that a lot of students that went from Jane Junior High to Westview had quit school by Christmas in Grade 10. He figured that after having three years of

---

170 Whitehead interview.
171 A. S. Neill, *Summerhill: A Radical Approach to Child Rearing* (New York: Hart Publishing, 1960).
172 Whitehead interview.

unstructured learning, they were just finding it too hard. This was also a period when there were a lot of jobs available to young people.

"A sixteen-year-old could get their license, they could drive a car, they could get factory jobs, and there were just a lot of kids who just wanted to work, because they wanted to leave home and they wanted to start their lives. So, very quickly, kids from the neighbourhood just weren't going to school after Christmas of Grade 10. So, there were just a few that I went to school with from here."[173]

Westview Centennial Secondary School [174]

Grade	Dropouts	Average Age
9	29	16.2
10	88	16.7
11	64	17.6
12	29	18.6
13	18	19.2
School Avg.	228	17.3

Media

The *Toronto Star* published an article on "Ratings of schools in North York" on Feb 28, 1978. It said, "Westview Centennial in the Jane and Finch area, that some call a corridor and others an urban ghetto appears to be at the bottom of the heap. This area has the highest density in Metro and Karl Kinzinger (Director of the North York Board of Education) says that the students suffer educationally from it."[175]

---

173 Whitehead interview.
174 Blue Book chart, *DWAC Statistics*
175 "Ratings of Schools in North York" (*Toronto Star*, February 28, 1978).

Marcelline Hinds, a resident, took issue with the label "corridor" and "urban ghetto," as that did not describe where she lived in the community of Jane-Finch. She wanted to know where this "urban ghetto" was located. "Is it the income of the people in the area; is it the mixture of the ethnic groups in the area; could it be the presence of Ontario Housing units; could it be the crime rate; could it be the high density?"[176] In terms of ethnic groups, she felt that was impossible, as this was Toronto in a Canada of multicultural heritage. Surely, having low-income people living in social housing would be discrimination, which would be against the Human Rights Code. She wondered how the local crime rates compared, per capita, with others in Metro.

Hinds felt that the Star had published a very provocative statement in a supposedly responsible newspaper.

> These remarks also belittle our community school—a school whose staff should be commended for trying to work with our 2,200 students in a building designed to accommodate considerably less. Westview has nineteen portables to cope with their inflated population. Many of those students read this interpretation of the statistics and felt very bad. Surely more constructive recommendations should be forthcoming. Mr. Kinzinger notes in that article that if people believe in something it will probably become a self-fulfilling prophecy. Let the news media continue to tell us how bad conditions are, and we shall see whether our children will find a place to stand and a place to grow.[177]

Newcomers in the education system

Many newcomer families did not initially get involved with the schools. Many believed that it was the teacher's job to teach and to deal with the children while they were at school. Parents were acclimatizing to a new country, looking for employment, or employed in challenging working conditions. Attending parent meetings, challenging the school system on policies such as streaming and discrimination was overwhelming for many newcomers at that

---

176   Marcelline Hinds, Letter to the Editor (*Jane Corridor*, April 1978).
177   Marcelline Hinds, Letter to the Editor.

time, and this continues to be so. However, education for their children was one of their major reasons for coming to Canada.

The early newcomers, as with the early settlers from Britain and the United States in the 1800s, came from rural areas, for the most part. They did not have an opportunity to get a good education, but they wanted this for their children, and they worked hard to ensure that their children succeeded. As more newcomers came to Canada from urban areas, many parents were well-educated and had training and experience as doctors, accountants, engineers, lawyers, or teachers. The Canadian government however did not recognize their qualifications and as a result, they could not get employment in their field. They drove cabs and worked in factories until they could upgrade their credentials. Education was not only important for their children, but for themselves.

Community response to education

One such person who believed in education was the indomitable Fay Cole. Cole reluctantly sent in an application to Ontario Housing. She did not want the stigma attached to living in social housing, but she applied anyway because their children, who were getting older by the minute, needed more room to grow and to play. Both Fay and her husband Douglas had grown up in large families on the beautiful island of Jamaica, where children played outside, not confined to an overcrowded and tired-looking apartment building.

"Douglas, we're moving!" Fay stated. Douglas looked up in surprise. He had just come from a ten-hour shift at the factory. He was tired and hungry, and the last thing he wanted to hear was that they were moving. They and their six children were living in a small three-bedroom apartment at Oakwood and Rogers Road, and while they were surviving, they were also struggling—struggling for too long to make ends meet and to provide a comfortable place for their children to grow up.

Cole was the homemaker and volunteered in their children's school. She was determined to make sure that her children received a good education in this new country while Douglas worked long hours trying to make ends meet. Ontario Housing offered them a four-bedroom townhouse in the

Firgrove neighbourhood in the Jane-Finch community, but she was reluctant about moving to the notorious Jane-Finch area.

She told Douglas, "I really think that we are going backwards by moving into social housing, so when we move, the only thing I'm going to get involved with is the school. And, I keep hearing things in the media about how bad that area is—what if the boys get in trouble?"

Douglas, who was now ready for bed, looked at her over his late meal of delicious oxtail stew and said, "Look, the rent is going to be half of what we pay now, lets just move."

Fay walked away, thinking, *"It will be me keeping the kids out of trouble, not him!"*[178]

The move turned out to be uneventful, and an earlier visit to the unit only reinforced their decision to move into this new townhouse development. There was a recreation centre near their townhouse, and the younger children did not have to cross any roads to go to school. So, after they moved in, she made her way to the Firgrove Public School to register her children, but not before meeting her first neighbour, Luciana.

Luciana was a young Latin American woman with two children, a little one in a stroller and a toddler hanging on. She had three bags of groceries, one tightly wrapped in the bottom of the stroller, one behind the baby and another in her hand. As they chatted, Cole found out that Luciana lived on the upper level of the four-storey stacked townhouses. A "stacked" structure at Firgrove meant two townhouses of two stories each, one on top of the other. The townhomes were on four levels. The entrance to the Coles' front door was in a hallway on the first floor. The first floor contained the living room and kitchen and the backdoor opened into a good-sized backyard. The second floor had their bedrooms.

To get to the third level, there were stairs at both ends of the hallway. The entrance to the second stacked townhouse was on the third floor. When you entered the front door to the upper townhouse, you found the bedrooms and a bathroom. To get to their living room, you walked up the final flight of

---

178   Fay Cole interview (Toronto: York Woods Library, Black Creek Living History Project, September 2009).

stairs within their unit to get to the living room and the kitchen. There was a back door off the living room that had a good-sized patio, a feature those living in the stacked townhouses enjoyed.

The challenge was that four-storey buildings in Ontario did not require an elevator, so life for young families living in the upper townhouses proved to be difficult, especially when it involved strollers, babies, and groceries. The other problem came into play when you were watching television or listening to the radio and then had someone knocking on your front door. The door located at the bedroom level could easily wake up a child that you had spent time trying to get to sleep. It was indeed an awkward house design.

Cole could not leave Luciana with the impossible task of walking up four stories with children, a stroller, and bags of groceries. That would mean leaving the stroller downstairs with the groceries while she carried up her children, then leaving the children alone while she ran down to carry up the groceries, and then back down again for the stroller. While Fay knew that she could not help everybody, she could help Luciana by taking care of her children while she made the multiple trips upstairs. Afterward, she walked away toward the school, shaking her head and thinking that she was glad to be on the ground floor. She also thought that whoever designed these townhomes must have been a single man!

While Cole knew that this was a low-income area with many single parents and low-income families, she expected to find an active parents' council where she could get involved and influence her children's education. Cole met another mother in the hallway, Abebi from Nigeria, and asked her when the parents' council met at the school. Abebi looked at her, "What parents' council?"

A visit to the principal's office gave Cole the opportunity to express her concern about a lack of parent involvement in the school. The principal responded with the usual, "Parents are not interested" and "Parents will not come out." Cole's response was that she would work with him to organize a meeting. She was thrilled by the attendance at that first meeting, with over twenty-five parents attending. They named themselves the Firgrove School and Family Association and Fay, with a commitment to work as a team, became its first president.

Cole settled nicely into her new home and was determined to keep her involvement centred on the school with a focus on her children. She knew there were programs for women starting up in the community, but that was not for her. Her usual response when someone knocked on her door inviting her to a group was, "Yes, I'll come," but she never showed up. She just did not want to engage with others, until one day a young woman knocked on her door to tell her about a new Life Skills program for women that was starting in her neighbourhood. Fay's response was different this time because the young woman talked about the childcare element of the program. While the women were in the group, she would provide a stimulating program for the kids that prepared them for school. She told Fay, "In the children's program, they are going to learn and, who knows, with a head start one of your boys might become prime minister one day."

This young worker must have said all the right things, because Fay, though reluctantly, started participating in the Life Skills program. She initially tended to sit away from the other women, but over time, she found that she was learning, even though her son was screaming in the childcare room. The class was for a sixteen-week period, and at the end the group facilitator, or "coach," invited Fay to join a Life Skills class, where she would learn how to become a Life Skills coach herself. She was not ready for that but became the coach's assistant at the next Life Skills class in another local neighbourhood before finally getting her Life Skills Coach certificate. Fay, much to her chagrin, was certainly getting involved in the Jane-Finch community, but she was not quite finished with the school.

Parents were concerned that most of the public-school children attending the school were in portables, because the public school was also occupied by students from the Catholic school board. The registration for the Catholic school far exceeded the public-school children. There were no Catholic elementary schools close by, and given that the area had a large Italian population, the public school agreed to share the space. However, as families started to move into the new Firgrove units, the demand for public space grew, hence the portables.

Children in portables did not have equal access to the amenities within the school. While they used the bathrooms, gym, and library in the school, children in the portables first had to put boots and coats on, trek into the school to get to their destination, and then repeat the process returning, losing valuable teaching time. Nobody wanted to be stuck in a portable and parents did not want their children there either. The parents decided the Catholic School Board needed to build another school.

≈

Over time, and after lobbying with the school superintendent and school trustee, the parents' council was invited to do a presentation to the North York Board of Education. In preparation, they learned that there were 1,619 elementary school students on site for a school that had a capacity of 950 students. That left the other 669 students in portables. Not only were they almost seven hundred over capacity, but there was no end in sight, and a final total between 1,700 and 1,800 children might be reached.

With determination, they made their first presentation and learned that some of the trustees were not aware of their issue. Dave Logan, the school trustee for Jane-Finch, also had this to say.

> The lesson of Jane-Finch and Firgrove, and indeed much of North York, is clear. North York continues to suffer from the lack of sufficiently flexible long-term planning; it has adopted short-term planning whose long-term effects can be seen by walking through our community to observe the harvest of troubles we have reaped. We should never allow schools to get this big. They become completely impersonal and incapable of responding to the needs of individual students.[179]

The Catholic School Board built its own school, St. Francis de Sales, across the street from Firgrove. Their plan for Firgrove's newly acquired space was to incorporate enough space for community use and a home for the some of the social service agencies that served the area. The parents of the Firgrove Public School took great pride in winning this battle.

---

179 Dave Logan, "Poor Area Planning Troubles in the Schools" (North York: Jane Corridor, December 1975).

Cole became an active member on the board of directors for the Jane/ Finch Centre. She facilitated a women's group in Firgrove, worked for the Ontario Institute for Studies in Education (University of Toronto) as an outreach worker at Firgrove School, attended the first Bridging Course for Women through York University, worked for the Black Creek Venture Group, became a Life Skills Coach for the YWCA, and eventually secured a position on the Refugee Board for the federal government.

Cole stated that moving into and becoming involved in the Jane-Finch community was "life-changing," and that she would always call Jane-Finch home. "It was one of the best places I have ever lived, and many of the skills that I now have, I learned, gained from my involvements in that community."[180] Fay Cole made significant contributions to the Jane-Finch community before purchasing a home and moving with her family to Mississauga.

Planners respond

As the 1970s came to an end, the Social Planning Council of Metropolitan Toronto released a report entitled, "Suburbs in Transition, Part 1: Evolution and Overview" written by Marvyn Novick.[181] This report played an instrumental role in bringing attention to the suburbs in 1979. Novick was introduced to the Jane-Finch community in 1976 and assisted the newly formed Jane/Finch Centre to formulate an approach to its development.

While Novick continued his work in Jane-Finch, he proposed to the Social Planning Council that he do a report "…to tell people about the real story of the suburbs and who was living there." Novick had started work on the report in 1978. Part One came out in April 1979 and Part Two came out in April 1980. "All this came as a result of consulting in Jane-Finch. I had the benefit of meeting people on the ground."[182]

Novick understood that the suburbs had been forgotten although they were experiencing similar issues to Regent Park, and that other formerly

---

180 Cole interview.
181 Marvyn Novick, "Metro Suburbs in Transition—Part 1: Evolution and Overview," Social Planning Council of Metropolitan Toronto, 1979.
182 Novick interview.

suburban communities, such as Rexdale and Malvern, were also facing the same. His report, supported by a group of twelve, including residents Helen Ede and Pat O'Neill, changed the way in which the City thought about the suburbs and opened the doors to possible funding for those communities. This ground-breaking report served as a backgrounder to understanding trends and patterns of what was happening regarding planning in the period of 1950 to 1970 and the significant changes that had occurred.

Novick explained how he was motivated to describe the suburban experience.

> My consultations in Jane-Finch fuelled the decision to pursue the major suburb study that I did for the Social Planning Council. Once I was in Jane-Finch, it became clear that the rest of the world should know there was another reality up there, which few knew about. Mel Lastman [mayor] didn't know about the reality of Jane Finch. Paul Godfrey, who was Metro Chair, didn't know about the reality of Jane-Finch. These were North York political leaders who had basically abandoned the distant corners of their municipalities. They saw no political advantage from knowing about Jane-Finch, the Peanut [Don Mills] or Flemingdon Park. My job at the Social Planning Council was to help people across Metro know about this. There was a reality that wasn't being shared.[183]

As part of his research, he did group interviews at Brookview Middle School, getting over one hundred children and youth to talk about the community and their experiences. He and his colleagues conducted focus groups in the neighbourhoods and held interviews with front-line staff. Novick did not trust what agency directors would tell him.

> They would spin everything in contrast to front-line public health nurses, a committed teacher or a community police officer. It became clear that there was a need to get more community-based agencies going and that's how the Jane/Finch Centre started. There was good work going on from local workers such as Mary Lewis of Children's Aid and other committed practitioners. But there was

183 Novick interview.

no local agency that had ongoing resources to do both support and bring people together for public issues, when it was required.[184]

Novick documented that there was a lack of municipal recognition and that there were diverse populations in the suburbs, like other areas in Toronto, that needed a whole lot of community supports that any diverse population would need.

> This had started to become evident through the Local Initiative Programs (LIP) that began in 1973, helping people start community-based services and programs," stated Novick. "Some of these LIP projects were showing up in suburban areas as well—not many, but the notion that municipalities needed to build a social infra-structure in their communities was just starting to be discussed. The Social Planning Council had done a review of community services in Toronto. We suggested that cities had a responsibility to look after the social infrastructure and social development of their communi-ties and that should be a municipal responsibility. The idea was starting to creep in. The John Robarts Commission on Metropolitan Toronto in 1976 was beginning to say that this should be part of local government's responsibility, to be concerned about the social infrastructure and support systems in all communities.

> There was a growing demand that local government fund com-munity-based programs that had been started by Local Initiatives Projects, so the scope of local government funding of community support programs was increasing between 1975 and 1980. Before that, residents and workers in Jane-Finch didn't feel that their com-munity was getting its fair share of public services and support.

> When Metro Suburbs was released in 1979 and 1980, it changed everything. The report got enormous coverage changing perceptions of who lived in the City. It helped build metropolitan alliances. People in the downtown, Parkdale, Kensington, Regent, and east Toronto recognized that there were people similar to them in other parts of North York and Etobicoke. The building of alliances started,

---

184 Novick interview.

and this was quite important. But it just didn't happen overnight. It took the Metro Suburbs report to get people to recognize that inner city schools were in the outer areas for the Metro Toronto Board of Education to make inner city criteria apply to all schools so that extra resources could go to schools in North York, Etobicoke and Scarborough that had similar high need populations as Toronto.

The report really confirmed and changed whole public perceptions about people who had felt abandoned and isolated. Residents in suburban communities like Jane-Finch felt all along that North York didn't care about them, that Scarborough didn't care about them, that Etobicoke didn't even know they existed. So, the sense that they were part of something bigger was quite important.[185]

The broader Toronto population was quite unaware of the inner city being created around Jane Street and Finch Avenue. The Jane-Finch community had already been getting negative press and even the leading politicians from North York seemed not to realize the consequences of public policy decisions and the lack of social planning. This changed with the publication of Suburbs in Transition.

There were political leaders from North York like Paul Godfrey and Mel Lastman who were both indifferent and ignorant about what was going on in their own areas. That was the world that prevailed, but there was tremendous strength at the grassroots in the Jane-Finch community. There were strong community people who were vigorous and resisted further high-rises in Jane-Finch and started to demand that they needed community services in their area. They started the first suburban community and family centre. That's been the strength of the community—affirming and building upon its diversity, what the mainstream media never presents.

Political leaders denied it. Mel Lastman was quoted on the front page of the Toronto Star as calling the report, "baloney." So, did

---

185 Novick interview.

Gus Harris, Mayor of Scarborough. Paul Godfrey summoned us to a meeting of the Social Services Committee where he was going to cut the funding of Social Planning Council for producing this report. I think he is one of the worst political leaders we have ever had. This is the guy who imposed the Sky Dome on us. That has been this horrible failure—this thing that has bled large amounts of public money. He was going to cut us, but we were smart enough to visit religious leaders who spoke to suburban councillors at Metro who were coming to understand what was happening in their own area.

Godfrey discovered that he had lost his majority on the committee. Some of his people that he thought he could count on from Scarborough and North York weren't with him anymore, because they were coming to understand that what was being discussed was true. Religious leaders told them that this stuff was real and was happening in the community. So, it changed the political culture in the sense that people at high political levels were compelled to acknowledge the new realities. Mayors like Lastman had never understood what his municipality was about. He thought that if he could keep his political base in Willowdale and Downsview, he didn't have to worry about the rest of North York. Well, all of a sudden, political leaders in the suburbs had to start being concerned about everyone.[186]

Malcolm Shookner, who at the time worked with the provincial government as part of the reform of Children's Services in the Ministry of Community and Social Services (COMSOC), recognized the importance of this document.

On a larger scale, Jane-Finch was not the only neighbourhood in Metropolitan Toronto at that time that had development pressures and high concentrations of people living in low income, immigrants, and other kinds of social issues that were being collected in these neighbourhoods and not being adequately addressed. Of course, there was also the downtown versus the suburbs tensions and that

---

186 Novick interview.

was what *Suburbs in Transition* was trying to document, the need for Metro Council at that time to pay attention to the whole of Metropolitan Toronto, not to just look at the downtown issues.[187]

Representing Jane-Finch on the SPCMT research advisory committee, Helen Ede said, "I found social planning very interesting, and so I was pleased to sit on a Social Planning Council committee, which acted as a critic when Marvyn Novick was preparing *Suburbs in Transition*, which gave substance to the situations that befall densely populated suburban areas."[188]

The report said that the issues of jobs and affordable housing were critical, along with transportation issues. There were special needs of children, families, youth, immigrants, and senior adults that should receive consideration within the larger framework of suburban adaptation. The report pointed out that the suburbs contained fifty per cent of all inner-city students in Metro schools. Most of Metro's families had both parents in the labour force. In the suburbs, there were high numbers of single parent families, significant groups of unemployed people, alienated youth, and a multitude of cultures and races.

York University's response

Social Planning Council dedicated a great deal of time in bringing recognition to the Jane-Finch community, but they were not the only ones interested. Elspeth Heyworth, a York University professor doing community relations work, had an exceptional understanding of the Jane-Finch community. Heyworth presented a paper at the "Future of the Suburbs" conference, and in it, she pointed out the changes taking place in the former suburbs.

> What we are seeing now in the metropolitan suburbs of Toronto, at any rate, is the pattern of the recent city turned inside out—the problem areas are not only in the centre, but also at the periphery. As social workers, we have been invited to address these 'problem' areas—or what we are calling 'the new suburbs.' The one with which we are both most familiar is the Jane-Finch area of North York, and

187 Shookner interview.
188 Ede interview.

our experience with this community has had a significant impact on both the community and on York University.

Even now, including its surrounding area, there are only four main offices or branch offices of United Way-financed member agencies in contrast to an area roughly the same size in the city of Toronto where in 1976 there were 35 main offices of member agencies, eight branch offices and 10 offices of non-member agencies, which received funding. So, Jane-Finch, and other areas like it, was left with all the traditional problems of inner-city communities and without either the infrastructure or services or other advantages of the inner city. Their lack of the traditional amenities of urban culture—cinemas and bowling alleys, subways and streetcars, restaurants and bars, stores and service centres, even park benches and street corners—rob them of the 'exuberant diversity' which (Toronto author) Jane Jacobs cherishes in many inner cities.[189]

In her presentation, Heyworth described the community. Between 1968 and 1978, the population doubled, which meant it was growing at a rate forty per cent faster than the 1968 plan projected. By 1978, the population was 56,000 and 21,000 were children. They came for housing and clearly housing was not enough. The issues of education, housing, and employment were identified in Heyworth's presentation. "All of [the organizations responding to these issues] were community-initiated and are run by community boards and thus the whole area of education is broadened by the building of competence and confidence among citizens."[190]

Heyworth talked about the way in which the community influenced the special needs report by the North York Board of Education and worked with municipal bureaucracy to create change. The community also lobbied the university to make education more accessible and appropriate to their needs. An example was the Bridging Course for Women, which was started in Jane-Finch.

---

189   Elspeth Heyworth, "Future of the Suburbs Conference at York University" (North York: *Jane Echo*; February 20, March 20, April 20, 1982).
190   Heyworth, "Future of the Suburbs."

Another one of her observations was that the initial local organizations were started by women—women who worked at home and women who worked for pay. They were most concerned about the environment in which they were bringing up their children, and they wanted to create a community where programs and services were available in each of the seven neighbourhoods. Heyworth pointed out that "Jane-Finch women have made countless community initiatives. Women have shared their strengths and new-found skills with each other. Women have learned that personal is political, that private troubles can be turned into public issues."[191]

---

191   Heyworth, "Future of the Suburbs."

CHAPTER FIVE

Community Response and Action

Following Social Planning Council's first report, *Suburbs in Transition*, came the report "Planning Agenda for the Eighties, Part 2: Metro's Suburbs in Transition." It contained sixty-five recommendations from more than three years of research, planning, consultation, and exchange by Social Planning Council on social conditions in the municipalities.

Next came "Neighbourhoods Under Stress" (NUS), released in 1983.[192] It was a report of the Joint Task Force on Neighbourhood Support Services, built on Metro Suburbs in Transition. Novick (who later became the dean of the Faculty of Community Services at what was then Ryerson Polytechnic Institute) was the task force chair. The Joint Task Force included representatives from community planning and service organizations from across Metropolitan Toronto and Peter Clutterbuck, who helped with the research for Suburbs in Transition. Clutterbuck, who later became the executive director at Social Planning Toronto, was the research director for the task force.

The NUS report defined neighbourhood support programs as "locally initiated activities, controlled by participants and residents, which enable people to cope with daily needs and to contribute to community life."[193] Mary Lewis clarified why neighbourhoods were under stress as reported in the document.

> The essential argument presented was that there are three levels of human services and the 'ground level' deserved to be formally recognized and funded. The ground level included primary support

---

192 "Neighbourhoods Under Stress" (Toronto: Joint Task Force on Neighbourhood Support Services, 1983).
193 "Neighbourhoods Under Stress."

networks that address basic daily needs, historically met through extended families, long-term relationships, and stable neighbourhoods. The radical changes in family structure, forms of urban-suburban lifestyles and settlement patterns have led to an erosion of the primary support networks and neighbourhood-based voluntary support programs were emerging in response to these changing social and economic conditions, especially for more vulnerable groups such as older people, unemployed youth, single parent families, welfare recipients and immigrant people, among others.[194]

"Neighbourhoods Under Stress" described the funding crisis faced by these community-based organizations and proposed the establishment of a provincial-municipal neighbourhood support program and formally recognized them as essential services. The core budget proposed was between $67,300 and $74,500 annually.[195]

≈

Subsequently, the Province of Ontario, together with the municipality of Metropolitan Toronto and the United Way of Greater Toronto, agreed to fund the Community and Neighbourhood Support Services Program (CNSSP) as a demonstration project in 1985. The CNSSP provided administrative or core funding to locally based organizations with the intent to help both individuals and families meet their social needs and to encourage contributions to neighbourhood life. It was hoped that with funding from the CNSSP, it would increase the capacity of neighbourhoods to identify and respond to local needs.

In a further discussion of the "Neighbourhoods Under Stress," Lewis explained the impacts of the report.

> The report had an immediate impact, contributing to the existence of about twenty voluntary agencies that built community programs and services and promoted social support. It can also be argued that the report's impact went well beyond the decade following its release.

---

194 Email from Mary Lewis to Wanda MacNevin, 2018.
195 "Neighbourhoods Under Stress."

Several agencies funded have had a profound impact on their respective communities. In addition, many of the most significant policy efforts of the City of Toronto and United Way of Greater Toronto over the following three decades can trace roots to this initial report. Moreover, while the goal of formal acknowledgement of neighbourhood support services by the province was not achieved, neighbourhood support services and local leadership were incorporated as key components of several significant provincial programs.[196]

CNSSP was evaluated in 1992 by the Community and Neighbourhood Support Services Association and the Social Planning Council. The conclusion indicated that the program was successful in encouraging locally initiated programs, thereby promoting community responsibility and participation, and fostering social integration and prevention by providing services tailored to the specific needs of the local community.

There were lessons learned through the "Neighbourhoods Under Stress" report. According to Lewis, "A short-focused report can be extremely helpful in influencing social policy. Further, it can be argued that the process was as important as the product. The entire process of working on *Suburbs in Transition* and "Neighbourhoods Under Stress" built a strong coalition committed to action."[197]

She also reflected on whether the priorities to Metro's outer suburbs were addressed equitably.

> This recommendation was more central to *Suburbs in Transition* than to "Neighbourhoods Under Stress." Nevertheless, the report's analysis of the funding crisis facing support services states that smaller programs, mostly located in suburban communities, are threatened with termination. Data was also provided on grants by area municipalities to local social support programs in 1982 indicating Toronto was allocated more than half a million, with Etobicoke and Scarborough about $100,000 and North York well behind at $36,000. So, it does speak to the gap. So clearly even this initiative

---

196   Lewis interview.
197   Lewis interview.

that was introduced directly because of the report continued to flow funds along traditional patterns.[198]

CNSSP lasted ten years and was discontinued in 1995 as part of the Harris government's cuts to social services.

The Yorkgate lands again

The 1980s saw multiple actions by members of the Jane-Finch community, including dealing with the development on the Yorkgate lands. Six years after the initial discussions, the North York Planning Advisory Committee was met "…by a raucous crowd of 500 residents, led by the first-term Councillor Peter Li Preti. They had in hand a 9,000-name petition demanding that City Hall quash a 1983 bylaw that would allow Murphy Hull to build six condominium high-rises on the property."[199]

The Planning Committee agreed to recommend that Council hold a further hearing before deciding the fate of the bylaw. "Wanting to avoid further conflict, Council, in the lead-up to the hearing, set up 'peace negotiations' to be mediated by Mayor Mel Lastman and attended by three citizen representatives, Councillors Peter Li Preti, Maria Augimeri and Mario Sergio, and representatives of Hull's Elderbrook Developments."[200]

The talks resulted in several compromises, with the number of high-rises proposed for the site falling from six to three. The proclaimed success of Li Preti and his band of "Davids" over the "Goliaths" at City Hall and with Elderbrook was reported in the Toronto media, with headlines extolling Jane-Finch's newfound political muscle.

David Lewis Stein of the *Toronto Star* declared that "In Jane-Finch, once the angry, heavily-policed, self-pitying trouble spot of the city, there is emerging a self-confident, well-organized, politically sophisticated community."[201]

---

198   Mary Lewis, "Neighbourhoods Under Stress Commentary," unpublished paper, July 2018.

199   Mark Kear, "A Maker of History".

200   Mark Kear, "A Maker of History."

201   David Lewis Stein, (*Toronto Star*, 2008) as quoted in Mark Kear, "A maker of history in the York West community" (*York West Advocate*, September 2008)..

The North York Planning Board finally gave approval in 2008 for Elderbrook Development to build the long-awaited shopping centre. The board approved the proposal for two walkways, one from Jane Street and one from Finch Avenue. The shopping centre went ahead, but they did not have interested tenants for the bowling alley or the theatre. The mall was also to provide space for a community service organization.

When I inquired about the rent for a community service space, it was beyond what any community service organization could pay. At the time, Li Preti made a side deal with the developer that if they could not rent that space in the first year, it would revert to rental space for stores. However, one small space was made available to seniors, and a group of Italian seniors utilized that space to play cards until it reverted to a store many years later. This idea of having services provided in the mall did not come into affect until the early 2000s.

Community response to schools

Strong school engagement also continued into the 1980s. Rouvean Edwards, a woman whose roots were in the Caribbean and Nova Scotia, who grew up in Montreal, was a devoted activist in the community living in the Shoreham area. She had always been involved with her children's school, but she explained that schools were seen differently by other West Indian families.

> I found that a lot of the West Indian families didn't get involved in their schools back home, so they didn't think that they needed to get involved with the school system here and would leave it all up to the teachers. So, when they were asked to come in for parent-teacher interviews and association meetings, they didn't feel that they would be heard and so they didn't. There were not as many Black families as there is now within the school system. The other thing I found out was that there was a lot of streaming within the school system. They tried to stream the kids into non-academic programs, and I faced that with my kids. Although they were born here, some of the teachers felt they should be stream-lined into going into business or menial jobs—that type of thing. I really had to fight the school system to get my kids into the better schools—let's put it that way—which they

did. All of my five kids went to Jefferys [C. W. Jefferys Collegiate Institute], and I believe it gave them a better start.[202]

Parents in the school system can be innovative in how they mobilize their communities to achieve change. This is what happened at Driftwood Public School in December 1980. The Driftwood Parent-Teacher Association decided it would bring the teachers to the parents in their home community. They held two coffee parties at 15 Tobermory Drive for parents who had children in Driftwood. "Some people find it difficult to visit the teacher in the classroom and they often feel they are not wanted at association meetings. We wanted to show them that this was wrong," offered the parent-teacher association president at the time.[203] Unfortunately, this practice of hosting school meetings at 15 Tobermory did not continue.

This initiative was an attempt to engage parents, but they were not talking about the fact that schools in working-class, ethnic-minority neighbourhoods tended to be economically and socially disadvantaged. Families who live in poverty may be unable to provide nutritious meals. Newcomer and immigrant families may have had limited English language skills. They may not have the ability or knowledge of how the school system worked, so that they could advocate for their children while working multiple survival jobs. There would be limited opportunities to expose their children to stimulating experiences with visits to places such as the Science Centre or the Royal Ontario Museum.

The other disadvantage is the lack of ability to raise sufficient funds to support innovative opportunities in the schools. Schools located in higher income communities generate funds for their children to enjoy trips, to purchase equipment that adds value to the students learning, and to ensure that no child goes to school hungry. Clearly, children from economically and socially marginalized conditions require additional supports to level the playing field for successful outcomes.

It was also important to bring parents to the school board. Peggy Birnberg, the Jane/Finch Centre's first Child-Parent Coordinator, who had taught

---

202 Rouvean Edwards interview (Toronto: York Woods Library, Black Creek Living History Project, May 2018).

203 "The Teachers Bring School to Parents" (*Jane Echo*, December 1980).

school in New York City and was a bit of a rebel, tells the story of taking parents to a North York Board of Education meeting to ensure motions that they supported were passed.

> During a school trustee meeting, we brought 'real live' children with balloons into the boardroom. I remember specifically at least one trustee called me a communist for taking such radical action, and here I was, a New Yorker, and this was really mild activism for me. They wouldn't allow us to sit around in that downstairs room. We were relegated to the gallery, and of course everyone was so well-behaved because we said our job wasn't to disrupt, it was to support a motion so that it would pass. We were successful and did make an impact. I was at the North York Board of Education a lot—so went to various meetings, committee meetings, etc.—and my greatest pleasure, aside from actually working in the community, was occasionally parking in a spot that said, 'Mel Lastman Only—Reserved!'[204]

Education system response

Peggy Gemmell, an activist with Downsview Weston Action Community and editor of the community newspaper, did a term as a public-school board trustee for Ward 3. She shared some of the highlights from her term in the local paper. She reported that the North York Board of Education was acting on the need to allocate resources to inner-city schools. The bulk of this funding from the Province went to Metro for Toronto schools as North York had not claimed any inner-city schools. Schools were eventually identified, statistics were updated, and $700,000 from Metro was allocated for North York schools.

There were extra teachers assigned to keep grades 1 and 2 down to twenty to twenty-five children per class. They hired ten community school outreach workers, as parents were often newcomers who had difficulty understanding what was happening in the school and understanding how the system worked. English as a second language teachers were increased, and Ted

---

204 Peggy Birnberg interview (Toronto: York Woods Library, Black Creek Living History Project, March 2010).

Gould, a principal, was hired as a consultant for two years to give advice on future directions to the board. Gemmell indicated that this action was only the beginning and that much more work was to be done at the middle schools and high schools.[205]

After one year consulting with schools concerning students who had special needs, Gould's report indicated that the Westview Family of Schools in Jane-Finch had six of the board's fourteen schools with special needs, the largest concentration in North York. Recommendations were made to lower class size and hire forty-five to fifty additional teachers. There was a call for no more than twenty pupils in kindergarten, twenty-two in grades 1 to 3, and twenty-five in grades 4 to 6. Professional development was proposed for teachers along with a recommendation that teachers be given time to visit the parents in their homes, if desired.[206]

The Firgrove community got behind Gould's report with Joyce Arthur, an activist resident and president of the Firgrove School Association, who spoke eloquently to the North York School Board advocating that the resources made available in the pilot project must continue to be made available to all special needs schools. Another parent, who had a son in kindergarten, expressed concern for the teacher who had twenty-five children in her class with one teacher aide. "With a class of this size and a language problem with several of the children, how can my child be expected to get his full share of the teacher's attention? These young children need added attention in their first years at school, especially where language and culture are so different from their home environment."[207]

The recommendations were approved by the North York Board in April 1981 and implementation was set for Firgrove, Topcliff, Yorkwoods, Driftwood, and Shoreham Public Schools. Firgrove was the pilot school when the project started in 1979 and the research indicated that students'

---

205   Peggy Gemmell, "I Saw Many Changes—All of Them Good" (*Jane Echo*, December 1980).
206   "Report Seeks Smaller Classes" (*Jane Echo*, March 1981).
207   "Firgrove Students 'Happier and Better,' " (*Jane Echo*, April 1981).

self-image and reading level were higher and the increase in staff has "definitely made a difference," according to the principal, Laurie Hadden.[208]

Despite the challenges in the school system and the everyday challenges faced by low-income communities, residents continued to fight for what they needed in the schools. For example, parents wanted childcare centres to be in the schools, as childcare had become a significant issue in the mid 1980s. While DWAC advocated for more daycare centres and did get a few more in the community, it was not enough. Malcolm Shookner, the senior coordinator at the North York Inter-Agency and Community Council, fondly remembers actions taken by parents in the communities.

> I recall, for example, lots of residents showing up at the school board the night a debate was on about some sensitive issues that were affecting the community. Childcare was a big one, trying to get childcare into the community and issues related to childcare in the schools. I remember hundreds of residents showing up with balloons at the school board meeting to make their peaceful, yet visual case for community support for childcare that was required in the schools. There was a lot of competition around whether they could use school space, school policies that were inhibiting the use of school space for childcare, and all those kinds of issues tied up in a bundle. At that point, the childcare scene was really evolving quickly in the mid to late '80s and childcare was emerging as a dominant issue to the point that in 1989 and 1990, they were on the verge of having a national childcare policy. [...] They were that close to signing something off, but it never came about.[209]

The school system and the Black community

In June 1985, the Education/Black Community Steering Committee submitted a report to the North York Board of Education. The research indicated that a majority of the general Caucasian school population were in advanced streams and about fifteen per cent in the basic and vocational programs. The

---

208   "Some Class Sizes Here Go Down to 20 Pupils" (*Jane Echo*, June 1981).
209   Shookner interview.

report also noted that "restrictive data obtained from the Board" placed only four per cent of Black students in the advanced streams and sixty per cent in basic and vocational programs.[210]

Wayne Burnett, a young Black activist member of the community who became a teacher and later worked with the Bob Rae government, was interested in the research. He found that the "Final Report of the Consultative Committee on the Education of Black Students in Toronto Schools," published in May, had similar information: 28.5 per cent of Black students (more than any other racialized group) were attending schools offering basic level programs. It goes on to indicate that this "trend remained in 1981, 1982 and 1983."[211]

Burnett also noticed that there was a high number of Black students indicating an interest in university (fifty per cent in a 1982 report on Grade 8 students), contrasting with the alarmingly high number of these students in special education classes (34.6 per cent). Parents were obviously concerned with these findings. Burnett heard comments by justifiably angry parents: "Even in Toronto, to be Black and poor is tough. Students are forced into non-academic courses leading to dead-end jobs. The school expects the students to be low achievers. The school focuses on the failures of Black students."[212]

This remarkable young man, who grew up in Jane-Finch, understood that parents, students and others had much to contribute to resolving these issues and that people needed to start questioning what was going on with their children's education.

In 1981, a weekend conference was held in the community as people were feeling that educational opportunities were not structured to help Black children. There was a sense of optimism at the conference when Bev Folkes, a resident and chair of Caribbean Outreach had this to say. "...the majority agreed that leadership qualities in the Black community will improve in the next few years." While leadership qualities may have improved, Black

---

210 Wayne Burnett, "Public School System: Who's Failing Whom" (North York: *Norwester*, August–September 1988).
211 Wayne Burnett, "Public School System."
212 Wayne Burnett, "Public School System."

children in the school system continued to have poor outcomes, drop out [or be pushed out] of school, and experience discrimination in the schools.[213]

There were a lot of issues facing Black youth in the 1980s and 1990s. Dr. Carl James, a professor of education at York University, became familiar with Jane-Finch through his friends while working downtown at the Central Neighbourhood House. At this time, James got involved with the Maroons Community Organization that held programs at the newly built Driftwood Community Centre. In his book, *Life at the Intersection,* James described his experience with the Maroons in Jane-Finch.

> The program attracted hundreds of Black youth, many of them recent immigrants from the Caribbean, with profiles, needs and issues similar to the youth with whom I was working in downtown Toronto. The youth and their parents needed educational support that would assist them in their adjustment to the Ontario education system, as well as space for social, cultural and recreational activities. The Maroons organization, run by Alexander Francis, had programs geared to addressing these needs, but the organization was most famous for its annual basketball tournament at Tait McKenzie Recreation Centre at York University. The tournament drew teams from as far away as Montreal, Halifax, and the United States. I attended a number of these basketball tournaments with the senior basketball team from CNH, coached by my co-worker Denny Hunte. Hundreds of youth participate in Maroons' Thursday evening and Sunday afternoon program activities, to the extent that, as Francis noted, they sometimes had to close the doors of the Centre to comply with fire regulations. This large attendance, or as Francis put it, 'gathering of hundreds of Black youth in one place' was of such concerns to the Centre's administrator, as well as community members, that a meeting was called at the nearby school to discuss

---

213   Kathy Huntley, "Black Expectations Seen Lower by Caribbean Outreach Survey" (Jane Echo, June 1981).

'what to do with [N-word] night', " as Francis recalls. Nevertheless, the program continued for about nine years.[214]

Government engaging youth

The City of North York was concerned about what was happening with youth at the time, so in July of 1980 the North York Council hired seven youth "street workers" from across the city—Islington and Finch to Don Mills Road. Four of the youth surveyed the Jane-Finch area and three covered Lawrence Heights, the Don Mills "Peanut," and Humber Summit. The youth, who lived in the areas they investigated, talked to young people, tenants, homeowners, and business owners. They reported back to Council with their findings and there were no surprises.

The list of issues included a lack of jobs for young people. Youth from Jane-Finch said that to get a job, they had to leave their neighbourhood. There was a limited number of recreational programs available, especially late evenings. Getting permits for school gyms for basketball and soccer was difficult. There were confrontations between police and youth, often related to the enforcement of the *Trespass Act*. In terms of housing, there were infestations of mice and bugs, slow responses to repairs, and a poor attitude of management towards tenants.

Despite all the complaints, each worker expressed that, "…a strong sense of community spirit exists, and that people are willing to work towards solving the problems that are evident. They have volunteered to carry on helping in their own communities to get the job done." In an article on the survey, Councillor O'Neill said, "What remains to be seen is what North York's response will be to the recommendations that these young people are now preparing. Will they receive a pat on the back and a commendation for a job well done or will Council recognize that the time to act is NOW?"[215]

─────

214   Carl James, *Life at the Intersection: Community, Class and Schooling* (Halifax: Fernwood Pub., 2012, 13).
215   Pat O'Neill, "Go Elsewhere Young People to Find Work" (*Jane Echo*, September 1981).

The North York Mayor's Committee on Community, Race and Ethnic Relations had a lot to say about each of the above areas of concern. At the time, it was helpful that Stephnie Payne was on that committee. Payne, a resident of Jane-Finch, had worked with youth in the community and was the local school board trustee for decades.

> I was part of the North York Committee on Race Relations, and I do have a plaque down there (on the wall). The City was trying to elevate some of the issues that we were facing in North York because that's when the towers went up in the '60s and the housing started to develop. It was like warehousing people in Jane and Finch at the time, which started to create tensions between the homeowners and landlords. The majority of the landlords, at the time, I think, built these towers in the hopes that they would be privatized like condos, not thinking that it would become ghettoized later on in years. So, I think we have to go back to City Planning in North York—how did they ever allow this to happen? But, in hindsight, I don't think they thought it would be like this.[216]

The Mayor's committee on Community, Race and Ethnic Relations submitted a report that made recommendations with regards to the police, housing, parks and recreation, education, and race relations. The conclusion to the report addressed the challenges and opportunities.

> The Outreach Pilot Project, conducted over a brief time span, merely began to address concerns and perceptions in relatively few North York communities. A more concentrated outreach activity across North York is required in order to continue to facilitate responsiveness and accessibility of programs to other rapidly changing communities in North York. There is no question that racial tensions exist in the City of North York. There is no question that some residents in North York feel less equal than others. There is no question that there is widespread concern about the existence of weapons and drugs and increased crime in some areas of the city. There is no question that this concern has created great fear among residents who, in some

216 Stephnie Payne interview (Toronto: York Woods Library, Black Creek Living History Project, March 2011).

cases, are arming themselves in self-defence. There is no question that residents and institutions do not always clearly understand each others needs. But there is also no question that there is a willingness on all sides to deal with these frustrations.[217]

The committee put forward their recommendations as a roadmap for future action. "In responding to these recommendations, we would caution all concerned to note that failure to take positive action now will cost us and our children heavily in the future."[218]

On April 30, 1982, the Mayor's committee on Community, Race and Ethnic Relations and the Race Relations Division of the Ontario Human Rights Commission announced that they would sponsor four projects, hiring thirteen students to continue the previous year's outreach project; twenty-six students in a Youth Home Help Corps to run errands for seniors, do minor home repairs and gardening; twenty-four to do conservation work, including general cleanup in the greenbelt and valley lands; and twenty-one students, who came from the arts, were to create an original musical based on the experiences of residents in the area. Coordinators and managers were to be included to support the youth in doing their jobs. While helpful to some residents, and paid work for some youth, the recommendations took steps towards resolving race and ethnic relations issues that were identified in the surveys but were not nearly enough. Over time, the Mayor's Committee on Community, Race and Ethnic Relations ceased to exist.

Engaging community

Pat O'Neill, the alderman at the time, decided to organize a community forum to identify areas of concern with an intent to do something about it. The forum was held on May 4, 1982, at Firgrove Public School with over one hundred people attending, including representatives from more than thirty-five community groups and twenty agencies who served Ward 3. "The areas identified had been identified in previous meetings: youth

---

217   "Report on the Outreach Pilot Project" (North York: Mayor's Committee on Community, Race and Ethnic Relations—Appendix F, September 18, 1981).
218   "Report on the Outreach Pilot Project."

employment, social services, education, recreation, housing, and municipal concerns. At this forum, five work groups were set up to discuss concerns and make recommendations."[219]

O'Neill reiterated, "Many participants indicated that in order for these issues to be dealt with effectively, some basic work must be done to build trust and a capacity in the community for residents to work together. It was generally agreed that more resources were needed at the grass-roots, neighbourhood level in order to assess needs and develop effective responses."[220]

As a result of the community forum, O'Neill consulted with key community leaders and groups on the priority areas identified and, subsequently, a proposal was submitted to Metro Council's Community Services and Housing committee to hire five neighbourhood outreach workers to work in five neighbourhoods—Driftwood, Gosford, Firgrove, Yorkwoods and Northwoods. The proposal was submitted in September 1982 and up to a maximum of $85,000 was approved. Paul Godfrey supported her motion and in the end she received some of the funds, but for less than a year, to hire the outreach workers.[221]

The proposal pointed out that Jane-Finch was not one cohesive community; rather it consisted of several distinct neighbourhoods. Recreational facilities were extensively used and there was no money available for expansion of programs. Community leaders and representatives of neighbourhood groups must have a sense of "ownership" of the strategy and that training for potential leaders was important.

The purpose, for the small amount of $85,000, was to develop local leadership with the long-term goal of fostering a sense of community and a stronger community infrastructure. Other goals were to improve access to services and to develop summer employment programs for youth. A Jane-Finch Ad Hoc Task Force was formed to provide a mechanism for key government officials to respond to initiatives emerging from the work of the neighbourhood

---

219   Pat O'Neill, "Youth Hiring Headaches" (North York: *Jane Echo*, May 1982).

220   Pat O'Neill, "Youth Hiring Headaches."

221   Pat O'Neill, "Report to the Community Services and Housing Committee" (North York: Borough, September 8, 1982).

outreach workers while seeking financial and other supportive resources that would sustain the work.

The design of the project included a management board, a project advisory committee consisting of representatives of the agencies and institutions providing service in the area, and five neighbourhood committees. The neighbourhood committees would identify the needs of their area and negotiate with the management board for staff support time. The Neighbourhood Committee Development Officer would be responsible for the establishment of the committees. A committee, made up of each of the chairs from the five neighborhood committees, would look at issues and concerns of Ward 3, in general.

The overall objective was to assist the local community groups in dealing with agencies and institutions to help them to meet their own needs and objectives. Five local workers were hired to work in their own neighbourhoods in Ward 3. The neighbourhood committee would establish procedures and priorities for each of the workers by looking at needs of the whole neighbourhood, monitoring and evaluating the implementation of a workplan. These committees were also supposed to strengthen the community and present a stronger voice to funding sources, elected officials, agencies, institutions, and to the larger community.

The evaluation sub-committee of the Jane Finch Neighbourhood Outreach Project approved the appointment of the Ontario Community Education Centre to conduct the evaluation. Their job was to monitor the project activities in consultation with the committees, develop research instruments, gather data through interviews, questionnaires, meetings and analysis of minutes and other printed material, evaluate the outcomes and produce a written report.

The evaluation indicated that some progress had been made. The project was overly ambitious, with six specific goals to accomplish in less than one year and without sufficient training for staff to fully implement the goals. The community expressed the concern that projects this ambitious ought to be no less than three to five years.[222]

This project was not extended beyond the first year. It was another example of the community developing a well-thought-out proposal and not receiving the support it needed to respond to its identified issues.

Government response to housing

Meanwhile, the city bureaucrats and politicians continued to hear about the concerns regarding the quantity of social housing in Jane-Finch. Mayor Mel Lastman met with the Honourable Claude Bennett, Minister of Municipal Affairs and Housing, to discuss a possible reduction in the concentration of subsidized housing in the area in 1983. The minister referred the mayor to the Metropolitan Toronto Housing Authority (MTHA) board, and the board set up a sub-committee to investigate housing in Jane-Finch.

The local *Jane Echo* newspaper did extensive coverage of this issue in 1983. The sub-committee recommended that the board reduce the total number of subsidized housing units in the area, stating that the concentration in the Jane-Finch area was excessive, over 2,200 units. They also said that the number of available spaces should be increased in areas where there was currently a low number of subsidized units to compensate for those who moved from Jane-Finch. The article stated that the Jane-Finch area had 31.8 per cent of the total subsidized housing in North York and 13% of the Metro total. "[Twenty-five per cent] of the multiple housing units in Ward 3 are subsidized," Ward 3 Alderman Claudio Polsinelli observed.[223]

Polsinelli, elected as alderman for one term following Pat O'Neill, was a member of the MTHA sub-committee. He emphasized that the intent of the report was not to displace families but that any action taken should be done gradually and smoothly by waiting until tenants moved out of their own accord. He figured there was upward of an eight per cent natural turnover

---

222 "Evaluation Report for the Jane-Finch Neighbourhood Outreach Project" (Toronto: Ontario Community Education Centre, January 31, 1984).

223 "MTHA Asked to Cut 'Excessive' Concentration of Subsidized Housing" (*Jane Echo*, September 1983).

rate in Metro housing, which could mean the conversion of two hundred units per year from subsidized to market rate rentals. "It is also important to note that we are not recommending reducing the total number of units available in Metro Toronto," Polsinelli said.

> The final report back to MTHA provided four methods to reduce subsidized housing in Jane-Finch: utilize the natural turnover rate, replacing tenants in subsidized buildings with those who would pay a market rent and creating new subsidized housing elsewhere in Metro to ensure the same number of subsidized units.[224]

They would convert social housing to co-operative and condominium housing. Under such a proposal, Canada Mortgage and Housing Corporation would require that twenty-five per cent of the units in each project remain as rent-geared-to-income accommodation. The sale of OHC buildings was contemplated after conducting a demographic study with residents in the buildings in the Jane-Finch area. The committee was also concerned to note the high proportion of children to adults in several of the MTHA buildings (e.g., 1,444 children and 830 adults in one building).[225]

The committee also made some further recommendations.

> That the Authority support the creation of a broadly-based Community Council formed of residents and youth, serving as a channel of community; hiring of residents, particularly for maintenance purposes with MTHA acknowledging that they needed to review the current situation with respect to maintenance staff in buildings; and that there be a youth group fund providing small amounts of funding to youth groups in the area in return for a commitment to carry out custodial work in MTHA buildings."[226]

This left people believing that perhaps MTHA wanted to better maintain the buildings and property so that those who could pay market rent would move there. But what about the people who currently lived there?

---

224 "MTHA Asked to Cut 'Excessive' Concentration of Subsidized Housing" (*Jane Echo*, September 1983).
225 Claudio Polsinelli, "MTHA Committee Asks Reduction in Units Here" (*Jane Echo*, September 1983).
226 Claudio Polsinelli, "MTHA Committee".

More than twenty concerned residents attended a City Council meeting to hear discussion on the Human Services Committee recommendation regarding the mayor's special committee report on MTHA housing in Jane-Finch. Council passed a motion to accept the report, "as a catalyst for discussion." Polsinelli presented a petition with over one hundred names of residents from a condominium apartment building that was supportive of the proposal.[227]

The mayor wanted the social housing buildings in Jane-Finch to be investigated for violations of the *Public Health Act* and the *Property Standards Bylaw*. Gord Venner, then special assistant to Mayor Mel Lastman, said the mayor had issued instructions to the Building Department and Health Departments to look at the buildings in the Jane-Finch area, but there had been no response from the departments. An article published in the Noth York Mirror, cites how the "action comes in response to the MTHA's rejection of major recommendations in a report by a committee established to look at housing problems in the Jane-Finch community."[228] The report basically recommended that the amount of subsidized housing units be reduced in the Jane-Finch area and moved to different areas of Metro Toronto.

Yaman Uzumeri, a building commissioner for the City of North York, wrote that to the best of his knowledge, his department, "...hasn't received specific instruction from the Mayor's office to look at the buildings in this area." He also added that every building in the City of North York must meet certain requirements and that if the Ontario Housing Buildings in the Jane-Finch area had been receiving closer attention lately, it was only because of their rate of deterioration.[229]

The Medical Officer of Health was not available for comment on whether or not the OHC buildings in the Jane-Finch area were being investigated for violations of the Public Health Act. The senior project manager for the Edgeley Village residences, approximately six hundred units, said that no inspectors had specifically contacted him about the OHC buildings in the

227 "MTHA Asked to Cut".
228 "MTHA Asked to Cut".
229 "Lastman 'Gets Even' with OHC" (*Jane Echo*, December 1983).

Jane-Finch area. Mayor Mel Lastman was not available for comment to say what progress had been made on the investigation.[230]

No action was taken on the recommendations.

Community response to rent increases

Another action undertaken by residents was regarding the state of privately owned buildings and the needs of those who paid market rent. The Jane Finch Tenants Council received a grant of $35,476 from the Canada Works Program of the federal department of Employment and Immigration in August 1984. The intention was to hire three field workers to educate tenants about their rights and obligations and assist residents in setting up tenants' associations over a seven-month period.

The project began in early October 1984 with the project team going building to building, complex to complex, succeeding in compiling profiles on close to sixty low-and high-rise buildings within the greater Jane-Finch area, bounded by Steeles Avenue West to Wilson Avenue and Weston Road to Keele Street. Rochella, one of the team members and a fourth-year university student, gave this explanation.

> They may complain, but for some strange reason, when the land-lord chooses to ignore them, as is not uncommonly the case, many tenants take no further action. There is one tenant who has had no hot water in his kitchen for two years. Another, whose fridge stopped working, waited a whole year for the landlord to replace it—then bought her own. And she won't ask for a rebate. Nor is collective apathy uncommon. Although the use of an outdoor pool during the summer months was included in the rent of one building, tenants took no concrete action when the landlord last year decided simply to fill in the pool. And not with water, either. No one has sued or contacted the Residential Tenancies Commission on this matter. Not yet, anyway. We may change that, though.[231]

---

230   "Lastman 'Gets Even' with OHC".
231   Finn Schultz-Lorentzen, "Unshaven Tenant Wears Nothing but Underpants" (*Jane Echo*, March 1985).

The team found some carefully maintained buildings with reasonable rents and they have heard tenants speak quite highly of their management. The team had 20,000 pamphlets printed in English, Spanish, Italian, Hindi, and Urdu with plans to translate more.

～

The tenants' association of 2940 and 2970 Jane Street, privately owned rental buildings, planned to take their landlords to court to force them to repair and clean the two buildings. They told the media that garbage and incinerator rooms were infested with rats, apartments were overrun by mice and cockroaches, security doors were filthy and without locks, and the stairwells were poorly lit.

When they took a couple of reporters on a tour of the buildings, they found that the front door locks were broken, and one had no intercom service. Fire door closers and fire equipment were broken in both buildings, the garbage bins were piled high, and the smell was overpowering. While the property management company blamed the tenants and their children, one woman who moved in said, "I had to wait three weeks to move in because the apartment was being sprayed for cockroaches." She had paid rent for the full month and was promised a refund, which she never received. "Kitchen cupboard doors and drawers were missing or broken," she said, "and there's no freezer door in her fridge." She said that her worst problem was a balcony door with no screen or glass. Her ten-month-old daughter Hallie can climb through the doorway, and she was afraid for her child's safety. In an association newsletter, the tenants said, "We want a building we can be proud to live in ... not a dirty, disreputable place, in such a state of disrepair that we are ashamed to invite our friends and family to visit."[232]

Earlier in the 1980s, DWAC did some research regarding renters paying taxes because there was a misconception that people who rent an apartment do not pay taxes. Some homeowners felt that those who pay taxes should have a vote and that because people living in rentals did not pay taxes, they should not have a vote. DWAC's research pointed out that renters pay property tax

---

232 Kathy Huntley, "Tenants Plan to Sue Landlord" (*Jane Echo*, August 1981).

in their rent and are entitled to the same services as homeowners who pay proportionately less taxes. They do, indeed, have a right to vote.

Community coordination

Residents were organizing and so were local community organizations. One such group was the Coalition of Concerned Community Organizations, a short-lived group that attempted to enhance coordination, communication, and cooperation within the community. The group, providing neighbourhood support services in the area, was receiving funding for their organizations from the Ministry of Community and Social Services, Metro Community Services, the Ministry of Citizenship and Culture, the Federal Department of the Secretary of State, the Ministry of Health, the City of Toronto, and the United Way. They sent out letters in early 1987 to funding representatives and social planning agencies, such as the North York Inter-Agency and Community Council, to share the outcomes and recommendations from a workshop on community development in the Jane-Finch community sponsored by the Jane/Finch Centre in 1986.

The coalition felt it was significant that the issues identified and discussed at a consultation meeting convened by the Community Neighbourhood Support Services funders, were the same as those from the workshop. There was clear consensus that there was a critical need for "hands-on" support for grassroots organizing and for resources to coordinate community-based efforts in response to identified needs. The consultation meeting provided a unique opportunity for neighbourhood service providers to sit and discuss with funders their concept of community development and some of the essential ingredients of that process. The letter they sent said, "This statement is an indication of our commitment to ensuring that funding bodies acknowledge that community development and local co-ordination are legitimate and critical areas in which to allocate funding."[233]

They identified the need for multipurpose space that would provide an opportunity for people to meet both informally and formally and share ideas

---

233 Coalition of Concerned Community Organizations letter (North York: January 19, 1987).

and experiences that facilitate the community development process. "The lack of adequate, accessible, multipurpose space for use by community-based groups has been an ongoing, critical problem in the west end of the city since the area became a densely populated, multicultural suburb."[234]

Space had always been difficult to secure for programs, workshops, and community meetings, especially community meetings that generate large numbers of people. If you utilize the gym in the community centre, you are displacing the youth who would otherwise be engaged. Schools are not available during the day when they are needed and often there are fees attached when they are available. "We have seriously considered as a long-range plan constructing a facility that will meet our special needs as neighbourhood support services."[235]

A subsequent document was prepared in June 1987 for funding representatives articulating the vision for community development in Jane-Finch. The goal was to have community-based organizations in every neighbourhood providing opportunities for participation and leadership development, as well as support services. They wanted a community worker in every housing complex and opportunities to develop community enterprises, preferably in storefront settings. They wanted physical changes to the streetscape, with provisions for store-front operations thus creating an "active" community appearance, giving opportunities for browsing, and shifting the focus of activity from the Jane-Finch intersection area to areas that are underserved and have few resources. The document also contained the concept and the process for realizing this vision and the related goals.[236] While the local community-based organizations continued to work together, this vision was not supported by the different levels of government.

---

234 Coalition letter.
235 Coalition letter.
236 Coalition of Concerned Community Organizations, "Our Vision Re: Community Development" (statement to funding representatives, June 10, 1987).

Political response to community issues

Peter Li Preti was elected as city councillor for Ward 3 in 1985. In December 1986, Li Preti wrote a proposal to the City of North York for a two-year project for Jane-Finch in which he wrote,

> I have met with many homeowner associations, as well as condominium owners, visible minority groups and a number of residents in order to generate some thoughts on both the problems and solutions for our community. Through their contributions, i.e., knowledge about the community, needs and concerns, they have facilitated my efforts in trying to identify specific aims and objectives which are clearly defined in this paper and above all most achievable.[237]

The proposal made concrete recommendations for youth employment, housing, policing, media, and additional services to Jane-Finch. For example, with regards to housing, in 1986 there were 13,334 dwelling units, of which 2,372 were family rent-geared-to-income, with over ninety per cent of those being owned by Metro Toronto Housing Authority. Ward 3 was comprised of twenty-five to thirty per cent subsidized housing as compared to Ward 9, which had 0.2 per cent; Ward 7 had 0.7 per cent; and wards 6 and 8, had one per cent each. Toronto Housing (the City of Toronto's housing arm) owned 756 assisted senior citizens units.

There are approximately forty-five apartment buildings that are twelve-storeys or higher in the ward.

Li Preti proposed no additional development, such as the one proposed for the Yorkgate lands; no additional subsidized housing; secure rentals at 35 Shoreham for seniors only, except for ten per cent capacity for York students if the units were vacant. He recommended that fifteen per cent of units at Edgeley Village (just west of the university) go to York students as units became vacant, so that York students could become role models for the children. He said that attempts had to be made to attract people who did not need a one hundred per cent subsidy (the reputation of the area was making it difficult to fill units), and that the housing authorities investigate

---

237   Peter Li Preti, "Two Year Proposal for Jane Finch to the City of North York," December 11, 1986.

selling units to instill a sense of pride and ownership. He also wanted Metro Housing to hire locally.[238] His proposal was not approved.

Councillor Li Preti continued in his desire to improve the Jane-Finch community, so he made a motion on November 3, 1986, that proposed a Northwest Committee to assess present needs and recommend strategies. That committee would include five councillors and report to the Board of Control, who would then report to Council. The motion was carried.

The establishment of the Northwest Committee was one of his first accomplishments as a councillor. A local Northwest Advisory Committee was also established to include area residents, representatives from community organizations and service agencies, and elected officials. One objective was encouraging broad participation of issues and concerns expressed by the residents at the local community level. Residents felt they needed to be heard by their local politicians.

In October 1988, Susan Nwosu, a local Jane-Finch resident, community activist, and member of the Jane/Finch Centre board of directors, prepared an evaluation report of the Northwest Advisory Committee. It was pointed out that the committee, formed to look at the unique needs and issues of concern to residents of Wards 1, 3 and 5, was highly diverse in terms of race, ethnicity, culture, and socio-economic status.

> A major strength of the Northwest Advisory Committee is that it has been recognized and supported by civic authorities as a means of ensuring the broadest representation possible for all citizens of North York. The model used by the Northwest Advisory Committee can be used in other areas of North York. The City of North York has recognized, through the committee, the unique problems and strengths of the Northwest community, as well as the need for communication between many segments of the whole community. Despite the high level of grassroots organization in the northwest community, and a philosophical commitment to serving the whole of the community,

---

238   Peter Li Preti, "Two Year Proposal."

no formal mechanism existed to join groups having the resources and authority needed to implement changes, to groups who could identify needs. There is no structural connection to the civic authority as represented by Council, municipal departments reporting to council police, North York Inter-Agency and Community Council, York University, North York Committee on Race Relations and others. The Northwest Advisory Committee is the effective mechanism integrating the segments of the Northwest community into the whole and linking the community to the various 'authorities.'[239]

Some of the work that came from this initiative included launching a new community newspaper, *The Norwester*, receiving funds from the City to support Downsview Weston Information Post, and a motion from Council allowing the North York Parks and Recreation to assist the York Community Connection day camp. The City provided funds for the development of the Downsview-Weston Community Health Centre (later named the Black Creek Community Health Centre), a job fair was organized, and support was given to the Coalition of Concerned Parents trying to upgrade school-age childcare and to COSTI IIAS for their youth groups.

They also noted that work had to continue to deal with housing, policing, drug misuse, employment, and the need to engage with the North York Committee on Race Relations and the provincial Race Relations Directorate.

> We believe that the Northwest Advisory Committee must be reconstituted by the North York City Council immediately following the November 1988 municipal election so that we can continue to work on these major issues and others. We would also request the continuing support to the committee by the City Clerk's Department and the continuation of a small operating budget of $1,000.[240]

---

239   Susan Nwosu, *Evaluation of Northwest Advisory Committee* (North York: October 14, 1988).
240   Nwosu, Evaluation.

In 1989, after the 1988 fall elections, the Northwest Committee met and adopted several items including: providing one hundred dollars for each of their meetings for childcare and refreshments, secretarial service to the Committee, and increasing the membership on the Northwest Committee from four to five, with the fifth being the chair of the Northwest Advisory Committee.[241]

≫

In 1989, Li Preti received funding from the City of North York to organize a conference called, "Project Rebirth—A Community In Action." This conference was supported and encouraged by the community and was held on September 23, 1989, at Westview Centennial Secondary School. It had ambitious goals to ensure broad participation through outreach, establish consensus for improvements, recognize the accomplishment of the community, and strengthen networks. They planned to initiate short-term improvement projects that would enhance the community.

> Jane Finch was built predominantly during the suburbanization process of the 1960s and 1970s. For many, it has come to symbolize many of the inherent weaknesses and mistakes of this process, e.g., inadequate and fragmented planning, the production of high-rises, a lack of proper social and community support resources. Project Rebirth will, however, pull together and draw on the expertise of these organizations and groups to pressure governments to provide Jane-Finch with the opportunity to help itself. Through these collective efforts, some of the existing groups will be provided with resources to build this community in character and strength, and to serve the community better.[242]

The conference had over two hundred participants who collectively articulated the concerns and discussed potential solutions. There were three themes. One was that solutions to community issues required community input on strategic bodies. "Community residents were united in the belief

241 Nwosu, Evaluation.
242 Project Rebirth, "A Community in Action Report: An Assessment of the Needs and Problems of Jane and Finch" (North York: March 1990).

that successful strategies required community consultation and involvement. Attempts in the past in which governments or institutions-imposed solutions were rarely successful. Residents said that area residents should be members of committees, task forces and nearby institutional governing boards."[243]

Secondly, they wanted partnerships with, and resources from, governments and institutions. The community deserved an increase of services, community spaces, and funding. A recent report, prepared with the assistance of the Community Relations Office at York University clearly illustrated the under-funding that this community suffered when compared to other similar communities. This conference was held in 1989, but Jane-Finch residents had been saying this since the early 1970s.

The third theme focused on the fact that no one set of solutions would work given the diversity of people and viewpoints in the community—a diversity that required a variety of solutions to community concerns. Funders had to provide funds on a multi-year basis for new initiatives, some of which appeared to overlap, but offered differing solutions to difficult challenges. These issues continue to persist into the 2020s.

While the day was ambitious, with thirteen breakout groups, there were numerous concrete actions resulting from Project Rebirth that led to the formation of action committees to work on issues identified. There was also an agreement to work in partnership to improve conditions in the Jane-Finch community.[244]

A lot of work was needed to be done, but there were initiatives already being implemented according to information obtained from Councillor Li Preti. Capital improvements were being done by the North York Council, with financial support from the Province and Metro Toronto. There were also initiatives taken to improve job training and education in collaboration with the schools.

A steering committee was formed in the community to coordinate the various initiatives developing anti-drug abuse programs, community cleanup

---

243   Project Rebirth.
244   Project Rebirth.

initiatives, and others. While some of this work was implemented, it could not be sustained due to insufficient funding.

Support from NYIACC

While this process was happening in the late 1980s, the Jane/Finch Centre recognized that the community needed allies and saw the North York Inter-Agency and Community Council (NYIACC) as a resource. It was originally called the "North York Inter-Agency Council," but was later renamed to better reflect the participation of community members.

NYIACC provided a gathering place for communities in North York to come together; for local leaders to meet and better understand one another; for bringing together neighbourhood organizations with "mainstream" agencies and institutions in order to develop mutual trust and respect; and for providing a forum for broad, issue-based discussion and problem-solving.[245]

Malcolm Shookner, senior coordinator at NYIACC at the time, learned a lot from working with communities like Jane-Finch.

> One of the other things that really was an important lesson for me is when I arrived in North York in '82, a lot of the work was in reaction to issues at the time. Gradually people started saying, "This is what we want" rather than, "This is what we don't want." Thinking in terms of goals, it became proactive community development; what people now call asset-based community development. So, to me, the work that was going on in Jane-Finch at that time was an early example of communities trying to take control of their own resources and their own destinies, taking control away from distant forces of institutions and agencies and developers and others that had created conditions that were bad for communities and people who lived there.[246]

People in the Jane-Finch area utilized the skills and expertise of Shookner, and he was clear about his role with the community.

---

245 Mary Lewis, "Case for Community Work" (extract from personal papers).
246 Shookner interview.

People know what they need and that the solutions come from the people who are experiencing the problems. The role of professionals like myself was, first of all, listen and hear what people were saying and help people to articulate what it was that they needed and wanted for themselves. So, I learned those skills of being someone from outside the community who would be there as a resource to help people to achieve their goals.[247]

Support for a women's shelter

External collaboration was invaluable, but the community also looked for support from within. The Jane/Finch Centre played a major role in providing hands-on organizational assistance—guiding and supporting volunteers in convening meetings and agenda preparation, assisting chairpersons in conducting group meetings, and helping to prepare newsletters. Workshops were organized on topics such as leadership, anti-racism, mobilizing action, and advocacy. Peggy Edwards, the Community Development Coordinator at the Jane/Finch Centre, helped with those initiatives along with writing funding proposals.

The Jane/Finch Centre took great pride in supporting the development of the North York Women's Shelter, with Edwards playing a significant role. A resident, Rita Duenish, had spoken with Edwards about the need for a women's shelter. Edwards agreed and acted to find a way to make that happen. Following a meeting she attended with other staff working in North York, she expressed frustration with just talking about domestic violence issues and not taking action. Edwards was aware that shelters were located downtown and women, even though they were referred to them, did not go because it meant uprooting their children and leaving their community.

I was sitting next to a public health nurse in the community, and I remember saying to her that I was tired of us talking and talking about the need for a shelter. "So let's do something.' I asked her, "Will you do it with me?" And she said, "Are you serious?" I said, "Yes, lets do something." So, she said that if I did something, she would support

---

247 Shookner interview.

me. It was that conversation that led to that whole four years of work for the development of the North York Women's Shelter.[248]

As a member of the Cross-Cultural Coordinating Committee of NYIACC, Edwards was aware of a Women's Needs and Resources Committee sponsored by NYIACC that was not functioning at the time due to a lack of focus. She spoke with Michael Aiken, the Mental Health Coordinator at NYIACC, to find out if this initiative could revive the Women's Needs and Resources Committee. The issue of mental health was a hot topic in the 1980s and NYIACC received funding from the Province to hire Michael Aiken. He thought this shelter was a great idea and convened a meeting of people who used to be on the committee. Edwards put her proposal forward and the idea of a shelter in the west end of North York became the focus of their meetings, with Edwards providing staff time over the next few years.

It required a significant contribution of staff time from the Jane/Finch Centre: establishing a board of directors, navigating the search for land to build on, going through the required zoning process, visiting and learning from other shelters, and writing funding proposals. Edwards said it was a tremendous learning experience and a marvellous community development initiative.

> Rita (Duenish), a member of the community with a deep interest in domestic violence, was the first chairperson of the incorporated shelter board [of directors]. Women without a lot of planning experience, or academic qualifications, or work experience took on leadership roles in the steering committee for the development of the shelter. They spoke to the media. They spoke to Rotary Clubs and other groups and did things that they didn't do before. I was also able to plan with that steering committee and board in helping them grow.[249]

The first coordinator for the North York Women's Shelter was Isobel Meltz who shared an office with Edwards at the Jane/Finch Centre for two years while the shelter was being built. The North York Women's Shelter opened

---

248   Peggy Edwards interview.
249   Peggy Edwards interview.

for occupancy on September 10, 1984, and it was immediately filled with twenty-eight women and their children.

Development of community services

In 1981, five women from the community were hired as "community workers" to help make the lives of parents and children easier and more contented by connecting them with other people through the creation of a network. This demonstration research project, the Child Care Network Project, was designed by the University of Toronto, DWAC, and the Ontario Ministry of Community and Social Services. The aim was to examine the role of informal networks as a support for families in the community.

Marie Cerny, one of the people hired, was a well-educated and thoughtful woman who lived in the community and had an interest in research. She was concerned about women connecting to each other for support.

> The ideas sprouted mostly in conversations around kitchen tables. Small groups of moms, with the support of a community worker, talked to each other about the needs of their children: "What can we do together to make this neighbourhood a better place?" As workers, we valued the mothers and their knowledge and we were there to work with them, not for them. At the time, different words were used, but from the beginning the Network believed in and lived the principles of empowerment, capacity building, valuing diversity, and collaboration. All of the staff were from the community, reflecting the diversity of its residents, and approached their work knowing the mothers were the experts in what was wanted and needed to make their lives better, not the staff.[250]

In 1985, the network incorporated as a non-profit organization to become Delta Child Care Network with Cerny as the executive coordinator and located in Stanley Road Public School. They not only provided direct service to parents and children, but also did community development—reaching out to families in the Jane Street and Sheppard Avenue area, the Keele Street

---

250 "Celebrating Our Past: Shaping Our Future—25th Anniversary (1981–2005)" (North York: Delta Family Resource Centre, 2005).

and Sheppard Avenue area, and the Daystrom, Chalkfarm and Falstaff neighbourhoods—to involve residents in responding to issues affecting their lives.

Delta was instrumental in creating organizations within those neighbourhoods and then encouraged and supported their incorporation: Daystrom Family Resource Centre in 1988, Chalkfarm Community Centre in 1991, and the Falstaff Family Centre, which became part of the Falstaff Community Services Organization in 1994.

꧁

With Delta well on its way and following the successful development of the Jane/Finch Centre, Helen Ede thought it prudent to put some time into the formation of a Centre south of the Jane-Finch community. In 1982, the Northwood Golf and Country Club near Sheppard and Arleta, was sold to the city of Toronto for one dollar. The land was sold to a developer to build houses and a country club was considered a community benefit for this new development.

"The club consisted of several buildings, as well as the private golf course that went into the ravine," explained Ede. "The land was sold to the City of North York and was overseen by Parks and Recreation. Space could be booked by community groups and others. A community group had asked that one building be set aside solely for community organizations, but this did not occur."[251]

The new homeowners who purchased the houses around the golf and country club protested to their politicians about not wanting social services in their new community. The one building envisioned by others for community organizations was demolished. That did not deter other residents, so Ede, along with a few other interested residents and agency supporters, secured a small grant where Ede was hired as the researcher, along with another resident, to do outreach in the community. This group led to the formation of the Northwood Neighbourhood Services (NNS) in 1982.

What was learned in the north part of Jane-Finch about developing new non-profit community organizations was used at the newly established NNS

251 Ede interview.

but tailored to suit the residential mix of the area. NNS had its first office at Sheppard Avenue West and Jane Street, where they developed expertise in serving newcomers throughout the area. They moved to an industrial area west on Sheppard Avenue and eventually moved to Wilson Avenue, west of Jane Street. There they had a focus on settlement services, child/parent programs and programs for youth, women, and seniors.

Around the same time that Delta Family Resource Centre and Northwood Neighbourhood Services came into being, also developed were the Asian Community Centre (now the Elspeth Heyworth Centre for Women), the Latin American Community Centre, Canadian Cambodian Association, Jane Finch Community Legal Services, Jane Finch Concerned Citizens Organization, Conflict Mediation Services, and the Black Creek Community Health Centre. Each of them had a story to tell.

⁓

Veena Dutta, a young mother in the South Asian community in Jane-Finch, was home with her child and learned that there were many struggling South Asian families in the community. She wanted to do something about that. In a conversation with her friend Aruna, she explained, "My son started to go to school all day, then I started to go by the store [Towers Department Store in the Jane Finch Mall]. We went there and one of the ladies asked me in my language about buying a can of chickpeas. So, I helped her, and I was thinking, 'Look at that, there are so many people you see and there is no help for them whatsoever'."[252]

Dutta, with support from Aruna, decided to do something for the people from South Asia, especially for abused women. These women felt it was too much for them—no supports, poor English skills, and for many reasons they felt helpless. Then Dutta met Elspeth Heyworth.

Heyworth, York University's community relations officer and a professor in the social work faculty, was also interested in the South Asian community. She had been born in Goa, a former Portuguese colony in southwest India,

---

252 Veena Dutta interview (Toronto: York Woods Library, Black Creek Living History Project, September 2011).

to missionary parents from England, and fondly remembered India. Goa has fabulous beaches on its beautiful seacoast and is a popular vacation spot with foreign tourists.

Dutta was delighted to meet Heyworth and told her, "You see so many people, Indian/South Asian people on the road, sitting in the park, or on the bench in the mall, and they were sort of like lost because of lack of language. They couldn't communicate. And worse than that, some women told me that people were charging them five dollars to fill out a simple form or a pension form for fifty dollars!"[253]

Heyworth was a social worker by profession, with incredible insight and passion. She said, "There are things we can do to help the women and their families—let's get organized and figure out how best to respond to the most important issues."

Over the kitchen table at Dutta's home in the Gosford Avenue townhouses, and with her friend Aruna, Elspeth explained how to do outreach, a term foreign to both. Elspeth said, "Outreach is a way to reach people by knocking on their doors and distributing flyers."

They went out and tried it. Veena excitedly shared her first outreach experience with her husband later that evening. "Elspeth came with us when we went to the buildings on the southwest corner of Jane and Firgrove. We heard the building was considered to be not very safe, but we knew there were a lot of South Asian people living there. We made note of the Indian names in the lobby, then we went to the top floor of the building and crisscrossed at each level so that you know where you are. We knocked at the doors, saying, 'My name is Veena [or Aruna], and I want to talk to you to see if we can join hands to help each other.' We printed hand-written flyers, and we left them under the doors." She went on to say that they met so many women and were looking forward to doing more outreach.

They started by offering support and information at the Driftwood Community Centre. On their first day, the space was jam-packed, people were even standing outside in the snow as Dutta and Aruna made their way to the door. "Aruna, what do we do? What have we done?" Aruna calmly

---

253 Dutta interview.

suggested that they take one person into the room at a time, take their name, address, contact information, and ask about their problem.

Collectively, they learned about the many issues and concerns of South Asian people and from there established the Asian Community Centre with Heyworth's help and support from Peggy Edwards and Alderman O'Neill.

The new Asian Community Centre was not the only thing Dutta got involved with. Heyworth recruited Veena to the board of directors of the York Community Connection whose purpose was building bridges between the university and the community. From there, Dutta met Ann Wirsig, an empathetic listener who was also the executive director of Northwood Neighbourhood Services. They provided Dutta with a table and a couple of chairs at their new location on Rivalda Drive. The space was not very accessible, so she was soon providing services in whatever location she could find.

Over time, news about their work reached the United Way and with some funding they found their own first small office on Milvan Drive, on the same block as the Latin American Community Centre. They didn't have any office equipment initially, so would walk across the road, make a copy and then come back. When they obtained additional funding, they hired two workers, established a viable workspace, and Dutta was made the coordinator and later the executive director of the Asian Community Centre.

The Latin American Community Centre (LACC) was established earlier by leaders in the growing population of Latin Americans living in the community. At that time, the only other organization that provided services specifically for Latin American people was the Centre for Spanish Speaking Peoples, founded by four women in 1973 and located in downtown Toronto.

The Latin Americans came from countries all over South America, often with serious political differences. While the issues affecting Latin Americans living in the Downsview area were similar (e.g., poverty, housing, employment, over-policing), the ways in which they approached the issues were different, depending on their politics or country of origin. As a result, there were difficulties with the management of the organization. The board president (also a director on the Jane/Finch Centre board) reached out to the Jane/Finch Centre and to Margarita Mendez, a Salvadoran who was hired by the Centre as an outreach worker when she arrived from Mexico. She had extensive education, experience doing community work, and an abundance of passion. (She later became the child/parent coordinator and then the executive director of the Jane/Finch Centre.) Mendez offered to organize a meeting with the funders along with the United Way. They also requested that someone from the Centre's board of directors chair the annual general meeting.

After some discussion between the Jane/Finch Centre and the LACC, it was agreed to ask Richard De Gaetano, the chair of the Jane/Finch Centre's board to facilitate their annual general meeting. De Gaetano had some train- ing in conflict mediation and knowledge of political struggles worldwide through his earlier work with social justice movements, but he was unpre- pared for this meeting. Despite his knowledge of Latin America, he did not speak Spanish, a fact known prior to the meeting by board members. The United Way and the City of Toronto were the only funding representatives present at the meeting. The meeting imploded over differences between fac- tions in the group and ended abruptly.

The funding bodies decided to defund the LACC, and while they were preparing to close its doors, the community strongly advocated that some of the funding remain in the Jane-Finch community to support the Latin American people. As a result, the Jane/Finch Centre and Northwood Neighbourhood Services received some funding, so that they could each have a full-time Latin American worker.

Mendez reflected on both the Asian Community Centre and the Latin American Community Centre.

> There were two big ethno-specific organizations serving people—the Asian Community Centre and the Latin American Community Centre. They both disappeared. Jane/Finch Centre was very much involved in those two organizations by trying to provide support so that they would be viable and receiving funding as they were sig- nificant service providers for residents in the community. Those two ethno-specific organizations disappeared and for me that highlighted

the importance of having more multi-service organizations, because when you have organizations that are geared to one specific culture—not all Latin Americans are the same, and that's why those two organizations disappeared. The same for the Asian Community Centre—you have so many differences in religion and political and economical approaches. In all these countries, there is not a diverse community, but there are the diverse approaches. Class is a big issue, religion is a big issue, so how can you be serving them. That's why I believe these two organizations failed. In addition to [these problems] the Latin American Community Centre management was not properly done. That really had a big impact in the funding.[254]

Other ethno-cultural communities came to Jane-Finch. Vietnamese "boat people"—mostly middle-class and anti-communist—came after the defeat of the United States forces in their country in the later 1970s. Many settled in Jane-Finch. Following that migration, was an influx of Cambodian people who migrated because of the violent Pol Pot regime in the late 1970s. Cambodians who emigrated to Canada were also known as "boat people," similar to the Vietnamese, and almost all settled in this community. Given the amount of affordable housing available, newcomers from around the world frequently settled in Jane-Finch.

Many Cambodians, like other newcomers who fled countries suffering from extremely violent governments, may have been suffering from mental health problems (today, we call it post-traumatic stress disorder). Between 1.5 to two million Cambodians died of starvation, execution, disease, or overwork. In the 1970s, there were no mental health professionals nor settlement workers in Jane-Finch who spoke their language and who understood their culture and their traumas. There were major generational differences between parents from a traditional Cambodian culture and children growing up in the Canadian cultural environment. This created serious difficulties

---

254 Margarita Mendez interview (Toronto: York Woods Library, Black Creek Living History Project, January 2011).

and tensions between parents and children, combined with poverty, jobless-ness, and discrimination against racialized newcomers.

There was a significant impact on the children and youth in Cambodian families in Jane-Finch. However, there were also Cambodian professionals and businesspeople living in the community who recognized the importance of providing support to those who were having difficulty settling in the new community.

The Chhom family was well-known in the Cambodian community, and they played a lead role in establishing and incorporating the Canadian Cambodian Association of Ontario in 1979. The office was on the second floor in the Yorkwoods Plaza, where it operated for many years. Unfortunately, funding was not sustainable, and while the organization still exists, at this time it does not have funding for operations.

Sue Wilkinson, a young woman with incredible energy and insight who later became the executive director of the Jane/Finch Centre, met members from the Cambodian community when she did a student placement at the London Cross Cultural Learning Centre. They were doing a partnership with the Cambodian Association in Toronto at the time. As a result, she visited the association in Jane-Finch numerous times. When she graduated, she was hired by the Cambodian Association as a program manager to build partnerships, access resources, and secure funding. That work also included building rela-tionships between the Cambodian, Laotian, and Vietnamese communities.

Wilkinson sought funding for youth-related initiatives in order to bring the three communities together and overcome inter-cultural tensions between them and because they all faced similar issues. Youth were dropping out of school, absenteeism was an issue, and youth were sniffing glue and abusing alcohol.

Glue sniffing was a big issue in the 1980s in Toronto and in this com-munity, as it was easily available and affordable. Wilkinson explained, "So, gas stations, for example would find bottles of glue products and not really understand why. So, talking to businesses about the signs that they have problems on their land was interesting." Funding was made available to hire local youth who spoke Cambodian and who spoke the Khmer language and who understood the issues.[255]

⟳

More services were needed. DWAC initiated the idea for a legal clinic to serve Jane-Finch and established a committee consisting of residents and workers in the area. At the same time, the Jamaican Canadian Association, Firgrove United, and the Maroons were each planning to organize a legal-aid clinic. DWAC encouraged them to work together and a new joint committee was formed that established the Northwest Community Legal Services. In late 1980, the Ontario Legal Aid Clinic Funding Committee approved sixty thousand dollars to hire staff and to pay for a suitable location. There was money for one lawyer, two community legal workers, and a secretary at the clinic for a six-month period. The Ontario Legal Aid Plan said, "The clinic shall provide direct legal services within the Jane-Finch area as a matter of priority, but clients residing in the northwest section of North York shall not be turned away."[256]

With a small name change, the Jane Finch Community Legal Services officially opened on March 26, 1981, in the Norfinch Plaza. At that time, they offered help with problems involving immigration, human rights, criminal injuries compensation, welfare and family benefits, tenant rights, police complaints, unemployment insurance, and legal-aid certificate appeals. They later moved to 1315 Finch Avenue at Keele and Finch, as they needed additional space to continue to provide legal services to the community.

⟳

For working-class Black and racialized people, legal services were often too late or inaccessible. An organization that would advocate for and engage the Black community was needed. Tragedy was not new to some who lived in the Jane-Finch community. For example, when Linda Morowei's brother

255 Sue Wilkinson interview (Toronto: York Woods Library, Black Creek Living History Project, June 2016).
256 "Three New Programs for Our Area" (*Jane Echo*, September 1980).

was shot and killed by the police, she and Dudley Laws from the Black Action Defense Committee co-founded the Jane Finch Concerned Citizens Organization (JFCCO). It was established in 1978, incorporated in 1982, and the office was set up on the second floor of the Yorkwoods Plaza in Jane-Finch. Morowei, a resident of the community and mourning the loss of her brother, was concerned about Black youth and their educational needs. Black children and youth were more often labelled within the school system and assumed to be "troubled" children coming from poor families. This was racial profiling of children, which would be carried on in different ways throughout the lives of Black people.

When they got older, Black youth (and other minority youth) would frequently be stopped on the street by the police who assumed they "looked" guilty or were "just gathering" personal information and contacts for future reference. Criminologists, Black academics, and diverse anti-racist activists called this "carding" from the contact cards filled out by police after stopping people on the street.

This most often resulted in, first of all, intimidation of young Black men (and sometimes young women) who were just walking or hanging around their neighbourhoods doing nothing wrong. Second, any information the resident gave would go into a police database and could be shared among all other enforcement agencies, employers, or immigration officers. Third, any resistance to giving the information could result in a physical altercation and subsequent arrest by the police. The youth would then have a criminal record, maybe jail time, and have problems in employment (or even volunteering) for the rest of their lives.

❧

The Jamaican Canadian Association (JCA) was operating Caribbean Outreach Booster programs in communities across the city and Morowei worked tirelessly along with another local activist, Bev Folkes, whose focus was on incarcerated youth, to ensure that one of those programs landed in Jane-Finch. The program ran on Saturday mornings giving young people a sense of identity and self worth, helping them gain confidence in themselves.

Morowei dreamed about taking a group of youth to Ghana, Africa, to make a life-changing journey to discover the Motherland. She wrote an article for *Share* (a Black community news magazine) with her ideas and hoped to find other like-minded people. One person who responded was Winston LaRose, who was known for documenting important moments in Black community history. Together they planned the trip to Ghana, with LaRose prepared to document the experience with youth from Toronto and Jamaica. The youth reflected on their experience of the journey.

"It was a profound trip; feels like home."

"I recognize how important culture was and that's what makes us distinctly human."

"I experienced firsthand what television or even a book could never give me."

"It gave me an awakening—I learned more about my customs and to recognize African traditions as my traditions."

Years later, LaRose followed up with the youth and found that most had become doctors and lawyers.[257]

JFCCO engaged youth in sporting events. For example, it participated in the Fifth Annual Firgrove Invitational Sports Festival, a two-day event featuring basketball and soccer teams from Canada and the United States that was held at Westview Centennial Secondary School. The event was sponsored by the Jane Finch Concerned Citizens Organization and local mosque Masjid Muhammad, as well as its traditional sponsor, the Firgrove United Sports and Cultural Club. A banquet was held following the Saturday games at the Driftwood Community Centre for all to celebrate their achievements.[258]

Over time, the JFCCO lost its legal and charitable status and Morowei moved back to Jamaica to live with family, but eventually returned to Toronto. In 1998, La Rose, who regularly commuted from Burlington, retired from professional life as a registered nurse, business owner, and documentarian, took over as the leader of the JFCCO. Without funding he secured space in the Yorkgate Mall in 2000 and as a committed volunteer he worked passionately to advocate for,

---

257 Telephone Conversation with Winston LaRose, 2019.
258 "Firgrove Expects Thousands" (*Jane Echo*, August 1981).

and inspire, members of the Black community. As of 2020, JFCCO continues to exist, but without its own space or paid staff.

≫ఽ

Neighbourhood disputes and tenant-landlord complaints were issues for many people in the community. The Mennonite Church, with funding from the Mennonite Conference of Ontario, hired Dalton Jantzi to be a community chaplain at the twenty-five-storey MTHA building at 15 Tobermory Drive in 1980. Jantzi provided pastoral care and worked with residents to develop activities that improved their quality of life. Through Jantzi, the community came to know about the church's commitment to conflict resolution, so with support from the Mennonite Church, Conflict Mediation Services of Downsview (CMSD) was established in 1987, with Evan Heise as the coordinator. This service was initially housed out of the Driftwood Community Centre, then a store location at 2885 Jane Street, and lastly, in a commercial unit on Eddystone Avenue. CMSD provided conflict resolution and mediation services for families, neighbours, and workplaces; victim-offender dialogue for youth referred by the justice system; peer mediation training for youth; and training for volunteer mediators in the community. They trained and utilized around seventy volunteers who provided the services in various languages.[259]

Pat O'Neill got a job with CMSD working with children in grades four to six. The three-way, three-year partnership between CMSD, the Hincks-Dellcrest Centre, and the Toronto District School Board enabled O'Neill to spend time in schools. When middle school students (ages eleven to thirteen) were asked, "What kind of conflict or problems do you see in your school?", they replied, "fighting" at seventy-two per cent, "bullying" at thirty-four per cent, "swearing" at twenty-six per cent, and "threats" at twelve per cent. The project goal was to provide a holistic program for children, youths, and their families to promote positive peer culture and non-violent approaches to conflict.[260]

---

259   "Community Services Notebook" (*Norwester*, August–September 1988).
260   "Kids Become Partners in Conflict Resolution" (*Jane Finch Caring Community*, June–August 2001).

While this was vastly different from what she did as a city councillor, O'Neill certainly knew how to resolve conflicts and had personal experience from raising her own six children. Her approach was to train about thirty children in conflict management techniques and how to solve problems on the playground. O'Neill tells the story about one little boy,

> So, we had these thirty kids, and at the end of the program we did an evaluation of what the kids had learned in the program. I'll never forget this one little boy from 15 Tobermory—Spanish background—and he said to me, "I found this program really helpful because I learned how to deal with problems without punching someone out." Success! And this was one of the bullies. But he also said to me that it helped him at home too, because he was able to talk about problems instead of getting mad and yelling.[261]

The CMSD had City funding, but it was not enough to pay staff, program expenses, and the rent at Eddystone Avenue. The community recognized the value of conflict resolution and advocated to keep the program in the community, but in the end, it was decided to reallocate the funding to St. Stephen's Neighbourhood House, an organization downtown that had a great deal of experience providing conflict medication services across the city, including in Jane-Finch.

⁓

Leaders in the community were talking about the health of the community and having conversations about the need for a community health centre (CHC). The CHC model in Ontario provides comprehensive primary health care, prevention programs, and education by a team of health professionals that is locally led by a board of directors. Ede and O'Neill requested support from Malcolm Shookner, from NYIACC, to help the community figure out how to make this happen. Cerny, who helped establish Delta Family Resource Centre, joined the team along with Peggy Edwards from the Jane/Finch Centre. Initially, it was referred to as the Downsview Weston Community Health Centre.

---

261 O'Neill interview.

NYIACC generously agreed to provide staff time to work with the community to develop this centre. Shookner recalls,

> I started having meetings with residents, parents, people who lived in different buildings like 4400 Jane Street, 15 Tobermory and a couple of other places to hear what they had in mind and what they thought when you say, 'community health centre.' Residents talked about wanting a place to go to get their health issues looked after, where the community is in charge of this community-based, not hospital-based program.[262]

Shookner did research, sharing models that already existed in Ontario in the 1970s.

A group of committed champions worked to articulate the vision of a health centre and how to get from where they were to the creation of a CHC. That journey included speaking with the Ministry of Health about requirements to make the case to the Ministry. Shookner remembers, "The documentation of needs turned out to be a four- or five-year exercise, mostly in frustration, because the Ministry of Health was not very helpful to us. Without funding to do the work, the team utilized York University students to conduct research along with community volunteers and supporters to make the case."

Another big obstacle was getting the support of the local hospital. The community believed that the hospital administration saw the CHC as a threat.

> The hospital thought that they could run 'ambulatory clinics,' but the only time people go to their hospital was when they think they had an emergency. We did manage to find evidence that most people in the emergency room didn't have emergencies and that if we could create a community-based model where people could go with their health needs, it would take a lot of pressure off the hospital. It took us a couple of years of dealing with the vice president and others in that hospital to get them to come around to the view that a community

---

262   Shookner interview.

health centre would not be a competitor, but rather an ally to the hospital in meeting the health needs of people in the community.[263]

In 1987, Shookner excitedly shared with the team. "Minister of Health Larry Grossman stood up in the House and announced that the province was starting a new policy to support community health centres across the province." Following that announcement, the community began working with the Ministry of Health, which then became an ally and supporter and gave the community some funding to complete the development work and to further develop the funding proposal.[264]

Within two years of the announcement, and after eight years of work, the funding application was approved and the newly incorporated organization, the Black Creek Community Health Centre, opened its doors at the Jane-Sheppard Mall in 1991. This new non-profit organization was led by the founding Executive Director Cary Milner, PhD, who clearly understood the importance of growing both the primary health services (e.g., doctors, nurses, counsellors, chiropodist, dietician) and health promotion services (community health workers) to develop programs focusing on the determinants of health and responding to local issues.[265]

'Cries from the Corridor'

Peter McLaren published a book called, *Cries from the Corridor* (Toronto: Methuen, 1980). McLaren was a teacher at Driftwood Public School for four years and he wrote about the children who attended his class. He emphasized that his intention was to bring attention to the issues both teachers and children were facing as a result of people living in poverty. However, the book was the subject of a great deal of controversy, not just in Toronto, but across Canada, once again drawing negative attention to Jane-Finch.

The community held him to account by inviting him to be on a panel at a public discussion on how community and schools can support each other, organized by DWAC. He believed that the book was not just a Jane-Finch

---

263 Shookner interview.
264 Shookner interview.
265 Cary Milner retired in 2011, after 22 years as executive director.

BY US! FOR US!

story, but a metaphor or paradigm of what was happening in major urban
centres across the country.

> While my book has been described as a powerful document and
> praised as perhaps the most powerful statement on education to
> emerge in many years, it has also been criticized for allegedly dam-
> aging the reputation of a particular school and wounding the self-
> images of scores of children, parents and some teachers. The book
> focuses on frightening, harsh, yet often ignored aspects of what life
> is like for some children and their parents in a growing segment of
> our urban society. *Cries from the Corridor* was written to shock and
> pummel an indifferent and apathetic middle-class public into an
> understanding of what it's like to grow up poor in an area created by
> greedy developers and insensitive, self-serving politicians. [266]

One resident stormed out of the meeting declaring that "Our children are
not drug addicts and vandalizers." Another said that she would not read the
book, "…because I refuse to have anything to do with professional parasites
who are making money out of our poverty." Marvyn Novick, research director of the Social Planning Council, reiterated that many of the "shocking"
facts quoted about Jane-Finch are not unique to that area. Jane-Finch did not
have the highest vandalism cost, nor the highest unemployment rate, nor the
highest immigration, nor the highest crime rate, indicating that there were
pockets all across Metro, especially along Highway 401, where these issues
are just as bad or worse.[267]

One eighteen-year-old attended the panel discussion. "I've lived here for
12 years and my friend for 11 years. I went to school at Driftwood, and it
wasn't the way you've told it in your book. We aren't bad—and we're sick of
being labelled. I'm sick of hearing 'Oh you poor thing' when I say I live in
Jane-Finch or having people expecting we are rotten kids."[268]

Carl James, a professor of education at York University wrote about
McLaren in his book called *Life at the Intersection.*

---

266 Peter McLaren, "My Commitment Deep, Detractors Myopic: Author" (*Jane Echo*,
       May 1980)
267 "Meeting Plans Government Pressure" (*Jane Echo*, June 1980).
268 "Meeting Plans Government Pressure."

Nevertheless, his series of journal entries about the students' problems and his daily experiences with their socially unacceptable behaviours and educational disengagement provided a rich account of how the educational system (including some the attitudes and expectations of his colleagues) were failing to meet the needs of the students. In fact, unlike media reporters' representations of the 'corridor,' McLaren demonstrated how the learning and teaching situation was directly related to the circumstances of his students lives, and he called for teachers to change their understandings of the students.[269]

Ted Gould, the consultant for the special need schools in the North York Board also attended the meeting. "North York is just coming to grips with [a] changing society. It's hard to find people who provide services and professionals with the right background," he said. "They need training to deal effectively with the new problems." And, Novick summed it up, saying, "Parents have the power [to deal with these issues], if they discover it and use it."[270]

Dalton Jantzi, the Mennonite community chaplain at 15 Tobermory, where many of the parents had children who attended Driftwood Public School, also attended the meeting.

> I remember being somewhat unnerved by reading the book [*Cries from the Corridor*], which had just been published. I kept thinking to myself, perhaps those things happen in a school or in a community everyday, but the way in which it was written there was a sense of hopelessness. It sounded as though these kids got into serious trouble every moment of the day, every day of the week, every time they went into the classroom, and it was a bit overwhelming, actually. I was feeling a sense of optimism, saying 'Okay, what do I have to find out here in order to know what the reality is?' So, what I did was talk to the local agencies, at least the ones I became aware of, I talked to local church leaders, at least some of them, not all of them shared my passion about being in the community. I remember talking to some principals in the schools. I tried to learn what the City was doing by

269 Carl James, *Life at the Intersection*, 13.
270 "Meeting plans government pressure"

way of Parks and Recreation, and I got a sense that there were some good things happening, perhaps not enough, but there were some good things happening that the City in general was not aware of.[271]

The public discussion at that community meeting gave residents an opportunity to respond to what was written in the book and utilize that opportunity to raise awareness about what was happening within the school system.

Gradually over the years, McLaren changed his perspective on this experience. He renounced his original venture, *Cries from the Corridor,* saying that he "grew to dislike the book," and went so far as to state that it now "disgusted" him because it totally lacked "a coherent philosophy of praxis" [practice based on theory]. For the next thirty years, through six rewrites, and as a key component of a larger book, *Life in Schools,* he managed to expunge the bad parts and generate a radical analysis to prepare teachers for resistance to global capitalism and its attendant problems. In 2013, McLaren was appointed Distinguished Fellow in Critical Studies [in the Education faculty] at Chapman University in Orange, California.[272]

Media

The Jane-Finch community has a long history of nationwide media coverage and public attention negatively depicting the community as a place of poverty, crime, and social dysfunction. In the 1980s, a murder could happen at Jane and Lawrence, but be reported as happening in Jane-Finch, over six kilometres away. When Boudreau, Keil, and Young did their research for *Changing Toronto—Governing Neoliberalism,* they conducted a search for articles about the community in two Toronto newspapers for the 1970s and 1980s. Of all the articles found, there was only negative coverage.

The first archived use of the term "Jane-Finch" in a major daily newspaper appeared on April 30, 1965. The newspaper was *The Toronto Daily Star* (later called the *Toronto Star*). The story was about an expectant mother of eight children who was living in a house owned by the Ontario Housing

---

271 Dalton Jantzi interview, Toronto: (Black Creek Living History Project, September 2009).

272 https://en.wikipedia.org/wiki/Peter_McLaren.

Corporation in Scarborough and had to move, as it was being demolished. Initially, she explained that she needed to move to north Etobicoke so her daughter could be close to a treatment centre. The closest available OHC housing available was in Jane-Finch. She was offered a four-bedroom townhouse in Jane-Finch on Driftwood Avenue for $120 a month but refused to move there.[273]

The impact of negative media coverage is felt in many ways. When youth or adults apply for a job, their address may be used against them. When you say, "I live in Jane-Finch," people routinely say something like, "Oh, that's a bad place to live," or "That must be awful," or look at you with sympathy— poor you! You are labelled by where you live.

If you live in the Bridle Path neighbourhood (an expensive area with mansions), you are seen as being wealthy and having good connections. But if you live in Jane-Finch then something is wrong with you. It is well-known that Black youth are harassed by the police there. Property values are lower than in other parts of the city. Tom Rakocevic, member of provincial parliament was elected in 2018 and thoroughly documented that car insurance is known to be higher than other areas of the city. There are no high-end shops or restaurants or movie theatres.

People who live outside of Jane-Finch generally do not come to the malls and restaurants unless they work there or have some other reason for being in the community. Yet people who have moved away come back to visit friends or relatives, or both, and spend time in the community. Many who grew up in the community, or lived there for a time, have fond memories of the people and places there. People in the community recognize that there are contradictions between external perceptions and internal realities.

⁓

There was a period in the mid-late 1980s when drug use was prominently portrayed in the media reporting on Jane-Finch. One resident, Carol Scott, an activist living in the Firgrove housing complex, was fed up with the

---

273   Chris Richardson, "Canada's Toughest Neighbourhood: Surveillance, Myth and Orientalism in Jane Finch," 2008.

negative media coverage around the drug issue, so she organized a "Say No to Drugs" march in the community in September 1988.

"People have to know that they can make a difference," said Scott, who took the lead in the parade, with over fifteen hundred fellow residents participating. She felt strongly about this issue because she was finding syringes in the schoolyard in the mornings, and that had to stop. Bernie Densmore, a supportive community relations worker with Toronto Housing, explained that the parade was a way for people to take a stand. "The majority of the residents are good, decent, hardworking people who felt alone in their feelings about drugs," she said. "Now they know they aren't alone."[274]

Both Densmore and Scott blamed the media for playing on people's fear and for painting a dim view of the community. Most of the people buying drugs came from other parts of the city, or other cities, encouraged by the media attention that told them that Jane-Finch is where you go to get drugs. "The press never talks about the kid who is president of his student body or the one who took tenants' groceries up to the apartments when the elevators were broken," explained Scott. The residents and the workers were not the only ones chiming in on the negative media during this period.

The staff inspector for 31 Division Police, Julian Fantino, wrote a letter to the local Norwester newspaper in 1988 that gave a more nuanced view of the community. In the letter Fantino said,

> A great deal of media attention, most of it negative, has greatly influenced the perception of the public at large into believing that the Jane-Finch community is populated in the main by drug dealers, purse snatchers, murderers and prostitutes. In essence a place where crime, fear, and feelings of hopelessness have taken a stranglehold. Of late, media accounts of Jamaican gangs (posses), drug wars and territorial disputes have propelled the reputation of the Jane-Finch community into an unprecedented character assassination. Yes, the Jane-Finch area is experiencing a serious crime problem.

---

274   Grace Cameron, "Taking a Stand Against Drugs" (*Norwester*, November 1988).

Yes, there is reason for concern. Having said the foregoing, we must acknowledge that, although unacceptable, the situation is not unique to this particular community. *Crime statistics for the whole of Metropolitan Toronto indicate that incidents of violent crime have risen 92% in the past five years.* [emphasis added] If we were to further fine tune this information, I know that much of the problem relating to crime everywhere in our society at this time is closely connected to a worldwide flourishing drug trade.

[...] Anyone who is objective will readily conclude that the many difficulties experienced in this community have evolved from the original concept and planning strategies that have since materialized into many unforeseen problems. The decisions, input and initiatives taken to develop the community to its present state, were in the main, assumed by individuals, ministries and governments outside the residents. So, let me get the facts straight. If finger pointing is in order, and I don't think it is, those who are so engaged, might be well advised to point outside the community itself. In brief, as far as I am concerned, the media especially have given the Jane-Finch community unfair treatment.[275]

⁓

In December 1981, the local *Jane Echo* newspaper covered a meeting held by the alderman Pat O'Neill in cooperation with the Downsview Weston Action Community. The front-page article was titled, "GUNS: No one here has seen them." The police and politicians present said, "There seems to be no basis for it." Irene Pengelly, Chair of the 31 Division Police Committee on Race Relations and Policing, declared that the fear and publicity may create a problem by leading "crazies" to get guns for protection. O'Neill called for the meeting because of reports that residents were "arming themselves in fear."[276] Where did this fear come from?

---

275 Julian Fantino, "Open Letter from Police to Jane Finch Residents" (*Norwester*, November 1988).
276 Peggy Gemmell, "GUNS: No One Here Has Seen Them"; "Report says residents see press as enemy" (*Jane Echo*, December 1981).

A report was presented to the Mayor's Committee on Community, Race and Ethnic Relations that said, "Jane-Finch residents see the press as an enemy because of misrepresentation that encourages fear and perpetrates injustice." For example, the *Toronto Sun* had a headline, "Neighbourhood Cringes" stating that in the community, "Parents live under a pall of fear, terrified that violence and death could strike again at any moment."[277]

A December 14, 1981, article in the *Toronto Star* said that Lastman feared a bloody winter of shootings. "There are guns all over the place," said Mayor Mel Lastman. "People are coming into that area (Jane-Finch) with guns, and those people intend to use them." Bob Strupat, who was his executive assistant, said that the mayor's fear is a "sense" that there are an increasing number of guns in the area based on street workers' reports and increasing tales of "episodes" involving guns. Interestingly, the police responded that they knew of no increase in illegal guns in the area, nor in the number of violent crimes. Bill Traynor, director at the Driftwood Community Centre, said that in four and a half years at Driftwood he had never seen a gun. He volunteers in youth programs in other parts of the city and has been in other locations where he said he had seen guns but, "never at Driftwood."[278]

Furthermore, Irene Pengelly, who also volunteered at an after-school program, said the response of young people in the program to recent publicity is to say, 'Why can't they leave us alone?' They are proud of their community and resent outside people and the press making it look bad."

The December 1981 *Jane Echo* article went on to say,

> The street [outreach] workers reported that residents feel the press has degraded and misrepresented their areas, that it has encouraged fear, and in some respects has encouraged people to stay away… This negative halo…is terribly resented by residents. In their minds the press are not the defenders of justice, but the perpetrators of

---

277 Henry Stancu, "Neighbourhood Cringes" (*Toronto Sun*, November 27, 1981, 4), quoted in Peggy Gemmell, "Report says residents see press as enemy" (*Jane Echo*, December 1981).

278 Cecil Foster, "Lastman Fears Bloody Winter of Shootings" (*Toronto Star*, December 3, 1981, A6), quoted in Peggy Gemmell, "GUNS: No One Here Has Seen Them" (*Jane Echo*, December 1981)

injustice. Residents acknowledge significant problems that their communities have to deal with, however, they express pride in living there and in growing up in these areas. This pride is rarely reflected in press reports. The reputation of fear in these areas is often far greater than the actual experience. The negative talk encouraged by this fear is producing some unfortunate behaviour. Some residents are acquiring guns and other types of weapons to (as they see it) defend themselves.[279]

The article recommended that the North York Mirror and North York Bureau of the Toronto Star balance their coverage with positive stories and spend some time getting to know the community.

In another article, residents were said to, "...complain that the powers that be know about their neighbourhoods only through sensationalized reports in the media," [280] and officials of the municipality seldom take the time to walk through neighbourhoods to see the problems at close hand. It recommended that the Board of Control, commissioners, and local aldermen meet with members of the community, particularly youth, on a regular basis.

Information about the community did not just come from newspapers. A film called, *Home Feeling: Struggle for a Community,* was produced in 1983 by two filmmakers, Jennifer Hodge and Roger MacTair, through CBC's Fifth Estate. The film was supposed to highlight the strength, resilience and vitality of people under pressure. However, this documentary stirred controversary by exposing racial tensions and challenges with 31 Division police and residents in the community.

The video portrayed police insensitivity to community needs and the stigmatizing of the community generally, and public housing, specifically. The movie was also billed as a documentary look at the Jane-Finch community. Some of the criticism focused on the fact that the movie centred on the Black community in Jane-Finch and therefore was not a look at the whole

---

279   Peggy Gemmell, "Report Says Residents See Press as Enemy".
280   Peggy Gemmell, "GUNS:".

Jane-Finch community, but of only a sizeable minority of it. Yet, it was the primary image people got from the film.

The first screening at the library was supposed to be for the residents of the area, according to advance flyers. Stanley White, of Tobermory Drive, was angry when he arrived to find that seats were reserved, and you had to have tickets. "If I'd looked in that room and seen it full of people from the area, I wouldn't have said anything," he said. But there were empty seats and fifty per cent of the people were invited guests or social workers and civil servants from outside the area. Ward 3 alderman Claudio Polsinelli was shouted down when he tried to make a point using the experience of Italian immigrants in Toronto. White agreed with him. "The system isn't working," White said. "Police race relations efforts aren't working."[281]

Michael Spensieri, MPP of Yorkview, also wrote an article for the *Jane Echo*.

The film sets out to ambitiously tackle the concerns of the Black community in Jane-Finch. It flops miserably, not as a vignette but as a political and social statement which everyone expected it to be. It raises certain issues; the vignette has received widespread attention and has stirred reactions from all sectors. Among its critics are community volunteers, social agencies, and indeed the police who feel that the movie portrayed them negatively. While overlooking outreach programs, community relations work, etc., especially among the youth, the movie leaves one of the impressions that nothing is being done to alleviate the problems as the community continues to be victimized by the police, themselves only a manifestation of the all-oppressive 'system.' While no one holds any answer to the problems illustrated, it is irresponsible to suggest that the themes are not being addressed. It is noteworthy that the Honourable Jim Fleming, former minister of multiculturalism, and MP for York West, has commissioned a Government Committee of Parliament to investigate discrimination of visible minorities. It is with great

---

281　"Billing Rouses Anger" (*Jane Echo*, Aug 1983).

disappointment that other efforts by government, volunteers, and agencies were not cited in the movie.[282]

In the September 1983 issue of the *Jane Echo*, Sadie Deen, a resident and community volunteer submitted an article after attending the viewing of *Home Feeling*. She said she had "...a deep regret and concern—regret that Canada's once renowned police force has fallen so much in public esteem and concern for the Canadian youth, many of whom are unemployed and who must cope with the added frustration of police harassment!"

She went on to say,

> The police could be of immense help but as long as they continue to view the Jane-Finch youth with disdain, not all the services the community has provided will be of any benefit. Without a doubt, a Jane-Finch address carries a stigma and, as was evident in the film, a simple offence from someone of such an address could be blown out of proportion by the police and the media and it is the police evidence that counts. The present mutual mistrust between the police and Jane-Finch youth must be eradicated and until some initiative is taken by the police and the media, there can be little room for change. The deteriorating police-community relationship can no longer be ignored. When resources are lacking, it takes much to extract that potential—it requires a deep understanding of human problems and a clear understanding of the special need every human being has to preserve his or her dignity and identity intact. Unless changes are implemented in the important forces responsible for exercising controls and maintaining peace and order, Jane-Finch will continue to justify the media's image of the 'bad address.'[283]

Policing and community

Metro Toronto's 31 Police Division, first located at Jane Street and Sheppard Avenue West and later moved to Norfinch Drive, near Jane Street and Finch

---

282   Michael Spensieri, "Movie Flops Miserably as Social Statement" (*Jane Echo*, August 1983).
283   Sadie Deen, Letter to the Editor (*Jane Echo*, September 1983).

Avenue, has a mandate to respond to emergencies, enforce laws, prevent crimes, and provide support services for the northwest area of the former North York. However, the tension between the police and the community of Jane-Finch has a long history. Perhaps that's because of the socioeconomic and political system and the police culture or that constables come from other areas, cities, or towns, and are moved every few years between divisions across the city. Could that be to ensure that they do not develop positive relationships with the local residents?

There were attempts from the early years to develop relationships with the police at 31 Police Division. Brian Whitehead described his experience from the 1970s.

> I never had any negative interaction with the police, just because I just didn't. Other people did, and I guess it was the beginning of foot patrols and North York's Mayor's Committee (Mayor Mel Lastman's Committee on Race Relations). We had a 31 Police Division group that would meet and Julian Fantino at the time was the Detachment Commander. Irene Pengelly was in that group, as you may know, and Lenore Suddes used to go to that and John and Jean Campbell. All kinds of people went in and out—it was a good committee. I think they were trying to introduce community policing, getting the officers out to walk and meet kids, instead of just coming in to arrest kids.[284]

The 31 Division Community Liaison Committee started in the 1980s. Stephnie Payne explained its origins.

> You know, it wasn't until about the '80s that I think I had a positive impact, because I really got active seeing my two girls growing up and I thought, I'm not missing anything. It was at one group program at Oakdale Park that Irene Pengelly, who you would probably remember worked at Oakdale Park, and she was very fond of Greg Bobb, a local youth. I remember specifically one day Greg Bobb came in

---

284 Whitehead interview.

and he had gotten himself in a little scuffle and the police really went down on him. So Irene advocated for Greg Bobb and that's when I sat with Irene, and I said, "We need to look at different strategies to work with our various communities and bring in some sort of common sense to the issues of police brutality of Black males." I remember Irene said, "Yes, Stephnie, I agree with you—what could we do?" We needed to form some kind of committee, and I think it was between Irene and I, I don't remember who else, that we started meeting with police and forming the 31 Division Community Liaison. I was part of that with Irene and bringing some of these issues out at the meetings.[285]

Love Koduah, an activist who co-founded the Ghanaian Women's Association to support Ghanaians new to the community, shared her perspective of problems with policing in the community. "In the '70s and '80s, it was policing. The crime was very high, maybe higher than now. We weren't able to communicate with the police. The fear is still there, and when people see you talking to the police, they think we are informers. Maybe you are telling them that at nighttime, we need security, or we need more lighting."

While navigating these kinds of issues, she started the Asante Multi-Cultural Association of Toronto, which eventually built a housing cooperative at Weston Road and Finch Avenue. Koduah became the queen of the Asante Multi-Cultural Association, and her role was to focus on women's issues.[286]

Richard De Gaetano had moved into the Glen Gardens Housing Cooperative in 1990 and became aware that there were issues of racism and discrimination with the police. He had a long history of involvement with fighting anti-Black racism and was a social justice activist and trade union organizer. He joined with other members in the co-op and participated in a protest responding to an incident of police brutality to a Black man who lived in the co-op.

There was an incident that took place sometime in the spring of '93, when one of the co-op members was driving back to the building

---

286 Love Koduah interview (Toronto: York Woods Library, Black Creek Living History Project, April 2011).

and was being followed by the police, who proceeded to handcuff him in our parking lot. Then one of the cops took him behind an emergency exit that stood out in the parking lot and started beating him. I didn't see this or hear it. But some of the members heard the member screaming while he was being beaten and went out onto their balconies and yelled at the police and went downstairs to the parking lot to make it clear they were watching. The police quickly took the handcuffed young man off to the police station. I knew there had been a history of police problems in the community, because the community had a large Black population, and I had been involved in anti-Black racism work since I was quite young. So this was an important issue for me and even though the guy was known, or assumed, to be a drug dealer, he was still a member of our co-op community, and he was being treated unfairly and unjustly. The people in the co-op felt they had to protest this and, although I didn't try to take on any leadership position on this, I offered whatever help I could in the organizing a protest. Which we did. It involved quite a few people from the co-op and the community. It was quite an interesting first experience in Jane-Finch.[287]

A series of meetings were held at the co-op with people such as Dudley Laws, a leader of the Black Action Defense Committee. Letters were written to politicians and press releases were sent to media. Further action included marching up to 31 Division carrying placards denouncing police violence against lower-income people. "It's not a Black thing and it's not a white thing. It's happening to the working poor and it just has to stop," Rose Allen-Gordon told a news conference held just before the march up Jane Street.[288] While Allen-Gordon made a valid point about the working poor, most people in the community felt strongly that Black working-class members of the community were the primary target.

⁓

287 Richard De Gaetano, interview (Toronto: York Woods Library, Black Creek Living History Project, July 2014).
288 Moira Welsh, " 'Working Poor' stage protest" (*Toronto Star*, June 13, 1993).

Beth Bow, who conducted some research in the area, noted the way police dealt with residents in a paper for her class.

> When an organization like Firgrove United is set up to try to give the residents entertainment and sources of recreation, hopefully resulting in the cutting down of the number of social problems in the area, they are almost immediately investigated by the police. When a meeting was called with the police to discuss what the problem was, local resident and political activist Lennox Farrell politely asked what they were being investigated for. The answer he got was they were not going to sit there and be insulted; they did not have to stand for this, and proceeded to walk out. Such actions can only serve to dissuade others and frustrate, to the point of giving up, those like Lennox who were trying.[289]

The community, especially Black residents, also experienced issues with the court system.

> Pengelly, chairman of the Division 31 Committee on Race Relations and Law Enforcement, said she failed three times to reach provincial Judge C. J. Morrison Monday by phone after he cancelled an appointment with herself and Clive Banton, coordinator for the committee, set for last Friday. Morrison was criticized by Jane-Finch residents after a report in the *Toronto Star* on Feb. 25 quoted him as saying in court that Blacks in this area seem to have a 'chip on their shoulders' for the police. Pengelly said someone in Morrison's office finally told her the judge did not want to discuss the matter further. Earlier this month the Jane-Finch Concerned Citizens Organization called for his immediate removal from the bench. In a press release the association said, 'Such statements coming from a highly placed member of the judiciary can only serve to further demoralize the Black community and are open attacks upon their dignity and integrity.' Carol Libbert, of Driftwood Avenue, a member of the association said, 'This puts us on the defensive. If a judge could make such a statement, could we expect justice in this man's court?'[290]

---

289 Bow, "Community Spirit of the Jane Finch Corridor".
290 "Judge Cancels Interview" (*Jane Echo*, March 1981).

The government was giving the impression of trying to respond to the challenging issues around policing. "The Ontario Youth Secretariat has once again provided funds to hire 35 youths to work with the Metropolitan Toronto Police for 8 weeks during the months of June, July and August."[291] The government aimed to provide summer employment for youth, improve relations between youth and the police and to connect youth with seniors. To do this work, youth distributed a 'Vial of Life' kit designed to carry pertinent medical information on every family member to be attached to a refrigerator door to alert emergency personnel should they come to their home. "In an emergency, if a victim is unable to provide information the vial will serve as a spokesman for the person needing emergency care. The program was a tremendous success last year."[292]

Leticia Deawuo, an astute and passionate activist from Ghana and living in the community, elaborated on her perspective of the police.

> I come at it from a very systemic and political analysis of what the police is and what the police mean and why the police came about and who the police are here to protect and to keep in check. So, to be real, the police were not made to serve and protect low-income people. The police were made to protect the interests of the rich and to protect their property from the poor. I think if we look historically, this system was set up to be against low-income people, and in the context of North America, low-income people are racialized and indigenous people and to keep them away from the rich and the ruling class property and to protect them and serve them then you already know how a disaster is made to be. And it goes to explain why we have police in some neighbourhoods and in some neighbourhoods, we don't.
>
> That comes from one other systemic issue of where poverty is the reality. At the end of the day, the individual police officer who comes

---

291   "Police Repeat 'Vial of Life,' " (*Jane Echo*, May 1984)
292   "Police Repeat"

to arrest him, is doing his job and his job is to book this kid, especially if they are a repeat offender, then it ends up on his record, which then has a long-lasting life impact. I feel like no matter what, and this is just my personal opinion, that no matter what we do, it's the system that was set up. If you look at policing from different parts of the world—it's the same. They are all set up the same way. Each country has their own issues.

I was reading a story from Ghana where a young mother and her child were brutalized by police officers. So, police brutality in the United States, in Canada, in Africa and other parts of the world is the same issue that people have with them, because structurally, that's how they are set up. In terms of this community, I think if we don't change things systemically, the work with individual officers— yes, some of them are nice, some of them are just bad, but they all represent the same institution. [293]

Byron Gray, an activist who became a manager of youth services for the Jane/Finch Centre, grew up during that period of time.

I remember growing up and there was always this sense of belonging that needed to happen. I think with a lot of displacement of where people were living and having to form new alliances with new families and new friendships, it caused a bit of disruption to the way of life for many people. Then, smaller gangs were forming in the late 1980s and early '90s. We had the Vice Lords, Triph Kids, Loonie Toonz, M & M's, like they were all different, smaller gangs in small pockets. The Bloods and Crips came after that, where it was more definitive of, like, if you are on this side of the street, you were a Blood, and if you were on that side of the street, you were a Crip, right?

That came later on, but a lot of that came from the economic situations most people were in. Not being able to find employment, education being a bit more dismal at the time and just wanting to

293   Leticia Deawuo interview (Toronto: York Woods Library, Black Creek Living History Project, July 2015).

be part of a family. Parents were working two or three jobs, rarely home. You were being raised by your neighbours or by the kids on the street. There was a bit of a loss there—not a lot of infrastructure and support in the community to support the numbers that we had.[294]

Church leadership

One form of support for residents came from church ministries. Following years of traditional church 'planting' by many Christian denominations in northwest Toronto, and in response to the rapid population growth of this area, there was a call for some church officials to step outside their church buildings to reach out to the community. Values such as social justice, kindness, humility, showing hospitality, forgiveness, forbearance, truthfulness, and gratefulness are rooted in the Judeo-Christian tradition and in other faiths. The call to do this kind of work could be found in many religious documents, whether or not adherents accepted that calling.

A bold type of ministry was required where church leaders meet the community members on their turf, be prepared to step into non-religious arenas, and be concerned about assisting individuals to achieve their basic human needs.

Some of the churches that truly followed this approach to establish ministries in the community that served people where they lived was the Mennonite Church, the United Church and, for a shorter time, the Anglican Church. While the focal point of traditional faith communities is Friday, Saturday, or Sunday worship, the main focus of the community ministries that came to Jane-Finch was a presence that included community engagement and community development, standing in solidarity with low-income and oppressed peoples throughout the week.

The Mennonite Church first came into the community because of their interest in building a community ministry in an area that had been identified as marginalized, racialized, and experiencing a great deal of poverty. Hubert and June Schwartzentruber, kind and generous people, were mission

---

294   Byron Gray interview (Toronto: York Woods Library, Black Creek Living History Project, September 2015).

consultants with the Mennonite Missions Board of Ontario in 1980. They spent considerable time researching the area as a potential location for the Mennonite church to establish a "presence."

They approached Dalton Jantzi to further explore options. Jantzi, a compassionate Mennonite with strong social justice beliefs, was working at Warden Woods. He had worked there since 1966 as a preschool teacher, youth worker, program coordinator, and also shared pastoral care duties. His experience and orientation in the Scarborough public housing community of two thousand people had prepared him to accept the responsibility of taking on a community chaplain role in the Jane-Finch community.

Jantzi met with four community relations workers from Ontario Housing Corporation, where he outlined his background and his desire to be located within a social housing building. His primary question was, "Is there a particular high-rise building in the community that they would see as being: (a) most removed geographically from existing support services (b) where persons find it very difficult (for a number of reasons) to get connected with the resources which they need, and (c) where there seems to be a 'greater than usual' amount of loneliness, frustration, fear, apathy, and general sense of 'lack of community'? " In other words, 'Where are we most needed'?"

All agreed that 15 Tobermory Drive, located in the Jane-Finch community, was the best place to locate this ministry.[295]

In the first year, working out of a small office on the main floor of this twenty-five-storey building, Jantzi heard many people complain:

"Since I've moved into 15 Tobermory, my family won't come to visit me because of my address."

"When I want to find a job, I can't find employment because of my address."

"When I go to school, when my kids go to school, it almost feels like the address tells the school about something they can expect."

---

295 Dalton Jantzi, "Chaplaincy in a Highrise Community—One Approach to Urban Ministry" (Toronto: personal papers, 1982).

15 Tobermory (Jane-Finch)

Jantzi strived to minister with integrity and relevance. He thought that those stereotypes were terribly unfair and focused his ministry on working with residents of 15 Tobermory to help them create their community. Some of their ideas included safe places to socialize, going on trips with their children, starting a little store in the building where they could purchase needed household items, having a preschool program, youth programs, and programs for women—all on site.

The main floor included a large recreation room, two meeting rooms, a kitchen, and an office. It was currently being used by a private day care centre. Jantzi knew that the space was not serving many people in the building and set out to secure the space for this community of over 1,200 people living there. Having a good relationship with housing officials enabled him to advocate for the space. He contacted Betty Nidrey, a representative from Ontario Housing Corporation and set up a meeting. Jantzi knew Nidrey from his work in another community and believed she had compassion and a social conscience that enabled them to secure the space.

"We believe that you, Betty Nidrey, have the kind of compassion and social conscience for a community like this and you can make this happen. We'd like to leave it with you," Jantzi explained. "Within three weeks, Nidrey sent a letter saying that when this day care's lease term was up, the space would be available for the community for use. That was one of the early moments of celebration within that community. It just seemed like the right moment to do something."[296]

Meetings were facilitated by Jantzi with service providers who had the resources to offer programs in this newly opened space. Before long, the Jane/Finch Centre was offering a preschool program and a women's group. The residents were engaged by informing and participating in the growing programs and, as a result, formed a group called Tobermory Community Activities (TCA) Planning Council. The TCA met monthly to discuss challenges and successes, to make decisions about the use of space, and to identify gaps.

> That council was a group of volunteers who just came together and began meeting and working and, of course, working through some personality issues too. Once you haven't had any power or any clout and you get into that position, you enjoy it. Sometimes, more weight gets focused on one person's need, so there were issues to work through by way of hearing each other out, speaking and listening with care, so that everyone's opinion mattered. It became obvious after some time that my role as chaplain was extending to that of community development, not that I saw myself as a community developer, but as a kind of catalyst to link people and to be in touch with community organizations and agencies who would have something to offer, whether it was public health or recreation.[297]

Support for this ministry from the larger Mennonite constituency was forthcoming. As individuals, families and congregations throughout Ontario learned about what was happening they shared generously. This resulted in financial gifts and practical support and enabled the purchase of toys and equipment for the space.

It was important for people to not only receive, but to contribute to their community explained Jantzi.

---

296 Jantzi interview.
297 Jantzi interview.

We were saying to people who moved into the community (and who had stated clearly that they were only here a short time and would then be moving), 'What do you need from this community while you are here and what could you contribute?' They answered, 'We are never asked to contribute to anything. We're seen as those people who are takers but have nothing to give.' What we discovered was that they had many good ideas— to sit on committees, to sit on steering groups, to offer opinions. A few of the residents were on the first steering committee that implemented Conflict Mediation Services of Downsview, for example, and made a valuable contribution.

There were other times when people in Tobermory were tapped on their shoulders to say, 'Would you mind coming to this. Would you mind giving a word about this. Would you mind having your opinion expressed around this matter?' I remember one of the men saying, 'This is the first time I've ever been asked for my opinion, and I felt like it counted. I mattered to somebody; I mattered for something. Do you have any idea of how that makes me feel?' He said it with a lot of feeling, and this was an older man.[298]

The Mennonite Conference continued to provide valuable support by inviting Norma Reesor-McDowell to work with Jantzi. Reesor-McDowell, a Mennonite who lit up any meeting room she entered, grew up in the Markham area. Her husband was a student at York University, so this part-time position as coordinator made sense. While her time there was too short, she made a significant contribution to the community by working closely with agencies and organizations to increase their resources and supports to this community. She also became a friend to many in the community.

TCA decided that they needed to have a community coordinator to continue and enhance the work Reesor-McDowell had started, but they did not want to incorporate to receive funding. The Jane/Finch Centre submitted their proposal for a community coordinator to the City of Toronto requesting funding to support that position. With those new funds, Joanna Reesor-McDowell, another Mennonite and cousin to Norma, came to Tobermory

---

298   Jantzi interview.

and worked for many years in the capacity of community coordinator. Joanna brought strong administrative and organizational skills along with her warm and welcoming smile. Jantzi reflected, "Each of those persons brought their unique skill sets and related well to the residents. In terms of coordinating skills and being able to work as a team, I felt like the team we had going there really spoke loudly to the larger community about what was possible."[299]

Jantzi also set out to connect the Tobermory community to other Mennonite churches. An early one was with the Floradale Mennonite Church in the Elmira area north of Waterloo, Ontario that became a partner church to 15 Tobermory. The exchange started in 1981, when residents were invited to Floradale for a weekend and were matched with families with whom they established lasting relationships. Each December, a bus brought the families from Floradale to Tobermory for a Sunday afternoon to sing, share stories, and enjoy a wonderful meal together. The families from Floradale brought the desserts, provided a pre-Christmas program, and the Tobermory folks created a hearty ethnocultural dinner.

Relationships were being built, but more work was needed with regard to the scarcity of relationships. Jantzi recognized that people of all ages who had moved into Tobermory from war-torn countries, or who had been separated from their families, had to struggle with what it meant being in a new community. 15 Tobermory had more people than the town closest to the farm where Jantzi grew up. And, his town had an arena, a library, a little theatre, a fairground, baseball diamonds and soccer fields, several schools, and lots of churches. The "town" of Tobermory had four elevator shafts that carried over twelve-hundred people to and from their one, two, or three-bedroom apartments, twenty-four hours a day, seven days a week. Jantzi was aware of the challenges.

> If you are a mother on the 18th floor raising a three and a five-year-old, it's not easy or simple to tell your children to go play in the backyard. I found that people were incredibly innovative in making the best of a situation that was not easy. Often these were parents, moms who had been abandoned by a partner, or the partner ended

---

299 Jantzi interview.

up getting into trouble and couldn't be there with them, or the partner who they hoped would be a long-time supporter in that family disappeared. So, there were shattered relationships and broken dreams and heartfelt anger and grief around circumstances over which people had no control. I think the lack of control of things that affected everyday living was one of the major issues that I think of right now as something that sticks with me.[300]

There are many stories of newcomer professionals arriving in Canada and not finding jobs, and the frustrations that comes from that situation. Jantzi remembers having a conversation with a resident who was trying to start a business.

I do remember having conversations with the family of a man that we tried to help start a business—we helped to collect some money and helped him buy a hot-dog machine. It didn't get off the ground because he got beaten by some kids the first day he had it set up. That was a bit of a shattered dream for him. He was someone who said, 'I feel ashamed to be living in this building with my three boys and my wife. My wife struggles with mental health issues, my boys are embarrassed to be living here because back home I was an accounts receivable person with a corner office in Tehran and here I'm a nobody—I can't even find a decent job to support my family. I don't know why I came here. I was hoping it was a better life for my boys, but all we talk about is how angry they are at me.

Jantzi shared another story about a family from Sri Lanka.

I don't know to what extent that has changed, but I know another family that arrived here from Sri Lanka, where the father had been a high-school teacher. He had to take retraining after he got here because of his lack of 'Canadian experience.' There are many taxi drivers on our streets who were teachers and doctors back home, and the impact of being underemployed in our community has always been an issue that I know social agencies, more so than the churches, have sought to address.[301]

While many churches are sensitive to these issues and understand the challenges, there are some who blame the victim. Jantzi reflected on a conversation he had with a local minister.

> I remember going to a local church, one of the first weeks I was there in 1980, and meeting with the local pastor and saying, 'This is why I'm here and this is what I'm hoping to do.' He caught me a bit off guard a bit by saying, 'Wouldn't you agree, Dalton, that when you look at a place like 15 Tobermory where you are working, that most of the people have ended up living there because of sin in their lives?' I was stunned for a moment, and then I caught my breathe and said, "You know, that hadn't occurred to me. It had occurred to me that they might be living there because of sin in my life, because we have a very difficult time, as so-called Christian churches, to find ways of leveling the economic playing field and providing opportunities where doors and windows have been slammed shut. I'm there to try to make a difference in that field.[302]

Alternatives were important and it was comments like that and conversations with residents about relationships of trust, confidence building, and an interest of residents who wanted to further explore their spirituality, that led to the Black Creek Faith Community being formed at Tobermory. This ecumenical group that met each Sunday to worship together was later renamed the Jane Finch Faith Community.

The Missions Committee of the Mennonite Conference of Eastern Canada completed an evaluation in 1990 with a view to determine whether expectations, which were set for the ministry, were being met and to recommend possible directions for the ministry's future. An evaluation committee was established that included some residents and staff. Twenty-three residents were interviewed, nine individually and the rest in a series of small groups,

---

301 Jantzi interview.
302 Jantzi interview.

along with interviewing volunteers and other agency workers who were active in the area. It also interviewed Mennonite church representatives.

The findings of this evaluation indicated a positive impact on residents, agency workers, the wider Jane-Finch community, and the Mennonite Church. The original goals set for the ministry were clearly achieved through the personal relationships established and the activities carried out or nurtured by the chaplaincy.

Jantzi left this ministry in 1997. Amy and Clayton Kipfer, a Mennonite couple who were pastors, replaced him and moved into a home in the Jane-Finch community, where they remained for five years. The Mennonite Conference of Eastern Canada did an enormous amount of life-changing work. Skills were developed, and doors were opened for countless numbers of people who benefited from the Mennonite presence in their community. Those who shared this experience said they would do it all over again. Those who came after this church ministry, continue to survive in this small village, twenty-five stories high.

The work of the Mennonite Church did not go unnoticed by the United Church of Canada. In the 1970s, they had an outreach ministry to the Caribbean community that operated out of Beverley Hills United Church at Jane Street and Wilson Avenue. They hired two Jamaican workers to reach out to the community. Taking children to Sunday school was not the kind of outreach ministry they wanted to do, so when Doug Kingsbury, a leader in the United Church, came across the model of the Mennonite community ministry with Dalton Jantzi, he became interested. Placing a minister in a community, not to build a congregation, but to work in solidarity with the community, was more in keeping with the kind of ministry they were interested in adopting. Before long, the Jane Finch Community Ministry became part of the Toronto West Presbytery of the United Church of Canada.

After some discussions with Jantzi and identifying the Firgrove community as a suitable location for this type of ministry, they hired Peggy Campbell as the first Community Minister in 1982. Campbell was just returning after a twelve-year period working in Jamaica. With her exuberant personality, she quickly established herself, working from the two meeting rooms in 5 Needlefirway. Firgrove consisted of 382 families living in townhouses and an apartment building, owned and operated by Toronto Housing.

Campbell set out to establish programs and, like Jantzi, encouraged local service organizations to come into Firgrove to provide the services needed. She also had a deep affinity for youth and arranged trips to places as far away as the Maritimes, so that youth could expand their horizons and enhance their experiences. In 1988, Campbell moved away and David Murata, who had done his internship with Campbell, continued with the work until 1994. With his leaving, the Presbytery reviewed whether they should continue, but continue they did with the hiring of Barry Rieder in 1995, who remains in this position to this day.

~

The work being done by the Mennonite Church and the United Church was expanded for a short period of time to include St. Stephen's Anglican Church, located on Jane Street, north of Wilson Avenue. Jantzi, when he began his work, met with various ministers in the community, and he fondly remembered Reverend Jim Garland at St. Stephens. He was followed by Reverend Tim Grew, who was equally supportive of the concept of community ministries. Reverend Brad Lennon worked alongside Reverend Grew and eventually moved to a church in Guildwood Village, in Scarborough. Then along came Reverend Betty Jordan in 1991. Jantzi described her as an activist-type person who 'walked the walk.'

> I remember her offering candid opinions, helpful advice, asking all kinds of good questions as only Betty was able to do—no holds barred. Making a difference by her presence, because when she was there, when she was talking to a parishioner or a community resident, it was like they were the only person in the room. She brought something special into our neighbourhoods. I experienced her, as well as Tim Grew and Brad Lennon, as very affirming of the work we were doing at 15 Tobermory. It was a mutually beneficial relationship.[303]

---

303 Jantzi interview.

St. Stephen's Anglican Church focused some of their work in the Chalkfarm community, located one block south of their church. They also joined the newly formed Jane Finch Ecumenical Advisory Council, which had consisted of the Mennonite Church and the United Church. The monthly meetings included representatives from each of the neighbourhoods and a community agency staff. This meeting provided a forum for discussion, planning, and opportunities for cooperation.

While Reverend Jordan was in the process of becoming a priest within the Anglican Church, she utilized every opportunity at St. Stephen's to learn and to practice what it meant being among people in low-income communities. She explained her point of view regarding religion that was also informed from her previous time as a 'street nurse' in downtown Toronto.

> Personally, I don't draw a lot of lines between denominations and along faith lines. I think there is one God and we're all going in the same direction. We might be wearing different coats and taking different streets, but we're all going in the same direction. So, there weren't any preconceived ideas that might not work. We all had the same kind of theology and philosophy in working in this kind of community.[304]

Reverends Lennon and Jordan did outreach in the Chalkfarm community, sat on committees in the community, and did some of the legwork that came from decisions by the committees. Learning how to change systems, how to enable people to organize, and get governments to pay more attention to the needs of the community was a learning curve for Jordan.

One thing she quickly learned about and came to deeply understand was the impact of racism. She learned early that "to be Black was to be less than," and shared a story that illustrates this fact.

> Tim [Reverend Grew] was accompanying a young fellow who happened to be at the wrong place at the wrong time and had been arrested holding a gun in his hand, when in fact a friend had run past him and handed him the gun as the police was chasing him. So,

---

304   Betty Jordan interview (Toronto: York Woods Library, Black Creek Living History Project, August 2010).

this kid got charged with possession. The result here was a kid who lost his Grade 13 year because of the court case. With Tim being 6' 5", a heavy-set guy, white, with a clergy shirt on, he sat in court with this single mom every single time she went to court. I can't remember what he was convicted of—it was really a light sentence, and we realize that the reason he got that sentence was because there was a white priest sitting beside the mother. So, the whole racial issue was front and centre as far as I could see.[305]

Reverend Jordan soon recognized that there was strength in the community, a strength totally unknown outside of the community.

In order to live in a situation of public housing, being poor, a single parent and having black skin—to get through the day was a major, major accomplishment—absolutely major. And to raise your kids in that kind of situation and have your kids not to be in jail was another major accomplishment. I don't think that to this day that this is appreciated—not appreciated at all. To get up every day, under those kinds of conditions and get your children off to school and do your laundry and clean your home and have them come back home and make them supper and all that kind of stuff in those kinds of conditions—they are heroes—absolute heroes.[306]

Woman abuse was also an issue Jordan reflected on.

Christina's children were abducted, and I walked through that tragedy with her for two years. I think that by us walking together enabled her to do that journey, even though it ended in tragedy for herself. I did write to her parents a year after her death (they were in Spain). All three of her children had been abducted to Iran (her husband was Iranian) and they (Christina's parents) had bought one of the children for $50,000 and they were going to purchase the other two so that they could have their part of Christina with them. That was closure for me and that was also very good for me to know what was happening for those kids. But that two-year walk with

305 Jordan interview.
306 Jordan interview.

Christina that I had was difficult. It was hard for both of us, but we enabled each other to walk it. She was the mom, and I was just walking beside her."[307]

Sadly, Christina had been brutally murdered by a man from a previous relationship.

Reverends Grew, Lennon, and Jordan eventually left for other ministries. Jordan said that when she was ordained as a priest and moved to Flemingdon Park to begin a community ministry there, she walked away much more knowledgeable about community and community development than when she started. "I learned much more about what kinds of things needs to happen in order for a community to be able to stand up and be okay." Jordan indicated that when she left, they had not brought the parish along so that the work could be sustained by new priests coming to St. Stephen's. She later became the Reverend Canon Betty Jordan.

York Finch hospital

The 1970s to 1990s brought unprecedented growth to the Toronto and surrounding communities. As the local hospital rose to the challenges of caring for an ever-changing and diversifying community, the demand for new services, expansions and technologies was constant.

Michael O'Keefe, from the downtown Parkdale area, started his new position as executive director at York Finch Hospital on August 15, 1983. O'Keefe was no stranger to this area, having owned a home on Grandravine Drive in 1970, and said he was familiar with the Jane-Finch area and people. When he started, he identified three tasks to be tackled as part of his job: problems of equipment replacement in radiology and other laboratories, insufficient space in the emergency and other departments, and not enough out-patient care for psychiatric patients. He said the hospital had 303 beds and was the fifth busiest in all of Ontario.[308]

In 1984, the hospital had more than twelve thousand inpatients, performed five thousand same-day surgical operations, 42,000 X-rays and

---

307 Jordan interview.
308 "York Finch Hospital Welcomes New Administrator" (*Jane Echo*, September 1982).

serving as "family doctor" to thousands of people in the community. Michael Spensieri wrote about this in the *Jane Echo* paper.

> York-Finch has the busiest Emergency Department for any hospital of its size in Ontario. With 74,000 patients per year, the Emergency and Out-Patient Department is well used; however, its equipment needs updating and replacement. The replacement would cost $2,563,863. Many have asked me why the government is not providing funding for this most important endeavour. Unfortunately, the government funds have already been spent on repairing old equipment and replacing other equipment as much as possible.[309]

The article stated that the board, doctors, staff, and volunteers have contributed and was now asking the community for some financial support. This was an early indication that the government did not have the best interests of the health of residents in Jane-Finch, expecting the hospital to ask people in a low-income, working-class community to pay for equipment that the government should be providing.

The community was acutely aware that the board of the hospital did not represent the diversity of the community. The Northwest Advisory Committee wrote a letter to the Board of Governors at the hospital on June 30, 1987, regarding the appointment of board members. The letter requested the hospital amend its bylaws to allow four additional members from the community, the hospital be acknowledged as a community hospital, and recognize a strong need to make the board representative of the community it serves. The letter also pointed out there were no members of the visible minority communities presently sitting on the board. These recommendations were not accepted.[310]

For many years, there were tensions, complaints, and issues raised about the hospital by members of the community and in the 1980s attempts were made to improve communications and build bridges between the hospital and the community.

---

309   Michael Spensieri, "York Finch Updates Equipment" (*Jane Echo*, February 1984).
310   Wayne Burnett, Letter to the York-Finch Hospital Board of Governors, June 30, 1987.

Support from York University

The community recognized that research was important. In the late 1980s, Jackie Rankine, who became the Community Relations Officer at York University, worked with student, Reya Ali, to produce a report called, "Funding Levels Among Community-Based Services: A Comparison between an Inner City and a Suburban Neighbourhood."

Ward	Population	Funding
7	56,829	$3,470,550
1, 3, 5	149,160	$1,970,302

The report compared funding levels between community groups in Ward 7 in the City of Toronto, bounded by the Lakeshore, Sherbourne, Bloor, and Logan and selected neighbourhoods of Wards 1, 3 and 5 in the City of North York for the calendar year 1986. It included the funds received within that year but used into 1987. The former Ward 7 was used as a comparator because it was in the very heart of the inner city downtown and had been established longer in terms of its community services.

Funding levels for the organizations designated as Ward 7 community service providers were drawn from a report by Metropolitan Toronto Community and Social Services. Consideration was given for services that were offered beyond the geographic boundaries. The report indicated that it was by no means a precisely comparative report, as all factors must be exactly comparable to do such a report and it was thus not comprehensive. Its intent was to explore the funding levels within the city and the suburbs.[311]

According to the research, the broader Jane-Finch area in 1986 had more than double the population with only about sixty per cent of the equivalent funding.

---

311 Reya Ali, "Funding Levels Among Community-Based Services: A Comparison Between an Inner City and a Suburban Neighbourhood" (Research report for Community Relations Office, York University, n.d.).

The suburbs continued to be underfunded. An earlier comparison had been done between Jane-Finch and Regent Park with similar findings. According to Peggy Edwards, who had conducted the study, that despite the documented evidence of poverty, unemployment, single mothers, and lack of programs and services, the Jane-Finch area was not adequately funded compared to Regent Park.

Affordable housing

Affordable housing continues to be a dominant issue in the Jane-Finch community. In the late 1980s, two members serving on the Jane/Finch Centre's board of directors and some staff learned that the housing cooperative movement wanted to build a cooperative on the empty lot at 2750 Jane Street. Cooperative housing is member controlled—where members collectively own the building, are responsible for running it, and where there is a mix of market rent and subsidized rent. Public housing is fully rent-geared-to income, but residents have no legal control over their housing. Some of those living in public housing wanted another option for bringing up their children and others simply wanted to live in a cooperative environment. The founding board of the Glen Gardens Co-operative was formed from these different groups. When the local homeowners learned about this development, they fiercely opposed it. They clearly did not understand what a housing cooperative was, and they did not want low-income people moving into their immediate vicinity.

The founding board members learned that the land needed a rezoning amendment to build an eight-storey building. Despite City Council approving the rezoning, the Glen Gardens board and the homeowners brought their conflicting positions to the Ontario Municipal Board (OMB). The OMB was an arms-length provincial body that heard applications and appeals on municipal and planning disputes. The meeting at City Hall brought out both opposing groups, homeowners against residents wanting to live there. Lawyers put forth their case, and residents on both sides gave compelling arguments about the pros and cons of establishing such a building on Jane Street. After a long and tiring day, the OMB voted to give final approval to build the Glen Gardens Housing Co-operative.

Mario Sergio, the city councillor at the time who later became the local member of provincial parliament, had a somewhat different recollection. He was on the North York Planning Board at the time and the only housing development that happened during his term was Glen Gardens. It was approved because it was already zoned. "I remember that they came back to Planning or Council because they wanted to add one extra floor. There was a lot of resistance from people, and I said, 'They're going to be building the building—it's just one floor.' But politics being politics, I said, 'Let it go.' But I was telling my friends on Council to approve it. It didn't make sense. That was the only building while I was on City Council."[312] Glen Gardens Co-operative opened for occupancy in 1989.

One of the founding members of the board was Rouvean Edwards. She described her involvement.

> When I heard about it, can't remember who filled me in, but I know when they were building Pioneer Co-op and I asked about it, they said it was co-op housing. I asked what that was. So, they explained it to me. Then when they were thinking about Glen Gardens, somebody mentioned it to me, and I went to a couple of meetings at Pioneer Co-op and that was interesting. We were all excited, looking at the blueprints and the dynamics of all of that.
>
> It was educational, meeting with contractors and things like that and the people we met with were from social housing. Janet and Linda were awesome people to work with. I find Glen Gardens home and raised the rest of the kids here, until one by one, they moved out. My daughter liked it so much that she moved back in again."[313]

Fundraising in the community

With the Jane/Finch Centre's growth during the 1980s, the board recognized a need to supplement its funding sources through some fundraising. The board members at the time did not have expertise in that area, so with a small

---

312   Mario Sergio interview (Toronto: York Woods Library, Black Creek Living History Project, December 2019).
313   Rouvean Edwards interview.

grant, they hired Terry Lee as a consultant, who then brought in Malcolm Shookner, former staff of NYIACC, as a partner to help the Centre learn how to fundraise. Lee introduced the board to Pat MacKay, a compassionate and articulate advocate who understood the importance of enabling people and championing causes.

> The consultants called me and asked me if I would get involved in terms of being a mentor and in bringing some other people to help with fundraising. Basically, it was to teach fundraising, not to do it ourselves. That's what was very appealing to me. Most agencies who want help, want you to do the fundraising for them and just hand over the money. What was unique about this in my experience, I don't think I have ever encountered it anywhere else, but the Jane/Finch Community and Family Centre said very clearly, "please don't do it for us, teach us how to do it."[314]

A small committee was established with staff and residents, along with the consultants, and the Friends of the Centre was born. Chris McMeans, a friend of MacKay's, generously agreed to host a luncheon in her home with her friends and acquaintances. Given my long history in the community, I attended the first luncheon and talked about realities of Jane-Finch. It was an opportunity for those attending to get a better understanding of the challenges faced by people living in the area and the barriers they faced moving from poverty to employment.

The luncheon was a big success, and from that experience, one of the women who learned a great deal from this agreed to host her circle of friends for another luncheon. The luncheons continued until such time it was agreed this wide circle of friends had generated a significant list of future supporters. The Centre did not ask for funds at that time, rather it was agreed that with their permission, the new friends would receive a letter at the end of the year asking for a donation and they would receive only one letter each year. Lynn Ross, with an abundance of compassion, was a long-time supporter of the Friends of the Centre. This initiative continued into the 2020s.

---

314 Pat McKay interview (Toronto: York Woods Library, Black Creek Living History Project, March 2015).

Under Mackay's tutelage, we learned how to successfully approach corporations and how to organize a local fundraiser (we hosted the infamous *Polka Dot Door* at Driftwood Community Centre). The Jane/Finch Centre hosted a community meeting to share what they were learning with other organizations. MacKay also attended to offer her insights into this work. Sharing information so that others could benefit was always important to the community.

MacKay, with her quick mind and generous soul, continued to support the Jane/Finch Centre's annual Friends of the Centre campaign and champion worthy causes right up to her death at ninety-five years of age in September 2019.

Clearly, through the 1980s, the Jane-Finch residents participated on many committees, led and participated in numerous actions, advocated for what they needed, and developed new community organizations to respond to the needs of residents. This community was being left behind by people in authority, despite evidence presented to all levels of government of the difficult challenges many residents faced, so it was necessary for residents to continue to organize on their own behalf.

CHAPTER SIX

Struggling Against Austerity

Community deals with drugs and alcohol problems

In the late 1980s, the Jane/Finch Centre organized a forum to discuss the increased use of drugs and alcohol in the community. The result of this forum was the establishment of an Anti-Drug Advisory Committee. In the 1990s, the Province announced major funding for selected communities to "focus" on drug and alcohol abuse. The Anti-Drug Advisory Committee applied for a small six-month project called the Black Creek Community Groups United Against Drugs. This initiative then led to being chosen as a "focus community" by the provincial Anti-Drug Secretariat along with Parkdale, Regent Park, and O'Connor [east end of Toronto] for a two-year project.[315]

There were two criteria: a drug and alcohol problem and a track record as a community that had worked well together in the past. The coordination and collaboration between community organizations at that time augured well for this proposal. Dr. Ruth Morris—a local resident, activist, and a Quaker—was one of the world's leading spokespersons for prison abolition and transformative justice. She taught at universities, wrote books, and was hired as the executive director for this project, remaining there until her retirement in 2000.

Black Creek Anti-Drug Focus Community Group became incorporated with an anti-poverty, anti-drug, and anti-alcohol mandate in 1993. Later, it made a slight name change to the Black Creek Anti-Drug Focus Community Coalition [known as FOCUS], gaining non-profit charitable status in 1995. Their strategy was to prevent addiction by building a stronger, healthier community and by offering a range of programs and services. They hired

---

315   Ruth Morris, "A Short History of Black Creek Focus/PEACH" (North York: November 30, 1998).

local people to work with youth in the schools, within neighbourhoods, and across neighbourhoods.

Their primary concern was drug and alcohol misuse. FOCUS created ARAPO (the Association to Reduce Alcohol Promotion in Ontario) with attention given to alcohol prevention. Their secondary concern was to build a community where addiction would not take root because the core needs of residents were being met.

While working on the drug and alcohol issues, FOCUS hired seven residents born in seven different countries, plus a coordinator (also a resident), representing diverse populations in the community to run a Neighbour-to-Neighbour Project. That included bringing people together from different neighbourhoods and different socioeconomic and cultural backgrounds to share experiences and build trust within the community. They purchased translation equipment to be used at the meetings to support residents speaking different languages. Morris related that, "We showed our commitment to language respect by buying, with our first grant, an expensive simultaneous translation equipment set, which has been lent to groups all over ever since, as well as used in our community. We demonstrated this further by putting out our first newsletter for several years in five languages."[316]

The original health ministry funding agreement came to an end. Once the Harris Progressive Conservative Party came into power, funding for health promotion and prevention activities was slashed. Funded through the Ministry of Health's health promotion and prevention grants, FOCUS projects throughout the province were being forced to amalgamate their funding with other Ministry of Health-funded agencies. Initially, the Ministry of Health offered FOCUS three partner options: Humber River Regional Hospital, Toronto Public Health, or the Black Creek Community Health Centre. None of the negotiations with these three were successful, so FOCUS approached the Jane/Finch Centre because of their similar philosophies and services. FOCUS was integrated into the Mental Health component of the

---

316   Ruth Morris, "A Short History."

Jane/Finch Centre, with a focus on drug and alcohol use and misuse directed at children and youth. This helped the Centre move towards establishing a new youth component, which in 2005 became known as The Spot: Where Youth Wanna Be.

Sustainable funding was difficult to find at that time due to government policies and, after the funding from the Ministry of Health was discontinued, the Black Creek FOCUS reviewed its purpose. In 1998, the board changed the name to Promoting Economic Action and Community Health (PEACH) with added objectives of organizing free community education seminars on skills development, free community workshops on how to barter with local skills, and developing and publicizing an inventory of skills available in the community.

Ruth Morris also brought the concept of "neighbourhoodism" to the community. The Coalition Against Neighbourhoodism (CAN) was born in 1994, when two neighbourhoods in Toronto realized they had something in common. The stories used by the corporate media portrayed Jane-Finch and Lawrence Heights negatively and reinforced harmful stereotypes. Barry Rieder, who worked in Lawrence Heights prior to becoming a community minister in Jane-Finch, explained how this came about.

> I was part of this coalition called Coalition Against Neighbourhoodism and that coalition looked at the stigma the media has created, but also that which society has on culturally diverse, low-income communities. One of the things we found was that we were beating ourselves up because we were saying things like, "Lawrence Heights is not as bad as Regent Park," or "We're not as bad as Jane and Finch," and Jane-Finch was saying, "We're not as bad as Parkdale." Really, what we had to do was to come together as a community and fight back against the negative stereotypes of these communities.[317]

---

317   Barry Rieder interview (Toronto: York Woods Library, Black Creek Living History Project, June 7, 2018).

The media usually focused on negative events and some events happening in other neighbourhoods close by were labelled as Jane-Finch. The media did not cover the positive activities happening in these communities or the successes of the residents who lived there.

One CAN initiative was a new network of community newspapers with support from Tom Kear, Marilyn Eisenstat (a local teacher), and Ruth Morris. Morris described what CAN was doing.

> CAN has organized a movement to challenge media misrepresentations, met with the Managing Editor of the Globe and Mail, and the Ombudsman of the Toronto Star, trained residents on how to deal with media, and organized a major conference on Neighbourhoodism, keynoted by internationally famous John McKnight. [318]

In 1998, CAN sponsored a conference on neighbourhoodism featuring four short talks on how four neighbourhoods worked to overcome neighbourhoodism. "Each community's story is one of community residents working together, creatively, selflessly, and cooperatively, to build a more positive image of our home neighbourhoods," reflected Morris.[319]

Media

While new organizations were being formed and residents were becoming engaged in the community, the media were ever present with articles like, "Immigrants' dreams lead to ghetto life."[320] Ward 3 Councillor Li Preti, together with residents of the community in a bid to battle the negative media reporting on the area, put forward a motion that asked Council to condemn the sensationalized press coverage of the area. "Reference is always made to Ontario Housing and the Black community. By emphasizing the

---

318   Ruth Morris, "CAN tells the real Jane-Finch story" (Jane Finch Caring Community Newsletter, February–March 2000).
319   Ruth Morris, "CAN tells the real Jane-Finch story."
320   Elaine Carey, "Immigrants' Dreams Lead to Ghetto Life" (*Toronto Star*, April 10, 1979).

problems faced by the Black community, the media attributes blame to this small segment of the population."[321]

Frances Henry and Carol Tator argue in *Discourses of Domination: Racial Bias in the Canadian English-Language Press* that one of the most important factors in the racialization of crime is the over-reporting of crime allegedly committed by people of colour—especially Blacks. The authors argue that the media construct Blacks in ways that are damaging to their personal identity and their social status in the community. An examination of newspaper articles from the *Toronto Star, Toronto Sun*, and the *Globe and Mail* for two months of each of the years 1994, 1996, 1997 indicated that:

- 39% of articles in the Star and the Sun about Jamaicans related to issues such as crime, justice, immigration, and deportation.

- Racial identifiers were used twice as often in reports of individuals from subordinate racialized groups, particularly African Canadians, than whites.

- 46% of all crimes reported in the *Globe*, 38.5% in the *Star* and 25.6% in the *Sun* used a racial or ethnic descriptor [that] involved Black people or people of Caribbean origin[322]

The story of Jane-Finch included a description of the area and about how cooperatively people worked together for the benefit of the whole community. At that time, the divide between users of service and service providers did not exist. In Jane-Finch, you might be a client in one organization, a staff member working for another organization, and sit on the board of directors or other volunteer work for a third organization.

Capacity building

Neighbourhoodism also drew the attention of academics. The CAN generously supported a three-year research project called Toward Indicators of Community Capacity: A Study in Four Toronto Communities, with a report

---

321   Peter Li Preti, Letter to North York Council, December 11, 1986.
322   Frances Henry and Carol Tator, *Discourses of Domination: Racial Bias in the Canadian English-Language Press* (University of Toronto Press—Canadian Ethnic Studies Association, 2002).

published in 1999.[323] Two of the neighbourhoods were in Jane-Finch. Staff from the Centre for Health Promotion and Department of Public Health Sciences of the University of Toronto undertook this research initiative to include four Toronto communities or neighbourhoods: Parkdale, Regent Park, and in Jane-Finch, the Tobermory and Firgrove neighbourhoods. The purpose of the study was to develop a model of community capacity and ways to measure it based on community experience.

The engagement activities listed in all four neighbourhoods was extensive. Firgrove was referred to as, "the community that flies," and Tobermory, "the community that cares." They articulated what their communities had done to engage people. They identified their strengths, talents, and skills, and reported on the social and physical environment. They also recognized key people, their diversity, political awareness, and safety.

A new definition of community capacity was developed out of this research. The definition spoke to the community's ability to build on its strengths in order to achieve its goals.

> Talents, strengths and abilities are present in community members and form the bedrock upon which the community in all of its diversity can develop its goals and act to achieve them. These abilities are helped by facilitating conditions inside the community (such as having meeting space, services and programs). At the same time these abilities are hindered or blocked by barrier conditions inside the community (such as meeting times or places feel unsafe) and outside the community (such as a negative image of the community by outsiders).[324]

The media did pay attention, and incidents that happened, for example at Jane and Wilson, were no longer labelled as happening in Jane-Finch. Residents learned how to only say positive things to the media when they called to get information.

---

323 Suzanne Jackson, Shelley Cleverly, David Burman, Richard Edwards, Blake Poland and Ann Robertson, Toward Indicators of Community Capacity: A Study of Four Toronto Communities (Toronto: Centre for Health Promotion, August 1999).
324 Jackson et al, Toward Indicators.

Banking initiatives

Another important initiative led by Morris was the Banking Project. Prior to the name change from the Black Creek Anti-Drug Focus Community Coalition to Promoting Economic Action and Community Health, the organization started a banking project in 1995 because Morris witnessed the way in which someone was treated trying to open an account. She had a conversation with local community chaplain, Dalton Jantzi and they sent a letter to the Task Force on Church and Corporate Responsibility (TCCR) representing Canada's national church bodies in raising issues of corporate ethics. They do things like buying token shares in corporations to be able to speak out at shareholders meetings on ethical issues. Three people were then invited to present at a conference called Investors for Social Responsibility. Morris spoke and afterward she was bombarded with questions.

"Bankers rushed up to us after every bad news story we shared asking 'Is it our bank? Was it us'?" explained Morris.[325] From there, the Banking Project engaged with the Royal Bank's Jack Klassen, a regional vice president, and follow-up meetings were held with local bankers from many branches serving northwest Toronto.

Staff from the Banking Project brought welfare officials to the table and covered three areas: technological systems, policy changes and training options. Training sessions were held in 1995—with over five hundred residents attending—on issues such as accessing basic banking services. Shortly afterward, the Royal Bank started to pay the community for training on class and cultural sensitivity in 1997.

Morris soon learned about a press release by the Canadian Banking Association (CBA) to push for legislation to make the banks serve low-income communities more effectively. The federal government had hearings about the issue, and both sides wanted Morris' testimony about the Jane-Finch experience. Soon afterward, the banking association took steps to issue new standards, reducing the number of pieces of identification required for accounts and eliminating picture requirements.

---

325   Ruth Morris (Toronto: Your Community Newsletter, January 1998).

Morris proudly observed, "We had been saying we couldn't change the policies, but we had been a part of nationwide forces, which had created larger changes than we had thought realistically possible in such a short time."[326]

At PEACH's first annual general meeting in 1998, Morris and other board members celebrated their big win of getting a bank charter changed. Rieder attended the meeting.

> Fred Hayes, part of this banking coalition, brought one of the vice presidents of the Royal Bank to the dinner. Fred gravitated to me because I was the only person he knew and so I sat with the Vice President of the Royal Bank and he was asking me questions around, 'So, what do you do?' I said, 'I'm kind of a facilitator resource helping the community to build on their assets.' 'How's it funded?' 'Well, it's actually funded by surplus church property—kind of changing bricks and mortar into human resources.' Never thought much of it and we talked about some of the work, but a couple weeks later, Ruth Morris says to me, "I don't know what you did, but this guy is going around saying, 'I met this Minister without Portfolio, and if the church can put a minister in the community without a congregation, why can't the bank put a bank manager in the community without a bank'."[327]

The Royal Bank had property on Weston Road and Arrow Road that became surplus. They sold it and used the proceeds to create a community banking project, not only in Jane-Finch, but in Regent Park and Parkdale in Toronto, and in Regina and Montreal.

Rieder explained the concept of a community banker.

> The whole idea was to second a bank manager to work in the community and also to pay for a community banker apprentice to work alongside that manager and to work on economic development. Murray McAdam was hired as the community bank apprentice. It was a short-lived project—it had a few gains. Fred Hayes eventually moved on to head office because part of what Ruth Morris said,

---

326 Morris (Your Community Newsletter).
327 Rieder interview.

'We don't just want your charity, what's most important is how do we influence the systems themselves.' And so, Fred Hayes began working in the Royal Bank head office around what kind of policies and changes were needed within the Royal Bank for low-income and diverse communities. Murray McAdam stayed for a while and then moved on eventually to the Anglican Diocese of Toronto, where he had a social justice portfolio.

I was about to go on sabbatical when Murray McAdam approached me. The Anglican Church had a micro-lending program and they had about $40,000 that was still left in the program and Murray was trying to position us that they would give the money to Jane-Finch to start a micro-lending program. I came back from sabbatical and the bishops had decided they could use the $40,000 elsewhere. Sunder Singh, with the Elspeth Heyworth Centre, had worked in Riverdale with a micro-lending program and said, 'No problem, you have $1,000, you have $200, you have $2,000—we'll start our own micro-lending program.' So, what happened is that we started with the support of York University. We then did some market research including getting some graduate students working with some community members to research the community about what kinds of needs they had seen and whether or not they were supportive of it.

Initially, with the micro-lending program, we thought that people were going to be banging down our door for these loans. One of things that we found out is that most of our work is not so much in giving out the money but is more helping people to determine whether or not they are ready to start a business. In many cases, a business may not be the best thing for them to get into. I would say that out of every ten people that come to us, interested in starting a business, probably three moved forward and one gets approved.[328]

As of 2020, the micro-lending program ended due to funding restraints.

---

328   Rieder interview.

Cultural impacts on youth

During the early years of FOCUS, specific programming was needed to support newcomer youth. Sue Wilkinson had worked for the Cambodian Association as a student, then as a program manager, before being hired by the Jane/Finch Centre.

> In that role, it was mostly partnerships and bringing in new revenue, so lots of new partnerships and new resourcing. A lot of the work I did focused on building relationships between the Cambodian Association, the Laotian community, and the Vietnamese community. We got funding for several youth related initiatives that brought the three communities together because there were intercultural tensions between them and there was a lot to learn amongst the different communities because they had evolved in very different ways. That was a big part of it.[329]

Work was focused on youth leadership, bringing the three communities together to build capacity, develop skills and undertake initiatives. Academic challenges were a big issue.

> Youth were being kicked out of school for certain behaviours or not succeeding in school. Absenteeism was a huge problem, so youths as young as twelve were dropping out of school—a really big issue. Another big issue at that time was glue sniffing, believe it or not. We started some programs related to glue sniffing awareness as well, largely in the Cambodian community at that time. It was a big problem with kids as young as seven and eight. This is one of the programs funded. Can't remember who funded it (a glue-sniffing awareness initiative) but it was a partnership in Toronto, so there were others in the city, other regions that had similar issues. But it was even just raising awareness.[330]

Parents struggled in raising youth in a country and a culture so different from their own, sometimes without a partner or without elders around for guidance. On top of that, many Cambodians came from rural communities

---

329 Wilkinson interview.
330 Wilkinson interview.

and had no experience with urban environments. Wilkinson described her experience in this area.

The biggest issue women were facing was how do you raise a teenager? People did not know how to do that in the context of these intergenerational and cross-cultural tensions. You have youth who have only known Canada, and then you have parents who come from very traditional backgrounds and don't understand Canada. They don't understand our education system, leading to an incredible amount of stress and tension for everyone involved, for parents and their youth. [331]

Along with the focus on youth in the 1990s, there was also a focus on cultural sensitivity training. Margarita Mendez, a former outreach worker for the Jane/Finch Centre, and later the executive director, explained why this was an issue.

I started talking to people and listening to their issues that they have. It became very evident to me that because there were a lot of complaints about how they have been having difficulties with the public health department, with the board of education, and with many of those big institutions, that the piece of the culture was not part of the big institutions. Even with Hincks-Dellcrest at that time, when they felt residents had to be dealing with those organizations, there has to be a transition. Many of the countries where people were coming from and, arriving at Jane-Finch, the issue of physical discipline of children and many other cultural issues were not taken into consideration. A lot of people were being involved, without being bad parents, because there was not a teaching process for the parents. And, a teaching process for a lot of the agencies—there was a lot of conflict.[332]

---

331 Wilkinson interview.
332 Mendez interview.

Mendez found that the issues the Latin American residents had in dealing with agencies, such as the Children's Aid, was due to the contradiction of how they parented in their home countries versus what was expected in their new country. Utilizing a community development approach, she figured out that her time would best be used by training people within the organizations that Latin Americans were accessing or being referred to instead of doing case-by-case advocacy. This idea of cultural sensitivity training for mainstream agencies and institutions—including mental health agencies, schools, and the hospital—expanded to include trainings on different groups of newcomers for local organizations in the community.

≈

In the early 1990s, the Asian Community Centre was being challenged by a group of South Asian men, who confronted the women who ran the Asian Community Centre, accusing them of having a lot of money and not saying where it was going. Veena Dutta, the executive director and founder, was forewarned that at their annual general meeting there could be a takeover. It could be dangerous, and they did not know what could happen. While Dutta knew their financial books were in order, and that programs and services were being provided, they also knew that memberships were being taken out to "stack" the votes at the annual general meeting against the leadership. To ensure safety, Dutta invited the police, other supportive service providers, and funders to witness this event and to provide support. The meeting was held in the gym at the Driftwood Community Centre, and while nothing violent happened, a group of South Asian men took over the board of directors.

Dutta was distraught and concerned that all they had been working for would be lost. She was escorted out by the police to ensure she got home safely, and when she went home, her husband met her at the door. He said, "What?" and she said, "We lost it." Veena later shared that her telephone was ringing up to 2:30 or 3:00 a.m., because people from the ministry and others in the community wanted to know that she got home safely and that she was all right.[333]

---

333   Dutta interview

Sadly, Elspeth Heyworth, who had supported Veena in the development of the Asian Community Centre, had gone on vacation to Goa in 1990 and had drowned while swimming there. Some time passed, but with her usual determination, Dutta started the Elspeth Heyworth Centre for Women in 1992. Dutta wanted to honour Elspeth for all the work she had done in helping them establish programs for South Asians in the community.

The Asian Community Centre and the Elspeth Heyworth Centre ran simultaneously, but with the funding going to the Asian Community Centre. There were financial discrepancies and questions about management and the Asian Community Centre closed two years after the takeover. Funding soon came to the Elspeth Heyworth Centre for Women with Veena Dutta once again at the helm.

They moved into an office at Keele Street and Finch Avenue for a number of years, and later to their current office at Weston Road and Finch Avenue, where they provide a range of programs and services to both women and men. Dutta retired at age sixty-five, leaving the centre in the good hands of Sunder Singh, a passionate and determined woman who took over as the executive director.

Government response to youth

In 1992, the provincial government, under the leadership of Premier Bob Rae of the New Democratic Party, was concerned about the impact from the recent rebellion in Toronto in early May, referred to as the "Yonge Street riot" of 1992. Rodney King, a Black man in Los Angeles, had been beaten by four white police officers (famously caught on video) who were later acquitted. Closer to home, two Peel police officers were acquitted of killing seventeen-year-old Michael Wade Lawson, two weeks earlier. And two days prior to the Rodney King beating, Raymond Lawrence had been shot and killed by Toronto police. Police killings and brutality had stirred up a hornet's nest of angry youth and much of the Black community.

A response to this violence was organized by the Black Action Defence Committee, which coordinated a peaceful protest at City Hall attended by a few hundred people in solidarity with what happened in Los Angeles and Peel. The crowd grew to a thousand people as they marched to the United

States Embassy to show solidarity with Rodney King, and then they held a peaceful sit-in at Yonge and Bloor. By 7:00 p.m., the formal demonstration was ended.

Around 9:00 p.m., young protesters were still milling around and still angry. They went over to Yonge Street, the main shopping area, and began to chant "No Justice! No Peace!" Soon some were breaking store and bank windows and throwing objects at the police. The Black Action Defence Committee tried to move the protesters away from the violence and back into marching. [334]

These actions escalated over a six-hour period, leaving more than one hundred Yonge Street stores damaged and plundered with thirty-two arrests and many injured people on the streets. "While all races were represented, the majority were white youths and skinheads with covered faces, according to observers, who also noted that some Black people tried to 'stop the madness.' " In this article, Dudley Laws, of the Black Action Defence Committee stated, "People have been very, very angry for a long, long time" over the government's inaction in countering racism, particularly among police officers. [335]

Their anger was understandable.

≈

Deeply concerned, Premier Rae approached Stephen Lewis, who had been the leader of the Ontario New Democratic Party in the 1970s and who had become an inspirational speaker and celebrated humanitarian. Lewis agreed to take on the role of advisor on race relations and consulted widely to determine what needed to be done.

Over a period of one month, Lewis held more than seventy meetings with individuals and groups, including those who were most affected by racial discrimination. His working group of seven included Wayne Burnett, a resident activist from the Black community who grew up in Jane-Finch,

334 Shree Paradkar, "The Yonge St. Riot of 1992…or Was It an Uprising?" (*Toronto Star*, May 8, 2017)

335 Carola Vyhnak, "The 1992 Riot that Served as a Wake-Up Call for Police" (*Toronto Star,* May 19, 2017).

and Grace-Edward Galabuzi, another leader in the Black community who worked as a special assistant with Bob Rae at the time and later became a professor at Ryerson University. This group of seven remarkable people also included other people with both lived experience and insights on the issue of race relations.[336]

Lewis pursued this topic relentlessly and asked questions about the criminal justice system. This system was supposedly set up to serve and protect. Those from minority and racialized communities did not feel served or protected.

He found through his research into the police that the institution sadly lacked training for its officers in terms of race relations, the system for complaints, the use of firearms, and the use of force. Lewis also found that criminal investigations of police conduct was most controversial within the system and that change needed to happen. He realized that the police units had insufficient funds to do their work with any credibility. Lewis found that there was supposed to be funding from the Ministry of Citizenship that was to go to the Ministry of Correctional Services to provide ethno-specific counselling, but that it had been cancelled.

Even today, many in jail are awaiting their "day in court," incarcerated, but not convicted of any crime. The proportion of inmates in the criminal justice system of Black and Indigenous men and Indigenous women is far beyond their numbers in the general population.

> As of the most recent census in 2016, Indigenous and Black people accounted for 4.8 per cent and 3.5 per cent of the Canadian population, according to Statistics Canada, but made up 25.5 per cent and 8.7 per cent of those in federal prison, respectively, according to the correctional database that same year. [...] The Office of the Correctional Investigator, a federal watchdog, estimates Indigenous people will account for a full third of inmates sometime in the next

---

336 Stephen Lewis, "Report of the Advisor on Race Relations to the Premier of Ontario" (Toronto: June 9, 1992).

three years and that Black people are approaching 10 per cent of the prison population. [337]

An employment equity program for the Ontario Public Service had been in place since 1987. Lewis found this to be disappointing for racial minority designated groups. He explained that "...the program over the last five years reminds me uncomfortably of the Federal government employment equity legislation: the gains are marginal at best."[338] He found that civil servants of visible minority backgrounds were discouraged from implementing the employment equity program.

In terms of the education system, he observed that despite the rhetoric debated in schools about equity and fairness, change was not coming fast enough. For many years, Black students (and their parents) wanted courses on Black history. They wanted teachers who looked like them. They wanted guidance counsellors that understood their culture. They inquired why Black students were being streamed out of academic courses, discouraged from attending college or university, and were concerned about their future.

The Rae government rose to the challenge of trying to understand the impact of racial discrimination, and because of this research they developed twenty-two thoughtful recommendations, of which nine were related to the education system.

As a result of his investigation, Lewis articulated some observations of which one spoke to the primary cause of the issues.

> First, what we are dealing with, at root, and fundamentally, is anti-Black racism. While it is obviously true that every visible minority community experiences the indignities and wounds of system discrimination throughout South Ontario, it is the Black community which is the focus. It is Blacks who are being shot, it is Black youth that is unemployed in excessive numbers, it is Black students who are being inappropriately streamed in schools, it is Black kids who are disproportionately dropping out, it is housing communities with

---

337 Tom Cardoso, "Bias behind bars: A Globe investigation finds a prison system stacked against Black and Indigenous inmates" (*Globe & Mail*, October 24, 2020).
338 Stephen Lewis, "Report of the Advisor".

large concentrations of Black residents where the sense of vulnerability and disadvantage is most acute, it is Black employees, professional and non-professional, on whom the doors of upward equity slam shut. Just as the soothing balm of 'multiculturalism' cannot mask racism, so racism cannot mask its primary target. It is important, I believe, to acknowledge not only that racism is pervasive, but that at different times in different places, it violates certain minority communities more than others. As one member of the Urban Alliance on Race Relations said: "The Blacks are out front, and we're all lined up behind."[339]

Education continued to be a concern throughout the 1990s. The Province, under the NDP government, established the Royal Commission on Learning "to ensure that Ontario's youth are well-prepared for the challenges of the twenty-first century." They released a report that had a vision and action plan to guide the reform of elementary and secondary education. This included values, goals, and programs for schools, as well as systems of accountability and educational governance.[340]

The report indicated that Black students, parents, and community leaders expressed "serious concerns" about the level of educational achievement of their students and "frustration over lack of improvement over the years, during which time they have voiced their concerns to school boards and to the Ministry." The Commission went on to recommend that, in areas with large numbers of Black students, "innovative strategies" be used and "special programmes" be established that would address the "urgent need to substantially improve the academic performance of Black students."[341]

Some of the recommendations were adopted. For example, Wayne Burnett, who was working for the NDP government, undertook to review

339   Stephen Lewis, "Report of the Advisor".
340   Monique Begin and Gerald L. Caplan, "For the Love of Learning" (Toronto: Royal Commission on Learning, 1995), 433; as quoted in Carl James, Life at the Intersection, 107.
341   Begin and Caplan, 439; as quoted in Carl James, Life at the Intersection, 107.

the curriculum and make recommendations to improve it. One of the recommendations was to introduce the concept of life skills into the classroom, including topics such as conflict mediation, problem-solving, and communication. But in June 1995, a Progressive Conservative government came into power under Premier Michael Harris, who slashed funds for programs that impacted low-income, marginalized, and racialized people. That groundbreaking report on education remained on a shelf to collect dust, as do many royal reports, white papers, and other social research from government.

Governments come and go, but the community continued to be challenged by the same issues facing youth. One of those issues was education.

Fight for a community college

Members of the Network of Community-Based Organizations (NCBO) learned in 1992 that Seneca College wanted to consolidate its west-end campuses into one location. The only land that was available in Jane-Finch was the Yorkgate lands, thirty-eight acres of vacant land on the northwest corner of Finch West and York Gate Blvd. that remained undeveloped after the Yorkgate Mall was built. Councillor Peter Li Preti was on board and asked an architect to provide the community with a preliminary drawing of what the campus could look like on that site. Community residents were excited about this possibility, with the land being close to Westview Centennial Secondary School and across from the Humber River Regional Hospital.

Councillor Anthony Perruzza, who was the York West MPP, at the time was working on this as the Parliamentary Assistant to the Minister of Colleges and Universities in the NDP government. Perruzza, who was elected by Jane-Finch residents, explained the process the NDP government went through.

> Pat O'Neill [former councillor then Perruzza's assistant] had been chatting me up about a possible college consolidation in our area. Seneca College was looking for a new home and a place where they could consolidate their educational opportunities. They had a bunch of small campuses throughout the Greater Toronto Area, and I remember having a conversation with the president of Seneca at the time, I think a fellow named [Stephen] Quinlan, and they were committed to doing something like that.

Pat and I went to a breakfast meeting with Minister Richard Allen, and basically asked him for the start-up money to conduct a study to consolidate that campus. He gave us the money and we hired a fellow at the time, Peter Cannif, a principal at Seneca College's, King Campus. He went out and consulted the community and people vocalized that they wanted the new campus to be located on the site directly across from the Yorkgate Mall, on the last vacant parcel of land. Staff looked at the three or four other site options that were in the final report.[342]

Cannif looked at a potential partnership with York University. Initially, York was not receptive to the idea of a college being located on their university campus at Keele Street and Steeles Avenue West. Cannif determined that York was the best location and after some meetings, York concluded that it would be beneficial.

At York, there was an opportunity to be able to open a new campus site and instead of having to pay for the land, convert those moneys to York in-kind. York ended up getting a new science building instead of government funding for that land. There was a win-win associated with that; York would have a Seneca campus next door to their institution, plus an additional building of their own for the value of the land.[343]

While Perruzza wanted to support the community's recommendation, Cannif determined that if they did not go with this plan, there would be no college. Perruzza continued, saying, "That project took up a considerable amount of my time as an MPP because I had to push it along. Our team prepared the final report and we had to find $100 million to make it happen, which was a tough one."[344]

Finding the hundred million dollars for a Seneca campus at York University came as a result of the Toronto Argonauts winning the Grey Cup that year. Perruzza explained:

---

342 Anthony Perruzza interview (Toronto: York Woods Library, Black Creek Living History Project, April 2019).
343 Perruzza interview.
344 Perruzza interview.

When the Argonauts won the Grey Cup and some young people ran up and down Yonge Street, there ended up being a bit of a riot. Bob Rae appointed Stephen Lewis to look at that situation and the overall state of our youth. Lewis penned a letter to Premier Bob Rae, we used to call it the 'Dear Bob' letter, and it said that we needed more educational opportunities for youth, and that's something that Bob needed to look at. As soon as I read that letter, I immediately took the letter and rushed the Seneca Study Report over to Bob's office and said, "Have I got an educational opportunity for you."

A few short months later, the minister, premier, and everyone else involved were up at York making the official announcement to consolidate a Seneca College campus at York University. [345]

This did not happen without a fight from the community that wanted Seneca to build a full-sized campus on the Yorkgate lands. While Cannif's consultations were happening, the community asked for a meeting with the minister of education, Dave Cooke, to put their case to him. A community forum was held with over eighty community people at the Glen Gardens Housing Co-op, with Councillor Perruzza and MPP Cooke participating. By the end of the meeting, people left discouraged, feeling like a decision had already been made, but not in their favour.

Councillors Li Preti and Augimeri did a telephone campaign with a request to meet with Premier Bob Rae, but it was Minister Dave Cooke who met with the contingent of ten on April 11, 1994. Cooke explained that the ministry was moving toward a new system in post-secondary education, where colleges and universities would share services and staff. The community expressed that this could also happen at a Yorkgate campus, but it was not to be. The announcement to locate the campus at York was made on April 12, 1994. [346]

When others in the community learned of this decision, there was anger and there was grief—another loss for the Jane-Finch area. York University was still seen as not being part of the community, rather on the outskirts

345 Perruzza interview.
346 Dan Hoddinott, "GONE!" (*Norwester*, April 1994).

of the community, with conservation land and the Black Creek in between. "The government has not shown respect for our visions and our dreams," was Ruth Morris' reaction. NDP supporter and Metro Councillor Maria Augimeri said she felt the government lost, "…a big chance to better our community. Basically, I was very disappointed."[347]

After conversations with several people, it was agreed that the community needed to say goodbye to this splendid idea. A group of residents and workers decided to say the goodbye to the architectural renderings for the proposed Seneca campus on the York Gate lands. Bob McElhinny, a local activist and United Church minister, volunteered to facilitate the "funeral" ceremony with the community and to grace us with some words in recognition of this loss. Of course, the residents were wise enough to invite the media to join the event on what turned out to be a bright and sunny day. A contingent of workers and residents solemnly gathered at the corner of York Gate Boulevard and Finch Avenue, and with shovels in hand, they dug a hole for the drawings of the vision that the community wanted. After the hole was filled, the media interviewed several residents, took pictures, and the next day there were articles in both the local paper and the *Toronto Star* newspaper.

Some community members, along with Perruzza, believe that this action led to Seneca College establishing a small satellite campus in the Yorkgate Mall. While the community did not win this battle, they succeeded in securing a small satellite college in the centre of the community as a compensation for not developing a significant campus there. For residents who wanted upgrading courses, and even some main courses, the new satellite facility in the mall provided easy access within the community.

Government cuts

Community development was important to the Jane/Finch Centre, so they hired Farid Partovi Chaharlangi as a community development worker in 1995. Chaharlangi came from Iran as a political refugee. He initially spent time getting to know the community by visiting different neighbourhoods

---

347   Dan Hoddinott, "GONE!"

and talking to residents in those neighbourhoods. His manner was quiet and reflective, but his passion for social justice was unwaveringly clear.

> I did a lot of door-to-door outreach. I could say that I went door-to-door in all the buildings in the community, including public housing buildings and private buildings. I'm talking about thousands and thousands of people in buildings at the time I started doing my work in the community. That helped a lot in terms of getting to know different areas of the community and also talking to people with one-on-one information sessions and things like that.[348]

He also spent time getting to know the organizations in the community, went to meetings to learn about what they were doing, and visited existing programs. Soon after, he organized public education workshops and did leadership development training.

The year 1996 saw the Metro Days of Action take place, the year after Chaharlangi was hired. Michael Harris had been elected premier of Ontario in 1995 and he proceeded to make drastic cuts to government programs and funding that affected low-income communities.

In October of 1996, Chaharlangi helped to organize a local protest made up of residents, clergy, high school teachers, social workers, and unionists. In a small way, they showed the power of people, when the protesters joined hands and formed a human chain, first across Finch Avenue, then Jane Street, where traffic was halted for five minutes until the police arrived. It was a short and peaceful civil disobedience demonstration, where people ate breakfast, sang songs, and formed a human chain that blocked traffic in all directions. Hundreds of protest actions took place around the city and the province.

There were two other protests in the community happening at the same time. One was at York University, where students were upset about cutbacks in education, and further west, the TTC bus garages on Arrow Road were blockaded by union pickets from the Canadian Auto Workers and the Steelworkers. The unions were concerned about cuts to worker's compensation benefits and changes in the provincial health and safety standards. While

---

348 Farid Partovi Chaharlangi interview (Toronto: York Woods Library, Black Creek Living History Project, May 2018).

the other two actions continued, those from the Jane-Finch intersection joined a larger rally at the Mel Lastman Square along with some 5,000 gathered there to protest the new Conservative policies.[349]

Errol Young, a tireless resident-activist and a photographer for the community, was a North York school board trustee for fifteen years who quit when Harris became the premier.

> I quit the board because of Mike Harris. I knew that he was going to slowly starve schools with firing staff, lowering building standards, and making schools more dangerous and less effective. In 1997, Mike Harris took all funding powers away from the board. When I was a trustee, I was a fully elected official. What that means is that you have the ability to tax and spend. Right now, trustees have no ability to tax, just spend. The budget is set by a formula set by the Province. So, if they spend too much money on something, they have to give it up somewhere else, and while you always have to do that in a budget, they have a smaller and smaller budget per student every year.[350]

Members of the Jane-Finch community did not just protest in Jane-Finch and downtown Toronto—they also marched in Ottawa against federal government policies. The World March of Women was organized in Ottawa on October 12, 2000, where women from across Canada gathered on Parliament Hill to protest women's poverty, violence against women, and government cutbacks to programs like childcare and benefits for older women. The contingent from Jane-Finch was about one hundred strong, with almost half of them being seniors from 35 Shoreham Drive, a Toronto Housing seniors residence.

One woman, with the aid of a walker, was asked if she preferred to remain on the bus. Her reply was, "This is what I came here for. I'll manage." And manage she did, with thousands of women and men from across the country. The group travelled by buses paid for by the Steelworkers Union and

---

349 Steve Pitt, "Action Stalls Traffic at Jane-Finch" (*Norwester*, November 2, 1996).
350 Errol Young interview (Toronto: York Woods Library, Black Creek Living History Project, October 2019).

organized by the Jane/Finch Centre. They left the community at 6:30 a.m. and returned weary, but stronger later that evening.[351]

❧

Chaharlangi had vivid memories of his experiences during the Harris era. People were living below the poverty line through government programs, such as Ontario Works [welfare] and the Ontario Disability program; and the provincial government set a very low minimum wage for those who were working. Chaharlangi stated that there were only one to three per cent increases that added up to only a few dollars a month, but after 2000, the cost of living in Toronto had significantly increased. The cost of housing had gone up and the cost of healthy food increased as well.

> I started at the height of the Mike Harris government, when there were lots of attacks on poor and working people, racialized people, people on social assistance, and disability benefits. Rent control was abolished around the same time. We witnessed that lots of people were being evicted; people were cut from social assistance. I had to do community development, but I ended up doing a lot of one-to-one support for the community residents, as well. It was really overwhelming—very limited resources. And, at the same time, we kept talking about the fact that we needed to address these issues on the broader systemic level, because our capacity to provide one-on-one support was very limited and the issues were overwhelming. So we needed to push for systemic changes.

> Our community development approach was, while we were working with community residents from where they were at in terms of their knowledge base and their real conditions at the time, we support them and work with them on those issues. But also at the same time, we push for more community cohesion, for social justice work, anti-poverty work, and also supporting grassroots organizing—particularly resident-led grassroots organizing. So, we wanted to make

---

351 Sharmila Shewprasad, "Jane-Finch Women March" (Jane Finch Caring Community, November -December 2000).

sure that a lot of the work that we do with the number of community groups, resident activists would emerge as leading figures and spokespersons for the community, as opposed to only from the Jane/Finch Centre. So, the approach was very much around collaboration and being a resource for the community, but also pushing for a social justice agenda as well.

There were changes, obviously, at the provincial level in terms of the aggressive neo-liberal austerity agenda that we saw in the Mike Harris era. It softened a little bit after the Liberals got elected, but they continued in a different sense. For instance, by the time the Liberals came to power under the McGuinty government, people on social assistance were already fifty per cent behind on the poverty line."[352]

A lot of work was also done to support people on the Ontario Disability Support Program to get access to funds through the special diet benefit. Chaharlangi and others worked with local organizations and city-wide organizations, such as the Ontario Coalition Against Poverty, until such time that the provincial government changed the program, making it difficult for those on Ontario Disability to access the special diet funds.

Helen Kennedy, a community resident and labour activist for many years, became the chairperson of the North York Fights Back, an umbrella association that was leading the fight in North York against government cutbacks to public education, healthcare and social services.

The full impact of provincial downloading, education cuts and hospital closings has not really hit us yet. When they do, North York taxpayers need to be reminded that they have a right to public education, health care and social services. To fight the cuts, we're going to go back and start knocking on doors again. We're going to win this battle door by door and person by person.[353]

---

352   Chaharlangi interview.
353   Ruth Morris (Your Community Newsletter, February 1998).

North York Fights Back also participated in a major demonstration that was held on Friday, October 25, 1996, and many Jane-Finch residents and workers participated in the march down Yonge Street to join a rally at the North York City Hall. This day of action was part of the Metro Days of Action and participants extensively distributed a flyer listing ten reasons why people should participate in the actions.

Under the Harris government, elected in 1995, the amalgamation of the cities in Metro Toronto was proposed. One of the most notable people to be won over by the persuasive Kennedy was Mel Lastman during the recent amalgamation debate. Ruth Morris writes,

> The mayor was completely against holding a referendum until a last-minute public meeting at North York City Hall. We made sure we had all our people out and completely filled the council chamber. When Mr. Lastman saw the support for a referendum, he completely reversed his opinion. The mayor's joining our side proved to me that community activism works. [354]

In 1998, amalgamation of the five cities and the regional government took place despite broad public opposition in all of them.

Impacts from the cuts

Former York West MPP Mario Sergio described the impact of the Harris years.

> The years with former Premier Mike Harris were frustrating. I was talking with Al Leach, Minister of Municipal Affairs. At the time we were dealing with the amalgamation of Metropolitan Toronto. The Harris Government was bent on shoving it down the throat of the Toronto City Council, against their will.

> I said, "Don't do it. But if you want to do it, give notice to the City of Toronto, where they have three or four years until the next election to decide how they want to see the City of Toronto amalgamated." "No," Al Leach replied. "We're going to do it now and the way we want to." I told him that he was really choking people and not giving

---

354   Ruth Morris (Your Community Newsletter, April 1998).

them a chance. "Well, that's what Mike Harris wants. It's got to be our way and done now, because if we leave it to the City of Toronto, they will never do it." I told him that it's wrong.

Leach said it was going to be revenue neutral. And I said, "Al, come on, you know better than that." It wasn't, we can see that now. I told him, "You are going to be practically undoing six or seven munici-palities, which are functioning very well. Metro was doing very well, so why do you want to push this on the people who don't want it." And, the people didn't want it. But the government went ahead with it.

Of course, I remember the first sitting of the legislative assembly, when Mike Harris announced the cancellation of every housing project, even the ones that already had approval and the funding, the mortgage and everything. I said, "How can you do that?" "We're doing it." And, they did it with one scoop, including 21.8% [cut to] social services. It was chaos—we were powerless. You have a majority government. You're very bullied and you can sympathize as much as you want with people, and you feel it's a crime. There is nothing you can do.[355]

Barry Rieder was someone with deep passion and a strong commitment to social justice. He described what he was hearing from residents about the Harris attacks.

The first thing that comes to mind when I think about the commu-nity impact was the Mike Harris government cutting the allowance that young moms were getting. I remember some of those young women coming down to my office and to a discussion group we had in the chapel, literally crying and saying things like, 'We now have to decide if it's fresh fruits and vegetables for our kids or shoes.' I had

---

355 Sergio interview.

never observed that kind of impact from a political and economic decision and I will never forget what that did.[356]

The impact of the cuts demoralized residents. Workers in the area focused on supporting residents one at a time to respond to the prevailing issues of poverty. They also decided that a forum was needed to exchange information and advocate for needed programs and services. Initially, the newly formed Network of Community-Based Organizations consisted of more executive directors and managers, but it grew to include some frontline workers who were prepared to do the work.

Caring Community Award

The Network took pride in submitting a proposal to the Ontario Trillium Foundation for the Caring Community Award in 1998. The Ontario Trillium Foundation invited communities across the province to submit a proposal identifying why their area should receive this award. The award was to go to an area with significant community achievements, especially in the face of limited resources and difficult circumstances. The Network's proposal highlighted accomplishments of community residents:

- The Firgrove neighbourhood increased voter turn-out in 1995 from five percent to fifty percent through the hard work of two residents, Patricia Rodriguez and Kathleen Blair

- Black Creek Anti-Drug Focus established the innovative Community Banking Project in Jane-Finch

- Residents at 15 Tobermory established welcome tables in the lobby of the building, run by volunteers, to discourage people from selling drugs in front of their building [at the front door]

356   Rieder interview.

- The Neighbour-to-Neighbour project brought diverse groups in the community together to talk about their experiences and challenges, and

- Residents established the Westview/Brookview Parents Council to keep children in school and to raise achievement levels.

The Jane-Finch community was chosen as the winner of the 1998 Caring Community Award out of dozens of submissions from across Ontario.

The Ontario Trillium Foundation summed it up well when it announced that the Jane-Finch community had won the award. "Perhaps one of the most significant accomplishments of this community is the tenacity of the residents to transcend adverse circumstances and to create a community that continues time and time again to inspire hope in its members."[357]

This award received positive media coverage and instilled a strong sense of pride in the community.

Marvyn Novick told us, "When the Caring Community Award was given to Jane-Finch in 1998, I thought that for the first time the real Jane-Finch was publicly recognized and that this was an important moment."[358] Pat Capponi, an author, and mental health and anti-poverty activist also chimed in. "Despite the concrete and the strip malls, Jane-Finch has community soul other neighbourhoods only dream of.[359]

The Jane-Finch community was the only community in the City of Toronto to receive the award. Councillor Augimeri sponsored a motion at City Council to honour this achievement by placing four large signs at each of the four corners of Jane Street and Finch Avenue to acknowledge and commemorate the award. Barry Rieder shared his memory of that award.

> One of the things we did was just kind of highlight some of the collective action that was happening in the community, and the piece that happened out of Firgrove was increasing the voter turn-out. What we had done with the tenant's association was that we did a knock and drop at every household in Firgrove and explained that

357 Ontario Trillium Foundation news release (1998).
358 Novick interview.
359 Pat Capponi, "Clean City, Beautiful City" (Toronto: *Now Magazine*, July 1999).

voting mattered. We said, "We don't care how you vote, but what's most important is to vote, because when politicians pay attention to the polls right after the election, they spend their time and their money in communities that vote." We were actually able to increase the voter turn-out in Firgrove from 5% to 50%. So, there was a ten-fold increase around that. It's the impact we make with individuals in the communities that continue to make impact in their other communities or the community as a whole.[360]

∾

Another significant effort undertaken by the Network of Community-Based Organizations was advocating with the Ministry of Health to keep funding for youth in the community. The Youth Clinical Services had been asked by the hospital to leave their space in the portables, located behind the York Finch Hospital. They left for a new location at Finch and Weston Road, close to Emery Secondary School, but people were concerned that with them leaving, so would the funding that was to service youth in the Jane-Finch community. It was anticipated that unless youth went to Emery, they would not access the Clinic.

With Youth Clinical Services leaving Jane-Finch, the Network invited the Ministry of Health to attend one of their meetings. Network members made it abundantly clear that Jane-Finch could not afford to lose any funding that supported youth in the community and that the community expected them to allocate those funds to a local and reputable youth-serving organization. The Ministry eventually put out a call for proposals, and people watched in anticipation. The Ministry approved funding for a joint initiative called Y-Connect that would be operated by the Griffin Centre and Across Boundaries, two youth-serving agencies located outside of the community. They secured space at San Romanoway, the high-rise development on the north-east corner of Jane Street and Finch Avenue to ensure accessibility for resident youth.

---

360   Rieder interview.

Eventually, the Network stopped functioning. As Rieder said, "What started to happen was instead of managers or executive directors being at the table, it was more workers. And while a workers' table is important, it has no power and it lost some of its momentum. Some other things ended up replacing that later on."[361]

Responding to youth issues in the 1990s

The 1990s brought continuing challenges to the City of North York, pushing them to adequately respond to youth issues in the community and to youth who were new to Canada. While newcomer youth were struggling with their own challenges, youth who had arrived earlier from the Caribbean or youth born in Canada of Caribbean parents, continued to face issues of racism and discrimination. Unlike European immigrants and their second-generation offspring, racialized youth, both foreign and Canadian-born, faced continual discrimination.

In July 1997, Mel Lastman, the mayor of North York, released over 23,000 square feet of space from a former metal stamping plant to provide skills training and mentoring for disadvantaged youth. The lease rate was a 'legendary' seven cents a year for the Marcus Garvey Centre for Leadership and Education, and the city spent $500,000 on structural repairs at 160 Rivalda Road. Marcus Garvey was a Jamaican political activist, publisher, journalist, and the leader of the Universal Negro Improvement Association in the 1920s and 1930s.

They opened their doors in 2002. The motto of the Marcus Garvey Centre, a quote from Marcus Garvey, states, "Education is the medium by which a people are prepared for the creation of their own particular civilization and the advancement and glory of their own family, community, and country."[362]

In 2006, the Marcus Garvey Centre held a fundraiser with prominent people attending: Dudley Laws, Charles Roach, Dr. Charmaine Marie, Brad Melnychuk, Ruel Grey, Sylvia Searles, and Dr. Emile McIntosh. Dr.

---

361 Rieder interview.
362 Kurt Huggins, "Marcus Garvey Centre looks forward to a new path" (*York West Advocate*, May 2009).

Sandra Romano-Anthony, [a former electoral candidate in Jane-Finch] gave the keynote address focusing on "Building the Economic Future of our Community." Greetings were given by John Tory, past leader of the provincial Progressive Conservative Party, Ward 7 Councillor Peter Li Preti on behalf of Mayor David Miller, and Jean Fray on behalf of the Marcus Garvey Centre.

The organization's goal was to provide supportive training programs for youth and the fundraiser was to facilitate the ongoing renovation process for their space. Their intent was to build a kitchen and cafeteria to provide meals for the area youth and seniors in the community.

According to the *York West Advocate*, [a new Jane-Finch newspaper] the Garvey Centre was unable to provide the skills training and other services it committed to doing, and as a result some board members resigned. The relationship between the City and the Marcus Garvey Centre came to an end in April 2009, but there continued to be a group of members who made a commitment to further the work. "This conflict with the city has served to galvanize the Marcus Garvey Centre, and members are talking about being organized and working together."[363]

This is an example of North York responding to youth during the Lastman period, but in fact, 160 Rivalda Road is in an industrial area where there was limited bus service at the time. Neither did the Marcus Garvey Centre receive the necessary financial support to help them establish the organization in a sustainable way.

~≥e

Youth continued to experience challenges. Sam Tecle, an inquisitive young man, experienced firsthand what it was like attending school in the community. Tecle comes from an Eritrean family [more in Chapter 10].

> I remember growing up on the second floor at 15 Tobermory—I think seeing a bunch of different people from different places that I learned, that's how I learned about multiculturism. That's how I learned about people from different communities coming together, playing outside together. So, those are some of my formative

---

363   Huggins, "Marcus Garvey Centre".

experiences. I remember, as well, that the building had a community program and I remember back then—the early, early '90s—talking about the community stigma and all that, even at that age, as a child. Basically, I was not even eight or nine years old, so those were really formative. I mean, in the '90s, growing up in Jane and Finch, especially at Tobermory, you come up against—really close—to see stuff like people participating in different kinds of economy. You saw drugs, you saw people playing together, you saw that kind of, I guess, poverty or that side of it. All of that stuff was there, but then also a deep, deep sense of connectedness in community.[364]

Sam Tecle's experience was different because his father was a teacher and homeschooled him.

"It was weird, because, I think for me, going to school I was a quite ahead of the [other] students and ahead of the grade, as my Dad had homeschooled me. When I went to school here, I was quite ahead. I remember they put me in gifted stuff—I had to go to school on Saturdays, and I didn't understand that. I asked the teacher, "Well, if I'm already ahead of everybody, why do I have to come to school for an extra day?" But I also remember that the teachers always told me that my behaviour was "rambunctious." I got suspended, moved around, and I went to a lot of different elementary schools. So, I went to Firgrove, Topcliff, Yorkwoods. I got kicked out of Yorkwoods and came back to Yorkwoods to graduate.

They always had this narrative—I remember teachers telling me and my parents—"Oh, he's quite bright, but he should get out of the community." They always thought that whatever was wrong with me or why I was exhibiting the behaviour that I was, would be rectified if I had gone to a school outside of the community. By Grade 6, my parents sent me to Willowdale, which is a very different school, but they had this gifted program. I was in extended French, so I was learning how to speak French. A lot of that was my behaviour, yes, but also because of the teachers always saying that this place was

364   Sam Tecle interview (Toronto: York Woods Library, Black Creek Living History Project, April 2019).

causing that behaviour or, "He's bright and can get out of this area." In connecting with a lot of people who did go to school in the community, they had a very different experience than mine. I'm sure this was in no small part connected to ending up doing a PhD, doing a double major, doing all these things academically.[365]

Community and education

Education and community issues were important to Almaz Reda. Originally from Eritrea in Africa, Reda grew up in Ethiopia and brought a lot of skills to the table after having completed her education at the University of Calgary. As a single parent living in Jane-Finch and in social housing, Reda was most concerned that her son not be "labelled" by her circumstances and that he succeed in school. However, she was confronted with stereotypes and attitudes of the teachers.

> I suffered a lot and had some negative experiences relating to school issues. One time, my son was very young, Grade 3, and he was laughing at the shoes of another student. The teacher told me that he was disrupting the class, "He laughs all the time." I told her that he likes laughing, I sometimes got upset about it, and I apologized for that.
>
> She continued and said, "He even laughed when there was a kid, a child who had on old shoes and he looked at them and he laughed. This kid is very bad," the teacher told me.
>
> I said, "Okay." I have to respect the teacher, and I didn't want to argue—I didn't say anything.
>
> "Are you a single mom?" the teacher asked me. I told her, "Yes." "Oh, that explains how your son is behaving." I will never forget what she said. At that time, I was kind of new to Toronto and I kept quiet. I didn't know what to say. I actually didn't know what she meant by that because I was new to the community. So, when she says, 'single mom', I was married and divorced, so yes, I was a single

---

365   Tecle interview.

mom. I didn't relate to what a single mom means in this Jane-Finch community. I also didn't think a professional teacher would say that to insult a parent.

I was confused, and later on I was upset when I realized what she meant by that. I was very upset, and that was very wrong. You don't have to be a single mom to have your child misbehave. A child can misbehave for whatever reason—he can be silly, but it has no relationship to my being a single mom.[366]

Reda got involved in the community by doing volunteer work with the FOCUS program led by Ruth Morris. Through her work, she met people from the various organizations in Jane-Finch and ultimately became the volunteer coordinator for the Yorkgate Alliance, whose purpose was to coordinate community services and eliminate service duplication.

One issue discussed at the Alliance table was education. Reda shared how kids were being suspended, school was not supportive of parents, and there was a lot of domestic violence. She felt that if you challenged the school, you would not get anywhere, but would be labelled a troublemaker. "There were many parents that were banned and not allowed to come to the school, because they had an argument with the school. This was around 1993–94, where we had a lot of school issues and police issues with young people. Parents were in trouble, frustrated, and didn't know what to do."[367]

≈

It was then that the concept of the "Caring Village" emerged in Jane-Finch, around 1993.

It was a unique initiative embedded in the concept of community collaboration. It brought together community residents working alongside professionals who donated their time, in other words, volunteers who lived or worked in the local community and who brought to the table a broad cross-section of skills and competencies

---

366   Almaz Reda interview (Toronto: York Woods Library, Black Creek Living History Project, September 2019).
367   Reda interview.

reflecting a range of backgrounds and experiences. Fran Chaplin was the guidance head in the North York Board of Education, and she was very supportive. As a result, the local schools participated fully in all activities.[368]

Reda's lived experience encouraged her to advocate for systemic changes in education. She saw the Caring Village as a venue to "constructively advocate and challenge the system." It was agreed that the Caring Village would not be a program, but rather a "forum to do and promote advocacy for systemic change. Lasting change can only happen when you organize and inspire people to imagine a positive change that we all want and deserve."[369]

Reda became the coordinator of the Caring Village which had an initial focus on the areas of Shoreham Drive and Driftwood Avenue. She managed to bring partners around the table to ensure both children and parents were benefiting from community resources. For example, the public health nurses were providing workshops for parents. The police were providing information sessions, conflict mediation for families, and playing basketball with the children.

Besides managing the work of organizational partners, Reda felt that parent involvement in the children's schooling was very important to their success.

> During the years, we always promoted parental involvement in the schooling of their children and engaged residents in all aspects of our community activities. The Caring Village believes that it takes a village to raise a child, and parents are the first teachers and nurturers of their children. No one can help my child in my absence. Parents have to be part of the solution in helping their own children.[370]

Reda took pride in sharing that the exceptional transition program, Advanced Credit Experience (ACE), had its origins in the Caring Village starting in 2004.

> ACE is a collaborative community initiative built on the foundation of strong relationships between community, school and post

---

368   Reda interview.
369   Reda interview.
370   Reda interview.

secondary institutions. ACE seeks to address one key issue of interest to community residents—their children's educational success. It was rooted in an understanding that one's success in post secondary studies had a direct relationship between strong foundational skills and the ability to manage and balance the academic expectations of the post secondary educational environment.[371]

The ACE program's intent was to expose students to a college and university experience and show them that attending post-secondary education was an option they could consider. As part of their Grade 12 experience, they could take a course at York University. Reda reflects on this work.

> Fifteen years after its inception, The ACE program is run by York University and now involves schools from the Toronto District School Board and the Toronto Catholic School Board. It offers university entrance bursaries from $1,000–$5,000 for students who successfully completed the credit course. I am happy the program is doing well, and it is where it is supposed to be—at a university—as that is the mandate and purpose of universities. However, I feel it is important to give credit and acknowledgement to community members in Jane-Finch for their contribution to programs and initiatives like ACE.[372]

In 2006, the Caring Village was incorporated as a non-profit organization and received charitable status. It continues to promote non-violence through education and meaningful community engagement.

Talisha Ramsaroop, staff at the local York University–TD [Toronto Dominion] Community Engagement Centre, attended the ACE program after it transitioned to York University.

> The ACE program, called the Advanced Credit Experience, was a program that was offered in a few of the high schools—Emery, Westview, Jeffery's and McGuigan—and it was where, while you

---

371   Reda interview.
372   Reda interview.

were in Grade 11, they took you out of high school for a full semester and you were at York University. You were taking a single course at York University, a three-credit course, doing a co-op at York, and then having a sociology class that I was taking on campus. So, I took part in that program, and I had no idea that York University was so close to us. I didn't ever step foot on the campus prior to that.

When I learned about the university, we were always on campus. We spent every minute on campus just because of how much nicer it was than our high school. We did everything there. We weren't at the high school for the whole semester. That was a real eye opener experience and a really cool experience. I don't think I was on path—for sure I was not on path to going to university—because I was taking all applied classes prior to that. My average was around C prior to the ACE program, so that kind of changed things a lot for me because, I mean, in my mind, I really enjoyed the ACE program, and I had a really great time. I liked the class that I was taking and, in my mind—like, I got a C in the ACE program—but I was like, I was sixteen and if I can get a C, and when I'm eighteen, two years from now and actually in a university, I'll be able to do this no problem. It really helped to boost my morale, but then putting me in that environment made a really big change for me.[373]

Media

The community had expressed outrage about the video *Home Feelings*, produced in the 1980s. Another film came out in 1997 called *Jane Finch Again*. The filmmaker, Roger MacTair, returned to discover if Jane-Finch had changed or not changed, by talking to residents, former residents, police, and people who had appeared in the original film.

Jane Finch Again uncovered that many residents who had been interviewed for the first film were working and were doing well. One resident said, "Why do I need to move? I like it here." Several Toronto Housing neighbourhoods

---

373   Talisha Ramsaroop interview (Toronto: York Woods Library, Black Creek Living History Project, December 2019.

formed tenants' associations to improve safety and improve relationships with the police. The film was inspired by Greg Bobb, a resident of the area, whose "Unity Force" youth group educated and empowered a generation of youth to stand up for their rights and to make a life for themselves.[374]

Jasmine Ali watched both films as part of her research into the Jane-Finch community and explained her view from her lived experience.

> My lived experience and education influence how I interpreted these films. I am a Black woman who grew up in a similar neighbourhood, having seen my neighbourhood being terrorized by the police and having interactions of my own. I am highly sensitive to how Black communities are constantly under attack—it feels like from all sides at some points.
>
> People generally believe what they're told, especially if the information is coming from someone who has positioned themselves as the expert of the subject. When examining marginalized communities, a common trend that I have noticed is that "outsiders" seem to believe they have the best explanations and solutions to the issues facing such communities, so using their power, money and access to resources, the outsiders can convince others of that.
>
> When watching these documentaries, I was looking to answer a few questions. Who was presented as the expert? Who held the knowledge and was considered valuable or important enough to distill this information to the rest of us—those consuming this media?
>
> Overall, my reflections are that both videos help to tell a more complete story of Jane-Finch. There is no monolithic experience of Jane Finch. The first video highlights the issues of police brutality, which the second video does not. The first video has community members speaking candidly about their interactions with the police, both individually and as a group. The second video speaks to grassroots leadership creating solutions to their challenges. It looks at the investment being made in children who would hopefully have

---

374   Suzanne F. Jackson, "Yorkwoods-Grandravine neighbourhood in the broader Jane Finch community," Toronto: no date).

different experiences than the adults living in the community. It was multi-racial. There were success stories of all kinds—of those who "made it out" and those who chose to stay. It was shown as a neighbourhood that did not need to be escaped—you could live a happy, healthy and safe life living there.[375]

Policing Jane-Finch

Tensions continued between the community members and the police. In 1996, the local *Norwester* newspaper printed an article called, "Activist Deplores Police Shooting," about the police shooting a Black youth. A hastily called meeting was held one day after Andrew Bramwell, 23, of Kingston, Jamaica, was fatally shot by a 31 Division police officer across from the Jane Finch Mall. Linda Morowei was joined on the speakers' platform at a meeting called by Dudley Laws and Nzinga Walker, both of the Black Action Defence Committee, in response to the killing. Morowei's brother, twenty-three-year-old Tommy Barnett, had been fatally shot by police in January.

Laws described the killing of Bramwell as, "a continuation of killings of Black youths and men over the past several years." The police were not invited to this meeting. At the meeting, Morowei said, "I've been working in this community for 17 years trying to foster better relations with the police and it has been really frustrating. Our people are still being killed and something has to change before our young males become an endangered species."[376]

The usual government reaction was to give the police more money and manpower to patrol the neighbourhood, whether residents wanted that or not.

❧

On April 28, 1999, the Safer City Task Force (SCTF) was established by Toronto City Council to ensure safety for all residents and visitors. It was thought that some people did not see enough police officers in their

---

375 Jasmine Ali, research report.
376 Elizabeth Duncan, "Activist deplores police shooting" (North York: *Norwester*, March 1996).

community and that they were unable to enjoy public spaces in certain areas because of criminal activities. The task force concluded that there was an urgent need to supplement the City's existing safety initiatives that summer and recommended that the City support a Community Action Policing (CAP) project, a project that was built on previous consultations and recommendations made in the *Toronto. My City. A Safe City* report that was released in February 1999. This project would set up special police units in nineteen areas of the city, one of which was Jane-Finch.

On July 6, 1999, the Policy and Finance Committee at the City of Toronto submitted a report recommending CAP for all wards across the city from Toronto Mayor Lastman, who was chair of the SCTF. Two million dollars would be spent on CAP from the $3,500,000 new special reserve fund "Safer City Initiatives."[377]

Shooting of Brianna Davy

This infusion of funds across the city did little to minimize the impact of the murder of three-year-old Brianna Davy in the Yorkwoods Toronto Community Housing Corporation (TCHC) neighbourhood, nestled south of Finch Avenue and on the east side of Jane Street. It was a neighbourhood identified as one without adequate resources. Brianna Davy was killed on June 13, 1999, when she was hit in the head by one of four bullets fired at her father in the parking lot of this housing complex. Her father was shot in the back, chest, and shoulder and was left paralyzed from the waist down.

Yorkwoods TCHC neighbourhood has no internal roads but has narrow concrete pedestrian pathways winding throughout the development. The townhouses were aging, with tiny yards and no basements. The units themselves offered inadequate living space for large families to reside. Within the development, there was a recreation room that remained unused for many years.

Prior to the shooting, a steering committee of service providers had been meeting for the purpose of developing programs and services for that area. A

---

377   Policy and Finance Committee, "Community Action Policing (CAP)—All Wards" (Toronto: July 6, 1999).

needs assessment was initiated, but halted after forty surveys were completed, due to the murder. Safety, drug trafficking, alcohol, and the high number of youths hanging around with nothing to do, were of most concern to residents according to the surveys.[378]

This murder had an enormous impact on the community—emphasizing the community's concerns about crime and safety—and on the City of Toronto itself. Barry Rieder recalls that time.

> Downsview Ministerial supported the community when there were tragedies in the community. What had happened was that somebody had a beef with her dad and decided to take revenge and knew he was visiting his mother, Brianna's grandmother.[379]

> While he was putting her into the backseat of the car, he got shot and one bullet grazed the car, ricocheted, and hit Brianna. It was a real tragedy for the community."

Rieder was asked to attend a vigil for Brianna and brought along a church manual just in case it would be needed.

> So, I arrive and there is about two hundred people there on the street, laying teddy bears and putting flowers down. I'm looking around and there's no other clergy and Fred [known for organizing vigils] sees me, and he comes running up to me and I asked him, 'Did you ask anyone to officiate this?' He said, 'No, but would you?' So, I said, 'Let's go meet the family.'[380]

When the news of Mayor Lastman's plan to significantly increase policing in the neighbourhood where three-year old Brianna Davy was shot, the community's response was strong. A group of community leaders met and sent a message back to the mayor and the police saying, "Mayor Lastman, we really appreciate your concern about community safety, but please don't send in the troops until you've talked with us first."[381]

---

378   Wanda MacNevin, "Yorkwoods Safe Neighbourhood Project" (North York: Final Report, January 16, 2001).
379   Rieder interview.
380   Rieder interview.
381   "Residents nix police plan", (Jane-Finch Caring Community, August-September 1999).

Paulette Brown, a Presbyterian minister, reinforced that by saying, "I speak as a woman who has seen the pain in her own community, seen the sense of helplessness and struggles of our community, has tried to deal with the challenges before them." She went on to reiterate that the community did not need more basketball programs, nor did it need 'a top down' imposition of more police officers—but rather its members needed to become involved in its rehabilitation.[382]

A call to action

Dr. Ruth Morris urged that in memory of Brianna, the government must, "Prioritize education over corporate welfare; prioritize adequate income support for all in need over the tax breaks for the wealthy; prioritize health care over more perks for the well-off; prioritize housing supports and rent controls over the profits of land speculators and absentee landlords."[383]

Twenty years later, education, health care, and housing continue to be prominent unresolved issues in Jane-Finch, and across Toronto.

A call to action was initiated by Maria Augimeri, the City Councillor for this neighbourhood, by hosting a "think tank" meeting in July, shortly after Brianna Davy was killed. The meeting included the Toronto Police Services, local social service groups, church leaders, the commissioner of Community & Neighbourhood Services, Toronto Community Housing Corporation representatives, Parks and Recreation staff, school board officials, and a representative from the mayor's office. After much discussion, they agreed to work on three initiatives: a feasibility analysis to improve the physical infrastructure on City and TCHC lands through a pilot capital project, an assessment of community needs, and a community-based art project.

The community-based public art project received $150,000 in funding. The art project established a committee to find space and a design that would honour the death of Brianna. It had to offer a safe space for residents to come together to mourn in times of sadness and to celebrate in times of joy.

---

382   "Residents nix police plan" (Jane Finch Caring Community, August-September 1999).
383   Ruth Morris, "If Breanna had lived" (Jane Finch Caring Community, July–August 1999).

An artist from Montreal won the competition with her proposal, Circle of Words—Garden of Thought. She worked with residents to find the space and to design and create the art installation. While the community wanted the art within Yorkwoods, it was determined that the space needed could not be found there, so the art installation ended up on the north side of the Driftwood Community Centre. They made a Garden of Thought, comprising boulders with inscriptions of one or several words. The circular bench, made from Indiana limestone, "traces a 60-foot section of the circumference of a 25-foot diameter circle."[384] It was hoped that people from all over Jane-Finch would have a space to sit and reflect.

Garden of Thought

Robert Glover, the director of Urban Design for the City of Toronto at the time, said, "Creating this new landmark through public art reflects our desire to strengthen the Jane-Finch area, both as a social community and as a physical place in the city.[385] The peace memorial was to honour victims like Brianna and celebrate the champions of this multicultural community.

---

384 "Monument erected in Jane Finch" (North York: *Downsview Post*, June 2002).
385 "Jane-Finch launches a new landmark" (Jane Finch Caring Community, November–December 2000).

A pilot capital project proposed building new internal streets in Yorkwoods neighbourhood with additional lighting, sidewalks and trees, giving homes clear municipal addresses, reducing hiding spaces, redesigning unsafe breezeways, and reorienting some of the units. The internal streets did not get built as residents o verwhelmingly rejected that idea. While the planners and police argued that it would improve safety and access, residents were concerned about losing space and traffic safety for their children. The adjacent school was not in favour of the roads either, citing loss of park space where children play.

All three of the deliverables aimed to improve safety in the Yorkwoods area. Not only did the City attempt to revitalize the area, but others also got involved. The Toronto Raptors Foundation, along with Scotiabank Raptors TeamUp and Nike P.L.A.Y. Canada Program wanted to ensure a safe play space for this community, so they refurbished two playgrounds and resurfaced the basketball court. Plans were made for more than 250 students from five area schools to volunteer their time to team up, clean up, safeguard the area, plant some shrubs and bulbs, and "get their backs into some yard work for fellow neighbours as part of the Scotiabank-Raptors TeamUp launch." Several Toronto Raptors players and representatives from the bank unveiled the playgrounds and participated with children and youth on both the basketball court and the playground.[386]

While the City was involved in the above initiatives, the committee was approached by the federal National Crime Prevention Centre who expressed interest in supporting efforts in Yorkwoods. As a result, Black Creek Community Health Centre submitted a proposal in 2000 for a three-year Yorkwoods Safe Neighbourhood Project (YSNP) with the purpose of enhancing the quality of life for residents in the Yorkwoods neighbourhood utilizing a community development approach. The project was to increase the capacity of the Yorkwoods neighbourhood to develop a safe and healthy community by mobilizing its residents.

---

386 "Brianna Remembered with 'P.L.A.Y. Ground,' " (Toronto Raptors Basketball Club news release, Oct. 27, 1999). https://purpose.nike.com/play

With a federal grant of $49,950, staff were hired, and partner organizations stepped up to support this initiative. Doorsteps Neighbourhood Services agreed to act as the trustee, Delta Family Resource Centre provided office space, and Black Creek CHC provided the supervision of the coordinator. A residents group was formed, a youth leadership development program was started, community clean-ups and barbecues were held, new programs were started, and relationships between residents, agencies, and the police were improving. A door-to-door survey was completed in 2002, and the survey suggested that residents' perception of safety had improved. Residents attributed their feelings of safety to the new security cameras and lighting, increased security and police patrols, more activities for youth, and greater community involvement.

While the perception of safety was improved, residents did not feel completely safe. The Yorkwoods Safe Neighbourhood Project was evaluated by Dr. Suzanne Jackson who indicated that although residents' perceptions of safety had improved, crime rates had not. In her evaluation, Jackson ominously foreshadowed a crisis in the residents group. "There has not been enough history to ensure the long-term stability for this fledgling residents' group and its ambitions to create a safe neighbourhood."[387] While the residents group continued after the grant was over, with support from Delta Family Resource Centre, over time it was difficult to support the initiative without sufficient funding. This was yet another example of good community work and action, but with insufficient and short-term funding. The YSNP eventually came to an end.

The shooting of Brianna Davy galvanized community organizations to come together to create a reference group to address some of the concerns within the community. Their focus was to build on the area's strengths by placing emphasis on building on assets and capacities, prevention, community involvement, diversity, and community well-being.

---

387 Suzanne F. Jackson, "Yorkwoods Safe Neighbourhood Project—Interim Evaluation Report," Toronto; December 5, 2000).

CHAPTER SEVEN

Another Decade of Political and Social Action

The reference group became the Black Creek Community Capacity Building Project (BCCCBP) in the early 2000s and a community needs assessment was carried out by the newly formed group. The assessment considered not only elements and aspects of socioeconomic "need" or vulnerability, but also the potential or capacity of the community to build on its advantages and strengths.

Several phases of community action were initiated in 2003, including a demographic study of the community. A series of consultations throughout the community involving twelve focus groups was conducted between May and September of 2004. The development of a community action plan was made in 2005 from the results of the community consultation, with five priority objectives for the project:

- Economic independence and stability
- Development of services
- Healthy, safe, and aesthetic space and facilities
- Enhancement of information and services
- Showcasing the "Black Creek" community

There was an attempt to move away from using the name "Jane-Finch," which had been stigmatized by the media. So, after much discussion it was agreed to use Black Creek, acknowledging the beautiful creek that ran through and connected many of the neighbourhoods. A coordinating committee and five working groups were set up to focus on the objectives and develop a plan of action.

We are a coalition of residents, groups, and organizations focused on improving the quality of life for residents living in the Black Creek community. We work on different projects and initiatives that promote the strengths of the community and help to develop residents' ability to plan and act on areas that are important to them. We value and celebrate the diversity of this neighbourhood and strive to improve its well-being. The project is managed by the Black Creek Coordinating Committee who are local residents, local community agencies and various other community partners and supporters.[388]

Funding was received from the City of Toronto's Social Development Investment Program to oversee a work plan that would develop the coordinating committee and advance some of the initiatives identified in the Community Action Plan. The money was held in trust by Delta Family Resource Centre. In 2008, a resident advisory committee was functioning as a sub-committee of the Coordinating Committee, providing input and recommendations. All the working groups, except for the Showcasing the Black Creek Community working group, were functioning with positive outcomes.

Barry Rieder played a leadership role in the development and support for the Black Creek Community Capacity Building Project. When Delta Family Resource Centre (trustees of the grant from the City) moved away from the Jane-Finch community the funds went with them, leaving the group without the needed resources. The group morphed into the Black Creek Community Collaborative, a network that continues to meet.

❧

Also in the early 2000s, Councillor Maria Augimeri responded to violence impacting members of the African-Canadian community by working with leaders in that community. One initiative was the Building Hope Coalition, where Grace-Edward Galabuzi was the chief convenor. Augimeri said, "In an effort to confront incidents of violence, the coalition availed

---

388 "Black Creek Community Capacity Building Project" (North York: *Yorkwest Advocate*, September. 2008).

itself of opportunities to hear from affected community residents in their own communities."[389]

Lennox Farrell—a teacher, avid community activist, and an articulate member of the Building Hope Coalition—wrote a memo to Councillor Augimeri under the heading of "Draft Terms of Reference for Strategic Planning Committee."

> It is clear to us, if not all Toronto, that the violence plaguing the urban communities here is chronic. Occasionally it flares into crisis. Events for the past two months, with the number of killings, most unsolved, speak to this deep malaise, hopelessness and death. Many individuals and institutions in what are referred to as the wider community are also concerned.
>
> Some like the Province and police see traditional responses as being in order. These, addition of more officers, powers, and the like, have neither reduced nor even stemmed the crimes. It is our responsibility to stem the violence, which, along with an attendant hopelessness, are the nursing mothers of crime. Other public representatives like the *Toronto Star* have been supportive in assisting both the general community and ours to re-focus attention on structural causes as against the melodramatic results. They have an interest, as a result of a meeting with their editorial board, in working on at least three parts of an initiative with us.
>
> The MP [Member of Parliament] for York West, Judy Sgro, is an elected official well known to people who live in this area. She has been steadfast, consistent and available. We have a promise to meet with her by the end of September. In meeting with her, we showed the ways in which to break these cycles of violence by breaking the cycles of poverty. The cornerstone area for this includes home ownership, more accessible small business and other forms of loans, employment, and access to more services for women, children and men.

---

389 Maria Augimeri interview (Toronto: York Woods Library, Black Creek Living History Project, June 2019.

The strategic plan on which we are now at work must address the following, and for their accompanying reasons: every sector, including public, private and community; emphasize the role to be played by the private sector, in conjunction with that to be played by the public. Among the community sectors which must be brought more into this process of Building Hope are the [Black] churches. Their absence here is not concomitant with the presence of our people in them, and representative of our contributions to their upkeep and growth.[390]

In a memorandum to the City of Toronto's Economic Development, Culture and Tourism Committee in September 2001, the Building Hope Coalition highlighted that they had travelled across the city to places such as Regent Park, Alexandra Park, Lawrence Heights and community centres in Etobicoke and Malvern.

One concerted voice was heard at all of our meetings—that Black youth needed to see more commitment from all levels of government and that issues of great concern to Black youth must be brought to the forefront of our collective agenda immediately if we are to begin to turn around the violent course running through the city. Their request for the federal government was for more opportunities for skills training and jobs for youth. They were also asking the City for an increase in youth-oriented programming in its Parks and Recreation Department. They boldly went on to request the Committee consider support for the 2001 Youth Program Expansion Proposal for the 2001 Action Plan Report city-wide. This amounted to $1,593,362. That may be a large amount of money, but it was insufficient to adequately respond to youth programming across the city.[391]

A presentation was made to the Economic Development and Parks Committee by Councillor Augimeri. The presentation noted the significant

390   Lennox Farrell, "Strategic Planning Meeting Update" (North York: email communication, August 28, 2001).
391   Maria Augimeri, Memo to Members of the Economic Development, Culture and Tourism Standing Committee, September 6, 2001.

costs for policing in the country and in Toronto: $7.7 billion was spent in Canada on policing, courts, and corrections. At that time, the City spent over five hundred million dollars directly on police services and fifteen million on security for public housing. She presented a recommendation from the Building Hope Coalition that all levels of government provide better access to jobs, not jails; adequate life-skills training; and that job training and counselling be made readily available. She stated that school boards must respond to the disturbing number of Black students dropping out of school. There also needed to be a significant increase in youth programming. She pointed out that what they were asking for was less than ten per cent of the increase that the police received during the recent budgeting process.

Augimeri ended her presentation with the following.

> When one looks, proportionally, at the amount of money that is being discussed, one marvels at the relatively inexpensive solutions to society's maladies. A healthy social infrastructure—one in which housing, childcare, nutrition and a wide range of services for youth, play prominent roles will inevitably lead to a healthier society and a more committed and socially-involved group of adult taxpayers.[392]

Farrell, along with other well-known Black activists and leaders, felt strongly that they needed to be strategic with plans to bring their issues to then Premier Mike Harris, to Metro Council, and to the media. They also planned a meeting with MP Judy Sgro and a community meeting where their message was clearly, "Build Hope, Not Prisons." Mothers of Murdered Black Youth (MOMBY) would be present with plans to record their thoughts in the same way the slave narratives were done, providing an authentic, anecdotal record of their lives. All meetings would be held at the Jamaican Canadian Association.

The fight continued for Augimeri alongside the Building Hope Coalition. At a City budget meeting, Augimeri reiterated that Black youth needed to

392 Maria Augimeri, "Presentation to Economic Development & Parks Committee" (Toronto: 2002).

see committed action on their needs to begin turning around the crisis of violence in Toronto. She explained some of the factors affecting the state of employment for Black and racialized Torontonians. Almost sixty per cent of Ghanaians were unemployed, as compared to less than ten per cent of people of European backgrounds. Median unemployment for African, and Black Torontonians generally, was well over thirty per cent. For Jamaican Torontonians, it was almost forty per cent. Nine out of 10 Ghanaians lived in dire poverty. Seventy per cent of Ethiopians, over sixty per cent of Somalis, and just under sixty per cent of Tamils lived in poverty.

Augimeri was requesting $600,000 for advocacy programs, youth leadership, skills development and youth support programs, equivalent to the cost of incarcerating forty people. She ended her remarks with, "Where do you choose to put taxpayers' money—into prevention or into jailing our youth?"[393]

On May 8, 2002, Mayor Lastman and Brad Duguid, chair of the Task Force on Community Safety, announced a $4.45 million strategy to promote a safer Toronto for youth. The elements of the strategy included youth empowerment through skills development, innovative recreation programs, community awareness and public education initiatives that promote youth safety. It also included effective policing approaches for prevention and enforcement that support the Toronto Police Service in targeting high-risk youth and repeat youth offenders. A holistic approach in leadership, in which the City works with other senior levels of government, community agencies, school boards, the Toronto Police Services, the TTC and other partners to develop and co-ordinate initiatives for a safer city was part of the strategy.[394]

Three projects received some of the above funding for youth at the Jane/Finch Centre in 2002. One was for the Jane-Finch Khmer-Cambodian Youth Drug Prevention Project. The intent was to hire and train two peer youth workers for one day a week for forty weeks to conduct extensive outreach to Cambodian youth, provide a weekly drop-in program, and provide group

---

393 Maria Augimeri, "Youth Violence and Parks and Recreation Programs" (Toronto: City Budget, March 7, 2001).

394 "Mayor Announces Strategy to Promote a Safer Toronto for Youth" (City of Toronto: media release, May 8, 2002).

presentations. The second one was for Project YOU (Youth of Unity) to do glue sniffing awareness by hiring a coordinator and ten peer youth workers and to provide eight skill-building sessions for the youth workers and seven community presentations.[395]

The third grant was called The Jane Finch Gang Prevention Project. The purpose was to develop a community-wide youth council for the Jane-Finch area, so that youth would have a voice and be engaged in identifying issues and developing responses. Activities included training, education, supportive counselling, personal development, outreach and youth-led organizing. This grant ended with a symposium to establish an ongoing youth council.[396]

The first two grants totalled $33,062, and the third was $20,000, and they were limited in hours and duration. Youth programs need to be ongoing and adequately funded to be effective. A Youth Council was formed and continued to run for many years through The Spot that had the funding to support the group. While the grants engaged youth and accomplished some good work, it was like putting bandages on the complicated issues of the time. There were clearly identified consequences for not providing adequate support to youth in communities across the city.

In January 2004, Chris Brillinger, the City's executive director of Social Development, Finance and Administration sent Augimeri a memo responding to the Building Hope Coalition recommendations. He presented a list of actions to be taken by the City through the Ontario Works Incentive Funds to include programs to: support youth seeking employment, life-skills training, outreach, youth gang interview and exit strategy, drug-prevention grants, Jane Finch Mall "Youth Cents," prevention training for community and staff, and youth lifeguards' clubs. Parks and Recreation was to receive a budget expansion in 2003 to enhance program delivery to identified communities and youth outreach workers and youth employment workers were to focus on engaging in supporting the needs of "at-risk youth" populations in various

---

395   Letters of Understanding, Community and Neighbourhood Services (City of Toronto, June 24, 2002).
396   Social Development & Administration Division (City of Toronto, December 10, 2002).

high needs communities. [397] While this was a move forward, it was known that the dollar amounts allocated to the programs were far from enough to meet the needs of Black and racialized youth across the city.

Amalgamation of hospitals

Under the provincial Progressive Conservative government, actions had taken place in the early 2000s that had a negative affect on people living in the Jane-Finch community. In May 2001, the Toronto District Health Council (TDHC) was asked by Tony Clement, the minister for health and long-term care, to consider the Humber River Regional Hospital's proposal to move to another location in Downsview from its site in Jane-Finch. The TDHC was to give the government an analysis of the potential impact on access to services, other providers, and existing referral patterns of such a move. [398]

This had been discussed earlier in 1995, when the TDHC was mandated by the Harris government to do a review on Toronto hospitals, called the Metro District Health Council Report on Hospital Restructuring. They wanted to develop a strategic approach to priorities, eliminate duplication within the system, redeploy resources to meet emerging needs, and ensure a more coordinated, patient-focused system. In other words, this would mean reduced hospital costs for the Province by reducing the workforce.

With respect to northwest and north Metro Toronto, the Council made two recommendations: merge Northwestern General Hospital with Humber Memorial Hospital and consolidate activity at the Humber Memorial Hospital site, and merge North York Branson Hospital with York-Finch General Hospital and consolidate inpatient activity at the York-Finch Hospital Site. These were not implemented.

The Health Services Restructuring Commission (HSRC) was established in 1997 as an independent body "to make decisions about hospital restructuring and to advise the minister of health on restructuring other aspects

---

397   Chris Brillinger, "Responses to the Building Hope Coalition Recommendations" (Toronto: January 14, 2004).
398   "TDHC Review of Humber River Regional Hospital's Redevelopment Proposal: Final Report" (Toronto District Health Council, July 2001).

of Ontario's health services system." The HSRC supported the voluntary amalgamation of Humber Memorial, Northwestern General, and York-Finch General Hospitals.[399] This merger happened on March 31, 1997, to form the Humber River Regional Hospital (HRRH).[400]

Dr. Reuben Devlin, a well-known Progressive Conservative party leader, become the HRRH's new president and chief executive officer in August 1999. One of his priorities was to lead HRRH through the planning and implementation of a "visionary" strategy for the future of the hospital.

In September of 1999, local papers reported on the first of many community meetings where Dr. Devlin laid out a vision for the hospital's future. Renovation was out of the question. They were determined to build a new hospital somewhere else in Downsview, and close two or more of the three existing facilities. One site for consideration was the Downsview lands at Keele Street and Sheppard Avenue West.

Humber River proposed a new facility at a new site for several reasons. These included out-of-date facilities at the Church and Finch sites, transportation problems, an inability to accommodate new beds, and limited room for future expansion. The hospital felt that having all HRRH hospital services in one place would provide better service for patients and physicians and make the best use of healthcare dollars. A new hospital would replace the hospital's Church Street and Finch Avenue buildings. This would mean no walkable or local hospital in the Jane-Finch community.

Concerns were expressed about the loss of two very busy emergency rooms from the system, with the corollary concern about the ability of one emergency room to cope with the volumes from the original three sites. Transportation to the hospital would entail difficulties as many area consumers did not have access to cars and relied on public transit or taxis. Others were currently able to walk to the hospital. Another concern could be a diminished range of service options, especially regarding mental health, addictions, and access to diagnostic testing.

---

399   "TDHC Review".
400   IC Savings Heritage Display, Humber River Hospital, November 1, 2017.

The District Health Council recognized that there were advantages to a replacement facility, as the existing spaces had inadequacies and new facilities would help the hospital's recruitment and retention efforts. But consideration of those issues was outside of the scope of Council review. As a result of the review, the TDHC found "no compelling argument for HRRH to deviate from the Health Services Restructuring Commission's directions regarding the location of its services. On the contrary, it appears that the proposed relocation would have a detrimental effect on access to health services by a vulnerable population, referrals from community physicians, and neighbouring hospitals that would have to accommodate caseload ceded from HRRH." [401] Their recommendation was to plan the redevelopment of the Church Street and Finch Avenue sites.

⁓

"Build it Here! Build it Now!" was chanted loudly by the over one hundred residents gathered in front of the Finch site hospital on a cold winter day in January 2002. The CEO, Dr. Devlin, rejected the Toronto District Health Council report. Another surprise announcement was made by the Ministry saying there would be another delay in updating the facilities. [402]

A group of concerned residents convened a meeting to establish the Coalition to Save Our Hospital. They organized a community town hall meeting with a panel consisting of York West MPP Mario Sergio, City Councillor Peter Li Preti, and lawyer-activist Roger Rowe. The minister of health was also invited but did not attend.

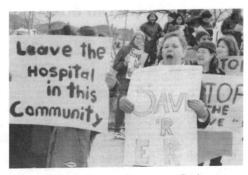

Hospital protest (Downsview Post)

Sergio said, "Don't do it! They say that they are listening to the people, but they do whatever they want." Councillor Li Preti expressed his concern that

---

401 "TDHC review".
402 "Save Our Hospital Protest" (*Downsview Post*, February 2002).

the hospital administration was letting the emergency room (ER) deteriorate based on his last experience there. Both felt that their advice was ignored by the administration. Rowe shared some statistics from the District Health Council's report that saw no merit in the plan. He pointed out that only five western Toronto ERs served the forty-two per cent of the population, while ten ERs served the fifty-eight per cent in the east. "This proposal will reduce the number of ERs to four. It is just not good planning." Someone from the audience voiced their concern with, "We want our money back!" The community had helped to raise twenty-five million dollars to build the expansion at the Finch site that the Hospital Restructuring Commission recommended four years earlier.[403]

While the coalition ended shortly after the TDHC recommendations, the community still did not trust that HRRH would honour the recommendations. The hospital board pursued their plans to amalgamate the three hospitals into one mega-hospital. The community organized a rally in front of the hospital, drawing media attention to this issue, and clearly demonstrating to "Save our Hospital." Residents were angry that the minister of health supported the move to amalgamate the three sites to build a "super" hospital. At that time, there were reports that they were looking to build the new hospital on the Ministry of Transportation site at Keele Street and Wilson Avenue.

On December 19, 2005, the hospital celebrated as Liberal leader Dalton McGuinty announced the approval of the hospital's redevelopment plans. Dr. Devlin was to come up with a "lean, green, digital building not just relevant on opening day, but also 25, 30 years from now." The government announced the commitment of greatly needed funding to improve health care in the northwest sector of the city. Community consultations were promised in that announcement.

"No such process has taken place. Yet we have been given every indication that decisions have been made behind closed doors without any opportunity for the voice of the community."[404]

---

403   "Community upset over hospital's plan to close Finch Ave. site" (*Downsview Post*, May 2002).
404   Humber River Health Coalition, "Advocating Transparency and Accountability in Healthcare" (North York: petition, April 25, 2007).

Li Preti, who attended the earlier protest, said that losing the hospital would be devastating for the community. Wilson Lee, a spokesman for Public Infrastructure Renewal Minister David Caplan, said that one of the three HRRH sites would likely close, but the Finch site could become an ambulatory care centre or outpatient clinic. He went on to say, "I realize that people develop a close relationship with their community hospital. Even if the hospital were to go on the Keele Street and Wilson Avenue site, and that decision hasn't been made, it doesn't mean the Finch site would be closed down."[405]

Rennie Terbogt, long-standing resident and community health professional who worked for the Humber River Footcare Clinic, had another idea. Terbogt knew that the hospital needed approximately forty-four acres, and he believed that acreage could be found on the still vacant Yorkgate lands. The proposed Keele and Wilson location had no doctor's offices, meaning more than one hundred doctors would have to spend over $50,000, each, to move. Terbogt spoke with Murphy Hull, owner of the land, at York Gate Boulevard and Finch Avenue, and he was interested in selling the Yorkgate land to the hospital. Hull originally donated the land for the existing York-Finch Hospital in the 1960s. Councillor Li Preti spoke in favour of the proposal. "I am convinced that this can happen. People said that the subway would never be extended and now it is planned. This makes a lot more sense than building one thousand housing units on the land. This site is probably the best for the hospital."[406]

The Humber River Health Coalition (HRHC) was formed in 2006 by another group of concerned residents and healthcare professionals, following the announcement by the Ontario government that a new Humber River Regional "mega hospital" would be built on a single site, and that one of the existing three hospitals would become an ambulatory care facility, which in the end did not happen. The HRHC was a non-partisan grassroots

405   Joe Friesen, "Residents Heartsick Over Fate of Hospital" (Toronto: *Globe and Mail*, June 7, 2006).
406   "A Better Plan to Keep Our Hospital at Jane and Finch—Revealed at Local Meeting" (*York West Advocate*, May 3, 2006).

organization that was advocating for a transparent consultation process between the Humber River hospital and the community that it served. Its concern was that there was a lack of transparency nor was there open public consultation by either the hospital, or the Ministry of Health and Long-Term Care, about which location or outcome would serve the community best.[407]

At the November 2006 HRHC meeting, a retired University of Toronto professor, John Balatinecz, discussed the importance of healthcare. From that discussion the members decided to organize a petition with support from the local churches, unions, residents, and community groups.[408]

Garry Green and Rosanna Vidale, long-standing community residents, stated in a petition that, "The HRRH Board and Administration are proposing significant changes to the health resources of our community without the consultation promised by the Government and the Board."[409]

In April 2007, the coalition presented a petition to the Ontario Legislature signed by 5,500 residents from the catchment area asking for a review and an open public discussion of the hospital board's decision to close and relocate its hospital services.

> There are other, more cost-efficient options that will better respond to health care than the directions that the HRRH Board seems intent on pushing through. The downsizing and possible closure of the Finch site will not improve health services for the catchment area, nor will it result in more efficient distribution and use of services. […] No opportunity has been given to present these options in open public discussion, and decisions are being made over the top of our community by individuals who in large part seem unconcerned by the local realities.
>
> The problem in large part stems from the governance structure instituted by the Ministry of Health. It is one shared by a number of communities across the province. After actions by the Health Services Restructuring commission in 1997, hospitals were directed

---

407 Humber River Health Coalition, "Advocating Transparency and Accountability in Healthcare" (North York: background to petition, April 25, 2007).
408 "Hospital Coalition to Broaden its Focus" (*York West Advocate*, November 2006).
409 Humber River Health Coalition, "Advocating Transparency."

to be self-governing. There were no checks and balances put in place to ensure that the community be represented or even involved in decision-making processes. The HRRH Board has become a closed, self-appointing body through its bylaws. Governance for a community should include responsibility to it.[410]

Letters were written to the board chair of HRRH; to the Minister of Health and Long-Term Care, George Smitherman; to the health critics of the Progressive Conservative and New Democratic parties of Ontario; as well as to local Liberal MPP, Mario Sergio. Sergio responded to a newspaper reporter. "These people [the coalition] are getting very political and it's got nothing to do with what's best for the community." [411] The coalition pointed out that their actions had everything to do with what's best for the community, as they lived in the community.

On August 31, 2007, the government announced that the site for the new hospital would be on the former property of the Ministry of Transportation at Keele Street and Wilson Avenue.

Push-pull between youth and police

Many actions happened simultaneously in the Jane-Finch community, often stressing community members beyond their capacity, given their own personal challenges. But, they persevered.

For example, when issues continued to be prominent between the police and youth, a Youth Forum was organized in April 2001 at the Jamaican Canadian Centre in hopes of improving communication between the police and the youth in the community. There were four breakout groups: the complaint process, youth violence, recruitment and affirmative action, and community policing. Youth talked about their negative experiences. "The police have a hostile, aggressive attitude towards youth, especially towards Black males."[412] They also expressed that there was no consistency within the

---

410   Humber River, "Advocating Transparency."
411   Humber River, "Advocating Transparency."
412   Perpetual Adom, "Narrowing the Gap Between Youth and Police" (Jane Finch Caring Community, June–August 2001).

community liaison officers, as they were constantly being transferred from one station to another. Relationships could not be built that way. One suggestion made was, "That policing be done according to the make-up of the community. For as long as the majority of police officers are white, Black males will always be subject to police discrimination and harassment."[413] Unfortunately, some Black police officers have proven to be as bad, or worse, due to the role and culture of policing in most countries, where their primary duty seems to be protecting the status quo.

There was a response from the police at this forum where the staff sergeant described community policing as, "Problem solving in partnership with the community."[414] They cited many examples of how the police participate in many programs, for example: in Rookie Ball, Rookie Puck, Rising Stars, Leaders in Partnership. The sergeant also explained they were trying to hire more visible minority officers stating that, in 2000, seventeen to twenty-two per cent of candidates were from visible minorities. Also, that officers were required to attend police college classes about crisis intervention and cultural sensitivity. And still Black and racialized people were shot in greater proportion by police.

Stacian Campbell, a young woman in the community who came from Jamaica in the early '90s and grew up in the community, wrote an article with the heading, "An interview with Stacian Campbell, a youth in our community."

> The treatment of Black and Hispanic people by the police is very unfair. They don't give them a chance to express themselves. They judge them solely on their appearance. For example, a Black youth is dressed in a certain way—then the police might think he's dealing drugs or maybe he's involved in other illegal activities.
>
> ...I don't think the foot patrol is a good idea because it intimidates the youth. They might not be doing anything illegal, just hanging out. Due to fear of the police, they might disperse as the police approach them. The police often interpret this in the wrong way,

---

413 Perpetual Adom, "Narrowing the Gap."

414 Perpetual Adom, "Response from 31 Division" (North York: Jane Finch Caring Community, June–August 2001), 4.

thinking that the youth are involved in illegal activities when in fact they are just hanging out.

I don't think the youth should change their appearance in order for the police to stop harassing them. This is what freedom of expression is all about. Everybody has the right to dress in the way they feel comfortable. It is their actions that should be considered, and not the way they are dressed or the way they carry themselves.

...There should be an equal amount of respect between the youth and the police. Only when this egalitarian relationship has been achieved can community policing in this neighbourhood work. Also, members of the community should know their rights. The police and the community members must understand that they are allies in the fight against crime. It should not be an 'us against them' thing. I hope that in the future, community members and the police will come together with one goal in mind: to reduce crimes.[415]

The relationship with the police could be called the good, the bad, and the ugly. Police youth programs are good, but when the police held a Town Hall in late 2002 and shut down a youth who was involved with the local Teen Violence Prevention Project who was asking a question, the community reacted. The Black Creek Community Health Centre and the Jane-Finch Street-Involved Youth Issues Coalition organized a community forum with five other organizations. The *Toronto Star* had published articles in the fall of 2002 about racial profiling and a reporter was at the town hall meeting. Community media were also represented there. The forum included a panel and a keynote speaker. Youth spoke freely about the issues they were experiencing. No matter how many forums or meetings were held, the tensions between the police and the community hardly seemed to improve.

---

415 Stacian Campbell, "An Interview with Stacian Campbell, a Youth in Our Community: In Her Own Words. A Young Jane/Finch Woman Speaks Her Mind" (Jane Finch Caring Community, June–August 2001), 4.

Jane-Finch.com is born

Paul Nguyen, who grew up in the Jane-Finch community and is an award-winning, community activist and journalist, launched a news and opinion web site called Jane-Finch.com in 2004. He wanted media to tell 'truths' about the community rather than the negative stories often put out by corporate mainstream media. When asked about his perception of mainstream media, Nguyen gave an extensive explanation.

> Well back then, I mean, especially if you're a kid growing up here, I don't think we paid attention to the news as much, because we were worried about our little lives—young people don't pay attention to the news. But as you grow older, you hear about what other people feel about the neighbourhood and you start to buy into the hype. So, you start to go "Yeah, maybe I am living in a dangerous place. Like I didn't realize it, but maybe it's not so great." So, you start buying into the hype, but then me, as a person who is frequently dealing with the news, I've been burned before. People twisting the story and manipulating and all that stuff.

> While making some friends in the news and understanding their business and their side of things we have to understand the opposite side and realize that they're doing their jobs and if there's a shooting they have to come down and do it. If there is a positive event, maybe they can't afford to come down and do it, because they can't afford the airtime and all this stuff. Right? So, I think it's to understand, and also if you want to promote positive stories you have to know how to market it as well, you can't just accept the news. It's not a service; they don't have to provide positive news right? It just depends on whatever the audience is watching.

> So, we are also responsible for consuming and demanding what we want to see on the news and in the media. And I think what we've done successfully at the website is to make boring or mundane things more interesting. So, like a tree planting—put a spin on it. Or how to promote something—the local elections, something like that. So, we always try to put a little spin and try to make it attractive enough

that mainstream eyeballs pay attention. So, it has a little bit to do with marketing, selling stuff, and knowing how the press works.[416]

Nguyen started the website because he could not find anything about the community on Google. "So, I did it, and then by accident it caught fire and it grew pretty fast in the first year."[417] While Nguyen has been able to capture another side of Jane-Finch through Janefinch.com, he also has a lot of pride in what this form of media can do for communities.

> I've gained a lot. I've been able to learn a lot, connect with people, grow my profile, be in a position where I can help other people grow their voices, which is the most satisfaction I receive.
>
> For example, my brother's friend [Jamal Campbell], who's a Black guy who lives around here, he was drafted by the Argos [Canadian Football League]. He played for the Argos, the Toronto football team, and they won the Grey Cup. So, he called me and said "Yo, man! I can have the cup for one day, what should I do?" and I said, "You just come here, and I'll connect you—maybe you can talk with some schools, and I'll try and get your ass on TV, I think it's a good story." I felt like it was interesting. So, I connected him with the local city councillors. He went to go speak at Elia [Middle School] and Jeffreys [C. W. Jefferys Collegiate] and we took pictures on the corner, got him on Metro Morning and CBC News. Great photo op! And it's not a win for me or a win for him, but a win for the community, because they see a young Black guy who's a very talented athlete who won a championship, bringing it to the freakin' corner of Jane-Finch. [...] Random people getting off the bus are like "What the hell?" They don't even know what the Grey Cup is, but they just want a picture anyway.
>
> So, I think we increased the morale and showed that Jane-Finch has winners. That was the goal of making the story. And for other people to see, like outsiders are like, "Oh shit! There are some cool cats there." And, also for the young people living here, who want to

---

416 Paul Nguyen interview (Toronto: York Woods Library, Black Creek Living History Project, June 2008).

417 Nguyen interview.

aspire to become an athlete or to do something with their lives, there are examples right here in your own backyard. You don't need to look to Kanye West or whatever. We've got a lot of local people like Dwight Drummond, now my friend Jamal Campbell, a lot of local Jane-Finch people that can serve as role models.[418]

PEACH struggles with school board policies

Programming and support continued to be needed for youth who were involved with substance abuse. The early 2000s was a time of instability in financing for non-profits and PEACH had to close down several of their projects. The board re-examined their goals and decided to place greater emphasis on providing programming towards at-risk youth.

This was a time when the Toronto District School Board implemented a Safe Schools Policy that was based on a rationale of "zero tolerance." The zero-tolerance policy provided principals and teachers with more authority to suspend and expel students. PEACH developed its Community Response to Zero Tolerance Project with funding from the National Crime Prevention Strategy and the Royal Bank. This included public legal education, as well as individual support to youth and families involved in the courts, and in the Safe Schools measures. Through partnership and training with Oolagen Community Services, PEACH also provided "Wraparound" support to youth in reaching their goals.

Community Response to Zero Tolerance was spearheaded by Roger Rowe, a local resident, lawyer, and Jane-Finch activist who became the chair of the PEACH Board of Directors. "That program helped us connect to a concept called 'Wraparound', " said Rowe. "We started to work with youth to form wraparound teams: meaning a trusted adult would work with the youth and bring other people onto the team to work to solve whatever issues the youth was facing at the time, whether it was court or home issues or school issues."[419]

---

418   Nguyen interview.
419   Marilyn Eisenstat, "PEACH Program Keeps Kids in School" (*York West Advocate*, September 2004).

One young man had a lot of difficulties with truancy. He had been suspended a couple of times each year and had earned no credits in the previous year. His wraparound support team found a web design program for him where he earned two credits and he then returned to his regular school schedule. 'It was nice to see all school staff take time out of their schedules to help my son,' said his parent. According to Andrea Daley, the project coordinator, the support for the work Wraparound is doing in the community has been incredible.

Marilyn Eisenstat, a community-minded, retired teacher from Westview Centennial Secondary School became the managing director of PEACH.

> Around 2001, the board did some strategic planning and changed the direction of PEACH to focus on youth who had been really disadvantaged by the *Safe Schools Act*, which had been recently introduced. So, there were a lot more youth who had been out of school, getting into trouble during the day, not knowing whether they could return to school. Parents were very confused about the new legislation. Because I had experienced the other end of it at school where kids had disappeared. They would be there one day and would be gone for months. I myself didn't experience the safe schools act as a teacher because I had retired before it was enacted, but I was concerned about those youth. That's what really hooked me to stick at PEACH and to help develop the programs that worked with youth who had been excluded from school in one way or another.[420]

Eisenstat saw the problems with the schools largely as a social justice issue. "The youth and their families have been rejected, so that they see themselves in a certain way. If their experience at PEACH helps to turn around how they see themselves and their future, then its important for our whole society."[421]

PEACH also developed the Get on the Bus employment project, the Suspended and Studying program to support youth who were suspended from school, the Summer Credit Recovery program with Grade 9 youth, and a music studio.[422]

---

420   Eisenstat, "PEACH program."
421   Eisenstat, "PEACH program."
422   Eisenstat, "PEACH program."

In 2007, they moved to larger quarters on Eddystone to accommodate the increased programming, and in 2009, the acronym of PEACH was changed to Promoting Education and Community Health (substituting "education" for "economic") to better reflect their major programs that work to support marginalized youth in the education system. This new space, built with capital funds from the Ontario Trillium Foundation, included a classroom with computers, a large instructional kitchen, quiet rooms for study and reflection, a meeting space for community youth and community partners, a semi-professional music studio that nurtures the amazing talents of youth, and an office for staff.

The Spot: "Where youth wanna be"

The continued focus on youth was important for Sue Wilkinson because of her previous work with youth in the community. The FOCUS funding had been integrated into the mental health component of the Centre concentrating on drug and alcohol use and misuse among youth and children. This helped to move towards establishing a new youth component for the Centre.

> The actual development of The Spot grew from multiple attempts to create safe spaces for youth. It was quite challenging to be honest. We tried Driftwood and we tried to use the offices at the Centre. The youth space started there, so they had a dedicated space in one of the offices to be used after hours. We used the basement at 4400 Jane for a long time, but nothing was theirs. It always felt like borrowed space, so you would come and the art on the walls would be Getting In Touch's art, or it's the community centre, it's the basement—it was never a youth space, it was never their space. Nothing was really for them, it was something that they were borrowing—someone else's space, always. So, there was a need to explore that a little bit around what would change if they were validated and respected in the way they deserved to be and be given a space of their own was part of the driving force.[423]

---

423   Wilkinson interview.

The "summer of the gun" exploded on the scene in the city in the summer of 2005. While there had often been gun violence in Toronto, that year seemed particularly bad. The timing was right to do something about it and to create a respectful space for Jane-Finch youth. Youth operating within their own ethnocultural or social groups were a driving force in specific neighbourhoods and territorial "turf" continued to be an issue. Having opportunities to bring youth from different neighbourhoods, and from various cultural backgrounds, into one space was important.

The Spot: Where Youth Wanna Be (called "The Spot") was developed based on a community development model of youth engagement work. Extensive consultation was done with many youth groups and any youth that staff could find to talk to about what a safe and friendly youth space would look like.

When this initiative started, there was no funding. Over time, funding was secured from the Ontario Trillium Foundation. Wilkinson, in consultation with youth, was able to secure space in the Yorkgate Mall in 2005; a location considered to be outside the "turf" of any single neighbourhood.

> It cost hundreds of thousands of dollars just to renovate the space. We were able to get a capital grant from Trillium and a small amount of start-up money, but basically there was no core funding at all. I remember even after The Spot was built, we were having our United Way panel interview. They came and sat at the table, and we talked about The Spot, and we talked about the fact that it had no funding, and that is when we got our first increase from the United Way that was dedicated for youth work.[424]

Byron Gray, a young and ambitious community college graduate who was running the after-school drop-in program at 4400 Jane, was hired as the first manager at The Spot. Gray had a deep understanding of youth issues. He strongly believed in youths' capacity and their ability to be engaged, and that

---

424 Wilkinson interview.

informed the operation of The Spot. He partnered with the Young Leaders, a small group of youth from Westview and the Griffin Centre to identify gaps.

> When we got together, we started talking about what we wanted to do, what kind of impact we would want to have, and we had a hard time figuring that out in the beginning. And I was kind of at a loss because there was so much happening and there were so many ways, we could have taken it. So, we decided to do a bit of an environmental scan to see what was available.
>
> We did a lot of surveying, focus groups, and different initiatives to give youth a voice and to be part of that process. We did about 350 surveys with young people in the Jane-Finch community to figure out the gaps in youth programs and services. They ended up saying that the top issues that they saw were violence, housing, health, racial profiling from a policing perspective, and then there were some other things around addiction, education and so on. What we ended up figuring out mostly was that young people needed space, or a place, where they could connect, but also to have access to resources and adult allies. Somewhere they could ask questions and find some guidance outside of their school, outside of their homes, a space where they could have ownership in a sense.
>
> The youth summarized all the information they heard and said that if they had a space where they could create and have ownership over, then it would resolve a lot of the issues they were finding and that was a priority. That's when we started talking. Some of our first questions was, 'What would we want the space to look like?' 'What are the symbols or the visuals that we want to see?' 'What are the programs we want to have in those spaces and what kind of people do we want supporting those spaces?' And so, they pretty much developed everything you can see when you go to The Spot at the Yorkgate Mall.[425]

A youth advisory committee was established and from there, youth were involved in making the space welcoming to themselves and other youth, and

---

425 Gray interview.

in advising staff about appropriate programs and services. Youth determined the "rules" for the space and because of that, they helped to reinforce the way in which The Spot would operate as a safe space.

~~~

That summer of 2005, a fifteen-year-old teenager named Jane Creba was shopping at the Eaton Centre in downtown Toronto when she was accidentally shot and killed in the crossfire of a running gunfight between young Black men. The shooting of this young teen from a white, "middle-class" family, brought all three levels of government together to form a community safety plan that allocated additional funding to fight crime. The subsequent initiatives included the Toronto Anti-Violence Intervention Strategy, a strategy later proven to, intentionally or unintentionally, target the Black community, especially young males. While the 2005 shootings pressured governments to respond, the response actually happened only after a young, white teen in downtown Toronto was shot, whereas most shootings had been happening to young Black males in the city with little or no significant response by the authorities beyond the regular harassment of Black people.

Violence in the schools

On May 23, 2007, the community faced another significant tragedy when Jordan Manners was shot and killed at the local C. W. Jefferys Collegiate Institute near Keele Street and Finch Avenue. This was the first time anyone had been murdered inside a school. As a result of his murder, a School Community Safety Advisory Panel was established to research and investigate the death of Jordan Manners and to make recommendations to the school board.

The panel was led by prominent lawyer Julian Falconer, Linda MacKinnon, a retired school superintendent, and Peggy Ashby Edwards, the former community development coordinator of the Jane/Finch Centre. They surveyed students and staff and conducted interviews—leading to a four-volume final report. The report addressed issues that the panel maintained fundamentally reflected and impacted on the health of school environments, generally, and school safety, particularly. As a result of the serious and most disturbing issues identified by both students and staff, 126 recommendations were made.[426]

There was extensive media coverage of the shooting. In an article, "Living with Diversity in Jane-Finch," in the journal *Architecture and the Built Environment*, the author explained the media's approach to covering issues in communities like Jane-Finch.

> The framing of Jordan Manners' death by the media is illustrative of essentialized and stereotypical representations of poor, ethnic-minority communities. As stressed by O'Grady et al, the 'cause' of the shooting was framed in a fashion that was suggestive of social and/or cultural inferiority (single-parent families, unwed mothers, welfare dependency, a high concentration of subsidized housing, etc.) [...] A dysfunctional local community was seen as ostensibly the root cause of Jordan Manners' death. The negative reputation of Jane-Finch is established and sustained along not only the axis of race and class, but also gender, since single mothers are the ones commonly blamed for the stigmatization and criminalization of the area, since they are seen as 'the producers of unruly youth.'[427]

Professor Carl James had something to say about Manners' death and the media coverage in *Life at the Intersection.*

> The media dubbed this incident as the first instance of a student being murdered in a Canadian school, even though in 1999 two students had been killed in a school shooting in Taber, Alberta. The difference between the Taber and Toronto shoots is, of course, context. The Tabor high school is in a small, mostly white town, where such an incident is supposedly highly unusual. Students at the Toronto 'urban' high school were considered 'at risk' because of the 'troubled' community where they lived and where such incidents tend to be seen as an inevitability—something just 'waiting to happen.' The notion of urban and 'urban school students' conjures up images of

426 Julian Falconer et al, "The Road to Health: A Final Report on School Safety, Executive Summary" (Toronto Board of Education, January 10, 2008).

427 Donya Ahmadi, "Living with Diversity in Jane Finch" (Amsterdam: Architecture and the Built Environment, November 2017, 33).

slums or ghettos found in American cities. These neighbourhoods are thought to be populated mostly by African Americans. And while African Canadians might not be the largest ethno-racial group at Jane and Finch, there is a tendency to categorize it as a 'Black' area. This is likely why, as noted above, Torontonians, the media and government representatives were looking at Jane and Finch during 'the year of the gun'.[428]

⁓

The impact from the "year of the gun" continued to be felt in the community through the remaining 2000s. While The Spot was still new in the community, Byron Gray decided to organize a camping trip for vulnerable youth.

There was still some trickling off from summer of the gun stuff—we had a lot of the young people that were involved in some of that activity, and it was right after Jordan Manners had passed. We said that we needed to get them out of the community and just heal. Phil Edwards [former resident and a Parks and Recreation worker in the community] and I were able to coordinate a trip. Sue Wilkinson helped us to get some funds to support the trip and we took them up to a Catholic site because there was no other space. So, we went to a Catholic camp and there was, like, Mary standing statues and everything everywhere—kind of scary up in the woods, but regardless we had fun.

We were able to get them up there, which was a bit of a struggle, because these guys are hard, and they don't want to go anywhere, and whatever the case may be. But we convinced them to have a fellowship with their boys up north and they turned into mice! They were just young people; they were crying, they were opening up, they were talking about the hardships, but the one thing that stood out for us was when they came back. Just hours before we came back, there was a shooting in Driftwood Court and many of them said they would have been there, because they got the call as soon as

---

428   Carl James, *Life at the Intersection*, 20.

they got back. They would have been there had we not taken them away. That was so impactful for us to know that we helped save some lives that weekend, just because we wanted to expose them to something different and to show them a different way.

To this day, a lot of those young men are doing well, starting their own businesses. I think only one of them, from what we know of, ended up on the wrong side of the law. It was an actual benefit to those young people that summer.[429]

San Romanoway revitalized

A lot of young people lived in one of the community's largest developments called Palisades, found on the northeast corner of Jane Street and Finch Avenue. Palisades was built in the 1970s as an upscale, gated community to include two high-rise condominiums and a thirty-three-storey rental building, where twenty-five per cent is subsidized housing. Palisades later became known simply as San Romanoway, the street that runs through the property. Between the two high-rise condo buildings (one eventually became a rental) and across from the thirty-three-storey rental building was a recreation centre that  included a swimming pool, exercise rooms, and rooms where fitness and other classes were held. The owners of the development, Greenwin Development, understood that childcare was needed as this new neighbourhood of almost five thousand people were working people. A portion of the space was renovated, and it became the Palisades Day Care Centre.

---

429 Gray interview.

Prior to establishing San Romanoway Revitalization Association (SRRA) in 2000, staff from Greenwin Development called a few service providers in the community to find out if those organizations could provide some of their programs and services in this new neighbourhood.

They called the Jane/Finch Centre and reception forwarded the call to me as I was a community worker at the time, running programs in the community. When I heard who was on the phone, I was eager to let them know what I thought, as I well remembered the fight to stop that development. I and others knew that placing thousands of people on the corner of a community that did not have social infrastructure and adequate resources would create problems. In my conversation with them, I assertively challenged Greenwin to fix the problem they had created by developing and offering programs

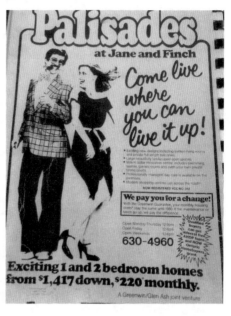

Ad on back of Tiny Toddlers Club recipe book

and services within their buildings. I also suggested that they pay for their own programs instead of depending on government funding to pay for their lack of planning and bad development.

Afterwards, reflecting on what I said, I regretted the way I responded to the person who made the call. After all, I was supposed to represent the Jane/Finch Centre and not my personal views. Residents in all neighbourhoods deserved good programs and services and government had a responsibility to provide them, or at least provide the funding, as they were the ones who approved the permit to build the development.

Greenwin found the right person, Stephnie Payne, who could help them deal with the problems they were facing in this newly built community. Payne, a formidable and passionate Toronto District School Board trustee at the time, had a run-in with Ross McLeod, the CEO for Teleguard, the company that provided security guards at the Jane Finch Mall, and who later became head of security for Greenwin. She did not meet McLeod in a social setting, rather she challenged his company to change the way his security was dealing with youth in the mall.

> How I got involved with Greenwin goes back to maybe 28–30 years ago when Ross McLeod, the Teleguard CEO started having security in the mall because of the social ills. It just so happened that one day, I was in the mall and these security guards were dragging a young Black man out and I could not stand for this. So, when I went to the security [guard] and held his hand, I said, "Let him go—you can't do this to humans." He just pushed me off and was going to arrest me. He finally let the guy go and I said you need to let me speak to the owner, who was Ross McLeod. Ross called me and we talked, and we met. I told him his guards needed some race relations and anti-racism training. So, I did that for these officers in 1994, and since that time we have become close. Ross would call me with various issues with his guards. And, Ross was managing Greenwin here, the security in here, because the social ills were hitting San Romanoway. Ross introduced me to Greenwin and said, "If you are going to do all this work to sustain some of the social ills, you can't do it without Stephnie Payne."[430]

Greenwin hired Payne as a consultant in 1999 and when San Romanoway Revitalization Association was established in 2000, she became the executive director. Payne soon learned that the crime there was 128 per cent above the national average in 2000, and so she made her intentions clear. "This is where you have to put your money where your mouth is. I know that you are losing big—vandalism, crime and everything—and the perception of the area is bad, so let's try to correct that."[431]

If they were determined to make the community safe for all its residents and to build a strong sense of community, they needed to understand the issues and then plan programs in response to the issues. They received funding in

430   Payne interview.
431   Payne interview.

2002 from the National Crime Prevention Centre and worked with the Law Commission of Canada to conduct a four-year study of the San Romanoway neighbourhood. That study included: identifying "physical modifications" in the physical environment of the buildings that could reduce opportunities of crime; conducting a Quality of Neighbourhood Life Survey, both before and after the intervention project; developing social development programs and services; and conducting an evaluation of the project.[432]

A preliminary report was prepared in 2004 showing there was an indication of good news in the community over the first two years, both for actual incidence of crime and victimization, as well as feelings of safety and perceptions of the community. Security features had been installed along with the development of new programs and services for all in the neighbourhood.

There was an overall decrease of 22.8 per cent in violent crime victimization over 2002, stranger assaults decreased by 33.3 per cent , robberies decreased by 31.3 per cent, and sexual assaults decreased by 37.8 per cent. While property crime in the neighbourhood was still above the Canadian average, it had decreased by 23.7 per cent from 2002 to 2004. Neighbourhood interaction improved, with neighbours getting to know each other at the programs, and programs for children and youth were well-attended.

The conclusion of the interim report highlighted the changes.

> There have been some rather dramatic changes in the San Romanoway community over the past two years: new programming, heightened community participation, a general improvement in feelings of safety, and reductions in violence and household crime victimization rates. In the general milieu of the Jane-Finch area, poor urban planning, relative deprivation, and concentrated suburban poverty have led to significant strains on community living. Nonetheless, the SRRA and the community crime prevention project have demonstrated that quality of neighbourhood life can improve, cultural diversity can be a tremendous asset, and progressive interventions can help and empower residents.[433]

---

432 George Rigakos et al, "The San Romanoway Community Revitalization Project: Interim Report" (Toronto: March 2004).

433 Rigakos et al, "San Romanoway."

Corporate media comes to visit

While there were many good things happening in the community, reporters came into San Romanoway only when bad things happened, until Joe Friesen from the *Globe and Mail* newspaper ventured into the community in 2006. Friesen met with staff and residents to seek approval for him to work out of a space in the SRRA office. SRRA took the risk and granted him permission to spend a few months in Jane-Finch. He wrote a series of sixteen stories titled "The Neighbourhood" written from April to August of 2006.

The intent was to tell the everyday life stories of Jane-Finch, rather than the negative stories. "The popular image of Jane-Finch has come to stand for the American ghetto. I hope to spend time to really understand Jane-Finch and give the rest of Canada a more complex portrait of the community," said Friesen.[434] While the articles did not remove the existing stigmas, they did highlight issues residents were facing in the community at the time.

To establish relationships in the community, he played basketball with youth, attended meetings, and came to know people in the community. Friesen brought attention to the work Toronto Housing's property manager Mwarigha was doing in the Firgrove community. Mwarigha worked towards opening up the property—removing wire grilles, adding doors with large windows, planting trees, hosting barbeques, and encouraging security guards to engage with youth. "We're trying to win the hearts and minds of all people here, to make it harder for people to think this is an easy place to commit crimes and fade into the scenery," Mwarigha said.[435]

Friesen wrote about an aspiring reggae singer and song writer living in San Romanoway, Jennifer Roberts. Her songs were featured in local college radio stations along with another song being rotated on several Jamaican radio stations[436] and about another resident, a local tenant representative, who made a compelling argument for much needed repairs to her housing development and succeeded.[437] He covered stories that impacted residents such as challenges from the smell of garbage, determining whether to have

---

434   "The Globe sends a reporter among us" (*York West Advocate*, May 3, 2006).
435   Joe Friesen, "A show of community, not force" (*Globe and Mail*, May 15, 2006).
436   Friesen, "Singer hopes her bubble won't burst" (*Globe and Mail*, May 8, 2006).
437   Friesen, "Wheeling and dealing to keep out the rain" (*Globe and Mail*, May 20, 2006).

more affordable housing in the area, to reporting on challenges facing youth in the community.

≈℮

Jasmine Ali, as part of her research for this book, thought the opportunity of having a reporter based in the community could be innovative journalism. She then shared her perspective of his reporting in Jane-Finch.

> The series titled 'The Neighbourhood' aimed to tell the everyday life stories of Jane-Finch, because the media too often told stories of negative things happening. There was an opportunity to provide a real insider's perspective. But the fact that most of his articles focused on, or returned to, the themes of violence, poverty and crime/drugs insinuated that this was the insider experience of the community. His writing told a story of Jane-Finch, but not all the stories of Jane-Finch. Taking one story, and branding it as the entire story, is what the Nigerian author Chimamanda Adichie refers to as 'creating a single story.' Outsiders who read these articles were having their beliefs confirmed because this 'insider' knowledge already lined up with what they came to believe, by other news sources. So, it legitimizes fear, legitimizes this 'us vs. them' ideology.[438]

She thought that his attempt seemed well-intentioned but missed the mark.

> At the end of the day, the same negative narrative was perpetuated amongst the masses. Those that did not know the neighbourhood personally, were left to feel fearful of what may happen to them should they step foot on the intersection.

Ali believed that his stories did not recognize where communities within Jane-Finch came together to create and to respond. The history of the community was not told, leaving the reader to imagine the government adequately responding to the needs of this community.

---

438   Jasmine Ali, research report.

Most of these initiatives were built from the ground up. From the community members that would benefit from these programs. From groups that were not afraid to cross dividing lines of ethnicities and neighbourhoods to work together for the betterment of the entire communities. Living in Jane Finch is not a monolithic experience, there is no one narrative that completely describes what it is like. Rather, there is a series of narratives, that change as the community changes, combine to create this community's reality.

The headlines were heartbreaking. Heartbreaking because they were always rooted in struggle, even the articles about hope and relatively positive things, always found its way back to sharing the struggles of the community. Telling the story of struggles is important, and necessary, however that is not the whole story. These articles reduce the communities to the struggles that they experience. One of the most telling was the article titled "Welfare mothers given chance to break the cycle." Why are the women featured in the story described as a 'welfare mother'? She and the other women participating in that community program are more than their financial struggle. They are mothers, who happen to be accessing social assistance. When you have an image of a young Black woman and her children under a title of "Welfare mothers..." what narrative and stereotypes is that saying?[439]

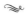

Chris Richardson, a university student attending Brock University, wrote a paper called "Canada's Toughest Neighbourhood" in 2008. He studied the media coverage of Jane-Finch in 2007, utilizing mainstream Canadian newspapers. "To refer to Jane-Finch as Canada's toughest neighbourhood—whether accurate or highly exaggerative—has a real effect on the community. Property values can drop. Outsiders may avoid the neighbourhood. And those who stand to benefit will use the area's notoriety to spread fear. In short,

---

439   Jasmine Ali, research report.

the more one believes Jane-Finch is Canada's toughest neighbourhood, the more it will become Canada's toughest neighbourhood."[440]

Richardson tells the story of Alwyn Barry, a local Jane-Finch resident who filmed his battle with colon cancer and passed away at the age of eighteen. Barry said, "I needed people to see what I went through day-to-day, to show another side of life in the neighbourhood centred at the Jane Street and Finch Avenue intersection." Barry recalls changing schools at one point so he would not have to deal with the stigma of telling people he went to school in Jane-Finch. "But kids asked where he lived."

Richardson found that, "…predominantly-negative connotations of the neighbourhood are reinforced through the perpetuation of dominant discourse, the use of "expert" knowledge sources, and the discounting of conquered knowledges or lived-experiences of residents."[441]

Development of the Yorkgate lands

As the only large, vacant parcel of land in Jane-Finch, there was a continual focus on the Yorkgate land. It got both local media attention and resident engagement into the 2000s. The Elderbrook Company, led by Murphy Hull, designed a 999-unit project to be in two high-rises rising over twenty stories. Hull, who owned the land for forty years at that time, was waiting for the right time to build. He originally proposed building six luxury condominium buildings in the 1970s but lost that fight. This new complex would have 220 freehold townhouses on the north end with 775 condominium apartments facing Finch Avenue. The official plan approved of this level of density and the City's planning staff were recommending the plan for approval in January 2005. Councillor Peter Li Preti was quick to reject the report based on community wishes.[442]

Ishwaar Bisram, president of the Condominium Corporation YCC 206, was actively involved with this fight. "We (members of different homeowner groups) just sent a letter to the City saying that we would agree to a total

---

440 Richardson, "Canada's Toughest Neighbourhood."
441 Richardson, "Canada's Toughest Neighbourhood."
442 "Community opposes the size of Yorkgate project" (*York West Advocate*, March 2005).

of only 775 units there, which would be detached, semi-detached, and townhouses," he said. "We don't want the high-rises which will look like a monolith along Finch. It is in our interest, as homeowners, that the pricing is helpful to our area. If the units are a decent size and price, they will lift the area up." Bisram continued to say that, "We know that there is a downturn in the market and for-sales signs are staying up longer. What we worry about is if they can't sell them and that could be used for rentals. We have enough rentals in the community."[443]

At the Council meeting, Li Preti shared the complicated history of the site, explaining how the city staff's interpretation was flawed and that the actual density was much lower. Councillor Howard Moscoe moved that the developer build the more community acceptable townhouses before starting in on the larger buildings. In the end, Murphy Hull did not build any housing on the land.

The land remained zoned as high density and the high density was granted new legitimacy by the City of Toronto's official plan, which called for high-density, mixed-use development along major roads.

The *York West Advocate* newspaper commented on Murphy Hull when he died in 2008.

> Murphy Hull, one of the area's first and largest private land developers, influenced our history for at least five decades. The first neighbourhood in the '60s to transform the farmers' fields into a budding suburb was the Hull project. Hullmar Drive, which winds its way through crescents and cul-de-sacs north of Finch, is named after him. It was built by his Elderbrook company. These and other developments in the area might well be considered sufficient to cement Hull's position as a key figure in our history. The development, however, for which he may be most remembered, is the development that has not happened. This is the development planned for Mr. Hull's vacant farmer's field known by local residents as the 'common.'[444]

---

443 "Community opposes the size".
444 Mark Kear, "A maker of history".

An Africentric school

People in Jane-Finch knew that low-income and high-density neighbour-hoods had negative impacts on the community. Stephnie Payne, with an enormous passion for children, knew about the disengagement, poor per-formance, and high drop-out rates of Black students. She had been elected as trustee in 1991 and served Ward 4, Toronto District School Board, until she retired in 2014. One of her focuses was on improving the educational outcomes for Black students in the community. Recalling a commencement at Westview a few years ago, she explained that she asked all the Black males in the audience to stand up, and in a cohort of about two hundred students, only three stood up. These were the only Black males graduating that year in a school where a large percentage of the students are from the Black popula-tion in the community. She knew that had to change.

She initiated and chaired a committee of community members, teachers, administrators, and board personnel to prepare a plan for a school that would be responsive to the schooling needs of underachieving students. As a result of this work, a number of Africentric summer programs and curriculum proj-ects were initiated and implemented in schools where there was a significant number of Black students with a disproportionately low level of educational achievement. The programs drew on African-centered sources of knowledge and perspectives to create a rich and diverse educational experience, building an environment of high academic achievement, increased student engage-ment and enriched cultural pride for all students. [445]

The TDSB Alternative Schools Advisory Committee, based on parent rep-resentation, approved the establishment of an Africentric alternative school in 2007, as it does with other alternative school requests. When the Toronto District School Board proposed introducing an Africentric alternative school as a way of dealing with low Black graduation, the idea brought a mix of different reactions.

Alternative schools were not new to Toronto. For example, there were alternative schools for the arts, for Indigenous students, for at-risk youth, and for those who are "gifted." Alternative schools use non-traditional, hands-on

---

445   Carl James, *Life at the Intersection*, 108.

approaches to learning the required Ministry of Education curriculum. Each school has a distinct identity and focus, such as democratic education, holistic learning, physical art, mindful living, entrepreneurship, social justice, community outreach, and more.[446]

It was hoped that the Africentric school would include the sources of knowledge, experience, and history of peoples of African descent as key to teaching and learning. "The Black students would see themselves reflected more often in all subject materials, that history would be taught with a more realistic reflection of the experiences and events that shaped the peoples of the world—not just Europe and North America—and in particular, those of African descent."[447] Africentric schools would also have teachers in greater numbers who looked like the students, who shared some of the experiences that the students experienced, and who could be role models.

A *Toronto Star* editorial claimed that "The idea smacks of segregation, which is contrary to the values of the school system and Canadian society as a whole." The *National Post* wrote, "The concept of special schools for Black students is one of those terrible ideas that refuse to die."[448] An editorial in the *Globe and Mail* (February 13, 2008) said, "Before declaring such failure, a system dedicated to treating all students equally regardless of skin colour has a duty to try harder to remove whatever obstacles exist in the regular classroom to the education of disaffected youths."

Speakers in favour of the school said it was misleading to equate it to segregation of Black students. "Its not about segregation, it's about self-determination," said Angela Wilson, who first proposed the idea to the school board. The trustees narrowly approved the contentious Africentric School proposal.[449]

The Africentric School opened in 2009 within the Sheppard Public School, with over one hundred students. In that same period, Stephnie Payne

446 TDSB website.
447 Sarah Kear, "Africentric Schools, Programs in Toronto" (York West Advocate, December 2007).
448 Carl James, Life at the Intersection, 107.
449 Caroline Alphonso and James Bradshaw, "Trustees Narrowly Approve Contentious Afro-centric School" (Globe and Mail, January 30, 2008).

thought that young Black women were doing slightly better than the males. Teenage pregnancy rates were lower around 2012, meaning fewer Black women would leave school and then come back later. More were heading toward college than university, although Payne advocated for young people to go to university instead of college. "It comes down to economics—college is more affordable than university." [450]

Another concern that she had as a school trustee was that African, Caribbean, and new immigrant children are constantly being streamed into special education or "behavioural" classes. She was also a huge proponent of combining public and Catholic school boards into one. "Parents are drawn to sending their children to Catholic school, assuming that this will help them become more religious people, but it is the Catholic board that does more streaming than the public. I believe that the Catholic Board also makes less of an effort to hire teachers that reflect the community." Payne's experience was that administrators from all boards made little effort to truly understand the needs of the Black community. "They need to come with a full understanding of what is going on in the community, and they should meet with community leaders and find out what is going on once they are in the community."[451]

Inner-city schools

The Toronto District School Board established a task force in November 2004 and a report called "Model Schools for the Inner City" was submitted to the board in May 2005. At the time, inner-city schools were identified by the school board as schools with a large concentration of students living in poverty. In identifying the issues, the report said,

> The challenge faced by urban schools today is to equip students from diverse backgrounds to participate fully and equally in an increasingly complex Canadian society. Teaching is not limited to the classroom but is embodied in every aspect of the school experience and student learning is impacted by disparate social factors. Poverty,

---

450   Payne interview.
451   Payne interview.

culture shock, family status, and youth violence increasingly play roles in the lives of our students and are especially significant in the lives of our inner-city students.[452]

The task force identified inner-city schools based on specific criteria, looked at resources already in the community, and then presented their findings in March 2005. The goals that guided the task force included achieving fairness and equity, school as the heart of the community, inclusive culture, and high educational expectations for the students.

In the Jane-Finch community, three schools were identified as Model Inner-City schools: Driftwood Public School, Firgrove Public School, and Yorkwoods Public School. Each of the schools received additional funding for staff to plan and design, through community and school consultation, the process for implementation.

Not every student attended one of the model inner-city schools. Suzanne Narain went through the regular school system, attending Gosford Elementary School, Brookview Middle School, Westview Centennial Secondary School, and then York University. All of them are in Jane-Finch, what academics call an inner-city community. She also lived with a large extended family—nineteen people—in their home at one time.

> At that time there were a lot of Italian immigrants in the neighbourhood. They would constantly call the police on us for various things like, the grass wasn't being cut, or the kids were running outside in their underwear, and the music being too loud, or cooking food that smelled. At that time, we didn't have the vocabulary to understand it as racism. My parents were very kind people and see Canada as a safe haven and just saw those people as just not being nice people, not racist.[453]

---

452 "Model Schools for Inner City Task Force Report" (Toronto: Toronto District School Board, May 2005).

453 Suzanne Narain interview (Toronto: York Woods Library, Black Creek Living History Project, September 2018).

Narain gave her perspective on growing up in Jane-Finch.

> In elementary school, you're very much innocent in your child-hood and your concerns are very different. But in middle school you become more aware of the media, more aware of the perception of the neighbourhood, more aware of what's happening to some of your friends, and things like that. So, I think I've always been kind of concerned with how people were thinking about the way in which the media was presenting folks in the community, and the reality. Or, it was contradictory of the reality that I knew of, that people who were bright, or people who were successful, and were not just violent or drug dealers, or these awful things they say about our neighbourhood.[454]

When she went to high school, she learned about the issue of profiling.

> Police violence or police surveillance, or hyper-surveillance, on profiling has been an issue. We'd get stopped all the time in high school, or get pulled over, get our backpack searched. That's always been an issue in our community, and I don't think people were taking us seriously until the Toronto Star did that report a long while ago—about the police racial profiling in the police service, particularly in the communities. And, that was back in the early 2000s.

Narain was a bit of a rebel in school and exposed to people who were arrested, or killed, and young women who got pregnant. According to Narain, the education system in communities like Jane-Finch have one social worker for five schools. The teachers have students facing critical life-impacting experiences: parents going through a divorce, kids living in shelters, sisters getting molested, brothers getting shot. Narain, who teaches children from kindergarten to Grade 6, believes that children are not being supported to the degree they need to be supported, largely due to cuts, large classroom sizes, and poor infrastructure, along with limited resources.

---

454   Narain interview.

Rosalie Griffith was one of Narain's high-school teachers who believed in her, and Narain credits Griffith for her success. Narain strongly believes that "If someone believes in you, there's no telling what you can do."[455]

Community actions

Residents in the community continued to fight, to advocate and to create. New social action groups were being formed to respond to the issues created by the poor planning. One such action was undertaken by Gary Green, a local resident who later decided to run for city council. He organized an event called United We Stand, where twenty-five issues, along with potential solutions were determined by residents and workers in the community.

One of the top six issues was employment opportunities, specifically among youth and newcomers. People were also concerned about the upkeep and safety within Toronto Community Housing buildings, including the concentration of low-income housing in small areas. Crime and perceived lack of safety/security was part of the top six issues, along with the need for better racial and socio-economic representation in the development of programs. Lastly, negative media images and coverage continued to negatively affect the area.[456]

United We Stand was not the only event where issues and solutions were identified. Community workers were organizing events such as movie nights and workshops that brought pertinent information to groups of residents. Farid Chaharlangi from the Jane/Finch Centre was in the midst of this work.

> Many community residents wanted to see positive systemic changes and they were frustrated around the fact that their voices were not heard. For that reason, we worked with resident activists and partner organizations to organize a community conference called, 'Jane Finch is Getting On' in March 2007.
>
> We got together around 2006 to see what we could do, and during this time, we were organizing a number of events for the

455 Narain interview.
456 Gary Green, "United We Stand" (North York: Report on a Community Meeting, July 26, 2006).

International Day for the Elimination of Racial Discrimination—lots of big community events and discussions. All of these were happening around the same time. People felt that we needed to be dealing with the racialization of poverty in Jane-Finch, which needed to be addressed.[457]

～

The Jane Finch is Getting On conference, funded by the City of Toronto and with the support of nine local organizations, focused on issues of access and equity faced by residents. The conference also called for commitments to identify and mobilize around solutions and effect change through community actions.

Leticia Deawuo completed her placement at the Jane/Finch Centre and graduated from the Social Service Worker program at college. The Centre hired her to organize the conference.

> At the time, the issues were around education, the state of housing in the community. It was around the criminalization of youth, and it was around employment. I remember there were five and I can't remember the fifth one, but those are the four I remember. The role I played was really getting residents engaged in the conversations and getting them to participate, so a lot of the work I did at the time was community outreach. Literally, we had multiple forms of outreach: tables in the malls, door to door leafleting, and one of the ones that I truly enjoyed was the one-on-one conversations with people around why they should attend the event, and why it was important. As somebody who was young, straight out of college with a lot of passion and yes, we could do something. And, then you talk to older folks in the community, and they say, nothing ever changes in this community; do you know how long we've been talking about this—forever! It was interesting for me and it didn't kill my passion for it. I just felt like there was something that we, as community,

---

457   Chaharlangi interview.

can still do to, one, bring about political accountability, and to also challenge the system that keeps the situation in place.[458]

Jane Finch is Getting On Conference had over one hundred residents and forty organizations and volunteers represented. It was moderated by Cheryl Prescod, a long-time resident and social activist, and began with a panel of community residents and workers, along with guest speaker and long-time political activist, Dr. Grace-Edward Galabuzi, professor at Ryerson University.[459]

During the conference, issues were identified that impacted residents, from the early years, up to and including issues affecting seniors. Issues were identified that impacted how people accessed information, received support, or accessed resources. Residents pointed out that the community lacked political power, that they felt stigmatized and stereotyped, and that they wanted safe and affordable housing. Youth issues were highlighted with residents expressing that there was over-policing of youth that led to incarceration. The list was long and supported by all those in attendance.

The conference facilitated an opportunity to generate potential solutions that included improving the image of the community in the media; holding politicians, agencies, and organizations accountable; listening to and valuing youth in decision-making; and taking collective action on the issues identified.

Residents described the impact of the day. "We need to organize ourselves. There is strength in numbers."

"The government needs to know what we want."

"I am so proud of my children. And I am proud of being from Jane-Finch."

"When kids are not heard, when they cannot express themselves, it makes them feel alone. Putting down kids never helps—it makes things worse."[460]

The community skillfully articulated the issues and came up with recommendations, however, the issues were not just felt by those who lived in

---

458   Deawuo interview
459   "Jane Finch is getting on: What's holding you back?" (Community Forum Report, May 2007).
460   "Jane Finch is getting on."

Jane-Finch community. They were impacting working people in all suburban neighbourhoods across the city, and in certain downtown areas. This was also the period following the Year of the Gun and, while resources were increasing, deep rooted systemic issues just did not get the attention they deserved.

~~≈~~

Jane Finch on the Move (JFOTM), a grassroots group, emerged from the Jane Finch is Getting On conference and focused on organizing to ensure residents issues were heard. They hosted a community forum with over three hundred community residents and representatives from community organizations attending and participating in the discussions. George Martell, a long-time education activist, spoke about how to break the class/race barriers in the schools. Professor J. David Hulchanski talked about the growing income gap in Toronto. Hulchanski had produced a report, *The Three Cities Within Toronto*, that provided a comprehensive examination of income polarization in Toronto's neighbourhoods from 1970 to 2005. The findings found three distinct "cities" within Toronto, based on income. Ward 3 was part of the forty per cent of the city that had low incomes, substantiating what the community already knew. [461] There continued to be an inequitable distribution of investments and resources to the community.

JFOTM became a fully independent, resident-led group to "give a voice to our community, telling our stories, and being known as individuals." A few years later, they produced a book called *Voices Matter: Jane-Finch Residents Speak Out*, where they shared their stories and opinions. JFOTM continued to function for a number of years, speaking out about poverty and supporting social justice work.

Chaharlangi from the Jane/Finch Centre attended both events.

> Following that, many community residents felt that we needed to do more work around various aspects of poverty in the community. The fact that some of the root causes of the problems that we had been facing in the community had to do with lack of access to

---

461   J. David Hulchanski, *The three cities within Toronto: income polarization among Toronto's neighbourhoods, 1970–2000* (Toronto: Cities Centre Press, December 2007).

employment, affordable food, poverty, and lack of investment in the community. So, some anti-poverty initiatives started to be formed around 2007-2008, out of which the Jane Finch Action Against Poverty (JFAAP) was formed.[462]

Mobilizing residents

Butterfly GoPaul, a community health worker and passionate community resident-activist, had also attended the events.

JFAAP started with a conversation with local organizations and agencies and maybe a few residents that might have worn different hats or just a few residents that sat at the table at the time. It was all these issues happening in the neighbourhood, the policies were only getting worse, and at the time, organizations and agencies were also feeling the pressure as well. Less money, more expectations. We also just moved away from where we couldn't even say 'advocacy' to a place where we were able to do some of the advocacy work. We started having a conversation about having an action in honour of the Eradication of Poverty in the Jane-Finch neighbourhood.

Residents were really engaged in this conversation, and we were meeting weekly. There was nothing that existed like JFAAP, so we were also trying to figure out what is JFAAP, as well, in these discussions. "Here are the issues but what does this look like in our neighbourhood." I think that was a big part of our conversations. But also, what was happening at that time. What we were hearing from residents was police brutality, what was happening in the raids, and what was happening with the blatant disregard for people's homes, and the attack on community.

That was one of our first actions, and after was organizing around police brutality, and in particular, 31 Division. That was also a huge movement that happened. We got thousands of signatures, we had petitions sent to the four corners of Jane-Finch to get signed, and we had all kinds of people supporting. People from York, residents,

---

462   Chaharlangi interview.

youth-led groups, arts groups in the neighbourhood. We went to 31 division, and we had demands, and it was the first time I have seen our neighbourhood organized and, on the page, but also very reactionary. We were able to respond very quickly, and we still didn't know what JFAAP was—it was the first six months of JFAAP."[463]

GoPaul continued to describe some of the motivating issues that got JFAAP going.

There was an incident or two that made us mobile at the time. I believe there was a raid that happened—and we were hearing from the Somali community that mothers and elders in the Somali community were being beaten up and brutalized in their homes. Children were being zipped-tied with their wrists and thrown behind cruisers. We heard that there was some kind of smoke-bomb that was thrown in a home, and a little boy was burned on the side of his face.

This was all around the time where there were police that came into the Jane Finch Mall and let off pepper spray, or something, some kind of smoke out of a gun. There was a lot of friction and there was a build up and I think that's what was happening. Just tightening policies and criminalizing different people, the coordination of security and the police in the neighbourhoods. We were hearing a lot. And every day, people were seeing it and bearing witness, so it wasn't just like the gangster just doing it but being in a mall and being impacted with the blatant disregard of people's safety and wellness.

So, we were hearing it from different ways, and I think with JFAAP's membership—people living in different neighbourhoods, coming from different kinds of experiences, from a single mom to a young person, to somebody who goes to a program—we were hearing these stories so much that we were able to connect these people and their stories. It was a difficult time.[464]

---

463   Butterfly GoPaul interview (Toronto: York Woods Library, Black Creek Living History Project, May 2016).
464   GoPaul interview.

Suzanne Narain shared another perspective with an analysis of neo-liberalism and the austerity policies of government.

> Some of the challenges have been living under a neo-liberal regime and having so many cuts. So many of our politicians who really don't listen to us, the change of government, the move to the more conservative government. I think a deeper challenge, or a more intimate challenge, is the fact that a lot of the people who are part of JFAAP are residents in the community and already have jobs or families and lives to take care of. We are the ones who have to advocate for the needs of our community after already being so, I guess, exhausted or overworked and under paid. I think one of the challenges is that it takes a real toll on your personal health and well-being.[465]

While most of the Jane/Finch Centre's work focused on program delivery, they wanted to expand their community development and capacity building work, acknowledging it was challenging to do work around grassroots organizing and supporting resident involvement. It was important that residents be the spokespeople for the community, but resources for this kind of work remained limited at the time.

Despite the limitations, the protests and rallies did not stop. There were a lot of initiatives such as: Jane Finch Save our Schools Campaign, Jane-Finch

---

465   Narain interview.

Community Forum on Immigration, Right Food/Food Right Campaign, May Day rallies, advocacy for the Special Diet program, all candidates election meetings, and Raising the Rate of Social Assistance. Farid Chaharlangi's support was always provided along with resident-activists from JFAAP and staff from the Black Creek Community Health Centre and CLASP, the Community Legal Aid Support Program of York University.

≈

Initiatives came from issues identified by residents. One of the issues was food security, including access to healthy food, fresh produce, and good quality products. Around 2008, the Heart and Stroke Foundation did research comparing the cost of healthy foods in different parts of the Greater Toronto Area. They found that the cost of healthy food in communities like Jane-Finch was higher than a well-off area in Scarborough or in Thornhill, one of the highest income areas in the GTA at the time. Chaharlangi, who noticed this research, pointed out that Jane-Finch is one of the lowest income neighbourhoods in the whole GTA. It had much higher prices for healthy foods than areas such as Thornhill.

Representatives from Heart and Stoke reached out to the Jane/Finch Centre and Black Creek Community Health Centre, and with funding from the Heart and Stroke Foundation, JFAAP initiated a project in 2009 called the "Food Right: Right Food Campaign." Residents went into different neighbourhoods across the GTA to compare food prices, verifying the initial research, and mobilizing residents to act. "Hundreds of community residents came together and talked about how they could address the issues related to healthy food." [466]

As a result of this work, JFAAP brought together residents to discuss food issues. According to surveys, 74.2% of respondents said they needed more vegetables in their diet, while 70.3% said they need an increase in provincial income assistance, as well as an increase to minimum wage rates to enable households to afford the basic costs of living including the ability to eat healthy and maintain a balanced diet. The results of the Food Right: Right

---

466   Chaharlangi interview.

Food campaign indicated that true food security is impossible without social and economic justice including the realization of food justice.[467]

JFAAP was successful in engaging community, helping residents become aware of the significant difference in food prices in different neighbourhoods, and making a link between the amount received by Ontario Works and the amount really needed for basic living. Many newcomers joined who had an interest in healthy and affordable food and learning how to access it.

The group then undertook an expansive project of consultation and community engagement, producing a report called Fighting for Food Justice in the Black Creek Community, funded by the City of Toronto. As a result of the consultation, they hosted community conversations, a Food Frequency radio show, and identified issues such as food, policing, and race and culture. "When discussing what food justice means to them, many community members made the connection to the criminalization of poverty and race and how that connects to accessing food."[468] They ended the project with a food justice day of action with over one hundred protestors and supporters to assert the human right of access to healthy food.

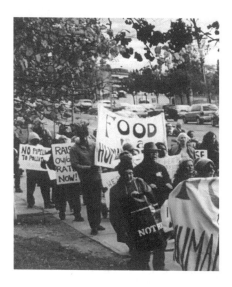

---

467   "Fighting for Food Justice in the Black Creek Community: Summary Report" (Toronto: Black Creek Food Justice Network, 2010).
468   "Fighting for Food Justice".

Actions continued around food justice. When the Black Creek Community Farm was formed at Jane Street and Steeles Avenue West [the northern boundary for Jane-Finch], residents got involved with the farm and the Black Creek Food Justice Network.

York University in Jane-Finch

While residents continued to work on accessibility of food and food justice, York University continued to find ways to engage with the community. The most progressive work initiated by the university, from a Jane-Finch perspective, was to establish a deeper relationship with the Jane-Finch neighbourhoods through increased connections between the university and residents.

For example, in the late 1990s, Professor Susan McGrath became engaged in the community through the Network of Community-Based Organizations, representing York University. She was appointed by the school of social work to support the Black Creek Community Capacity Building Project that followed the work of the Network of Community-Based Organizations. Her supportive work also helped influence York University to establish a community engagement centre in Jane-Finch.

Rhonda Lenton, dean of Atkinson College at the time, and now president of York University, was also committed to the idea of establishing a centre in the community. To do this work, York obtained a ten-year gift of one million dollars from the TD-Canada Trust bank in 2006. The gift was made to establish a teaching engagement centre with the goal of promoting accessibility and social justice through meaningful and transformative community-university partnerships.

After consultation between York and the community, the York University—TD Community Engagement Centre (CEC) opened its doors in the Yorkgate Mall in 2008. TD-Canada Trust funding paid for the rent and maintenance of the space, and York University matched this with funds from the President's Office to cover the salaries of a manager, a community projects coordinator, and an administrative assistant. Student placements were also utilized to support the CEC. While organizationally part of the

Atkinson Faculty of Liberal and Professional Studies, responsibility for the CEC was transferred to the Vice-President Academic and Provost offices in 2009, reporting to the Vice-Provost Academic.

Dr. Mamdouh Shoukri, (president of the university from 2007 to 2017) and a keen supporter of community engagement, came to the Yorkgate Mall for the grand opening.

> The Centre is a great opportunity for York University and its neighbouring communities to share information in a way that will benefit everyone. It will give the community members access to the knowledge and services they need, and an opportunity to share their experiences with students and faculty who want to enhance research and learning in a meaningful way.[469]

Sue Levesque was the first executive director of the CEC. She was a strong supporter of university–community partnerships by providing space and opportunities for collaboration and joint initiatives that enrich students' experiences, reducing barriers to post-secondary education for residents, and supporting actions in the community.

United Church's community ministry

York was not the only institution engaged in the community. The Jane Finch Community Ministry, a ministry of the United Church, continued its work by providing community development and community organizing support, offering pastoral care, and engaging in advocacy through coalitions and networks. Barry Rieder, the community minister explained his focus on youth violence. "Dealing with some of the violence in the community, it's kind of two steps forward and one step back. The violence in the community reflects some of the other social issues that end up happening. It's racialized poverty—that's the reason why Black youth end up killing themselves, or each other."[470]

---

469 David Ros, "York goes to the Mall. Is this community U?" (*York West Advocate*, September 2008).
470 Rieder interview.

Rieder formed the Street Involved Youth Issues Coalition with other concerned workers in the community. He explained that he had come from the downtown core, where there were resources and supports for youth, but not in Jane-Finch. Eventually, the youth issues coalition became the Neighbourhood Action Youth Employment Committee and along with that came funding to do training within high schools. The training included first aid, food handling and customer service. Training was also available for youth who were not working and were out of school, including forklift training, food handling, and smart serve (bartending) training.

> There's been a variety of youth violence, and it peeked around 2005 with the "year of the gun." That was where fifty young men, from across Toronto—Black men—had lost their lives. Unfortunately, it wasn't until a [white] woman, on boxing day downtown, got caught in the crossfire that all kinds of resources started to focus on youth.
>
> I remember an article in the *Globe and Mail* at that point in time that said they were not surprised that this kind of violence has ended up happening because unemployment rates for all youth is 17%, but for Black male youth, it was double that: 34% unemployment. So, out of every three young Black men, one can't get a job, not because of their ability or inability, but it's because of the colour of their skin. And, in many cases, it's because of the neighbourhoods they come from. That's one of the reasons why the Neighbourhood Action Youth Employment Committee got very involved in youth employment."
>
> It was well understood that if they were "middle-class" white, Canadian-born youth, they would not be discriminated against because of the neighbourhood where they lived.[471]

∾

While some work was progressing in the employment area, there was much work to do in the community. Through his work, Rieder built trust with youth who were gang-involved and tells the story of meeting a young woman named Andrea in Firgrove who wanted to organize a BBQ in the

---

471   Rieder interview.

community. Andrea was a spoken word artist who wrote poetry around ending violence, having experienced the impact of crime herself. Because of her experience, she had street credibility and the ability to bring youth from north of Finch to the south, into the Firgrove area.

Rieder met with her to help her write a letter to solicit donations that would support the BBQ. While Andrea thought that would be a one-time event, it was not. The event became known as the Unity BBQ, and it became an annual event to bring people together. This young woman, who was the founder of the event had been to enough funerals, but it was the death of a youth called Iron that encouraged her to push for Unity.

> She thought that was going to be the last event, but Iron was one of the young persons that was killed in our community. He was a youth that had connections to both Firgrove and Yorkwoods, and he was involved as a dealer and trying to hustle and make money that way.

> Mwarigha, one of the Toronto Housing Property Managers, had this project where the contractors had to hire youth as apprentices. There was a painting company that hired Iron as a painter apprentice and Iron looked at it as saying, "This is my ticket out of here, because if I continue with this lifestyle, I'm going to be either dead or in prison." Things were going really well. Iron painted the community ministry's walls—nice colour, great job—and he had gotten his contractor's license, he just got engaged, and he bought a condo. One night when he was having an argument with a friend of his, his friend stabbed him. His friend suffered from mental health issues and had been in and out of prison, and of course, prison doesn't help people with those issues. Iron's friend stabbed Iron in the chest and Iron drove himself to the hospital thinking it was just a little flesh wound and got stitched up there. The doctors wanted to keep him overnight and of course, Iron didn't want to get his friend in trouble, so he left, and he bled out internally. Iron was really a lovely person.[472]

～

---

472   Rieder interview.

One of the things that Rieder is very proud of in his ministry is the Back-to-School program. Lorraine Ferguson, who lived in Firgrove for many years, was at a Black Creek Community Capacity Project meeting and met Sharon Simpson who worked for the Labour Community Services, an agency of the Toronto and District Labour Council. Ferguson asked her, "Do you think there are any unions that could help out with some backpack supplies for school?"

Within a short period of time, Lorraine approached Rieder saying, "Good news—one of the unions wants to provide some support for backpacks." Rieder replied with, "That's great, but I'm going on holidays; there's not much I can do."

Apparently, the union wanted to channel the funds through a charitable organization and with an addition of four-hundred dollars from the ministry, funds were set aside with the Toronto West Presbytery. Rieder tells the story of how community residents, with strong determination, can make things happen.

> So, I went off on my holidays and they knocked on a few other doors to increase that money to about $3,000—doubled it. On their own, by bus and picking up backpacks at different stores, supplies, coming back in a taxi, they filled and distributed 164 backpacks filled with school supplies. So, I came back wanting to pat them on the shoulder and say great job and everything like that and said, "No, no—we don't want to stop there.' Maryan, who at that point in time was on social assistance said, "I've always wanted to start a scholarship program—a scholarship program, not for my son, but for other people in the community. I'm willing to put in twenty dollars a month of my social assistance into a bank account just to start this." I suggested that we talk to the Painters and Allied Trades Union because my understanding of this union wasn't wanting to do a one-off but wanted to journey with this community. So, we convinced them to provide us with enough resources to give out 500 backpacks filled with school supplies and three $1,000 scholarships, which actually turned into four. It was actually 700 backpacks filled with school supplies and also money for the Women's

Group—$400 so they could have money to provide some childcare and refreshments.[473]

The union eventually gave out up to one thousand backpacks filled with school supplies and ten one-thousand dollar scholarships. This event was run by the community with volunteers filling the backpacks and planning the event. The Painters and Allied Trades Union provided the most generous support with funds for this event. This program continued for ten years, ending in 2018.

Rebranding Jane-Finch

The mid-2000s brought the idea of rebranding the community by Councillor Anthony Perruzza in 2006. He wanted to change the name of Jane-Finch to University Heights. Perruzza said, "University Heights, and York University, they re-enforce positive thoughts. I'm hoping that it will kick-start a renaissance of the area."[474] The City was slated to change some of the neighbourhood street signs to feature the new University Heights label. However, the suggested sign had a picture of a farmer and of a student. While the intent was to picture someone moving up, the fact was that in 2006 only twenty per cent of residents in Ward 8 (which included the university) had a university degree. In 2016, 27.3 per cent of residents in Ward 8 had a post-secondary certificate, diploma, or degree. It could also be assumed from the design that a student was to be held in a higher esteem than workers. In Jane-Finch, workers represent far more of the population.

"I thought maybe it was just a PR thing," said Paul Nguyen. "All this rebranding and all this political correctness actually makes things worse, and it just distracts from the real problem. Calling it University Heights is not going to do 'jack'! "[475]

Chaharlangi agreed with Nguyen. "I'm not sure it's going to make any difference due to some of the fundamental issues that people in the community

---

473   Rieder interview.
474   David Ros, "Jane and Finch to become 'University Heights' " (Toronto: Excalibur, York student newspaper, October 16, 2007).
475   Ros, "Jane and Finch".

are facing, such as unemployment, poverty and housing issues. These aren't going away."[476] Clearly, rebranding the community to University Heights does not resolve the ongoing systemic and social issues impacting the community from its beginnings.

It was also known that students in the local schools or women on welfare were not being encouraged to attend post secondary education, rather they were pushed to simply get a job or training that would lead to a job. Shazia, a participant from the Women Moving Forward program, explained that when she told her social services worker about her aspirations to pursue a university degree, she was told that university would be an impossible choice for a single mother.[477] Women Moving Forward was started by the Jane/Finch Centre and became an award-winning program that provided an integrated and comprehensive program for young single mothers that would lead them to self-sufficiency.

While Perruzza admitted that a name change was not going to solve the problems, he felt that the name change could offer a sense of pride of place. Others felt differently. Suzanne Narain, an engaged community activist, had this to say. "Community members were not given an opportunity to take part in creating the new image of Jane and Finch. Most importantly, I submit that because the efforts to rebrand Jane and Finch did not involve members of the community, it is lacking the fundamentals of a democratic process."[478]

While the Jane-Finch area was not rebranded as University Heights, the City of Toronto has formally named the area of Steeles to Finch, Highway 400 to the Black Creek as the Black Creek neighbourhood; the area defined by Finch to Sheppard and Highway 400 to Black Creek as the Glenfield-Jane Heights neighbourhood. Steeles to Grandravine and Black Creek to Keele is referred to as the York University Heights neighbourhood, and the area of Grandravine to Highway 401 and Highway 400 to Dufferin as the Downsview–Roding neighbourhood.

---

476 Ros, "Jane and Finch."
477 Tonika Morgan and Heather Miller, "From Poverty to Prosperity, Women Moving Forward" (Toronto: Jane/Finch Community and Family Centre, 2011).
478 Suzanne Narain, "The Re-Branding Project: The Genealogy of Creating a Neoliberal Jane and Finch" (Toronto, 2012).

Narain says, "If the Ward 8 district truly wants to create a new image of Jane and Finch, it is vital to identify the deep systemic issues that affect the lives of its residents and work from that point to find solutions to break the chains of poverty and violence."[479]

Save our schools

Community meeting to protest school closure. (Photo by Errol Young)

In 2009 and 2010, a Pupil Accommodation Review Committee (PARC) was set up by the Toronto District School Board to review schools. From that review, they determined that there were five Jane-Finch schools that were under enrolled and therefore targeted for closure, including Shoreham Public School, the school serving the children in Edgeley Village. According to Narain, this was part of a rebranding initiative.

> Selling Shoreham Public School would benefit the rebranding of Jane and Finch by providing the community surrounding York University with access to a new and improved school. While the school board may not have had any direct involvement in the rebranding project,

---

479   Narain, "The Re-Branding Project".

the process of closing schools does fit into the larger neoliberal ploy in the Jane and Finch area.[480]

The residents formed a coalition called Save Our Schools, organized meetings of up to three hundred people and protested the reviews. None of the schools were closed.

Public transit

Enhanced public transit was needed for residents in this area of the city as well as for those in York Region who had inadequate transit connection to downtown Toronto. Thousands of students from across the Greater Toronto areas travelled to York University, daily. It is known that people living in Jane-Finch travel great distances to work. Buses are often packed to capacity along Finch, leaving people to wait for the next bus in hopes there is room for them to board.

The Toronto Transit Commission did not play a part in the attempt at rebranding, however having a subway in the community has a direct affect on residents and for students attending York University from across the City.

Interestingly, the idea for a subway was raised by then Councillor Mario Sergio back in 1979.

> I said to Mel [the mayor], "One thing that is affecting my area is a lack of transportation." And I said, "What do you think if we get the subway up all the way to York University?" "What a good idea," Mel said, "and how are we going to do it?" So, we worked on that.
>
> I remember, I went to speak to former Mayor Lorna Jackson at the Vaughan City Hall, and I said, "Lorna, we are heavily supporting a subway extension to York University and loop it around Steeles Avenue, and then all the way to Yonge Street." She said, "I want nothing to do with the subway—I'm not going to spend half of the money to please the people of Toronto."
>
> And I said, "No, its not really pleasing the people of Toronto—we're going to be bringing the subway to your doorsteps." She wanted

---

480   Narain, "The Re-Branding Project".

nothing to do with it. That was back in 1979, when I planted the seed to bring the subway to York University. Those were some of the big issues. It takes a long time and I learned that in politics, a good idea takes a long time to come to reality."[481]

When MP Judy Sgro became a member of parliament, she wanted to bring federal dollars to the community and one of the things the community needed was good transportation.

You need transportation networks that's done properly, and you need the infrastructure to go along with it. We got the subway, an issue I worked on from day one, over thirty years ago to getting the subway to York University. I never really imagined it could happen in my lifetime, but it did. I worked with Peter Li Preti, Greg Sorbara and the University administration to get the subway up to there and to make sure we had the funding to do it.[482]

Councillor Perruzza also played a significant role in getting the subway in the community over many years.

There were a lot of hot topics, for example, like the subway extension to York University. Mayor David Miller and other folks here at City Hall were looking to redirect the funds that the provincial government had made available to extend the subway. We built that extension, and it works especially well for York University students and the surrounding community. While I agree that ten years ago, when reviewing the numbers on paper, many would question the purpose of the extension. We know that ridership will increase over time. That was a signature transit project for us, there's no question about it. I fought to get the chairmanship of the Spadina Subway Committee at the TTC to make sure that if there was anybody that was going to hinder the project that I would be the first to hear about it.[483]

481 Sergio interview.
482 Judy Sgro interview (Toronto: York Woods Library, Black Creek Living History Project, November 2019).
483 Perruzza interview.

City government's response to housing conditions

Some of the work dealing with issues impacting residents included improving where they lived. Helen Kennedy's work in the early 1980s fight to improve the conditions in private apartment buildings, was taken on in different ways by Councillor Anthony Perruzza.

When I first got here in 2006, I went into Mayor David Miller's office and said, "Look, I want to introduce a program called Landlord Licencing here at the City." This was another big topic for me. He said, "Tell me a little more about that idea...I have never heard of that before."

I told him that there were some places, like Los Angeles, where the local government had a system in place to hold landlords accountable for rental housing conditions. Miller said that if I really wanted to work on that, I should get on the Licensing Committee.

I said, "That's precisely why I'm here, I'd like to be on the Licensing Committee, and I'd like to kick-start that program. I'd like to introduce that to the city and see where it goes."

In my ward, we had unacceptable housing conditions and we needed to find a way to do something about it. After getting on the Licensing Committee, I think my first press conference here at City Hall was about landlord licensing. I built a coalition with an organization called ACORN [Association of Community Organizations for Reform Now] and introduced them into the neighbourhood. I brought them up into our part of the world, and with ACORN, we rolled up our sleeves and we started to work on organizing tenants.

Councillor Howard Moscoe chaired the Licensing Committee at the time, and we created a program called MRAP—the Multi Residential Audit Program. Nothing like this had existed before. This program involved a special unit of inspectors who had the authority to audit rental buildings. Prior to that, if you lived in an apartment and you felt your building wasn't clean or being maintained or had adequate heat, you would call an inspector. An inspector would visit your unit and deal with your particular complaint. In our area, most tenants wouldn't call an inspector for fear of reprisals from the landlord. Instead, they would complain to the local politician but would be very reluctant to pick up a phone themselves and actually request an inspector.

What the MRAP program allowed us to do was to have a team of staff audit buildings and common areas. While we didn't get a lot of buy-in from the tenants who would let the inspectors into their own units to see their apartment, the inspectors themselves started to go out on a mandate and over a span of a couple of years they audited every single rental building in the city. These inspectors wrote thousands of work orders. I started this program in 2007 and it eventually became the municipal audit program.

I gave up the chairmanship of the committee about two or three years ago and the new chair renamed the program to what it is currently known as, RentSafe TO. Initially, I always got resistance from the bureaucrats telling me why we couldn't do it. "No Councillor, we don't have the legislative authority. We can't do landlord licencing. We don't have the ability to bring in a licencing regime. We can't have the same law as Los Angeles, we don't have that authority." As it turned out, because of the rental audit program that I had essentially started, the City was in a position where they had issued all of these orders that landlords were not acting on. We had all these orders up on the City's website—thousands of orders—and then we had a limited ability to get that landlord to act on it, other than through the City's prosecution route.

The bureaucrats themselves came back and said to me, "Councillor, I think we can do landlord licencing. I think we can do a licencing system, where we can get landlords to be licenced and as a condition of their licence, if they don't adhere to the work order, we can remove [their licence] and have them face the repercussions." That additional process took a long time to achieve, but it was well worth the fight. I am proud to have helped accomplish that.[484]

United Way response to the community's issues

Political support was needed in the community, along with support from various institutions if any improvements were to happen. For example, community development and resident engagement needed additional resources to carry on the work and the Jane/Finch Centre saw the opportunity to expand its work through the Action for Neighbourhood Change (ANC) project. The ANC was an initiative of the United Way of Greater Toronto's Building Strong Neighbourhoods Strategy. This project, launched in 2007, was about supporting residents to create positive changes in their communities. United Way made a commitment to fund ANC for ten years in identified at-risk neighbourhoods across Toronto, a commitment rarely made by any government or private funding body.

Jane-Finch was one of the thirteen identified priority neighbourhoods. The United Way wanted to promote this funding opportunity, so the Jane/ Finch Centre hosted an information session for the United Way and invited all community-based organizations that might be interested in applying for the funds to the meeting. The funding for this project was $276,000 per year over a period of two years, after which time it would be reduced to $100,000 annually. While a few organizations applied for the funds, the Jane/Finch Centre received the funding and agreed to work across five neighbourhoods: Gosford, Firgrove, Tobermory, Edgeley Village and Yorkwoods/Grandravine.

The funding enabled the Centre to open an ANC office in the Norfinch Plaza [corner of Jane Street and Finch Avenue] and a resident association was formed with representatives from across all the neighbourhoods. Residents were hired as animators who carried out four hundred surveys to establish priorities. Twelve focus groups were held across the neighbourhoods with seventy-five youth and seventy adults participating to identify safety issues and prevention strategies through a peace building initiative of the ANC. A community safety conference was held with almost one hundred residents. There were festivals in each of the neighbourhoods, and the first ever Jane's Walk was held in the community. Jane's Walk is a series of neighbourhood walking tours, named after urban activist and writer Jane Jacobs. The walks encourage people to share stories about their neighbourhoods, and to connect with neighbours. ANC was important to the community, enabling residents to take leadership and create the change they wanted to see for their neighbourhoods.

Two years later, when funding was reduced, the office was relocated to 415 Driftwood Avenue, a Toronto Community Housing building. With the reduced funding, it was decided to focus on fewer neighbourhoods and, after consultation with many groups, it was determined to direct their work to Edgeley Village, including the Driftwood and Shoreham neighbourhoods.

Anna-Kay Brown, an Edgeley Village resident, was reluctant to get involved with ANC. Brown, like many other people moving to Jane-Finch, believed it would be a temporary move so no need to get involved. Residents wanted to secure a job and make enough money to leave because people wanted their kids to go to a better school outside the area. People wanted more programs for their children and better access to services. Residents were simply too busy trying to navigate oppressive systems, working in unsafe environments for low salaries, or simply trying to survive one day to the next. Brown, an insightful young woman, aptly describes how she felt about moving into the Jane-Finch community 2008.

> At first I heard all the stories about Jane-Finch, and I was like, "No, I did not want it," I protested. I carried on, but I was seven months pregnant, so the chances within that time to get another place… My housing worker really suggested that I take it. So, I did. I was quite unhappy for the first few months—for the first two years—until I started to get to know my neighbours. It just so happened when I moved here a string of violence started to happen and there were more shootings. This was around 2008. That really just stressed me out because it added on to all the negative things that I had heard about the community. My friends, they didn't want to come to visit me here, so I was trying to get out of here as fast as possible. But, as I said, after the two years passed by and I got to know the community more and started to engage more with my fellow neighbours, I started to realize, you know, it's not so bad. I had a good neighbour who said to me, "You know, there's ANC—Action for Neighbourhood

Change—you should come and check it out and volunteer with us." That's what I did, and my volunteering started from there.[485]

For many years, the ANC provided training for residents to strengthen their skills. They worked with residents to respond to issues in the community, including hosting forums, advocating around issues, and building leadership capacity.

Anna-Kay Brown was a long-term and determined volunteer with Action for Neighbourhood Change. She described some of the activities of the ANC.

> If you want to talk about some of the work that we did—one of the biggest things that we did was a back-to-school event where we tried to give out over 200 backpacks to the residents. We would have workshops and CPR courses. We tried to figure out what the community needed and then to cater to that. A lot of those things that were needed was certain training for jobs they were doing, so you would always get people for those activities—financial literacy courses, March break workshops from Monday to Friday for that week at Brookview Middle School.[486]

Neighbourhoods under stress

The United Way continued to conduct research to bring attention to the issue of poverty, develop new initiatives, and offer those new programs or projects to low-income communities across the city. In 2004, Frances Lankin, then president and CEO of the United Way of Greater Toronto, stated, "Healthy neighbourhoods are the hallmark of Toronto's civic success. Their strength comes from the rich mixtures of cultures, safe streets, abundance of green space, diversity of shops and cultural amenities, and the social infrastructure of community services and programs."[487] Lankin, as Minister of Health in the Rae (NDP) government supported the establishment of community

---

485   Anna-Kay Brown interview (Toronto: York Woods Library, Black Creek Living History Project, September 2019).
486   Brown interview.
487   "Strong neighbourhoods: A call to action" (United Way of Greater Toronto, 2004).

health centres and attended the Black Creek Community Health Centre's grand opening in 1991.

Mayor David Miller also understood the importance of healthy neighbourhoods. "Neighbourhoods are what make this city great. We must value what is distinct about our neighbourhoods and recognize that which has value beyond its cost."[488]

MP Judy Sgro, in her "Task Force Report on Urban Issues," pointed to the need to address the marginalization of the poor in cities, as a critical element of the broader reinvestment needed to ensure the long-term sustainability of our cities. She warned that, "Our urban areas are home to a growing number of vulnerable people, and more must be done to address social problems such as poverty, drug and alcohol abuse, and marginalization."

Sgro's report noted that the concentration of poverty in North York between 1981 and 2001 was increasing. "There were four more neighbourhoods in 2001 that had more than half of their families living in poverty. Two of these are in the former City of North York—one in the Flemingdon Park community, with a family poverty rate of 57.8%, and the other in the Glenfield-Jane Heights area (Jane-Finch), with a 50.1% poverty rate." The report indicated that children and youth, single mothers, recent immigrants, and low-income elderly were typically over-represented in the neighbourhoods and experienced day-to-day hardship. Low incomes concentrated poverty and intensified the problems people face every day.

Poverty intensified in five communities, with the most prominent being the Jane-Finch community, where formerly "high" poverty neighbourhoods evolved into "very high" poverty areas, and where others that had "lower" or moderate" levels had "high" poverty. "Between 1981 and 2001, the total population of North York grew by 8.7%; economic families by 9%; but "poor" economic families by 80.5%."[489]

≈

488   David Miller, "Inaugural Address" (City of Toronto, news release, December 2, 2003).
489   Judy Sgro, Task Force Report on Urban Issues (North York: 2002).

The study, "Poverty by Postal Code: Geography of Neighbourhood Poverty," came out in 2004. It was done by the Canadian Council on Social Development for the United Way and reported that there were higher-poverty neighbourhoods in the former City of North York than in any of the other former cities.

Poverty By Postal Code also revealed that in 1991, there were 80,590 children living in higher poverty neighbourhoods in Toronto, but by 2001 the number had increased to 160,890—almost a one hundred per cent increase in just ten years. The number of adults also increased by that amount, youth by sixty per cent, but the number of seniors by only thirty-six per cent.

The story of newcomers revealed inequity in pay and in occupation.

> Data from the 2001 census shows that even with a university degree, recent newcomers earn only 71% of what Canadian-born university graduates earn, and 60% of newcomers to Canada do not work in the same occupational field as they did before coming to Canada. The number of immigrant family persons living in poverty increased 125% over the 20-year period, compared to a far smaller 13% rise in the number of Canadian-born family persons in poverty.

> Immigration is essential to the future prosperity of Canada, yet the findings from this study show that immigrant families are experiencing increasing difficulty getting a firm economic foothold in their new homeland. The high cost of housing, coupled with many barriers to entering the labour market in the occupational fields in which they are trained are all contributing to growing poverty and growing poverty concentration. [490]

The Strong Neighbourhood Task Force was formed in April 2004 to take up the challenge of a report released by the Toronto City Summit Alliance called, "Enough Talk: An Action Plan for the Toronto Region.[491] The Task Force, consisting of the United Way and the City of Toronto, with the

---

490 United Way of Greater Toronto and the Canadian Council on Social Development, Poverty By Postal Code: The Geography of Neighbourhood Poverty, 1981–2001 (Toronto: United Way, April 2004)

Toronto City Summit Alliance, "Enough Talk: An Action Plan for the Toronto Region (Toronto, 2003)

support of the provincial government, released a report in 2005 "The Strong Neighbourhoods—A Call to Action." Their goal was to build an action plan for revitalizing Toronto neighbourhoods. Their report indicated "…we are united in a common belief that Toronto's health and prosperity are closely tied to the well being of its neighbourhoods."

This report led to the "Building Strong Neighbourhoods Strategy," launched in 2005, which outlined a three-pronged approach for revitalizing the thirteen priority neighbourhoods with a long-term commitment to strengthen them through coordinated investment and local resident leadership.

Laurel Rothman, a former resident and one of the founding board members of the Jane/Finch Centre, submitted a report to the Strong Neighbourhoods Task Force in February 2005, while she was working for the Family Services Association of Toronto [now call Family Service Toronto].

> Addressing issues of basic needs is fundamental in any community regeneration plan. The community infrastructure must be present to ensure that people have easy access to food, income supports and housing. For most individuals and families, secure housing is necessary to enable them to connect to other types of community infrastructure. Clearly, income security is related to the ability to find and keep secure housing. Meeting these basic needs is a precursor to strengthening social networks which are important qualitative contributions to neighbourhood vitality. In other words, if people do not have secure housing or income, they are not likely to have time or resources to contribute to social networks.[492]

The report also defined community infrastructure. As part of that definition, Rothman noted that, "Municipalities developing 'strong' infrastructure will integrate physical and social planning and development and will invest adequately in both. Thus, for a strong infrastructure to exist in a locality it

---

492   Laurel Rothman, "Strong Neighbourhoods Task Force: Research Product Two: The Role of Community Infrastructure in Building Strong Neighbourhoods" (Family Services Association of Toronto, 2005).

is critical that there is adequate investment in both physical and social types of infrastructure."[493]

Another report was prepared for the Strong Neighbourhoods Task Force in November 2004 and submitted by Christa Freiler, a former researcher for the Social Planning Council of Metropolitan Toronto. In her report, it spoke to the impacts of highly concentrated poverty.

> Concentrated poverty has a 'multiplying effect,' particularly when there are clusters of high poverty neighbourhoods beside each other. High concentration poverty neighbourhoods are also presumed to lead to social and economic polarization, divisions among people along racial and other lines, and a threat to community and national social cohesion. It is feared that concentrated poverty will lead to increased crime, racial tensions, 'anti-social behaviour,' and health problems among individuals living in these neighbourhoods. The effects on children's development and future life prospects are particularly worrying.[494]

The community did, in fact, have several community-based organizations attempting to respond to both the needs of the community and to the many reports and funding opportunities coming its way, but short-term funding did not and could not resolve the systemic issues facing the community. Yet, short-term grants continued to be the norm with the exception of the Action for Neighbourhood Change funding.

Neighbourhood-oriented youth strategies

The United Way announced the Youth Challenge Fund (YCF) in 2006 and designated its funding towards the thirteen priority neighbourhoods. In the Jane-Finch community, some initiatives that benefited from capital investments from the YCF were The Spot, Firgrove Enrichment Program, PEACH, and San Romanoway Revitalization Association. Other groups of youth-serving organizations received funding for programs and services.

---

493 Rothman, "Strong Neighbourhoods."
494 Christa Freiler, "Why Strong Neighbourhoods Matter: Implications for Policy and Practice" (Toronto: Strong Neighbourhoods Task Force, November 4, 2004).

On February 14, 2006, City Council adopted the Toronto Youth Strategy that included a youth strategy panel. The panel of thirteen people included youth, community-based youth-serving organizations, city councillors, one funder representative, the labour sector, and the private sector. It was established to advise the mayor and the city council on actions required to implement the strategy. The implementation of the Toronto Youth Strategy was guided by five principles: access, equity, communication, opportunity, and action.

In 2007, the Toronto Community Housing Corporation approved its implementation plan for a new children and youth strategy with clear deliverables for a three-year transition process. Its intent was to transition the delivery of children's programming to alternate partners; enhance youth programming; support economic development opportunities for youth; and build a new organizational structure. By 2010, it was hoped that TCHC would have decreased their children's programs by eighty per cent while at the same time, increase youth programming from twelve to thirty-five locations. [495]

Police take aggressive action

With provincial funding, the Toronto Police also added a new initiative called the Toronto Anti-Violence Intervention Strategy, known as TAVIS. It was set up in 2006 to curb violence in high-crime areas as determined by the police. It was formed following the "Summer of the Gun" in the city in 2005, and after the murder of Jane Creba. Of the city's seventy-eight homicides, sixty-seven per cent were gun-related, a rate double that of the previous year. TAVIS was funded by the McGuinty Liberal government with the intention of being a multi-pronged, "community-based" approach to reducing violence.

From a community perspective, it was basically an armed occupation force invading the community. The implementation of TAVIS meant arbitrary stops and searches, "carding," and police violence against Black and racialized youth. Carding involved police stopping, questioning, and documenting

---

495   Board of Directors, "Children and Youth Strategy—Implementation Update" (Toronto Community Housing, February 13, 2008).

individuals when no offense was actually being investigated. This new practice was largely directed at male members of the Black community, a reflection of the demographics of where police were most often deployed. The data that was collected went into a permanent database that police said was used when searching for connections and possible witnesses and suspects, following crimes.[496] That database was accessible by other police forces and anyone requesting "criminal checks." Meanwhile, Black and racialized youth tell stories of being subjected to police raids, random searches, intimidations, and questions when stopped on the street.

John Sewell, head of the Toronto Police Accountability Strategy group and a former Toronto mayor said, "It's not creating stability and security in neighbourhoods; it's really causing upset. I'm not sure it was ever useful, the idea of just streaming in cops who don't know the area. I don't get it."[497]

While TAVIS was "adjusted" over the years, the response from people in certain neighbourhoods around the city like Rexdale and Jane-Finch indicated that it was too aggressive, and the youth felt criminalized and harassed in their own neighbourhoods and elsewhere.

Toronto Police Services Board Chair Alok Mukherjee came to believe that TAVIS did not serve the community. "The concern that I had, and I hear more and more, is that those other components of TAVIS did not get the same level of attention and were not taken with the same degree of seriousness as the enforcement piece. And TAVIS ultimately becomes simply synonymous with an enforcement piece. And that's when it becomes, in my mind, counterproductive."[498]

According to the *Toronto Star*, the latest available numbers they found were from 2008. "TAVIS officers made 108,796 community contacts, resulting in 2,640 arrests and 168 firearms seized. Put another way, one gun for every 650 contacts."[499]

496   Patty Winsa and Jim Rankin, "TAVIS Police Unit in Eye of the Storm" (Toronto Star, September 27, 2013).
497   Winsa and Rankin, "TAVIS."
498   Winsa and Rankin, "TAVIS."
499   Winsa and Rankin, "TAVIS."

The *Globe and Mail* reporter, Joe Friesen, was covering stories in Jane-Finch, and he wrote an article called, "A Show of Community, Not Force." The article described how a white van pulled into the Firgrove complex, the back doors opened, and twelve uniformed police officers entered the common courtyard that had children, teenagers, and parents. The officers were part of the TAVIS crew who searched a young man the night before and found a knife. "They come out as if they had just landed in Kandahar," said Mwarigha, the manager of Toronto Community Housing Unit 18. "They look like a real power force. If I was in trouble, I'd want them on my side. Of course, some of the youths are going to be scared." Mwarigha felt strongly that the show of force from police threatens to undo everything he was trying to build in Firgrove. Mwarigha went to see the 31 Division superintendent the following day to let them know that he was selling a different concept of community safety. "It would be a lot better if they would just work with us. (Ours) is not a Rambo approach to solutions."[500]

Shortly after TAVIS was initiated and following the shooting of Jordan Manners in 2007, another police initiative put police officers into the schools. The program was referred to as the School Resource Officer Program (SRO). The intent of the program was to have officers in the school to build relationships with the students. The officers participated in many activities; trips, camping, basketball games, school dances and parent-teacher nights. "We are not here to put armed officers in the school, to criminalize kids, or arrest kids. [People] should look beyond the outside, look beyond the uniform, look beyond the gun and see the person. We wear a uniform. We wear a gun; it's the tool of the trade. It's not the only thing that defines us."[501] Did they really think that armed police officers could be other than intimidating to children and racialized youth in a school setting?

From the beginning it was controversial. The Jordan Manners report (The Road to Health—The Report on School Safety), after extensive consultation with the schools and community, did not recommend this practice. Neither

---

500   "The Globe Sends a Reporter Among Us."
501   Carl James, Life at the Intersection, 98.

was the community consulted about this new initiative. "Ten years ago, our board made a mistake by not consulting the public, and not listening to the voices in the community," said TDSB trustee Tiffany Ford. She also indicated that the SRO program was flawed because it focused on having police at schools in only the most racialized and marginalized areas. "Our schools are meant to reinforce the power of education and not the power of stigmatization," she said.[502]

Black, marginalized, and criminalized youth, and families of those youth, knew the program was harmful to their children. Critics of the program argued that armed officers in schools intimidate students. They also raised concerns about racial and anti-immigrant bias.[503]

Carl James, in *Life at the Intersection,* explained the debate on police presence in the schools.

> Some argued that the presence of police would provide a level of safety and security to students and teachers, making the schooling environment more conducive to learning. Others argued that the presence of police in schools could instead cause students to be anxious, thereby making the environment even less hospitable for learning and possibly resulting in students choosing not to attend. Opponents also argued that a potential consequence of police presence in schools is the criminalization of students, which would contribute to the reputed school-to-prison pipeline. Generally, there was a fear that the presence of police would give the impression that the school is "bad," thereby validating the stigma of the community.[504]

A staff report was presented to the Toronto District School Board recommending that the controversial program end. The authors had consulted with students, staff and parents through surveys, held student focus groups and community meetings over a six-week period. While the results from the consultation indicated that the majority had a generally positive impression,

502 Andrea Gordon, "TDSB Votes Down Police Presence in High Schools" (Toronto Star, November 22, 2017)
503 John Pieti, "End Program that Puts Police Officers in Some Toronto Schools (Toronto: CBC News, Nov. 13, 2017).
504 Carl James, Life at the Intersection, 97.

forty-six per cent said they were not sure they wanted the program to continue. Eleven per cent, or 1,715 participants, said the presence of an officer intimidated them, and 2,207, or fourteen per cent, said that they felt watched and targeted as a result. The board indicated that their priority was "to mitigate against the differentiated and discriminatory impact of the SRO program" as described by students and communities. The SRO program ended in 2017, the same year that TAVIS ended.[505]

Sam Tecle shared a story of one of his experiences with the police.

> There was a heavy police presence—police were always around. They came up to us a lot and I know now that the things that they did back then were completely illegal. I mean, knocking on my door, coming in and asking us questions when I was young and at home taking care of my siblings. I was pretty young, as my parents had shiftwork and babysitting was expensive and all that. The police would have their badges and just put them in the peephole on the door, and 'Shoot, it's the police!' and I'd have to let them in. They would question us even though we were underage minors. So, the police were always close by, around, and that is an issue for young people.[506]

In November of 2005, Prime Minister Paul Martin came to the Jane-Finch community to announce fifty million dollars in funding for community agencies working against guns and gang violence and for youth justice projects. While he visited some institutions in the area and a housing complex, his visit brought undue negative attention to Jane-Finch. The announcement [of funding] was welcomed but making the announcement in an already marginalized and stigmatized neighbourhood further reinforces its stigmatization. Not a good choice. "The Prime Minister's visit served to re-confirm Jane and Finch as a national symbol of crime, poverty and violence."[507]

---

505 Shanifa Nasser, "TDSB Votes Down Police Presence in High Schools" (Toronto: CBC News, Nov. 2017).
506 Tecle interview.
507 Carl James, Life at the Intersection, 40.

People in authority at the city level also perpetuated the negative image of communities such as Jane-Finch. Reporter Rosie DiManno from the *Toronto Star* wrote about Police Chief Bill Blair's comments in "What's on the street starts at home."[508] The article spoke about gang and gun activity in the entertainment district on weekends and that the activity stems from people who live in the neighbourhoods of Jane-Finch, Rexdale, Scarborough, Brampton, or Mississauga who come down to the [entertainment] district on the weekend, along with their "weapons and propensity for violence down into this neighbourhood."[509] Of course visitors from out of province and other countries also came to this district.

There were also people in authority, like the former mayor David Miller, a University of Toronto Law School graduate, who grew up in a single-parent family and who adamantly rejected blaming single mothers for problems in Jane-Finch. There are professors who championed communities like Jane-Finch. For example, York professor Dennis Raphael said, "These communities are making people sick, but [...] it's more about raising people's incomes than razing buildings."[510] Doug Young, also a professor at York, argued that Jane-Finch was the result of three ideas that collided in the 1960s. They included the need for public housing, the desire to experiment with urban planning, and the opening up of Canada's immigration policy to non-whites."[511] Opening up the policy to non-whites did not create the problems, rather newcomers from poor countries who came to Canada, suffered racism, discrimination, and poverty.

Youth-supporting organizations

Young people cannot be blamed for the poor planning of this community. There have been several successful local youth initiatives that have been started by young people in the community. Some thrived such as The Spot, a program of the Jane/Finch Centre at the Yorkgate Mall, and others succeeded for a period before ending.

---

508 Richardson, "Canada's Toughest Neighbourhood."
509 Richardson, "Canada's Toughest Neighbourhood."
510 Richardson, "Canada's Toughest Neighbourhood."
511 Richardson, "Canada's Toughest Neighbourhood."

Friends in Trouble was started by Antonius Clarke, who moved to Canada with his family from Barbados and settled in the Jane-Finch community. He attended the local schools and in Grade 12 became the student-council president. He was "underwhelmed" by the student council, so he did something to challenge himself. "I created the Friends in Trouble to help me fill the void that I didn't get to fulfill through my role as school president. And doing the community involvement work also gave me some sort of, what I would call, courage." [512] He also wanted it to provide programs that would engage and captivate the attention of youth that would lead them to do what they wanted to do. Clarke became the executive director of Friends in Trouble and Friends in Trouble became a viable organization focused on youth for many years. Through that process, he and others learned a great deal about organizations, boards, administration, and programming.

The Belka Enrichment Centre (BEC) was initiated by two teachers who were beaten up once by youth in the community. One of those teachers, Dennis Keshinro, was born and grew up in Nigeria, moved to Toronto and lived in a high-rise on the corner of Jane and Finch. Rather than move from the area, they committed their time and resources to supporting youth to help them move beyond their anger and despair by providing positive alternatives. Keshinro remains the main force behind Belka Enrichment Centre. BEC was registered as a non-profit organization in 2001, with an aim to support children and youth of low income and inner-city communities secure economic self-reliance, equality, power, and civil rights. Its emphasis is placed on the belief that youth have the power within themselves to leave positive impacts on their communities.

Success Beyond Limits (SBL), located in Westview Centennial Secondary School, is another example of an innovative program established to reduce the impact of external factors that negatively affect the educational success of youth in Jane-Finch. Their beginnings started in a parking lot. A community meeting was held in 2005 with educators, community agency staff and parents whose youth attended Westview, to discuss the growing drop-out rates of students. After the meeting, some residents and community stakeholders debriefed in the parking lot and further discussed the challenge of

---

512   Antonius Clarke telephone interview, June 2019.

youth transitioning from Grade 8 to Grade 9. Youth were just not prepared. Studies have shown that youth in high school needed to have sixteen credits by the age of sixteen to reduce their chances of dropping out, and many did not have those credits. From those discussions came the inspiration for SBL.

By 2006, this group of activists, under the umbrella of a previous model, came up with an innovative idea to work with youth, prior to their entering high school, to earn a credit through a summer program. At the time, the TDSB had reservations about this idea, but the innovators went ahead with changing the structure of learning and providing the necessary supports, (e.g. food, transportation, and mentorship). They held their summer program at York University, which welcomed the youth to the campus. They started with about sixty youth, and over time, the program grew in numbers to 110, and the Grade 8 students were able to earn their first high school credit with the support of mentors—mentors who were in Grade 11 or 12.

In 2010, Success Beyond Limits became incorporated and received charitable status. Throughout the school year, it has an office in Westview where it operates a youth space—where staff support youth during the school day, run an after-school program, and where they connect youth to an array of diverse opportunities.

While moments of positive energy impacted the community, encouraged opportunities, and re-energized those who are engaged, the work to improve, challenge and fight for what is needed and deserved continued into the 2010s.

CHAPTER EIGHT

The Struggle Continues

A community farm

Food justice persisted as an issue in the community and members in the community learned that the Everdale Environmental Learning Centre was interested in the vacant land on the corner of Jane and Steeles next to the Black Creek Pioneer Village. Meetings and negotiations began and, in 2012, the newest community-based organization was established. The Black Creek Community Farm set up its office in the original farmhouse on the land and production began. Their purpose was to improve food security, reduce social isolation, and improve employment and education outcomes. Along with the farm, the Jane/Finch Centre, Black Creek Community Health Centre, and other partners formed the Black Creek Food Justice Network to fight for food security and food equity. The farm is another example of residents coming together to fight for what they wanted and needed.

The eight-acre property includes pristine farmland, a heritage farmhouse and barn, and a surrounding forest that extends down into the Black Creek ravine. It has certified organic vegetable fields, a forest trail and food forest, four-season greenhouses, an outdoor classroom, pavilion, and a bake oven, as well as a mushroom garden, chickens, and beehives. Executive director Leticia Deawuo, along with staff, took pride in welcoming thousands of visitors to the farm each year. Like Pioneer Village, the farm has become a place to visit in the Jane-Finch community, a place for social activities and community meetings for people of all ages.

Community schools under threat

When the Toronto District School Board suggested school enrollment was declining in this part of the city, a community meeting was held with over 250 participating. Prominent officials from across the city attended and heard articulate arguments from parents and students who were committed to keeping the schools open. Everyone knew that the subway was being extended and along with that would come residential development. Two more meetings were held with the second one ending in frustration, confusion, and uncertainty about the future of the schools in the area. The TDSB wanted to merge schools in hopes of opening new sources of much-needed revenue through the sale of properties. Five schools were in question: Blacksmith, Gosford, Driftwood and Shoreham Public Schools and Brookview Middle School that combined had more than two thousand students. All these schools were located north of Finch near Jane Street.

Trustee Payne indicated that there were twelve Accommodation Review Committee reviews happening across the City. "We've got some schools in our area that are at 61% enrollment and below, so it's just a matter of looking at how we can reconfigure these schools." Chris Spence, the director of education for the TDSB at that time, was advocating for a kindergarten to Grade 8 model. "I believe that fewer transitions, and the opportunity to have a critical mass of students in the school to drive staffing so we can have special teachers, is going to be beneficial to our students." Anthony Perruzza, city councillor and member of the review committee, pointed out that with the TTC subway system extending into the community along with the Light Rail trains (LRT) planned for Finch Avenue from Keele Street, there would be an increase in the population of families with children attending the local schools. The community won this battle—no schools were closed or integrated.[513]

Anna-Kay Brown became the co-chair of the Jane Finch Education Action group and shared her experience of the public-school system in 2019.

> Right now, we're dealing with the cuts. Before the cuts, we were dealing with infrastructure issues, which we'll still deal with because of the cuts. We're dealing with the lack of resources that we're still going to be dealing with because of the cuts. We were in a position where we were talking with the school board and the superintendents

513   "Three Democratic Heated Debates On the Future of Our Schools" (York West Advocate, April 2010).

about some of the issues that were in the schools, and how we can resolve them at a community level.

So, for example, I had a conversation with Westview [Centennial Secondary School]. They had three or four education assistants who helped kids who are having difficulty in how they learn. They had to let go two of those positions. They had to let go of caretakers, so that meant they had to close twelve classrooms. Their classrooms are looking at over 40–45 students per class. They also had to cut the majority of their classes and had to let go of teachers because of the mandatory classes that have to be done on-line. One of the things I brought up to them was how many computers do they have in their school that the kids in the school can use. The Yorkwoods Public Library is now closed for two years (kids used their computers) and also, how many kids at home even have computers or laptops or anything they can use for even the Internet.

These were some of the questions I left with the school to be able to figure out and how as a community we were going to address these things, because we know at the end of the day the school board, when it comes to us as a community, that we end up having to solve our own problems. That shouldn't be so, but it often times is. Due to bureaucracy, by the time everyone drags their feet, a whole year, two years, three years—all of those kids graduate, and nothing got done. I totally agree that it shouldn't be the community's work to do, but sometimes we have to advocate. The education system has not worked well in this community. The education system is not reflective of this community. There is nothing much there to stimulate the majority of the kids. For instance, like in high school, that should be a time when young people can get an idea of what they want to do after high school. This is where they should be able to go do an apprenticeship in mechanics or carpentry. This is where, maybe a grade 10 or 11, in their semester, they are doing these things. They have to find out what they are good at, and our schools are not equipped to be able to do those things for young people.[514]

514 Brown interview.

Byron Gray, manager for many years at The Spot, became the manager of the York University—TD Community Engagement Centre and had some thoughts about the impact of changes in the education system.

> I think the biggest shift that I've seen was removing the OAC (Ontario Academic Credit) from our curriculum and getting students at the age of seventeen into post-secondary, or the workforce, for that matter. That means that the level of maturity and time to develop mentally was shortened. And, they are going to be graduating at an even younger age. So, you're going to have therapists graduate and be twenty-three years old. How much life have they been able to live to use that as part of their experience and a part of their work or careers? I think that was a huge blow to the development of young people. It forced them to grow up a little faster than they should have. It has been a bit of a detriment to youth development on a whole, I think.
>
> Given our current political climate with Doug Ford and the cuts, they're feeling it. There are larger class sizes. There's a lack of teacher support. Some classrooms have closed in schools to maintain budgets, which give students less space to be in and to explore. With class limitations, you can't take a certain number of courses anymore, they are eliminated so they can relocate teachers. Students are having a hard time graduating with the right classes they need, or they have to wait a full semester before that course is offered. It's become challenging for them.
>
> On the other hand, it sparked a bit of civic engagement for a lot of young people—we saw huge walkouts by the students, but on the other hand, they are suffering in the actual academic piece—of graduating, taking their courses, having to take night school, which disrupts life because you're going to school in the morning or at night, having to do homework between that. If you had to have a job—it's another challenge. There is a lot of burden on the students now.[515]

---

515 Gray interview.

Talisha Ramsaroop, a former resident and a former community planner with Social Planning Toronto, works in York's TD-Community Engagement Centre. She also had something to say about the education system.

One of the other things that I see happening is the changes to education. Our schools are already underfunded. Our young people already have so many barriers to face, but now you are being put in class sizes where their classes are forty students. Or you put them in class sizes where you no longer have support for students with special needs or students who need special care, so that's something that worries me. There are so many issues young people are already facing that adding more cuts to their plate can only further hinder them.

One of the things that makes me really happy is spending a lot of time in the high schools now. One of the things I've been seeing is that young people are a lot more engaged and critical than I was when I was in high school. I didn't start thinking about these things until university, but all of our placement students that we've had from the ACE program, and all of the young people I see in the high schools when I'm going in to do scholarships clinics or workshops on what to expect in post secondary, they are all so politically aware and politically engaged. It is incredible!

All of our high schools walked out—every single one of them walked out with posters and were on the main corners about the education cuts. I don't think that kind of stuff was happening in our high schools, back in the day. I met this young woman who literally put Post-it notes on every single locker in Westview to remind her peers that the walkout was happening. That type of organizing—that type of political awareness—I think that our young people are now activists in this community. That is one of our strengths right now and I think in the future. I'm really excited for them to vote and for them to continue to make the changes that they are making.

In terms of the fight against racism, I think we manage to change in the sense that young people are talking about that very early as opposed to kind of learning about it in university or college or after high school and kind of focusing on it. Now we have a lot of teachers in our high schools that are from the community which is a really cool thing because they are now teaching. There are just a lot of people who are from the community who are now coming back to the community as teachers, or as social workers. That creates a unique perspective, but that's a change as well because when I was growing up, none of the teachers were from the area. That's a change for me and its never enough—we definitely need a lot more work to create a society that truly doesn't have racism and poverty. But with those little things we have managed to create change. Even the way media talks about Jane and Finch has changed a lot since I was younger.[516]

Inadequate responses to youth

Some things do not change. An issue is identified, and funding is allocated at the time of a crisis, but it is soon reduced or eliminated. The Roots of Youth Violence report was commissioned by the Dalton McGuinty government in 2007 and written by Dr. Alvin Curling (former speaker of the Ontario legislature) and Roy McMurtry (former chief justice of Ontario). It called for $15.8 million for implementation. Alvin Curling reflected, "I don't think they're addressing it in a forceful manner at all. If they were more aggressive, we would have been further along."[517]

The Roots of Youth Violence report spoke about many issues, for example gun violence, drugs and drug dealing, muggings, intimidation, gangs, and numerous other issues that stem from racism, inequality, and poverty. According to the *Toronto Star* editorial board, "If anything, the problems they identified have become even more pronounced as the city has become more economically and socially polarized. That trend has been going on for years, transforming what was once a largely middle-class city into one marked by islands of wealth surrounded by pockets of deep poverty."[518]

Those pockets of poverty have metastasized into oceans of poverty.

516   Ramsaroop interview.
517   Jennifer Pagliaro, "The Lost Decade" (*Toronto Star*, October 13, 2018).
518   Editorial Board, "Toronto Has Lost a Decade in the Fight Against Gun Violence" (Toronto Star, November 19, 2018).

≫

Many youth-oriented reports were developed, and projects continued into the 2010s. Some led to short-term projects where insufficient funding made them less successful, and some actually led to changes. For example, the *Ontario Youth Action Plan* (2012), *Stepping Up—A Strategic Framework to Help Youth Succeed* (2013), *Toronto Youth Equity Strategy* (2014) and the *Toronto Youth Engagement Strategy* (2014), to name a few. In the *Ontario's Youth Action Plan* report, it was noted how positive changes could be seen in various studies.

> Ontario has made progress in partnership with young people and their families. Our high school graduation rate has gone from 68 per cent in 2004 to 82 per cent in 2011, and our postsecondary participation rate of 64 per cent is among the highest in the world. Violent crime by youth is down 17 per cent compared to a decade ago. However, many youth—particularly minority and racialized youth—continue to face significant challenges and multiple barriers to success. Despite the leadership and efforts of individuals, communities, youth-serving organizations and different levels of government, too many kids in our province do not have access to the necessary supports, services and opportunities to succeed. In particular, the Review of Roots of Youth Violence report—authored in 2008 by former MPP and Speaker of the Legislative Assembly Dr. Alvin Curling and former Chief Justice of Ontario the Hon. Roy McMurtry—correctly identifies other challenges that disadvantaged youth face, such as racism and lack of culturally appropriate services." The report further said, "No child should be disadvantaged just because of where they live, the colour of their skin, their socioeconomic status or their religion.[519]

Children and youth are indeed disadvantaged because of where they live, the colour of their skin and their socioeconomic status. While some of the funds have made a difference, along with dedicated staff who do more than

---

519   Dr. Eric Hoskins and Madeleine Meilleur, "Ontario's Youth Action Report" (Toronto: August 22, 2012).

what they are funded to do, the community knows that short-term and inadequate resources ultimately leave the most vulnerable behind.

None of the strategies or plans addressed the systemic issues that impact youth from before the time they are born to when they grow up, if they live that long. Dr. Annette Bailey, an associate professor at the Daphne Cockwell School of Nursing at Ryerson University, suggested that, "Gun violence is a complex and multifaceted public health issue; one that is well-entrenched in social, political and economic conditions. Gun violence can be viewed as an infectious disease. It is widespread, deadly, and carries devastating consequences. This modern epidemic is killing Black youth more than anybody else and has inflicted trauma on family and friends." She stressed that gun violence has not received the same efforts "…that have worked to eradicate other deadly infectious diseases." Bailey's ten years of research into understanding grief and trauma experiences of adult and youth survivors of gun violence demonstrates how trauma is made worse by limited access to services, job losses, and often, marriage breakdowns. "The trauma is expressed as anxiety and feelings of hopelessness that leads to a domino of more gun violence."[520]

Loss in the community

Barry Rieder, community minister in the Firgrove community, both officiated and attended many funerals over the years, and after attending one funeral, Rieder thought about what happened and wrote a short reflection called "Grace and Forgiveness in the Midst of Tragedy."

> After the funeral of a 15-year-old, who was accidentally shot by his best friend, I was introduced to the father of the deceased and the father of the shooter at the funeral reception. After saying my condolences to the father of the deceased, I explained to the father of the shooter that I wanted to reach out to his son because in many ways there were two tragedies with this situation. After that, the father of the deceased said to the father of the shooter, "I am in great pain in losing my only son, but I do not blame you or your

---

520   Annette Bailey with Divine Velasco, "We need to Build a Culture of Peace to Fight Gun Violence" (Toronto: CBC Docs POV, 2018).

son for what happened. Now that I have no son, your son will now be my son." Then the two of them broke down and wept hugging each other as hard as they could. As I stepped back to give them the space they needed, they continued to embrace as they sobbed for what seemed like a good ten minutes. A group of community leaders also witnessed this powerful moment of grace and forgiveness. Eventually one of the Rasta elders in the community came and wrapped his arms around them giving them blessing and permission to move on.[521]

Rieder shared another sad experience.

In 2013, one of the things that happened was that there were six youth in the City of Toronto that lost their lives to gun violence. Four of them were from Jane-Finch; two of them were from Firgrove. The first was St. Aubyn, and St. Aubyn was such a lovable kid. He was actually killed by his best friend. What had happened was that they were fooling around with a gun, and you could ask why they had a gun, but part of the reason was that it's easier to get a gun than a job. But they were fooling around with the gun and they didn't realize there was a bullet still left in the chamber, so St. Aubyn died. Later in that summer, Tahj, another fifteen-year-old was killed at the Yorkwoods Plaza, right across from Firgrove. They were actually gunning for someone else and mistakenly shot him. I was part of the crisis response team, and I had taken a lead role with Tahj's family and supporting them through that.

During that time period, youth were doing tags on the buildings— at the rec centre, in tribute to Tahj and St. Aubyn like "Rest in peace, Skinny and Tubby"—that's what we called them in the community. Then housing would come along and whitewash over it; and then they would spray paint again, and then housing would whitewash over it; and they would spray paint it again and add some profanity, like "leave this the f... alone."

---

521   Rieder interview.

I approached the youth and asked, "Why don't we look at doing a memorial for the youth that would be more fitting?" So, we decided to do a memorial, but one of the conditions was that we not just focus on Tahj and St. Aubyn, knowing there had been some other youth in the community that had lost their lives. We decided to do a mural and focus on youth in the last fifteen years who had lost their lives due to violence. Unbeknownst to me is we came up with twelve names, and many I knew, some I hadn't. But it really struck me that a community of 382 households, over a period of fifteen years, twelve youths lost their lives to violence. Now if that happened in any other part of our country, outside a First Nations community, where youth are dying of suicide all the time, there would be complete outrage.[522]

The mural, called "Towards A Higher Journey" (using the acronym of Tahj's name), has twelve doves, each carrying a ribbon with a youth's name on the ribbon. Rieder read an article in the *Toronto Star* around that time that compared youth who died in Toronto to the Canadian soldiers killed in Afghanistan. In a ten-year period, approximately fifty-three youths in Toronto Housing had lost their lives to violence. During that same period of time, fifty-five Canadian soldiers lost their lives in Afghanistan. Rieder saw this as another war, "…that has ended up happening, that we don't talk about and that's called poverty."[523]

---

522   Rieder interview.
523   Rieder interview.

Tackling poverty

In 2014, the City of Toronto wanted to build strong neighbourhoods. Partnering with the Centre for Research on Inner City Health at St. Michael's Hospital, the United Way of Greater Toronto, and Woodgreen Community Services, they compared 140 city neighbourhoods through five different domains of neighbourhood well-being and measured inequalities between neighbourhoods. The domains included healthy lives, economic opportunities, social development, participating in decision-making and physical surroundings.

Each neighbourhood in the study was given a score within a range of 0 to 100, with the actual scores ranging from 21.38 to 92.0. Neighbourhoods with a score below 42.89 were identified as Neighbourhood Improvement Areas (NIAs). The lowest score (21.38) was the Black Creek neighbourhood, while the second lowest score of 24.39 was the Glenfield-Jane Heights neighbourhood—the north and south neighbourhoods of Jane-Finch. York University Heights and Downsview-Roding were also listed as NIAs, although not quite as low in score.[524]

When the Toronto Strong Neighbourhood Strategy (TSNS) was announced in 2013, the City planned to host consultations across the city, but for some reason the Jane-Finch community was not included for a consultation. Jane Finch Action Against Poverty wrote a letter to the City reminding them that Jane-Finch was a priority community and insisted that they be part of the consultations. The City agreed to this, so residents and workers worked hard doing door-to-door outreach—visiting youth, seniors, and parenting groups and as a result of this local outreach well over two hundred residents attended the consultation. It was the largest consultation done in the city, with more attending in Jane-Finch than all the other consultations on this issue across Toronto combined.

⌇

---

524   Social Development, Finance & Administration, "Toronto Strong Neighbourhoods Strategy 2020" (City of Toronto, 2011).

A few staff at the Jane/Finch Centre reviewed the City's TSNS Report and decided to host a meeting with several other organizations to discuss the report and to figure out how best to respond. One response was to do preliminary research to understand how funding was distributed, comparatively, in three other districts across the city. They looked at the number of staff and the funding received for services and programs in each of those areas and compared that information with the Jane-Finch area. Without extra funding, and with limited staff for this work, the Jane/Finch Centre took on that small piece of research.

Three areas were identified—wards 39 to 41 in the northeast; wards 20 to 31 in the south, and wards 13, 14, 18 in the southwest of the city—to compare with wards 7 to 9 in the northwest. With this preliminary research in hand, a meeting was organized, and representatives were invited from the federal, provincial, and municipal governments, along with the United Way. Only the United Way and Councillor Anthony Perruzza participated in the meeting. The community shared its information that clearly demonstrated less funding, and less staff supports for this part of Toronto.

The report, "Summary of Organizations and Services in Jane-Finch/Black Creek Area," (2014) can be criticized for not including institutions like community recreation centres, libraries or schools, but it was decided to focus on comparing community health centres and legal clinics' funding along with funding for community-based social service organizations randomly selected in each specific geographic area.

Ward	Population	Funding Allocation
7, 8, and 9 (northwest)	148,000	$951,055
39, 40, 41 (northeast)	185,150	$920,485
13, 14, 18 (downtown west)	152,005	$2,005,422
29, 30, 31 (downtown east)	151,795	$2,262,821

Community Partnership Investment program, City of Toronto[525]

525   Wanda MacNevin, "Summary of Organizations and Services in Jane-Finch/Black Creek Area" (North York: Jane/Finch Community and Family Centre, 2014).

While the populations were close in size, the amount of funds the City distributed in each of the areas downtown for that year were more than fifty per cent higher than those in the northwest and northeast wards. One could argue that rents for the long-established downtown community agencies were higher, their community services had been around longer, they had larger staff teams and they had larger facilities to maintain. Those working and living in the inner-city suburbs were trying to make the case that it was time for them to catch up; that the suburbs were vastly under-resourced by all levels of government.

By this time, the small planning group had expanded and agreed to conduct further research, calling itself the Jane Finch TSNS Task Force. With a small grant from York University's TD Community Engagement Centre, and a financial contribution from the Jane/Finch Centre, a research com mittee was formed that included staff from four local community organizations, university students, Professor Linda Peake from York University's City Institute, and staff from York's TD Community Engagement Centre. This project was led by the Jane/Finch Centre. Nathan Stern, who grew up in Jane-Finch and was attending York University, was hired to coordinate the literature review and the focus groups. Farid Chaharlangi, from the Jane/Finch Centre, was heavily involved in this initiative.

> We did lots of resident-led focus groups, did community-based research, and a report was produced, which talked about what community residents wanted to see in Jane Finch by 2020. That helped to give a direction, a mandate, to the Jane Finch TSNS Task Force in terms of the work that needs to be done. It was a strong mandate around social development, economic opportunities, social justice, addressing numerous issues from temporary agencies, workers' rights, inadequate minimum wage, healthy food, and public transit—which helped us also to form alliances during this time with groups like TTC Riders and the Fair Wage Coalition, etc. So, every time we get involved with some of these issues, we end up getting

involved in other campaigns, because they are all intersecting—kind of overwhelming in terms of the issues we are facing on all fronts.[526]

The final report included information from eight focus groups, encompassing diverse cultural, ethnic, and age groups; a description of the community; a policy context; and a description of the research methods, analysis, and recommendations.[527] This community-developed response was distributed widely to the premier's office, to the mayor's office, to MP Judy Sgro, to MPP Mario Sergio, and to the three city councillors in the area. It was also sent to bureaucrats relevant to the areas of study including Toronto Public Health, the Central Local Health Integration Network, and city services. Few responses were received from these politicians and bureaucrats.

The Jane-Finch TSNS Task Force table was expanded to include City staff. The United Way generously provided a pro-bono consultant who spent an afternoon with community representatives to further determine how this task force would function. The task force established sub-groups, each with a focus on a specific domain; all would come together monthly. While the Jane/Finch Centre staff led this process at the beginning, York University's Community Legal Aid Support Program staff took over the leadership in 2016 and co-led the process along with a community resident.

In 2018, the task force table decided to break away from the City of Toronto and operate on its own, as they found that the requirements from the City for their participation were too burdensome. The Task Force was re-named the Jane Finch Action Network (JFAN) and they advocated with all three levels of government, as well as institutions, to ensure that the social and economic health of the community was improved in whatever small ways they could accomplish.

---

526 Chaharlangi interview.
527 Jane Finch Task Force, Community Response to the TSNS 2020: What Neighbourhood Improvement Looks Like from the Perspective of Residents in Jane-Finch (North York: 2015).

New focus for neighbourhood change

Meanwhile, the United Way, building on conversations with residents and its learnings over the last ten years, brought the Action for Neighbourhood Change funding to an end. They decided to refocus to strengthen the capacity of communities to act on issues that matter to them and to be able to work alongside new partners to implement more effective solutions at the neighbourhood level.

In March 2019, under the new "Our Strong Neighbourhoods" initiative, Jane/Finch Centre applied for and received a two-year grant from the United Way. In developing its proposal for this grant, resident leaders and partners came together to select a key neighbourhood issue to focus on for the next few years. After looking deeply into existing resources and gaps in the community, the partners decided to tackle local economic opportunities and help strengthen pathways from education to employment.

Anna-Kay Brown got involved in this initiative and remains committed to this program.

> Our topic right now is economy—finding employment opportunities for community residents. So, we're working with York and working on the Finch West LRT with the Toronto Community Benefits Network (TCBN) around the initiatives they are doing with the LRT for employment. One of our next things was to create a roundtable of all people who were doing similar work to us and talk about how we can coordinate better so that we're not doing the same overlap work. Part of the problem in the community—there's always a few players doing the same work, and nobody is sharing among each other, so that we are not replicating the work or going after the same funding or resources. We're trying to see how we can really get those people at the table to have a serious conversation about working together.
>
> For now, we're at York creating a survey to find out what percentage of York staff is hired from the community. They can't tell us based on how they hire people with their data or system. Its going to be a survey—I'm not guessing the way its going to be set up as we are

in the process of working on it. We have two members from York that we meet with every month or every so often. We have [professor] Carl James on it and other people helping us and making sure it's ethical in the way we are proceeding with it. The overall goal of this survey is to find out how many people live in the community who are hired by York and even the possibility to find out their diverse backgrounds."[528]

University engagement continues

York University was another institution that recognized the value of collaboration and continued to find ways to support the community and to engage community residents. In 2010, the President's Task Force on Community Engagement released a report that reviewed current York University community initiatives. Among other suggestions, the report conveys that the inconsistencies throughout the university—both what is being done and how engagement is implemented—suggests that engagement should be more firmly embedded as a core tenet of the University Academic Plan, resource planning processes, and future strategic directions.

The report spoke to effective engagement that requires that the "inside be onside"—embracing diversity, responsibility for social justice, and democratic citizenship. The Task Force indicated that York University's ongoing relationship with its closest neighbour, the Jane-Finch community, remains one of its most important ones. They have "a civic responsibility to maintain close ties with the Jane-Finch community to support collaborative, community-based research, improved access to post-secondary education, community-capacity building initiatives, and sharing of university resources." [529]

York's position on community engagement "…provides an opportunity for York to distinguish itself and lead the dialogue with our community partners in shaping the role of higher education in building stronger communities."[530]

---

528 Brown interview.
529 "Towards An Engaged University: President's Task Force Report on Community Engagement, Final Report and Recommendations" (Toronto: York University, February 5, 2010).
530 "Towards An Engaged University".

In 2013, a one-day symposium in Jane-Finch called Connect the Dots brought together residents, organizers, community organizations, York faculty, and staff from the York University–TD Community Engagement Centre. A conference report was written by Suzanne Narain (Jane-Finch resident and York alumnus), and a student, Rajanie Kumar.

> The symposium sought to address both the historical and the contemporary oppressive structures, practices and relationships that have existed and continue to exist between York and the Jane-finch community. A key objective of this inaugural conference was to develop a dialogue between York and the Jane-Finch community surrounding issues of social justice, equitable research practices, and race and power relations in order to establish alternative practices that address the needs of the community and the university.[531]

Professor Michaela Hynie wrote an article, in consultation with local stakeholders, on the sustainability of a community-campus engagement centre in the changing environment in 2017. In that article, Dr. Hynie expanded on the multitude of initiatives between York and the community, including projects such as Connect the Dots.

> Residents expressed frustration in general at the disconnect between the high frequency with which they are consulted, studied and policed and the low rates of positive outcomes for residents. Some of the former two activities have been attributed to York University initiatives by faculty, students, or both. This is a caution to university members to refrain from 'doing research on' the community. It highlights the mistrust created by a history of research that has provided no benefit to community residents but is seen as promoting the careers of the researchers through publication and grants, a complaint that has often been raised in the context of community-based research.

531　Suzanne Narain and Rajanie Kumar, "Connect the Dots: Best Practices for Jane-Finch and York University Partnerships, Conference Report" (North York: December 11, 2013).

Since its inception, the CEC [York University–TD Community Engagement Centre] has been active in promoting community-based research in genuine partnership with community, supporting these research initiatives with funding, showcasing local examples of research partnership, offering a range of in-kind support to local research partnerships, and developing tools and activities to support collaborative research. This includes the Connect the Dots conference described under joint activities. Nonetheless, some frustration remains, and many university community members are still unfamiliar with partnership approaches to research. Finding spaces to air these issues is an ongoing and important issue.[532]

Through hard work and commitment, the CEC worked with local residents and service providers to establish guidelines for conducting research in the community. This started in 2013 at the Connect the Dots symposium and led to the Jane-Finch Community Research Partnership being established in 2016. "The need for a community ethics process is necessary to guide and inform how research is conducted in the community."[533] There was a desire for an institutional protocol for staff, students, and researchers whose work involved members of the Jane-Finch community. To develop that, the Community Research Partnership created an Ethics Advisory Board.

The Ethics Advisory Board identified five principles for conducting research in the Jane-Finch area that are contained in a document called, *Our Model: A Guide for Conducting Research in the Community*, released in 2019. The purpose of the partnership is to continue developing community-based research ethical procedures, processes, and principles that include community members as partners and knowledge creators in the research. In 2019, Ellie Perkins, a respected and community-minded professor, with assistance from community, along with other facilities at York, received a grant to continue this work. One goal was to provide support and create new ways for the

532 Michaela Hynie, "The Morning After: Stakeholder Reflections on the Sustainability of the Community-Campus Engagement Centre in the Changing Environment" (North York: 2017).

533 Sam Tecle, Abena Offeh-Gyimah, Talisha Ramsaroop, Lorna Schwartzentruber, Jane Finch Community Research Partnership, Symposium Report (North York: November 29, 2016).

community to access, and benefit from, research results. Another goal was to fight the stigmatization of Jane-Finch by outside researchers and allow community members to take the lead in building more respectful, ethical, and informed relationships between academic researchers and local community members and/or organizations.

≫

The ten-year grant that supported the York University–TD Community Engagement Centre ran out in 2016 and the university sustained it until 2019, when the university received an additional one-million dollar grant from the TD Bank to continue this valuable work. This speaks volumes about York's continued commitment to engage with the Jane-Finch community and about the generous contribution made by the Toronto Dominion Bank to this part of the city.

The success of the York University–TD CEC can also be contributed to its leadership. Following Sue Levesque, who was community oriented with passion, came Lorna Schwartzentruber as the new manager. She had great insight, sensitivity, and commitment to this community and grew many initiatives within the CEC. She left in 2018 to become the associate director of Access Programs and Community Engagement in the office of the Vice-Provost Academic at York, supporting York's commitment to build a more engaged university. The manager position was filled by Byron Gray, the long-time manager from the Jane/Finch Centre, who had an abundance of experience with youth and program innovation.

York University has come a long way in opening its doors to the community. Most recently, a safe space for youth, the Social Innovation Hub, opened at York University for Jane-Finch youth in January 2020. This was a partnership between Success Beyond Limits, an organization operating out of Westview Centennial Secondary School and the CEC, which aims to be a safe space for students from the community to access on-campus support. "We have a network of students from local high schools such as C. W. Jeffreys, Emery Collegiate, Downsview Secondary, and Westview Centennial," Talisha Ramsaroop from the Community Engagement Centre explained. The Hub is expected to provide workshops and research to help future students navigate post-secondary education, help them with resume writing, and accessing work-study programs. The space includes a lounge, a workstation, recreation amenities, and reading material. [534]

It was initially predicted in the 1960s that York would have a population of twenty-five thousand students. As of 2020, York University had Canada's third largest university, with 55,700 full and part-time students, eleven faculties and seven thousand faculty members and staff.

Humber River Hospital is built

While York University was building bridges to the community, the new state-of-the-art and fully digital Humber River Hospital opened its doors on October 18, 2015, on Wilson Avenue, just west of Keele Street. Tensions between the Jane-Finch community and the hospital continued to fester. MPP Mario Sergio wanted to build bridges between the community and the hospital, so he hosted a meeting with community organizations and residents in July 2016 with the new chief executive officer, Barbara Collins. That allowed Collins to explain their need to close the urgent care facility at the former York-Finch site because people were utilizing the urgent care at the new hospital. They could not afford to keep the Finch site open with only seeing twenty people or less at the urgent care every day. Meanwhile, they had four hundred people daily coming to the Urgent Care Department at the new hospital, along with eighty or ninety ambulances. Some residents in the community indicated that they did not feel safe going to the old hospital, as it was not well-maintained. They also felt they deserved to have access to the most updated equipment, rather than the old equipment at York-Finch.

~≈≈e

Members of the community spoke with staff at the Central Local Health Integration Network (Central LHIN is one of 14 LHINS established by the provincial government through the *Local Health System Integration Act*, 2006, to plan, fund and integrate health services at the local level) who agreed to attend a community meeting along with representatives from the hospital.

---

534   Ayesha Khan, "Social Innovation Hub" (*Downsview Advocate*, March 2020).

The intent was to urge the Central LHIN and the hospital to think about alternative ways for people in Jane-Finch to have access to urgent care and tests, without having to travel the six-plus kilometres to the new hospital. Travelling to the hospital meant having to take two buses or, in the case of sick children or adults, having to pay for a taxicab, should they not have access to a car. The meeting was useful in terms of raising awareness through an impactful presentation made by a local acting group called Nomanzland. Young people demonstrated through theatre, the impact of not having easier access to health care for people living in Jane-Finch.

HRH stepped forward to build bridges between the Jane-Finch community and the hospital by participating on committees, inviting community workers to the hospital for an orientation so that they could better utilize and refer residents, reaching out to hire locally, forming multiple patient-advisory committees, utilizing Black Creek Community Health Centre's Health Navigators to assist patients who utilized Urgent Care, as a few examples. Joe Gorman, Director of Public Affairs, became involved and accessible to the community. His ability to connect and engage began to win people over and to convince people that the hospital genuinely wanted to provide the best services possible to everyone in their catchment area.

Located near Keele Street and Wilson Avenue, HRH is a major acute care hospital with 1.8 million square feet with 656 patient beds. At that location, there were seven hundred physicians, 4,700 staff, 1,100 volunteers, 247,223 outpatient visits per year, 251,900 ambulatory and diagnostic visits and 4,297 births in 2020. As the first fully digital hospital in North American, Humber River Hospital wanted to ensure patients' comfort with eighty per cent of the rooms having a single bed with space for a family member to sleep. All rooms are "smart" with a bedside control terminal that allows patients to adjust lighting and set temperature, make video calls, access the internet, and review their medical records and test results.[535]

The Urgent Care closed in 2016 at the former Finch site. In 2017 several floors in the building were re-opened as a Reactivation Care Centre

---

535   Joe Gorman, Director of Public Affairs, Humber River Hospital (Email, November 2020).

for patients who no longer needed acute care services but found themselves waiting for an alternate facility for convalescence or long-term care.

For many years, the community complained about the racism, discrimination, and the lack of sensitivity at the hospital. The hospital hired Umwali Sauter in 2018 as Humber River's first ever manager of equity and inclusion. Her job was to ensure that an equity and inclusion lens is applied to every decision made at the hospital. Sauter attended local community meetings to engage with the community. There will always be complaints, but as long as the administration of the hospital is open to serving all people in the best way they can and, given their resources along with strong leadership at the top, Humber River Hospital may become better at serving a diverse population with respect and professionalism. Sauter stated, "I am here because Humber River Hospital wants to improve, wants to be fair, and wants to be equitable. I am proud to be here and to be part of making that happen."[536]

The HRH is no longer a local Jane-Finch community hospital, but a huge healthcare machine with the aim to improve the health of people who are sick and who come from great distances to seek care. Still, the loss of a local hospital within walking distance or an easy transit ride for multiple low-income communities in northwest Toronto remained a loss to the community. Residents can only hope that the hospital will provide the best possible care, regardless of where they live, their ethnicity, or their situation.

Planning to redevelop Firgrove

The Jane Finch Community Ministry of the United Church was embraced by the people of Firgrove and the broader Jane-Finch community. The ministry staff learned from the community and supported residents on issues of importance. When Toronto Community Housing announced that all the townhouses in Firgrove were going to be demolished and residents relocated, Barry Rieder worked diligently to assist residents in voicing their concerns and advocated alongside residents on their behalf.

This "award-winning" complex was built in the 1970s. Firgrove was the last social housing development built in Jane-Finch and yet, in recent years,

---

536   Umwali Sauter (Humber River Hospital website, 2020).

the townhouses started to crumble. Due to how poorly the buildings were constructed, coupled with normal wear and tear over the years, and neglect because of limited capital budgets, the buildings needed major improvements. The Mayor's Housing Task Force had allocated twenty-seven million dollars to repair the exterior and the interior of the townhouses. The community went through a planning process regarding the repairs; however, the engineers determined that they could not fix the townhouses as they were beyond repair.

Major repairs were already needed in the 1990s when Mike Harris was the premier of Ontario, but the Province did not allocate funds for maintenance to upgrade the townhouses. Rieder reiterated, "So, water damage from seeping through the roof basically rotted out the foundation of these buildings and the bricks. Even though we had 27 million to fix up the buildings, they were beyond repair."[537]

The townhouses were deemed uninhabitable, and residents were forced to relocate to various other Toronto Housing locations across the city. Rieder told the story about how people were assigned their new homes. "It was a deplorable process because how people were prioritized is that their names were attached to a number on a ping-pong ball in a bingo drum that was rolled around and whatever number popped up first, they got first pick of the available housing stock. They were quickly evicted and, in that process, was also the community ministry." No consideration was given to the needs of families with respect to any special needs of their children, nor distances to their places of work.

The most damaged townhouses, over one hundred units, were boarded up and fenced off, but no demolition had yet taken place as of 2021. The community was left wondering where the money had gone to improve the neighbourhood, when TCHC said they didn't have the funds to demolish the rotting townhouses.

> Just as recently as this spring [2018], they said they actually have money to rebuild Firgrove and they are now looking at demolishing the other half of the Grassways and the community is going to be

---

537   Rieder interview.

consulted around the designs and changes. It most likely won't be social housing, it will be a mixed community and I mean there are some benefits around that. But the concern is around what kind of supports and services and community amenities would be there for the community. So, they are probably looking at increasing the density, around four or five times in order to have the same kind of rent-geared-to-income units in the community. But the concern right now is that there is a swimming pool, a basketball court, the Firgrove Learning Centre—will those things be there in the community?[538]

Residents learned in the fall of 2020, that those remaining in Firgrove will be moved out by August 2021, and the demolition would begin in 2022. [As of October 2021, there are residents still remaining in the townhouses.] The Community Ministry found space in the local Firgrove Public School, adjacent to the community. While Rieder was grateful to secure the space, it is not accessible in the way his office was within the townhouse complex.

Precarious jobs predominate

Precarious employment in the community, and beyond the community, was a big concern to residents participating in the Jane Finch Action Against Poverty group. In 2018, it carried out research related to temporary and precarious workers and publicized their final report. Resident activists interviewed workers on their way to work, to learn about their issues, facilitated "Know your Rights" workshops, and advocated for enhancing workers rights, especially in the numerous temporary agencies in and around the Jane-Finch community. Farid Chaharlangi explained the efforts of JFAAP on this issue.

We've done a lot of outreach in the community, like at 5:00 in the morning, seeing hundreds of community residents going to the 905 areas [outside of the City of Toronto] because there aren't jobs in the community. JFAAP, with support from ANC around some of the funding aspects of it, BCCHC, as well as CLASP [Community Legal Assistance Support Program], we wanted to tackle this issue. We had done work on temp agencies for years. We knew lots of people in the

---

538   Rieder interview.

community who worked at temp agencies, but we decided that we would do even more outreach. Instead of doing door-to-door, this time we said, "Let's go to places where people are being picked up by temp agency buses and vans to go to work."[539]

This group of about fifteen people, mostly residents and activists, spread across the four intersections of Jane Street and Steeles Avenue West and, with lots of free coffee, talked to people about their issues, handed out flyers, and helped workers learn about their rights. One significant issue they learned about was that people walked a distance to the intersection at the border of Toronto and York Region prior to getting on a bus to go into the 905 regions. Otherwise, they had to pay a double fare.

Chaharlangi explains, "We called all of the temp agencies in the area, and the thing with the temp agencies is that some of them keep changing—they shut down and then re-open under different names. We called more than fifty of them and found that none of them were providing any jobs in the Jane Finch area. They were providing jobs in other parts of the city."[540]

Their research led to two reports of which one was produced by CLASP in partnership with JFAAP and the Jane/Finch Centre, and another one was led by residents and produced by JFAAP, describing experiences of people working in temporary agencies.

Leticia Deawuo shared her perspective of temporary employment agencies in the area.

> We have over a hundred temp agencies in our high immigrant community. The Workers Action Network studied the area from Steeles all the way to Wilson and Bathurst to Islington and in the bigger broader community, there are that many, even on Steeles [Avenue West]. Like I was walking along Steeles, and I was surprised how many temp agencies existed in one plaza alone. And then you see the sign boards of course. There are so many temp agencies operating in

---

539   Chaharlangi interview.
540   Chaharlangi interview.

our community and recruiting people from the community, so in terms of accessing employment, this is what people have access to.[541]

Temporary employment agencies know there are many workers in Jane-Finch who seek precarious jobs for various reasons, including lack of immigration status, difficulty finding regular permanent employment, racial and/or gender discrimination.

Jane Finch Action Against Poverty produced another temp agency report in 2019 that indicated that fifty-two per cent of workers in the Greater Toronto and Hamilton Area are employed on a temporary, part-time, or contract basis. The report also indicated that "There are as many as 100 temporary agencies in the Jane-Finch area. In past years, there have been over 200, but they are difficult to track as many constantly change their business names. Precarious employment, it seems, is the new standard."[542]

The foreword of the report states, "Precarity is concentrated in places like Toronto's Jane-Finch neighbourhood. In Jane-Finch, the 'new' precarious standard is not new at all; it has long been the norm. Jane-Finch can thus serve as a point of reference for understanding recent trends in the wider labour market."[543]

Community planning

One of the newer community groups, formed in 2012, was the York West Community Action Planning Group (CAPG), initially called Jane Finch 2020. CAPG grew out of the need to address the issue of poor planning in the Jane-Finch community. Richard De Gaetano, a community planner for Social Planning Toronto and a former Jane/Finch Centre board president, explained how the group came to be.

> About seven years ago, Wanda and I got together with Bob McElhinney and his wife Dorothy, Stephnie Payne [school board trustee and Black activist] and Errol Young [former school trustee

---

541 Deawuo interview.
542 "Permanently Temporary: Labour, Precarity and Resistance in Jane-Finch" (Toronto: Jane Finch Action Against Poverty, October 2019).
543 "Permanently Temporary."

and Jane-Finch Action Against Poverty activist] and just sat around in Bob's and Dorothy's living room, having tea and cookies and talking about how this community has never really had a voice in the planning and development that took place here.

We talked about all the kinds of mistakes that have been made because people, "experts" outside the community, came in and decided things were to be built in certain ways, that people were to live in certain ways, and sometimes it was a catastrophe for residents who had to live in the conditions that were supposedly so great, but turned out to be inappropriate. Then there was a lack of services and lack of infrastructure, a lack of transportation, transit issues, housing affordability issues, quality of housing issues. There were so many issues that just weren't being dealt with and we felt that residents needed to come together and see if we couldn't begin to push our politicians and encourage our residents, training residents to be able to speak for themselves and for the community on issues related to planning and development, whenever planning and development were going to take place.[544]

Initially, this small group of residents met in each others' homes and eventually arranged space in the York Woods Public Library for their monthly meetings. More activists were recruited to the idea. They met with politicians and with planners and established a relationship with York University. Their investigations led them to the issue of transit.

The initial plan for light rail transit (LRT) was promoted by Mayor David Miller in 2008 under the "Transit City" proposal. Plans included an LRT to be built on Jane Street between the Jane Station (on the Bloor-Danforth subway line) and Steeles Avenue West, and another on Finch Avenue between Finch Station (on the Yonge subway line) and Humber College, in north Etobicoke.[545] That plan did not come to be, but CAPG investigated and supported the concept of an LRT line on Finch Avenue, as it would speed up people's commuting time and help eliminate the crowding on the buses. The Finch bus, from Yonge Street to Humber College was known to be one

---

544   De Gaetano interview.
545   Frances Olimpo, "Next Stop: Transit City" (York West Advocate, September 2008).

of the busiest transit routes in Toronto—with buses packed with workers and students, meaning people often had to wait for another bus (sometimes several) during the rush hour traffic in the morning and evening.

CAPG found allies across the northwest and from around the city, to advocate and push for transit improvement in our community. De Gaetano took the lead on this. They called it the Northwest Transit Action group and committed to fight for light rail train lines in the northwest as the fastest and least expensive approach for rapid transit. Suzan Hall, an articulate former city councillor from north Etobicoke, joined the group and was a major asset in doing the political advocacy work that was required to succeed.

> So, we did a lot of outreach and got people from all over the city—from TTC Riders and from Code Red (two transit advocacy groups), from York University and Humber College, people who were residents from Rexdale and Jane-Finch, workers from agencies in Rexdale, Humber Summit, and Jane-Finch. We began advocating for the LRT from Keele and Finch subway to Humber College, and eventually we got official support from Humber College and York University, from the faith communities, and community-based social service organizations, and from our elected politicians.[546]

A successful transit forum was organized by CAPG reaching over fifty people and held at the local York Woods library in 2014, with Councillor Maria Augimeri (TTC chair), Jamie Robinson (Metrolinx), and a TTC planner as panellists. A local talented group, called Nomanzland, provided dramatization through skits about the challenges residents faced using the TTC.

The Province finally announced they were going to fund LRT development in Toronto, and one of the lines would be the Finch West line. Once they announced that and allocated the resources to it of $1.4 billion, CAPG decided that they had done enough to support getting an LRT line built, now they needed to do something else about plans for further development in the community.

---

546   De Gaetano interview.

The community learned that a maintenance and storage facility (MSF)—a large garage for the trains—was to be built on the land between York Gate Boulevard and Norfinch Drive, formerly known as the Yorkgate lands. CAPG thought a "train garage and rail yard" would not add anything beautifying or directly useful to residents of Jane-Finch, so they decided they would fight for a piece of that land on the Finch Avenue frontage for the community's benefit.

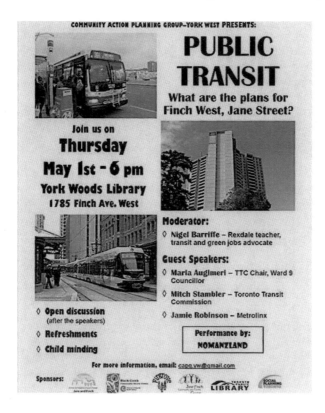

CAPG obtained funding from the York University—TD Community Engagement Centre to conduct two workshops to inform community residents about the Finch MSF, improve Metrolinx's preferred design for the MSF and to collectively advocate for community benefits. One benefit suggested and supported was for a community arts hub to be built on the land on Finch Avenue at York Gate Boulevard.

Based on information from the workshops, CAPG was committed to getting "community benefits," a concept that was used in Rexdale in a campaign for jobs and services at the proposed Woodbine Live casino and entertainment development. They started to push for a piece of the MSF land along Finch. The idea to build a community hub of service and a centre for the arts (CHCA) was discussed in partnership with the Toronto Community Benefits Network (TCBN).

TCBN had been set up by the Toronto and District Labour Council to bring together allies and partners concerned with jobs, apprenticeships, training, and social enterprises on the Eglinton LRT development project.

CAPG had joined early in TCBN's establishment. Both TCBN and CAPG wanted jobs and training (apprenticeships in the trades) for residents of Jane-Finch and Rexdale, opportunities for social enterprise by residents, as well as a social/health services and a cultural facility.

Tom Kear, a CAPG member, reached out to Eduardo Ortiz, a former resident and an architect who generously drew, without payment, a rendering of what a community hub and centre for the arts could look like in front of the MSF. The outstanding drawing was promoted and repeatedly used to illustrate this possibility.

CAPG decided to introduce and advocate for the hub with both local and external influencers. Members held meetings with the elected officials in the north-west area of the city, province and federal levels along with provincial and city bureaucrats to inform them of this work and to solicit support.

CAPG developed a set of principles for the MSF itself and forwarded them to Councillor Anthony Perruzza and Councillor Vince Crisanti of north Etobicoke to get them approved by the City. CAPG was concerned with the quality of the design and the environmental impact in the Jane-Finch community. The principles were later approved at Council.

Discussions began with Metrolinx, through various public events, both in terms of advocacy and in negotiations for a piece of the land. When it was time for the three consortia [groups of companies bidding on the contract to build the light rail line and the MSF] to meet stakeholders, the Toronto Community Benefits Network enabled members of CAPG to speak to contractors representatives. CAPG developed a presentation and three members spoke to it, calling for a fifty-metre setback of the proposed MSF construction from Finch Avenue and to give that strip of land on Finch to the community to build a community services hub and centre for the arts.

One of the members who spoke was Symone Walters, whose family had lived in the community for forty plus years and three generations. She stood at the podium and looked out at the audience. Quietly and yet with passion, she told the audience that her fifteen-year-old son, Tahj Loor-Walters, was at the plaza across the street from his home when he was mistakenly shot and killed. After a pause, she looked up at the representatives bidding on the land and said, "How far would you go to ensure the safety and well-being of your children? How far would you go to ensure your children had safe spaces to grow and to thrive?" Symone continued with her presentation articulating the importance of the community hub for the community residents.

Metrolinx eventually promised a minimum of thirty-two metres of setback from Finch Avenue with the proviso that the consortium that won the bid could give us more, if possible. The consortium who won the bid for the LRT/MSF, the Mosaic Transit Group, agreed to provide thirty-two metres of land for the community to build on.

CAPG wrote a grant to the Ontario Trillium Foundation, and in partnership with the Jane/Finch Centre, secured funding to conduct a feasibility study. An extensive feasibility study was completed after consulting with over 1,500 residents. CAPG then submitted a proposal to the City of Toronto to develop a business plan and a governance model. The grant was approved, and that work was done with input from residents. CAPG members were excited about this development and agreed that a Steering Committee should be established with expanded resident involvement to further pursue the hub and arts centre. Then, Metrolinx reversed their decision to donate the land.

The community was outraged when they learned this information. Tom Rakocevic, New Democrat MPP for Humber River-Black Creek (the re-named York West riding) declared, "Jane and Finch families are counting on this community hub, and the decision to abruptly change course on this visionary project is a devastating blow."[547]

In the spring of 2020, in the midst of the COVID-19 pandemic, the community came together to protest Metrolinx's betrayal with a rally held on the corner of Finch Avenue and York Gate Blvd. Residents and stake-holders spoke passionately about all the work that had been done and the importance of Metrolinx honouring their commitment. The media attended, interviewing residents and politicians, and articles were written giving the community's version of events.

The *Toronto Star* responded with strong commentary by columnist Royson James.

> If there is one neighbourhood that you dare not backstab, dupe, mislead and totally promise to help, only to turn your back, it is Jane and Finch. Not ever, considering its deficiencies. And certainly not at a time when the world is growing wise to what systemic anti-Black racism looks like—in all its ugly forms. And the LRT fiasco on Finch is so clearly among the ugliest.[548]

On July 24th, Phil Verster, president and CEO of Metrolinx, sent a letter to Councillor Perruzza indicating that its Transit Oriented Communities program was an example that could achieve the goals of the community and the city. It was understood that the sale of the land could be contingent on the developer including a community hub in its plans. Residents translated that to mean that Metrolinx could sell the lands on Finch Avenue to a devel-oper who would build a condominium, and the main floor would have a

---

547   Ben Spurr, "In Jane-Finch, Leaders Fume at 'Terrible Betrayal' After Metrolinx Goes Back On Plan to Donate Land For Community Centre" (Toronto Star, July 23, 2020).
548   Royson James, "Jane and Finch Dared to Dream—Now Metrolinx Dares to Double-Cross" (Toronto Star, July 3, 2020).

community hub. That way, the Province would get its money and the community would get their hub, however truncated and limited it was.

If such developers built a condo or office building on the Yorkgate land, one of the few neutral and central spaces left in the Jane-Finch community, the communities north and south of Jane-Finch may be less likely to use it as it would be seen as 'belonging' to the condo. Councillor Perruzza and MPP Rakocevic strongly advocated to members of the provincial government and Metrolinx to honour their original commitment to transfer the land to the City to facilitate the construction of a hub/arts centre for the whole community, and other nearby communities, to use.

Verster responded with a letter, dated August 6, 2020, indicating that, "Metrolinx remains 100% committed to ensuring that the community hub can be built on the land and at no cost for the land."[549] Councillor Perruzza assured residents that he would work with the City to facilitate the land transfer. The community wanted better clarification on this matter.

On September 8, 2020, the newly formed group, the Jane Finch Community Hub and Centre for the Arts Organizing Committee (HOC), sent a letter to Verster to inform him of the formation of the new group and to reinforce the importance of a collaborative process with the community. The letter then requested that the thirty-two-metre frontage be dedicated in its entirety as the site of the HOC as a benefit to the community. They also wanted Metrolinx to give its full support to the community's request at the upcoming meeting of Toronto City Council that it establish a community-directed task force mandated to plan and develop the HOC and establish a community-based governance model. The letter was distributed widely to all politicians and relevant senior Metrolinx representatives.

On March 11, 2021, the provincial government issued a news release "Ontario Provides Land for a Community Hub and Arts Centre in Toronto" including 2.174 acres of land at no cost to the city. It included the response from Mayor John Tory. "Thank you to Councillor Anthony Perruzza and the

---

549   Phil Verster letter to Councillor Perruzza (August 6, 2020).

Jane-Finch community for their strong advocacy for this hub that will be a key part of the neighbourhood's future along with the Finch West LRT."[550]

The Jane-Finch Community Hub Organizing Committee summed up the gains for the community.

> Today is an example of the strength of residents of Jane-Finch. We need to acknowledge the tremendous effort and work of the Jane-Finch community, a diverse and vibrant neighbourhood, towards securing this land. Today is an important step in this resident-led community initiative to create our Jane Finch Community Hub and Centre for the Arts. We look forward to continuing our stewardship of this process with the Province, City of Toronto and Metrolinx, and securing the necessary sustainable funding to build and operate the hub that our community has envisioned over many years.[551]

New City planning initiatives in Jane-Finch

Periodically, the City of Toronto conducts extensive planning in one part of the city or another to evaluate and revise the Official Master Plan and subsidiary plans (Secondary Plans, Avenue Plans, etc.). For example, the Keele Finch Plus planning study was launched in 2016 to respond to city-building opportunities because of the subway extension and the light rail transit line being developed along Finch Avenue from Keele Street to Humber College in Etobicoke. The study's work plan consisted of updating the planning around Keele Street and Finch Avenue to encourage growth and change, support community building, and leverage nearby transit investments. There were numerous neighbourhood consultations and communication between the Planning Department and residents.

In 2019, residents learned that the area around Jane-Finch would be the next site for planning. With the new LRT under construction, it was anticipated that the whole Finch Avenue route would undergo significant change and development in the coming years. In June 2020, City Council

---

550   News Release—"Ontario Provides Land for a Community Hub and Arts Centre in Toronto" (Toronto Star, March 11, 2021).
551   News Release.

approved the report, "Jane-Finch Initiative—Community Development Plan and Updated Land Use Planning Framework."

What sets this planning process apart is the approach to collaboration on a community planning exercise in Black Creek and Glenfield-Jane Heights, two key Jane-Finch neighbourhoods—something that was often forgotten in the past. In the "Report for Action to the Economic and Community Development Committee," the planning department articulated its plans.

> The first phase of engagement would build on the area's history of community-led advocacy and would integrate lessons learned from previous City-led consultations in the Jane-Finch area. City staff would consult with the community in the development of the engagement strategy to ensure that it reflects the expertise of local residents and businesses on the needs of the community and integrates engagement methods that would sustain the community's interest over the duration of the initiative.[552]

Perhaps the ideology above will ensure transparency and engagement so that mistakes from the past will not be repeated.

---

552 Planning Department, "Report for Action to the Economic and Community Development Committee" (Toronto Planning, February 25, 2020).

CHAPTER NINE

The State of the Community

There are still many challenges ahead for the Jane-Finch community. In preparation for the 2019 federal election, Jane Finch Action Against Poverty presented a document outlining some of the challenges. For example, it noted that in 1989, Parliament had passed a resolution to end child poverty by the year 2000. Thirty years later, one in five children in Canada still lives in poverty. The electoral district of Humber River-Black Creek has the highest rate of child and family poverty in Toronto. This includes all the Jane-Finch neighbourhoods.

JFAAP also found that this community had the highest number of families who are waiting for subsidized [rent-geared-to-income] housing. It is well known that the lack of affordable housing, rising rents, housing costs, stagnating incomes, and limited access to subsidized housing are major problems facing many residents.

Humber River-Black Creek had the highest number of children waiting for a childcare fee subsidy. Many families have difficulties pursuing education and/or employment opportunities without safe and affordable childcare.

The JFAAP document indicated that Humber River-Black Creek had a higher rate of poverty among racialized and Indigenous people than the rest of Canada. People in the community are witnessing more racism, inequality, anti-immigrant, and anti-refugee sentiments than most other communities.

Many people in the riding work for the minimum wage (or less) through precarious employment. The percentage of workers in Canada earning the minimum wage has doubled since 1998. JFAAP found that workers are mistreated, injured, and even killed on the job [mostly due to unsafe environments or lack of training and safety equipment], especially those hired through temp agencies. A temporary worker was killed on September 25, 2019, at the Fiera Foods, the fifth death of a worker in this company, which is located in the riding.

This community had the second highest unemployment rate for residents aged fifteen and older in the City of Toronto, along with one of the highest under-employment rates. Many people were not eligible for unemployment insurance due to overly stringent requirements. Those who are eligible receive inadequate benefits, while billions of dollars of "surplus" in the EI account were moved into general revenues and spent by the federal government on non-employment related expenditures.

JFAAP found that, increasingly, more seniors live in poverty as the Canada Pension Plan and Old Age Security are not sufficient to cover all the expenses people have. Many working people in this country do not have company pension plans to fall back on. It is also challenging to save through retirement saving plans and other financial instruments, due to low wages and the constantly increasing cost of living.

Their document ended noting that there is substantial demographic information documenting Jane-Finch as having enormous challenges, scarce resources, and insufficient supports to address the systemic issues that have impacted the community since its beginnings.

According to a report for action from the Jane-Finch Initiative, the Jane-Finch area differs significantly from Toronto as a whole.[553]

Challenges in the schools

Children face obstacles within the school system for multiple reasons. It is known that children born into poverty confront many challenges that can impact their ability to succeed in school and in life.

This was demonstrated in 2004 when the Province provided funding to implement the Early Development Instrument (EDI) across senior kindergarten classrooms to establish a baseline of Ontario children's readiness to

---

553   "Report for Action from the Jane-Finch Initiative—Community Development Plan and Updated Land Use Planning Framework (Toronto: Planning Department, February 25, 2020).

learn at school. In the first three years, the EDI was primarily implemented in the Toronto District School Board (TDSB) schools in the former North York and Toronto communities.[554]

The EDI is a questionnaire completed by kindergarten teachers measuring children's ability to meet age-appropriate developmental expectations in five key domains: physical health and well-being, social knowledge and competence, emotional health and maturity, language and cognitive development, communication skills, and general knowledge. The riding of York West covered seven neighbourhoods: Humber Summit, Humbermede, Palmo Park-Humberlea, Black Creek, Glenfield-Jane Heights, Downsview-Roding and York University Heights.

The results of the 2004/05 school-year EDI indicated that the Black Creek neighbourhood scored the lowest in all five domains. The 2007/08 EDI results indicated that Black Creek and Downsview-Roding had the highest percentage of children identified as having multiple challenges and that there was both a higher percentage of low-scoring children and a lower percentage of high-scoring children in this riding than in the whole of Toronto, across all domains. Three years later, the 2010/11 results showed that Black Creek still had the highest percentage of children identified as having multiple challenges. Relative to all other Toronto neighbourhoods, Black Creek falls in the bottom twenty on all domains in terms of the highest percentages of high-scoring children. It also falls in the bottom twenty on all domains except physical health and well-being in terms of the lowest percentages of low-scoring children.[555]

The Toronto District School Board is also facing challenges. In 2015, the former mayor of Toronto, Barbara Hall, worked with the Toronto District School Board's Governance Advisory Panel to report on improving school board governance at the TDSB. They heard from 550 people about how

---

554 Mothercraft, "Early Development Instrument (EDI) Results: 2004–2011 for York West" (2011). https://www.mothercraft.ca/assets/site/docs/resource-library/research-data/YorkWest_2010-11.pdf

555 Mothercraft, "Early Development Instrument".

issues within the school board had impacted public confidence and, perhaps student achievement. Twenty recommendations were made. Hall commented, "The threats to public education are real and serious and these are systemic issues that need to be taken very seriously."[556] Under the section Equity and Accessibility, the report noted some of these issues.

> The data showed that Aboriginal, Black and Latin American students were significantly overrepresented in Special Education Schools and Schools with Limited Academics, that is, those schools offering limited academic and university preparedness courses. With respect to the TDSB's two prestigious Specialized Arts Schools, self-identified Black students are significantly underrepresented.

> Many participants were particularly vocal about the lack of speciality programs in disadvantaged neighbourhoods. We heard frustration from those who believed that French Immersion, gifted and other specialized programs are, by great majority, offered in affluent neighbourhoods, leading to an inequity of access to learning opportunities that has a long-term detrimental effect on children from marginalized communities. We heard that this is because parents with greater resources are better able to advocate for their children.

Parents and community members expressed their concerns to the board.

> The board was not aware of or responsive to the unique needs of students with cultural difference or socio-economic challenges, and suggested that teaching, funding, programs, and resources should be carefully differentiated among unique communities to ensure that all students can reach their full potential." The board was told, "Some schools have laptops, some have nothing, some have smart boards, and some have no new textbooks.[557]

Skills for Change, an organization known for its work with newcomers, focused some of its research on educational attainment in the Jane-Finch area. It prepared a report for the People For Education conference held on

556 Barbara Hall, Toronto District School Board Governance Advisory Panel Report, August 19, 2015). (http://www.edu.gov.on.ca/eng/new/2015/TDSB2015.html).
557 Barbara Hall, Toronto District School Board.

November 2, 2019. Two researchers were hired, both of whom were Jane-Finch residents and had attended post-secondary school there. Some of their findings related to education and employment. In 2014, they found there was a lower-than-average high school graduation rate of 75.9 per cent. One local high school graduation rate was at 66.8 per cent, compared to the TDSB average of 84.2 per cent (TDSB, 2015). In 2017/18, [two] local secondary schools had some of the lowest literacy rates (59 per cent and fifty-five per cent) compared to the TDSB average of eighty-one per cent (TDSB 2018). In 2016, they found that only 11.7 per cent and 11.3 per cent, respectively, in Black Creek and Glenfield Jane Heights [Jane-Finch neighbourhoods] have a bachelor's degree or higher (compared to the city average of 44.1 per cent).[558]

The TDSB has a long way to go before parents in Jane-Finch can say that their children are in an educational system where access and equity is present for all.

Health indicators

Toronto Public Health completed a Ward 8, York West, Health Profile in June 2013 documenting the health status of residents in Jane-Finch. The report indicated that Ward 8 varies from the City of Toronto with higher numbers of risk indicators compared to the city. For example, York West had a higher proportion of children and young adults aged 0–29, a higher number of unemployed people, more people with less than a high school education, a higher number of racialized people, more recent and total immigrants, a higher proportion of low-birth-weight babies, and more teenagers giving birth. "Babies born with a low birth weight (less than 2,500 grams) are at higher risk for many short-term and long-term poor health outcomes."[559]

---

558 Fatema Venesha, "Reclaiming What Education Means to Youth: Findings from Participatory Action Research for the Jane/Finch Collaborative on Education to Employment—People for Education Conference" (Toronto: Skills for Change, November 2, 2019).

559 Toronto Public Health, "Ward Health Profile, Ward 8 York West, Part 1: Health Status and Public Health Services" (Toronto: June 2013).

The profile stated that there was a higher rate of respiratory disease hospitalization and cardiovascular disease hospitalization and mortality. "Some of the common respiratory diseases include asthma, chronic obstructive pulmonary disease, and lung conditions excluding cancer. Respiratory disease can be caused by smoking and environmental toxins."[560]

The report also indicated a lower median household income level, a lower rate of injuries to children and youth resulting in emergency department visits, and a lower rate of enteric (intestinal) diseases.[561]

Many residents had precarious employment with no health benefits, meaning they cannot afford to fill their prescriptions or afford time off to see a doctor when they are sick, which can lead to more serious illness. A lack of nutritious food also contributes to poor health and nutrition related diseases such as diabetes.

Residents in the community know this situation, they see these conditions, and they experience this reality. The question is, how does one change these conditions? We know that affordable housing, universal affordable childcare, increased minimum wage to the level of a living wage, strong anti-racism policies and practices, and the elimination of poverty would improve the health status for all. Is any government in the Canadian capitalist system concerned enough and bold enough to make any of this happen?

Gentrification—a rising threat

The concept of gentrification has once again emerged in Jane-Finch. Gentrification is a process of changing the character of a neighbourhood through the influx of more affluent residents and elite businesses. The potential for gentrification initially started in 2008 with the idea of Shoreham Public School closing to make way for development, and with the housing development just south of York University. Some argue that this will be a good for Jane-Finch, but anti-poverty activists argue that gentrification will displace people, such as what is happening in the Firgrove community—displacing hundreds of people so that developers can build condominiums.

560   Toronto Public Health, "Ward Health Profile".
561   Toronto Public Health, "Ward Health Profile".

Even if the same number of public housing units are built there along with the new privately owned units, many of the original residents and community amenities may be lost. Certainly, the rents in condo apartments and townhouses will be higher than public or cooperative housing, meaning low-income households are more likely to double up, or worse, potentially causing unhealthy living situations.

Transportation is one element of gentrification that changes a community. The subway has come to this area of the city, and light rail transit on Finch Avenue is slated to open in 2023. As a result, there is a slow growth of condominiums being planned on Keele Street, Finch Avenue, and on Jane Street that will change the community.

To the south on Keele Street, south of Sheppard Avenue, the Keeley Condominium is being built. Condominiums and townhouses have already sprung up on the former military base, now known as Downsview Park. When Bombardier, Downsview's aircraft manufacturing facility, was sold in 2018, it was anticipated that the airport would cease its operation in 2023, leaving more room for development of high-rise buildings. The height restrictions will be lifted as airplanes will no longer land at the Downsview Airport. The City of Toronto conducted a Keele Finch Plus Study that produced a report indicating high-rise intensification for the Keele-Finch intersection and surrounding area.

On Jane Street north of Sheppard Avenue, a developer is constructing the Yorkwoods condominium at Jane Street and Yorkwoods Gate, across the street from Firgrove. The plan for Firgrove, after the current townhouses are demolished, is for condominiums to be built alongside the new Toronto Community Housing apartment building that will house those who were displaced as well as those moving in for the first time.

While some anticipate this to be a positive change for the community, others think differently. For example, when the Tribute Village by the university was built, investors bought houses and townhouses, renovated them into multi-bedroom units, and rented them out to students and low-income workers. They became illegal rooming houses that are not regulated by any authority and create safety hazards for those who live there and in the adjacent neighbourhood.

Some in the community believe that will happen with the condominiums. Investors will purchase a few units and rent them out to families who will pay high rent, continuing to live in poverty. Or, multiple individuals, or multiple families, will share the condominium apartments to pay lower rent. Investors may not want to live in Jane-Finch, but they are happy to make money off working people while their investments grow. There are beautiful parks in the community; diverse people from all over the world; a community farm; and social and community services that help residents mobilize to fight injustice. Yet the increased population may outpace the ability of the community to respond to the ever-growing needs.

All levels of government have not adequately responded to the conditions created by governments since the 1960s. Without appropriate policies, such as protection for housing low-income residents, and adequate funding for community service, what benefit will intensification have for the population in Jane-Finch?

In June 2020, City Council directed staff to commence the Jane-Finch Initiative, which is undertaking resident and business engagement in planning for the future of the area and looking at how best to leverage the investment in light rail transit for the benefit of local communities. The stated goal of the Jane-Finch Initiative is to develop an integrated plan for the area that advances social equity and economic inclusion for current and future residents, encourages the appropriate kinds of growth and development in the area, and guides investment in community improvements.

If the City follows through with its new approach to planning through collaboration with the community's residents and workers, the Jane-Finch Planning Initiative might be an opportunity for the community to have a significant impact on the future, as it speaks to doing the work through an equity lens, including poverty reduction, affordable housing, and confronting anti-Black racism.[562]

The planning processes in the past often excluded low-income and working-class people and therefore made enormous mistakes that residents paid

---

562   Planning Department, "Jane-Finch Initiative Public Meeting #1" (City of Toronto, November 23, 2020).

for. This process has just begun and only conscious action by residents and workers to push the planners and politicians will make it more likely that the community will gain, not lose, in the process.

As long as the political system does not adequately respond to the systemic issues of our society—for example, poverty, racism, inequality, childcare, and housing—these obstacles will continue to impact communities such as Jane-Finch and the people who call Jane-Finch home. For example, Ontario premier Doug Ford announced an advisory council to study social and economic barriers for youth, called the Council on Equity of Opportunity. However, when elected, they cut twenty-five million dollars from the education programs. The government limited grants available for school programs, such as after-school jobs for youth in low-income neighbourhoods, cancelled free prescription medication given to those under twenty-five through the Pharmacare program, cut one billion dollars from social services across the board, cancelled the one-dollar increase in the minimum wage, and cut $84.5 million in funding for children and at-risk youth (including children's aid societies), just to name a few examples.[563] Too many studies, commissions, and reports have been created and never sufficiently implemented to influence critical systemic issues.

The Jane-Finch community is comprised of people from all over the world, speaking over one hundred languages or dialects, and is rich in culture and diversity. There is an abundance of skills, talents, experience, and social capital that has not been adequately recognized by society. The community has historically been a place where social groups have come together and established relationships. There is a shared sense of identity and a shared understanding of what it means to live in Jane-Finch, whether they are African-Diasporic, Italian, Latin American, South Asian, or Southeast Asian. Within and across those groups, and many others, there are shared values, trust and cooperation. Social capital is seen as "the links, shared values and understandings in

---

563   Fatima Syed, "Here's Everything the Doug Ford Government Cut in Its First Year in Office" (National Observer, June 7, 2019).

society that enable individuals and groups to trust each other and so work together."[564] Jane-Finch has demonstrated this concept repeatedly.

Betty Jane (BJ) Richmond, co-author of *What Counts: Social Accounting for Non-profits and Cooperatives,* was a professor in the Faculty of Education at York University with expertise in social capital. She explained her perspective of the Jane-Finch community.

> While developers made money in Jane-Finch, the intelligence, dignity, inventiveness and resourcefulness of the residents created tremendous social capital. Yet they were denigrated and stigmatized by their location. Many fine and even award-winning agencies and action groups continue today in Jane Finch because of the resilient responses of residents. For me, it furthers my study of the creation of social capital—Jane Finch presents a master class in creating social benefits. The volunteer hours and ingenuity applied alone would be worth mega-millions in any social capital audit.[565]

The COVID-19 pandemic came to Toronto and exposed many problems that existed in places like Jane-Finch. Such communities are full of poor-quality housing, often with multiple families living in one apartment or house because housing is scarce and/or unaffordable. Precarious workers take crowded buses to work in multiple jobs to try to make sufficient income for their families. It is known that production and warehouse jobs are crowded, and many do not have adequate PPE equipment, good ventilation, or the space for physical distancing to prevent infections from spreading. Poor nutrition, unhealthy living environments, and stress means that residents have more underlying health problems and poor health indicators, making them more vulnerable to infectious diseases such as COVID-19. Essential workers—in food production, health care (PSWs), grocery stores, etc.—often

---

564   OECD, https://www.oecd.org/insights/37966934.pdf
565   Jack Quarter, Laurie Mook and Betty Jane Richmond, What Counts: Social Accounting for Non-profits and Cooperatives (Upper Saddle River New Jersey: Pearson Education, 2003).

cannot afford to take time off for a test or to self-isolate, hence the virus spreads, regardless of the Province's lockdown measures.

Rachel Mendleson wrote an exclusive article for the Toronto Star. In that article was information about a letter written by Councillor Joe Cressy to Ontario's health minister and to the chief medical officer of health.

"The social determinants of health, like income, race and ethnicity, and housing, affect who gets sick and who does not," Councillor Cressy wrote. Also within that article, resident activist Leticia Deawuo spoke about not losing sight of the systemic changes needed to address anti-Black racism, as well as improving working conditions and living wages. "We know that there are these deep inequities that exist. So, what are they going to do in the long-term to make sure our communities can be healthy?"[566] Toronto Public Health also confirms Deawuo's concern about inequities.

> Communities with a high proportion of low-income, newcomer and racialized residents experience much higher levels of COVID-19. For example, while racialized people make up 52 percent of Toronto residents, they make up 83 percent of all COVID-19 cases. Conversely, while white people make up 48 percent of all Toronto residents, they constitute only 17 percent of COVID-19 cases.[567]

Butterfly GoPaul commented on the impact and response to COVID-19. "We need resources to make these changes happen. But the systemic reality is so deep that it's not going to happen with, you know, pixie dust and curry powder. We need to really break down what's been broken and stop trying to repair and create band-aid solutions. Because it's not working for communities like ours."[568]

566 Rachel Mendleson, "City turns to province for help in fighting COVID-19 in hard-hit northwest corner" (Toronto Star, July 9, 2020).
567 Heather McGregor, "Poverty Reduction Central to Building Back Better" (Toronto Star, August 17, 2020).
568 J. Yang, K. Allen, R. Mendleson and A. Bailey, "Toronto's COVID-19 Divide: The City's Northwest Corner Has Been 'Failed by the System', " (Toronto Star, June 28, 2020).

Concluding thoughts

Following the publication of *Suburbs in Transition* in the late 1970s, there were a number of significant public reports documenting the situation in Jane-Finch and other high needs areas. Some would lead to concrete actions and others would be ignored. The themes would be repeated again and again.

The broader political context halted progress and often set things back starting with the "social contract" of the Bob Rae NDP government and worsening in the second half of the 1990s with the Harris PC government. The Liberals, under Dalton McGuinty and Kathleen Wynne, did little to improve the situation for workers. With the election of Premier Doug Ford, more cuts came. Many community-based organizations help people survive and to eventually move to better circumstances but can do little about systemic barriers that continue to exist.

Until the government, and the people who vote them in, come to terms with the appalling socioeconomic impacts that affect the most vulnerable people in society, people in communities like Jane-Finch will have to be resilient. If successive governments offer token investments in programs, real change will not happen. If billions of dollars go to law enforcement agencies or to bail out big corporations, instead of providing affordable housing, jobs, and necessary services (such as childcare and good healthcare), change will not happen.

Because of the current state of low-income communities across the country, there are resident activists and community leaders working hard to bring attention to the issues impacting their communities, along with viable solutions. In the case of Jane-Finch, collaborative networks—the Jane Finch Action Network, the Black Creek Community Collaborative, Jane Finch Community Hub and Centre for the Arts Organizing Committee, Jane-Finch Housing Coalition, Black Creek Food Justice—and grassroots groups, such as Jane Finch Action Against Poverty and the Community Action Planning Group, will continue to advocate for what is needed in the community. They will also fight against the formidable systemic barriers that continue to grossly impact the lives of low-income, marginalized, working-class, and oppressed people of today.

Why do so many youth in Jane-Finch find themselves on the wrong side of the law?

For all the overwhelming problems faced by low-income families and precarious workers, their children suffer much more, denying them hope for a better future. Parents who are essential workers may not be present for their children while they work multiple jobs, long hours, and are underpaid. School systems may have improved somewhat, but they have a long way to go to equitably support Black and racialized students. The cultural challenges young newcomers face when arriving in Canada are daunting. The impact of policing (e.g., SROs, carding, discrimination, racism) has caused all of them harm. And trying to secure a good job as a Black person with a social housing address can be a formidable challenge.

Residents in Jane-Finch obviously experience their neighbourhood and their community in different ways, but the existing structures and dominant social relations of society impact them in a similar fashion as the vast majority are working people. Workers lives are more alike than not—their lives are vastly different from those who are wealthy.

Folks in Jane-Finch (in their vast majority) do not own businesses, employ other people for a large profit, live in mansions, or own summer homes in ritzy locales. There are differences in income, racialization, gender, age, language, culture, or national origin, but most live their lives in similar conditions. Residents take the same crowded buses or drive long commutes to work. They shop in the same over-priced local markets or have to travel outside of the community to find cheaper healthy food, better shops and restaurants, movie theatres, or music venues. They raise the children in the same neighbourhoods where the kids attend the same schools. Jane-Finch residents utilize the same recreation centres and libraries and many access the few social services that are available.

Divisions within society exist on many levels, sometimes affecting people in multiple ways. For example, racism impacts Black and Indigenous workers; racism and xenophobia also affect most immigrants from Asia, the Middle East, and Latin America. Those impacted by racism are the majority in Toronto, yet they get less of the social and economic benefits. Women, in all these groups, get less than men and, with the pandemic, I believe women have lost jobs faster and are carrying more of the domestic burden.

What has been wonderful about Jane-Finch is that despite the divisions and conflicts created by others throughout its history, or perhaps in reaction to them, working people in this community frequently come together and organize to resist the forces driving them apart. Many residents participated in support of organizations and grassroots groups mobilizing around key issues. Residents fought, and continue to fight, for what should rightfully be theirs as members of society. In so doing, they transform themselves and their community.

Unfortunately, many of the systemic issues created by the capitalist economy and state (including government and institutions) are not capable of being resolved by any single community, no matter how mobilized and effective the residents are. Jane-Finch residents and activists have had to struggle against the policies or lack of action of government and the impacts of economic changes. Communities such as this have insufficient political power and too few financial resources to actually build the things that are needed or to stop all the harms inflicted on residents.

Given the conditions of life in working-class communities, its important for the residents and workers in the community to join forces with others— other communities, unions, organizations, and workers elsewhere—to enhance the community's power and in the process strengthen the whole working class. What happens in Jane-Finch is often the result of what is happening elsewhere.

Events in the world have a direct impact on communities like Jane-Finch. When recessions, famine, wars, political instability, military regimes, or global corporations create unlivable conditions in other countries, immigration to Canada increases. Many newcomers settled in less expensive, more culturally compatible neighbourhoods, or where low-cost government housing was available, such as existed in Jane-Finch. Waves of immigration enriched this globally diverse community, bringing new cultural benefits, political knowledge, and experience of struggle to it.

Sometimes the arrival of a new surge of refugees, especially from rural or less-urbanized environments, would overwhelm the already inadequate social and settlement services and schools. Without supports from government, the increased population also put pressure on the community recreation programs and facilities. Transit and roads became more congested. School populations grew beyond their structural capacity (or staff's cultural competency), and students and teachers both suffered and school boards failed to act to supply the necessary resources required by a surge of students.

Experiences like these spurred a rising resistance to the lack of resources, neglect and discrimination that impacted people in Jane-Finch. Led by individuals who understood poverty and oppression—women, young people, and seniors—they mobilized neighbours and community activists to resist attempts to further marginalize the community. They organized protests and continue to do so today. They also developed programs and services to attempt to meet the needs of people ignored by mainstream society. Often, they were quite successful in forcing the public spotlight on the community, putting pressure on elected officials and bureaucrats. Organizations created to support residents did great work, but frequently, the limited resources allocated by funders would be for a limited, and inadequate, timeframe of a few years or less.

How do we get from where we are today to the place where Jane-Finch residents are seen as makers of history? History suggests that it will be the younger people—especially those from the Black population, South Asians, and Latin Americans—especially the women—who will move first, be most determined and persistent, will take on leadership responsibilities, and will encourage their elders to join them or support them.

There is much work to be done and given the strong and politically conscious young leadership of today, who can, with hope and with support, work towards creating an equitable society with justice for all.

CHAPTER TEN

How Anti-Black Racism Underdeveloped Jane-Finch

A critical issue in the development of the Jane-Finch community needs to be explained in greater depth than I felt I could give—anti-Black racism. Given the importance of this relevant topic, I reached out to a former long-term resident who has expertise in this area and who generously agreed to share his point of view. Sam Tecle will use his own words to share his insights.

⤝⤞

Sam Tecle grew up in Jane-Finch and has been a community worker and advocate in Toronto for over twenty years. He has worked with the Jane and Finch Boys and Girls Club, the Toronto District School Board (TDSB), Youth Leaps, Success Beyond Limits, and York University's Jean Augustine Chair in Education, Community & Diaspora. Sam has worked on research projects with Peel and York Region School Boards that have focused on Black students' school experiences. Notably, Sam spearheaded the first official program offered by the TDSB aimed to reintegrate youth who have had contact with the criminal justice system, offering both educational credits and reintegration services from a harm reduction anti-Black racism–informed lens.

Currently, Sam is a professor of Community Engaged Learning at New College, University of Toronto. His research and scholarly work focus on Black and Diaspora Studies, Urban Studies, and Sociology of Education. His forthcoming work, Black Grammars: On Difference and Belonging, *focuses on the experiences and perspectives relating to blackness and Black identification of East African Diasporas across the UK, Canada, and the US. Sam is a frequent commentator on youth issues, violence, and police interactions in multiple media outlets in Toronto.*

As I sit down to write this, there is considerable construction happening in and around the intersection of Jane and Finch. The Finch West LRT being developed by Metrolinx in partnership with the Province of Ontario has resulted in ripped and exposed concrete wide open on Finch from Keele (east of Jane and Finch) to Weston (west of Jane and Finch). The next major intersection east of Jane and Finch—Keele and Finch—is currently being "revitalized," a development project being led by the City of Toronto. Yorkwoods Public Library has been closed for at least the past year because it too is being remodelled and refreshed. At the same time, a large swath of affordable housing along Jane Street, just south of Jane and Finch in the Firgrove neighbourhood is currently being torn down with only a portion of it slated to be rebuilt. At first glance, all of this construction and development in what is a marginalized and neglected community, what city and provincial officials would call "revitalization," would indicate that Jane-Finch is a site of deep investment and the focus of all levels of government. This is only a mirage, because historically Jane-Finch has never been central to any political agenda, therefore has never been the site of investment.

In this chapter, I make the argument that Jane-Finch is a complex community made up of diverse neighbourhoods and peoples that has always faced stigma, structural neglect and continued and sustained disinvestment from all levels of government. I assert that anti-Black racism has been the organizing principle of Jane-Finch. Despite the appearance of development and revitalization we see now—what we call gentrification—both historically and contemporaneously anti-Black racism is the constant and the anchor that constitutes how Jane-Finch has been governed, the core reason why it has been neglected, and—despite current appearances—why it has ultimately been underdeveloped.

To begin to tell the story of how anti-Black racism underdeveloped Jane-Finch, I want to start with my own story of how I came to live and grow up in the community and glean from that what it tells us about how pervasive anti-Black racism is and continues to be, how it affects the ways this most rich and vibrant community comes to be seen and treated socially and politically.

My story in Toronto begins when my family landed here in the early 1990s, fleeing political conflict and war from our homeland Eritrea in East Africa. When I was born, Eritrea was embroiled in a long conflict for autonomy (for independence) from Ethiopia. At the time it was called the "longest war in modern history." This was a protracted armed conflict in which my parents participated, and then they had me. So, in fleeing all of those things, to raise a child, my parents sought refuge and ended up in Toronto. So, my youth, adolescence and teenage years in Toronto are filled with memories of countless stories, social functions, and gatherings that emphasized an Eritrean background borne of struggle. That shared connection with other Eritreans in Toronto formed for me my important *first* sense of community.

Jane-Finch, a community made up of different neighbourhoods filled with peoples from all over the world, was a pocket of the city where my family and I found comradeship, solidarity, and fellowship. Jane-Finch is made up of peoples who, like my parents, struggled and resisted in the place they once called home.

Growing up in this community meant growing up with peoples who had a fierce and fighting spirit, it meant growing up on a floor in a public housing building that had people from Ghana, Jamaica, El Salvador, and Nicaragua. I remembered thinking that this was the kind of multiculturalism from below that is such a defining, integral and valuable feature of communities like Jane-Finch. And how fortunate I was to have grown up in this place for the worldliness it offered me, the fellowship it provided.

What is unavoidable, and where the story often begins when people first hear the name Jane-Finch, is the community's reputation rooted in infamy and stigma. On so many levels, Jane-Finch is simply an intersection, but also it is never allowed to ever solely be an intersection. It is so much more.

Jane-Finch is one part of this self-professed world-class city that the public does not want to talk about in any substantive way. It is never discussed how Jane-Finch came to be known as a site of stigma, a site of danger, and a geographic space in the city to avoid. For me, I chart the beginning of this rendition of the community to Peter McLaren's book, published in 1980, titled *Cries From the Corridor: The New Suburban Ghettos*. McLaren, an elementary school teacher at the time was just beginning his career and his first book was a set of diary entries that he titled, *Cries from the Corridor*, detailing his experience teaching at an elementary school in Jane-Finch.

According to McLaren, he takes on the "challenge" of teaching in the famed Jane-Finch corridor. The book depicts staff that are exhausted, tired, and burned out. His principal warns him that he is entering a community like no other and with students who are the most difficult to contain or maintain, much less teach. And so, the idea of Jane-Finch being a site of chaos, danger, and darkness filled with cries that emanated from a corridor became commonplace. The media began to identify Jane-Finch as a corridor mainly based off the success of this problematic text.

Causing quite a stir, the book portrayed the students as delinquent, void of interest and drive in their education, and a wider community that was prone to violence and carelessness. This was perhaps one of the first widely available publications to cast Jane-Finch as a problematic community and unfortunately this has been the dominating narrative ever since. Although he came later to renounce this, McLaren never identified the book as constituted and centrally anchored by racism, and to be specific, anti-Black racism. McLaren never came to acknowledge the dominating narrative that was set into motion by his collection of diary reflections. Yet it is in the long shadow of that book that Jane-Finch exists.

For those who grow up, live, and work in a community with a negative reputation, it can hold you captive. It affects residents on such a deep level that my dad would tell friends and family that we lived at "Keele and Finch"—an intersection close to Jane and Finch so that they would be put at ease when coming over to visit. And this formed yet another sense of community for me, one informed by geography and shared social conditions, and the shared stigma of a single story. And when only a single story is told about a community, your community, one in which you take pride and, when that story is the only story, the only overarching, overbearing single story—that is a function of political and social power. What that has taught me is that communities like Jane-Finch, those that are predominantly populated by Black and racialized people, politically and socially marginalized people, is the important lesson that communities dominated by an overarching single story—is that there is always more to those communities. Every community like Jane-Finch is made of complex stories. And all of those stories matter.

These two narratives highlight some of the ways that I and those of us who grew up, live, work, play, and struggle come to make and define our communities. Some by circumstance, some by history, and some by identity. Growing up Black and working class in the 1990s in Toronto has an impact on how I come to think of community. It also helped to shape my own desire to attend teacher's college, and eventually go to graduate school.

Symbolic politics and structural violence

For any community that struggles with marginalization in the forms that I have detailed here: structured neglect and sustained disinvestment, anchored by anti-Black racism, results in underdevelopment, poverty and crime. The political right would ignore historical events and blame individuals and their lack of personal responsibility, their lack of drive and ambition, and their lack of ability to pull themselves up by their "bootstraps." On the left of the political spectrum, they would decry the foundational nature of historical disinvestment and the lack of social programs designed to address such histories. In Toronto—and Canada, more generally—the exercise of politics, or rather the game of it, mostly played by white men of wealth and power, is a banal exercise of trying to find the political middle.

As observed from Jane-Finch, the vantage point from which I make all of my political calculations, city and provincial politicians, be they from the right or the left, conservative or progressive, none have ever produced a political platform that substantively centres Jane-Finch, its people, or their needs.

And as a result, what we get in the form of political attention is constantly the cheap, symbolic gestures in place of sustained political programs that address the enduring structures that make life difficult in Jane-Finch. Very often we get symbolic responses to structural conditions. No recent event makes that more glaringly obvious than a recent shooting that took place in the community. It is a repeated pattern of our political representatives mounting symbolic gestures in the wake of spectacular violence.

On Sunday, November 8, 2020, Toronto mayor John Tory, NDP member of provincial parliament Tom Rakocevic, City Councillor Anthony Perruzza, and Interim Police Chief James Ramer held an impromptu "Safety Walk" with concerned residents and community members in Jane-Finch. The meeting was held at Jane Street and Stong Court, a few blocks north of Jane and Finch and was in response to a shooting that took place the day before where four people were hit, including a twelve-year-old boy who was walking home with his mother from the store. The young boy is being described as "an innocent victim." Reports indicated that two arrests have since been made in connection to this incident. The two young Black men who were arrested face twenty-eight charges with indications that more may follow.

I grew up and now teach and study in Jane-Finch. I have worked with youth in the area for most of my life. For those of us working on the ground, we do not have the luxury of framing violent incidents like this through the filter of "innocent" victimhood. Very often, we are the ones left working in the aftermath that this kind of violence leaves in its wake, and we do not ask questions about who did what to whom. We just show up, offer support, deploy care, and do what we can to help families and the community to get over the trauma.

The uncomfortable truth about this incident is that if it weren't for the twelve-year-old boy being accidentally shot across the street, this event would not have garnered any special attention or focus because our politicians at all levels accept these events as given in communities like Jane-Finch. The symbolic gesture of this "Safety Walk" was merely political theatre. We have yet to hear from representatives about what substantive investments, policy or otherwise, they will put in place that will change the conditions that make this kind of violence possible and predictable. We know that if we do not do something radically different, this kind of violence will repeat. And we will be here again, making the same phone calls, crying the same tears, and mounting the same vigils.

What if we framed this type of violence differently? What if we considered that when a young person picks up a gun and shoots at other young people in the middle of a beautiful Saturday afternoon on a busy street, we see that as a collective societal failure? What if we asked why communities like Jane-Finch are made so vulnerable to gun violence or global pandemics? What if we asked why youth who live here are always at such high risk of dying prematurely? What if we looked at these communities everyday instead of only in the wake of spectacular violence? What if we asked what might be possible if our politicians did more than offer symbolic gestures and political theatre when responding to incidents like this?

We need those charged with politically representing us and supposedly keeping us safe to consider communities like Jane-Finch and the people who live there every day, as a community that needs to be addressed and attended to beyond headline-making incidents of violence. Now that arrests have been made, what residents and community workers fear is that the spotlight, which shone so brightly on our community the last few days will fade and politicians will move on because arrests were made—with nothing substantively gained. That is why we are always skeptical of symbolic events like "safety walks" that offer politicians the chance to score cheap political points. These are platitudes in place of policy, which result in the same inaction, continued neglect and status quo that made the violence possible in the first place.

What might it take to have politicians and the broader public see the lives of Black, racialized poor and working-class people living in these communities as worthy of being engaged *before* violent incidents, not simply in the wake of them? When the focus and spotlight shines on vulnerable communities like mine only when there are "innocent" victims, tells us that our political representatives care little about our everyday lives.

It is easy to show up in the wake of spectacular violence; it's much more difficult to show up for people and their everyday struggles. The slow and less sensational effort it takes to effect social change and transform communities is the radical change we need to make an impact on overcrowded Jane buses; to invest in real, affordable, decent housing; address food insecurity; demand living-wage jobs; and provide the kind of mental health supports people dealing with isolation as a result of COVID-19 and poverty need. What might it take to urge City Council and Queen's Park to mount sustainable funding for programs and services in our community that will make real change possible? The choice has always been the same: either our politicians work with us to transform the conditions of our communities, or they're saying they do not care about us enough to show up before we die.

Another enduring feature of how Jane-Finch comes to be underdeveloped by anti-Black racism is how incidents like the one I detail above result in policy responses that make the lives of Black and racialized people in Jane-Finch ever more difficult. Let us take the issue of policing in Jane-Finch. According to the Ontario Human Rights Commission (OHRC), Black and racialized people who live in the city of Toronto are subject to racial profiling, over-policing, and increased incidents of police brutality. In that report produced by the OHRC, the most telling statistic, indeed a startling one, is that if a Black/racialized person is in the midst of a mental health crisis and encounters police, he or she is twenty times more likely to end up dead in that altercation with police than a white person is under similar pretenses.[569] I say that to highlight the fraught relationship police have with Black and racialized folks in Jane-Finch, in the City of Toronto, but really in any city in the Americas. Therefore, I find it a curious, in fact, racist, response that police and policing with its attendant logics are so often the policy response to the kinds of social problems I have detailed thus far in this chapter. To that end, I want to introduce here one example of such a racist response and how City Council repeated this familiar pattern in January of 2019.

Funding fading police/delegitimizing police

[I wrote this sometime in January of 2019 with equal parts frustration and rage because I knew I was putting pen to paper in advance of what would be yet another Black History Month filled with posturing and patronizing appearances by politicians at Black History Month events.]

---

569   See the Ontario Human Rights Commission's *A Disparate Impact: Second interim report on the inquiry into racial profiling and racial discrimination of Black persons by the Toronto Police Service* (Toronto: OHRC, August 10, 2020), which "confirms that Black people are more likely than others to be arrested, charged, over-charged, struck, shot or killed by Toronto police."
http://www.ohrc.on.ca/en/disparate-impact-second-interim-report-inquiry-racial-profiling-and-racial-discrimination-black

Recently, at the Toronto Police Services Board, a motion was put forward for a three per cent funding increase dedicated to policing in Toronto. This motion, which ultimately passed, requested an increase which would eventually push the 2019 Toronto Police Service's operating budget back above one billion dollars. And while Mayor Tory spearheaded this most recent increase, one to the tune of thirty million dollars, it is a complete about face from the mayor's first term. Back then, the mayor touted streamlining not only the force's budget, but also the force's responsibilities, tasks, and duties in an effort to "modernize" how policing operates in Toronto.

This about face from Mayor Tory—only the latest in a long line—comes as the Police Service's three-year transformational task force draws to an end. This task force was Toronto Police's effort to both modernize and pull the reins back on what has become a runaway budget. The central tenets of the transformation were a hiring freeze and "civilianization," which essentially meant the downloading of non-emergency work responsibilities to the City. It should be noted that the task force emerged under the previous Liberal government and was to be accompanied with legislation that would have, among other things, increased and sharpened police oversight, giving Ontario police chiefs more disciplinary powers, including the ability to suspend police officers who are being investigated of misconduct *without* pay. The legislation, which has now been placed on hold by the current Progressive Conservative government, would have been the first update to the *Police Services Act* in twenty-five years.

While we should always remain skeptical of institutions whose entire foundation is premised on the continued terror and surveillance of mainly poor and working-class Black and racialized communities, in the section that follows I want to think about all the ways the presence of police specifically, and the philosophy of policing generally, has been delegitimized of late from a plethora of different segments of society in Toronto. And if these latest rebukes of policing are to be taken seriously, then we are forced to conclude that this latest push *toward* increased policing—both in funding and standing in society—from Tory and all who are complicit, is a direct attack against those who experience the harsh and violent reality of policing most intimately—mainly Black and racialized people across this city, and specifically in Jane-Finch. The rest of this section details recent societal rebukes to policing, which are only the latest in a long line, which collectively send the same message: make (and keep) our lives free of policing.

One of my first introductions to pushing back on policing came as a young community worker in the late 1990s organizing and planning events. I worked at a small community organization in Jane-Finch that was very close in proximity to the police station. When we planned public events that encouraged residents and young people to come out, we would routinely partner with other organizations so that we could pool what little resources we had to put on a bigger and better event than any of our organizations could put on alone. Inevitably, word gets to that police division and its "community cultural relations officer" would come around asking if they could participate, either by contributing funding or providing volunteers.

Ultimately, this offer was always accompanied with a request to participate in the event in an "official" capacity. What that meant was having fully uniformed and armed police officers in attendance at our community event along with space on the always-coveted speaking list. I learned from elders, more experienced community workers, residents, and young people that allowing police to participate in the event, or even having them there at all, meant that community members would not come—and because of lateral safety and shared concern—would actively discourage others from doing the same. I learned that this position was informed by years of over-policing, racial profiling, police brutality, and abuse that they were subjected to by officers of that nearby division, the same officers asking to participate in an event "celebrating" community. As the community workers organizing that event, we could not have police at the event and maintain that it was about community. Not only did we decline police participation, volunteering or funding, we sought to ensure that nearby division was informed of the community's position based on history and requested they support us through their non-attendance.

I think of this early community work experience often, particularly when considering debates on policing in Toronto, especially when thinking about the recent debates surrounding police at Pride. The membership of Pride TO have twice voted down having police participate. Even amid heavy-handed attempts from its executive director and board, the membership has democratically stated that police at Pride is a non-starter. In his response to the second rebuke of police at Pride, Mayor Tory said he was "disappointed" in the decision to exclude uniformed police officers at Pride and that it was his job "to find a resolution not to concede." The language the mayor deploys here is telling. Who is he holding at the center when in response to a democratic vote, he declares there *still needs a resolution to be found*? To whom is the mayor declaring he will *not concede*? It is clear that Mayor Tory's main constituency in this matter is the police. What Mayor Tory is failing to grasp is that the results of these [democratic] votes represent the type of Pride experience the membership wants, one that does not include, symbolically or materially, the Toronto police. It is his role as mayor to abide by the mandate delivered by Pride TO, not to repeatedly convey his personal and politically calculated stance. Yet it is the latter tactic to which the mayor has decided to direct his efforts, to publicly cheerlead on the side of the Toronto police.

In 2018, the chorus of community voices pushing back the "School Resource Officer Program" (SRO)—a euphemism for fully uniformed and armed police officers in Toronto schools—were reaching a feverous pitch. Jane-Finch has three high schools located in its boundaries and all of those high schools had SROs, so in fact, an already overpoliced community had even more policing—now even in its schools. As of last year, the SRO program had been in place for ten years and came into effect following the Summer of the Gun and the death of Jordan Manners inside a TDSB school. Unsurprisingly, police officers were deployed to schools in communities where police-community relations were, at best, tenuous and antagonistic and, at worst, combative and violent. Because of the way the SRO program was rolled out and because of the history of policing in the communities in which they were stationed, the SRO program did not roll out smoothly. At schools where police officers were stationed, confusion arose when disciplinary incidents occurred as they inevitably do in high schools. For example, if an altercation arose between two students in the daily functioning of a school, teachers and administrators would affect whatever discipline was necessary. And in doling out discipline, school staff had a range of responses from which to choose and could consider any mitigating circumstances. Police have no such range, as officers of the peace they have a sworn duty to respond to any and all incidents through the purview of the penal code, their powers of arrest, and the criminal justice system. As then Police Chief Bill Blair said, "I have police officers; I don't have social workers."

Similar to policing generally, the SRO program was particularly damaging to Black and racialized youth across the system. Many more young people were "introduced" to the criminal justice system because of interactions they had with police in school—especially in Jane-Finch and other similar areas of the city. Community members began to track stories from Black students that the SROs in school were surveilling them. Evidenced by the fact that when young people were in their neighbourhoods in the evenings and on weekends, they were being identified by name, stopped, and questioned. Black youth were telling us it was clear that SROs were sharing "intel" with patrol officers in the wider community. Over the ten years the SRO program had been in place, community voices were decrying the program's harmful effects on Black and racialized youth and communities. The advocacy reached its apex when the TDSB approved a temporary pause and review of the SRO Program in August 2018. After over twenty student focus group sessions, one-on-one interviews, and eight community consultations in community, TDSB staff ultimately recommended to board trustees that the School Resource Officer Program in the Toronto District School Board be discontinued.

Recently, a similar public denouncing of policing has taken place at York University. Following a violent assault by multiple Toronto Police officers of a Black man on September 21, 2018, York University's Student Union formally acknowledged police misconduct on its campus. This was not the first time. Toronto Police have a long history of responding to altercations on that campus, where their chief function should be de-escalation, but their response has been one of escalation and violence. In this particular incident, York's Student Union requested York Security's notes—as security guards are required to record all incidents that occur on campus. Inexplicably, York Security had no notes to share. Because of this history and York Security's incompetence, or collusion in the form of willful ignorance, York University's Student Union took the issue up itself and passed a motion to formally acknowledge police misconduct, as well as a motion declaring that police had no place on their campus and questioning York Security's policy to call on Toronto Police for "de-escalation purposes." In addition, they are in the process of setting aside a dedicated fund for victims of on-campus police brutality. That such a fund is necessary tells us much of what the substance of policing is and what it might foretell.

In December 2018, the Ontario Human Rights Commission (OHRC) released its interim report on the inquiry into racial profiling and racial discrimination of Black persons by the Toronto Police Service titled, *A Collective Impact.*[570] This inquiry was the result of meetings with Black community members across the city, and the report was constructed with the aim of explicitly making Black voices central. The consultations were with community organizations and Black communities across the city. Some of the interim findings from this first set of consultations, as well as data obtained from the SIU, found that in the City of Toronto a Black person was "20 times more likely than a White person to be involved in a fatal shooting by the Toronto Police Service (TPS)."[571] And, that Black people were over-represented in use of force cases, shootings, deadly encounters, and fatalities. Clearly the OHRC report is only the latest in a long line of reports highlighting the Toronto Police Service's conduct.

The police force as an institution has a long history of dehumanizing Black people, and this OHRC interim report gives us only the latest numbers. While the OHRC does not have the mandate to implement direct change, the OHRC did call on the Toronto Police Service and its board to "acknowledge the racial disparities and community experiences," as well as calling on the Toronto Police Services Board to "require the Toronto Police to collect and publicly report on race-based data on all stops, searches, and use of force incidents."[572] The OHRC also did call on the police board to direct Toronto Police to implement recommendations in the *Report of the Independent Police Oversight Review* and the recommendations in the *Toronto*

---

570 Ontario Human Rights Commission, A Collective Impact: Interim report on the inquiry into racial profiling and racial discrimination of Black persons by the Toronto Police Service (Toronto: OHRC, December 2018). http://www.ohrc.on.ca/en/public-interest-inquiry-racial-profiling-and-discrimination-toronto-police-service/collective-impact-interim-report-inquiry-racial-profiling-and-racial-discrimination-black

571 OHRC, A Collective Impact.

572 OHRC, A Collective Impact.

Action Plan to Confront Anti-Black Racism.[573] Based on the Toronto Police and its board's immediate response, there is no indication of any serious uptake of any of the OHRC's calls to action.

I bring these events together to detail the undeniable reality that the already shaky standing police had in our society is fading and has been for some time. It is clear that police presence, and with it the rationales of policing and all its attendant logics, are no longer welcome in our Pride marches, our schools, our campuses, and in our community. The rebukes of policing are only getting louder, increasing in both frequency and intensity. That is why, from the perspective of Black and racialized peoples in Toronto—and especially from Jane-Finch—I cannot fathom the political actions of our mayor and the Police Board. To increase funding to a police force that has been rebuked by multiple segments in our society and whose core practice and methods have been condemned by the Ontario Human Rights Commission, is not only beyond the pale, but it is a violent attack on the health and well-being of Black and racialized people in this city—and it should be considered as such, by all who claim to care about us.

To show his face to Black Torontonians during Black History Month, the mayor, while relegating their communities to intensified police harassment and racial profiling, is a deep and profound contradiction. That despite longstanding pleas for change, this mayor and the Police Services Board made the choice to further push policing into communities that are harassed and violated by them daily. Our resisting policing in our schools, campuses, and communities will eventually push us to have a conversation about the logic and rationality of policing and if policing has a place anywhere in our society. Throwing more and more money into policing—blatantly and callously ignoring all democratic expression to the contrary, and by extension all the communities those bodies expressing them represent—is just wrong. And while political choices like more funding to police also has the effect of legitimizing police and reaffirming its standing in society, a serious conversation about the role of police in our society—if they are to have one at all—is coming. For many, this is a conversation that has been happening for a long

---

573   The report can be found here: https://www.toronto.ca/legdocs/mmis/2017/ex/bgrd/backgroundfile-109127.pdf

time, especially in communities like Jane-Finch. In one way or another, we have always been trying to resist what is an overbearing presence of policing in our lives, in our schools, and in our communities. In many ways, we have always been trying to defund and abolish police. This conversation—that might only now be reaching a feverous pitch—has been happening in our communities, if only in hushed tones for generations. Politicians ignore it at their own peril.

CCTV cameras to be installed by Toronto Police

The installation of police-controlled and monitored, closed-circuit television cameras (CCTV) in identified communities across Toronto was debated at Toronto City Council. Certainly, Jane-Finch was high on that list, despite years of lower crime rates than in other parts of the city. A notice was circulated in various parts of the city about this project. These are excerpts from a response to that proposal.

> What was the process by which our community was "identified?" The public should be aware of this process and the reasons behind them.

> What other communities in Toronto are slated to have CCTV cameras installed?

On top of those questions, this notice was asking for a lot of trust from the people who live and work in Jane-Finch. The Toronto Police were asking us to trust that they will not peer into our homes, that they will not keep data on file in permanent and secret databases. Ultimately that they will not trample on our right to privacy.

As reported by various media outlets like CBC and Global News, the recent Clearview AI scandal detailed Toronto Police's secretive use of controversial and unethical facial recognition software. This demonstrates to us that the Toronto Police cannot, and should not, be trusted. And it casts doubt on the ability of the Police Services Board to provide substantive oversight. It was Chief Mark Saunders himself who stated on the record that he was not aware of Clearview AI tech being used among his officers.

Jane-Finch is a predominantly Black and racialized community, and for decades the Toronto Police, in particular 31 Division, has had a fraught, at best, relationship with this community. Racial profiling has and continues to be rampant. The police abuse we experience in Jane-Finch is the kind that never results in any official record, so the recourse to lodge any kind of formal complaint is moot. These kinds of police interactions are an everyday occurrence and because of that, there is a rational, generational mistrust that is rooted in a history of police racism and constant excessive use of force. This is a community that exists, thrives, and lives in so many ways *despite* police, not because of them. If you've done any kind of community event in the Jane-Finch area, if you want it to be well attended, it is common knowledge that you do not invite police.

It is the firm belief of many community workers, grassroots groups, and residents that if this initiative is allowed to go ahead and cameras are installed in Jane-Finch—and what we assume to be other Black and racialized communities in Toronto—this will result in more racist policing, more racial profiling, and the increased harassment of Black and racialized youth.

And because of the history between police and Black and racialized communities, not only in Jane-Finch and other similarly constituted communities, but we must also implore to this body that this cannot stand.

The history to which I am referring to here has been noted by many other bodies: *Toronto Star,* Ontario Human Rights Commission, the CAPP Report, as well as too many researchers to enumerate here. In addition, this most recent Clearview AI Scandal is only the latest incident in a long line that continually reminds us that Black and racialized communities should not trust this police force.

With the various events I detailed above, from the historical to the contemporary, I wanted to make clear some of the ways anti-Black racism is a central feature of how Jane-Finch comes to be viewed, but also how it is governed, and how it comes to be seen from so many vantage points in society. It should go without saying (but it does not) that anti-Black racism, or even marginalization, neglect, or disinvestment, no matter how deeply they inform how Jane-Finch came to be the complex site it is, those are not the lenses by which we who live, work, play, and struggle there view ourselves or our community.

Jane and Finch, a neighbourhood full of joy and caring

August 14, 2003 is a date firmly etched in my mind, not only because it happened to be my birthday, but because it was also the day of the massive blackout that fell over much of the northeast region of North America. At the time, I was enrolled in summer courses at York University and that afternoon I was scheduled to take an exam, but the professor never showed up because, as I later learned, he was stuck on the subway.

So, amid complete darkness, I walked home. I strolled down Finch Avenue and then across Jane Street, and what I saw in my community surprised me, even after years of living there. I saw residents outside with makeshift bonfires that provided not only light, but also heat for cooking, and everyone was sharing food before it went bad in refrigerators that no longer had power.

There were cars lined up and down the street with all their doors open, blasting music and serenading impromptu barbecues. We didn't know why all the power was out or even how far the blackout stretched. But surrounded by darkness, Jane and Finch had decided to throw a block party, and everyone was invited (not to mention well fed).

There's no moment in my life that better demonstrates the most important lesson that growing up in Jane and Finch taught me: that words like "community" and "care" are action words—they're doing words. That moment also reminds me that, because of the work of so many of us in Jane-Finch, no matter what we've been through, what we face now, or what challenges may come, I knew then, like I know now, "We goin' be alright."

ACKNOWLEDGEMENTS

This book would not have transpired had it not been for a lot of exceptional people. The first are those I interviewed, many of whom were former residents, and some are current residents. Others interviewed either worked in the community (and gave much more than what was required by their job descriptions), and some interviewees cared deeply about the community and generously contributed their knowledge and support. Thank you so much for giving your time and for sharing your experiences to make this book come alive.

The list of thirty-nine exceptional and inspiring people is found in the appendices. Their full interviews can be found on the York Woods Public Library website: Black Creek Living History Project.

A big thank you to the York Woods library for agreeing to host the interviews, and especially to Jessica Rovito who prudently established the site and meticulously continued to upload all my material, even when she no longer worked at the York Woods Branch.

Special thanks to Katie Hayhurst, the area's alderman (councillor) in North York from 1973 to 1976. Katie was good enough to wade through her box of memories and provide relevant information about the early stages of development in Jane-Finch.

Local community newspapers, dating from the mid-1970s were invaluable. Tom Kear, in the publishing business, saved copies from the past—*Jane Corridor*, *Jane-Echo*, *Norwester*, *Downsview Post*, and the *York West Advocate*. Jesse Kear, a great source of information about the youth organization PEACH, generously shared some of her historical documents. Thank you both for your essential contributions.

I sent the first draft to three amazing women—trailblazers and innovators who played a significant and influential role in both the community and my life—Mary Lewis, Peggy Edwards, and Sue Wilkinson. Their insights, comments, and suggestions were invaluable and much appreciated. Mary, Peggy, and Sue—you have indeed influenced my life and I thank you deeply.

There was an initial chapter about community ministries and about the amazing work in Jane-Finch by the Mennonite Church, the Anglican Church, and the United Church of Canada. Dalton Jantzi, former Community Chaplin, The Reverend Canon Betty Jordan, and Community Minister Barry Rieder all reviewed this chapter and generously shared their opinions and knowledge. Their full interviews speak profoundly to their deep commitment to "community ministry," and to their belief in all people, regardless of income, race, or life circumstances. Thank you for all that you have done in the community and for inspiring me in my own life's journey.

Professor Narda Razack, former associate dean, Global and Community Engagement at York University, was enormously helpful in suggesting I apply for an intern to assist with research through the Liberal Arts and Professional Studies program. The internship awarded enabled me to hire Jasmine Ali in the summer of 2018. Thank you Narda for this gift.

Jasmine Ali was an undergraduate student at the time. She had a contagious enthusiasm with attention to detail, searching out archival information, analyzing research, reviewing media reports, assessing census data, and offering a young Black woman's perspective. Jasmine, a big heartfelt thank you.

Lorna Schwartzentruber, the associate director of Access Programs and Community Engagement (former manager of the York-TD Community Engagement Centre) generously read the stories I wrote about York University and provided me with helpful feedback. Thank you, Lorna, for your wisdom and support.

A revised and shorter version was read by Symone Walters and Bob McElhinney, both former Jane-Finch residents, and activists. They provided helpful feedback and encouragement—much appreciated.

Betty Jane ("B J") Richmond, former professor at York University, and a good friend, generously agreed to read the revised manuscript and offered constructive advice and suggestions. Thank you for your thoughtful ideas.

Pictures add so much to a book, and I found some with our own local *photographer extraordinaire*, Errol Young. Thank you, Errol, for recording our history pictorially.

The Honourable Dr. Jean Augustine generously wrote the Foreword for the book. My deepest thanks for your kind words of experience and hope.

My sincere thanks and much appreciation to community activist Sam Tecle for his contributions in Chapter Ten about anti-Black racism and his leadership role in the Jane-Finch community.

While preparing this book, I had many conversations with friends, relatives, acquaintances, and interested people. To all—a big thank you for your thoughts, ideas, and ongoing support.

Black activist, author Chris Williams was pleased there would be a book "about us and for us" that morphed into the title of this book. Thank you, Chris.

My appreciation for the valuable support from Rory Dickinson and the great work by the Friesen team.

Lastly, many thanks go to Richard De Gaetano, who reviewed the drafts, helped with wording, punctuation, checked accuracy, and gave me the confidence to send the manuscript to readers, and then to FriesenPress. This book would not have come to fruition without you.

I take full responsibility for any errors that may be found in this work.

APPENDIX A

Black Creek Living History Project (BCLHP) Interviews

1. Anderson, Doug, October 10, 2009.
2. Astrella, Joe, April 10, 2012.
3. Augimeri, Maria, June 2, 2019.
4. Birnberg, Peggy, March 2, 2010.
5. Brown, Anna-Kay, September 2019.
6. Chaharlangi, Farid Partovi, May 2018.
7. Cole, Fay, September 2009.
8. De Gaetano, Richard, July 2014.
9. Deawuo, Leticia, July 2015.
10. Dutta, Veena, September 29, 2011.
11. Ede, Helen, August 21, 2009.
12. Edwards, Peggy, June 2, 2010.
13. Edwards, Rouvean, May 2018.
14. GoPaul, Butterfly, May 2016.
15. Gray, Byron, September 9, 2015.
16. Jantzi, Dalton, September 2009.
17. Jordan, Betty, August 2, 2010.
18. Koduah, Love, April 18, 2011.
19. Lewis, Mary, January 14, 2009.
20. MacKay, Pat, March 3, 2015.

21. McLeod, Shane, February 2020.

22. Mendez, Margarita, January 22, 2011.

23. Narain, Suzanne, September 2018.

24. Nguyen, Paul, June 21, 2008.

25. Novick, Marvyn, June 2012.

26. O'Neill, Pat, August 24, 2009.

27. Payne, Stephnie, March 11, 2011.

28. Perruzza, Anthony, April 2019.

29. Ramsaroop, Talisha, December 9, 2019.

30. Reda, Almaz, September 13, 2019.

31. Rieder, Barry, June 7, 2018.

32. Sergio, Mario, December 2, 2019.

33. Sgro, Judy, November 29, 2019.

34. Shookner, Malcolm, February 7, 2010.

35. Tecle, Sam, September 2019.

36. Thompson, Marion Snider, June 9, 2010.

37. Whitehead, Brian, August 25, 2010.

38. Wilkinson, Sue, June 2016.

39. Young, Errol, October 2019.

APPENDIX B

Demographics

Humber River-Black Creek [based on 2016 Statistics Canada Census]

Population 108,035 *(Toronto = 2,956,024) [Toronto figures in italics]*

Ages 0-14 = 19% *(15%)*, 15-24 = 15% *(12%)*, 25-64 = 51% (58%), 65+ = 14% *(16%)*

Housing Renting = 51% *(47%)*, Owning = 49% *(53%)*

Avg. Rent $1,011   **Rent as % of income** > 30% of income = 45% *(46%)*

Mother tongue English = 45% *(53%)*, French = 1% *(1%)*, Other = 54% *(46%)*

Visible minority 74% *(51%)* **Immigrant** 58% *(47%)* **Non-immigrant** 39% *(49%)*

Visible minority population Black 22.8% *(8.9%)*, South Asian 14.2% *(12.6%)*, Latin American 9.5% *(8.9%)*, South East Asian 8.9% *(1.5%)*, Filipino 5.5% *(5.7%)*, Chinese 3.4% *(11.1%)*, West Asian 1.8% *(2.2%)*, Arab 1.5% *(1.3%)*, Korean 0.4% *(1.5%)*

Occupations management = 5.1% *(11.4%)*, business / financial / administration = 13.5% *(18%)*, natural/applied sciences = 4.2% *(8.2%)*, education / law / social / community / government = 8% *(13%)*, arts / culture / recreation / sports = 1.8% *(5.6%)*, sales / service 29.2% *(24%)*, trades / transportation / equipment operating = 18.3% *(9.1)*, manufacturing / utilities 14.1% *(4.3%)*

Unemployed 11% *(6.4%)* **Employed** 52% *(59%)* **Not in Labour Force** 42% *(35%)*

Income [$1,000s] < 20 = 13% *(13%)*, 20-49.9 = 34% *(25%)*, 50-79.9 = 24% *(21%)*,

80-124.9 = 19% *(19%)*, 125+ = 11% *(22%)*

Family type Couples w/children = 42.5% *(44%)* Without children = 22.8% *(34.8%)*

Lone parents = 34.7% *(21.1%)*

Households w/ 3+ children Couples = 21.9% *(16.3%)*, Lone parents = 20.7% *(11.5%)*

Top 10 birth places Italy, Vietnam, Jamaica, Philippines, Guyana, India, Pakistan, Iraq, Sri Lanka, Nigeria

Most recent immigrants Philippines, Iraq, Pakistan, Nigeria, Jamaica, India, Vietnam, Sri Lanka, Turkey, Afghanistan

Education level post-secondary = 38% *(59.1%)*, high school = 30% *(24.5%)*, no high school diploma or other certificate = 32.2% *(16.4%)*

Top 10 home languages *[single response 88.3%, multiple response 11.7%]* English 53.6%, Spanish 5.3%, Vietnamese 4.7%, Italian 4.5%, Urdu 2%, Cantonese 1.6%, Tamil 1.6%, Tagalog 1.5%, Punjabi 1.5%, Assyrian/Neo-Aramaic 1%

Avg. household income $65,458 *($102,721)* **Median** $53,500 *($65,800)*

Single-person household $32,100 *($55,400)*

Low-income population 27,670 *(543,365)*, **Per cent of population** = 25.7% *(20.2%)*

APPENDIX C

Measure	Jane-Finch area (NB 24/25)	Toronto
Population change, 2011 – 2016	-2.2%	4.5%
Visible Minority population	77.8%	51.5%
Immigrant population	58.9%	47.0%
Population under 25 years old	34.9%	27.1%
4+ person households	35.0%	21.9%
Families with children	80.1%	65.2%
Lone-parent families	41.3%	21.2%
Residential mobility – moved to a new residence (2011-2016)	31.7%	40.7%
Average household income	$60,997	$102,721
Incidence of low income	28.7%	20.2%
Unemployment rate	12.0%	8.2%
Labour force participation	55.0%	64.7%
Post-secondary attainment	39.0%	69.0%
Renters	56.0%	47.0%

Source:

Toronto Planning Department, "Report for Action: Jane-Finch Initiative—Community Development Plan and Updated Land Use Planning Framework," (Toronto: Feb 25, 2020)

REFERENCES

"A Better Plan to Keep Our Hospital at Jane and Finch—Revealed at Local Meeting" (*York West Advocate*, May 3, 2006).

Adom, Perpetual, "Narrowing the Gap Between Youth and Police" (*Jane Finch Caring Community*, June–August 2001).

Adom, Perpetual, "Response from 31 Division" (*Jane Finch Caring Community*, June–August 2001).

Agnew, Jean, "You Got Good and Bad in the Beef Ring" (*Jane Echo*, July 1982).

Ahmadi, Donya, "Living with Diversity in Jane Finch" (Amsterdam: Architecture and the Built Environment, November 2017).

"Alderman faces suit over high-rise stand," (*Toronto Star*, December 16, 1980: A13), quoted in "Interim Report" (North York: San Romanoway Revitalization Association, March 2004).

Ali, Jasmine, "Research Findings for Jane-Finch History Project" (North York: York University, 2018).

Ali, Reya, "Funding Levels Among Community-Based Services: A Comparison Between an Inner City and a Suburban Neighbourhood" (Research report for Community Relations Office, York University), n.d.

Alphonso, Caroline and James Bradshaw, "Trustees Narrowly Approve Contentious Afro-centric School" (*Globe and Mail*, January 30, 2008).

Amos, Michael A., *Both Sides of the Fence: Surviving the Trap* (Toronto: Famos Books, 2014).

"An Interview with Stacian Campbell, a Youth in Our Community: In Her Own Words. A Young Jane/Finch Woman Speaks Her Mind" (*Jane Finch Caring Community*, June–August 2001).

Augimeri, Maria, "Presentation to Economic Development & Parks Committee" (Toronto: 2002).

Augimeri, Maria, "Youth Violence and Parks and Recreation Programs" (Toronto: City Budget, March 7, 2001).

Augimeri, Maria, "Memo to Members of the Economic Development, Culture and Tourism Standing Committee", September 6, 2001.

Bailey, Annette with Divine Velasco, "We need to Build a Culture of Peace to Fight Gun Violence" (CBC Docs POV, 2018).

BCVG Proposal to North York Parks and Recreation, Youth Services Division (North York: 1980).

Begin, Monique and Gerald L. Caplan, "For the Love of Learning" (Toronto: Royal Commission on Learning, 1995).

"Black Creek Community Capacity Building Project" (*Yorkwest Advocate*, Sep. 2008).

Board of Directors, "Children and Youth Strategy—Implementation Update" (Toronto Community Housing, February 13, 2008).

Boudreau, Julie-Anne, Roger Keil and Douglas Young, "The In-Between City", in *Changing Toronto: Governing Urban Neoliberalism* (Toronto: University of Toronto Press, 2009).

Bow, Beth, "Community Spirit of the Jane Finch Corridor" (North York: paper for York University, 1984).

"Brianna Remembered with 'P.L.A.Y. Ground' ", Toronto Raptors Basketball Club news release (Toronto: October 27, 1999).

Brillinger, Chris, "Responses to the Building Hope Coalition Recommendations" (Toronto: January 14, 2004).

Burnett, Wayne, "Public School System: Who's Failing Whom" (North York: *Norwester*, August–September 1988).

Burnett, Wayne, Letter to the York-Finch Hospital Board of Governors (June 30, 1987).

Cameron, Grace, "Taking a Stand Against Drugs" (*Norwester*, November 1988).

Canzana, Lolanda interview (Toronto: York Woods Public Library, Black Creek Living History Project, November 2010).

Capponi, Pat, "Clean City, Beautiful City" (Toronto: *Now Magazine*, July 1999).

Cardoso, Tom, "Bias Behind Bars: A Globe Investigation Finds a Prison System Stacked Against Black and Indigenous Inmates" (*Globe & Mail*, October 24, 2020).

Carey, Elaine, "Immigrants' Dreams Lead to Ghetto Life" (*Toronto Star*, April 10, 1979).

Cecil Foster, "Lastman Fears Bloody Winter of Shootings" (*Toronto Star*, December 3, 1981, A6), quoted in Gemmell, "GUNS.".

"Celebrating Our Past: Shaping Our Future—25th Anniversary (1981–2005)" (North York: Delta Family Resource Centre, 2005).

City of Toronto, news release, "Huron-Wendat Day Honours Toronto's First Nations History" (Toronto: *NationTalk*, https://nationtalk.ca/story/huron-wendat-day-honours-torontos-first-nation-history, June 12, 2013).

City of Toronto, Policy and Finance Committee report (Toronto: July 6, 1999).

City of Toronto, "Toronto Action Plan To Confront Anti-Black Racism" (Toronto: 2017).

Clarke, Antonius telephone interview by author (2019).

Clement, Wallace, *Continental Corporate Power* (Toronto: McClelland and Stewart, 1977).

Coalition of Concerned Community Organizations letter (North York: January 19, 1987).

Coalition of Concerned Community Organizations, "Our Vision Re: Community Development", statement to funding representatives (North York: June 10, 1987).

"Community opposes the size of Yorkgate project" (*York West Advocate*, March 2005).

"Community Services Notebook" (*Norwester*, August–September 1988).

"Community Upset Over Hospital's Plan to Close Finch Ave. Site" (*Downsview Post*, May 2002).

Crucefix, Lanna, "The Parsons Site", *Journal of the Ontario Archeological Society*, Toronto. XXX.

Day, Arik C., *Social Innovation as Community Governance: Critical Success Factors in the Neoliberal City* (Amsterdam: University of Amsterdam, [Master's Thesis in Urban and Regional Planning], August 15, 2016).

De Guerre, Joan, interview (Toronto: York Woods Public Library, Black Creek Living History Project, November 2010).

Deen, Sadie, Letter to the Editor (*Jane Echo*, September 1983).

"District Plan 10" (North York: Metropolitan Toronto Planning Board, North York Planning Board, North York Board of Education and Metropolitan Separate School Board, February 1962), 22.

Duncan, Elizabeth, "Activist Deplores Police Shooting" (*Norwester*, March 1996).

Ede, Helen, "Inventory of Human Services in the Jane Finch Area" (*Jane Corridor*, January 1976).

Ede, Helen, "Neighbourhood Planning—Social Evolution of Jane Finch Area", June 1978).

Ede, Helen, Peggy Birnberg and Mary Lewis, "A Case Study of the Child/Parent Centre of the Jane/Finch Community and Family Centre", North York: Primary Prevention Institute, February 1980).

Ede, Helen, "*Workshop Five: Neighbourhood Planning—Social Evolution of Jane Finch Area*" (June 1978).

Editorial, "Toronto Has Lost a Decade in the Fight Against Gun Violence" (*Toronto Star*, November 19, 2018).

Eisenstat, Marilyn, "PEACH Program Keeps Kids in School" (*York West Advocate*, Sep. 2004).

"Evaluation Report for the Jane-Finch Neighbourhood Outreach Project" (Toronto: Ontario Community Education Centre, January 31, 1984).

Falconer, Julian et al, "The Road to Health: A Final Report on School Safety, Executive Summary" (Toronto Board of Education, January 10, 2008).

Fantino, Julian, "Open Letter from Police to Jane Finch Residents" (North York: *Norwester*, November 1988).

Farrell, Lennox, "Strategic Planning Meeting Update" (North York: [email communication] August 28, 2001).

"Fighting for Food Justice in the Black Creek Community: Summary Report" (Toronto: Black Creek Food Justice Network, 2010).

"Firgrove Expects Thousands" (*Jane Echo*, August 1981).

"Firgrove Students 'Happier and Better' " (*Jane Echo*, April 1981).

Freiler, Christa, "Why Strong Neighbourhoods Matter: Implications for Policy and Practice" (Toronto: Strong Neighbourhoods Task Force, November 4, 2004).

Friesen, Joe, "Singer Hopes Her Bubble Won't Burst" (*Globe and Mail*, May 8, 2006).

Friesen, Joe, "Wheeling and Dealing to Keep Out the Rain" (*Globe and Mail*, May 20, 2006).

Friesen, Joe, "A Show of Community, Not Force" (*Globe and Mail*, May 15, 2006).

Friesen, Joe, "Residents Heartsick Over Fate of Hospital" (*Globe and Mail*, June 7, 2006).

From Longhouse to Highrise: Pioneering in our Corner of North York (North York: Downsview Weston Action Community, 1986).

Gemmell, Peggy, "GUNS: No One Here Has Seen Them" (*Jane Echo*, December 1981).

Gemmell, Peggy, "Hull Back with Plaza Plans" (*Jane Echo*, January 1981).

Gemmell, Peggy, "I Saw Many Changes—All of Them Good" (*Jane Echo*, December 1980).

Gemmell, Peggy, "Report Says Residents See Press as Enemy" (*Jane Echo*, December 1981).

Gemmell, Susan, "Jane-Finch Decades Ago" (*Jane Echo*), June 1982.

Goldstein, Lawrence, "The Corridor—Pain, Anger...Hope" (*The Mirror*, May 17, 1978).

Gordon, Andrea, "TDSB Votes Down Police Presence in High Schools" (*Toronto Star*, November 22, 2017).

Gorman, Joe, Director of Corporate and Public Affairs, Humber River Hospital (Email, November 2020).

Green, Cynthia, "Neighbourhood Action Hearings" (*Jane Corridor*, May 1976; June 1976).

Green, Gary, "United We Stand" (Toronto: Report on a Community Meeting, July 26, 2006).

Hall, Barbara, "Toronto District School Board Governance Advisory Panel Report," (Toronto: August 19, 2015) (http://www.edu.gov.on.ca/eng/new/2015/TDSB2015.html).

Hancock, Macklin L., *Jane Finch Commercial Study* (Toronto: Project Planning Associates, for the City of North York Planning Board, February 1963).

Hardy Smith, Alana, "Pat O'Neill Interviewed" (*Jane Corridor*, New Year's 1976).

Hart, Patricia W., *Pioneering in North York; a History of the Borough* (North York: General Publishing, Canadian First Edition, 1971).

Hayhurst, Katie, email to Wanda MacNevin (2018).

Henry, Frances and Carol Tator, *Discourses of Domination: Racial Bias in the Canadian English-Language Press* (University of Toronto Press—Canadian Ethnic Studies Association, 2002).

Heyworth, Elspeth, "Future of the Suburbs Conference at York University" (*Jane Echo*; February 20, March 20, April 20, 1982).

Hinds, Marcelline, Letter to the Editor (*Jane Corridor*, April 1978).

History of Downsview Air Force Base (*Wikipedia*).

Hoddinott, Dan, "GONE!" (North York: *Norwester*, April 1994).

Hodge, Diane, interview (Toronto: York Woods Public Library, Black Creek Living History Project, November 2010).

Hoskins, Dr. Eric and Madeleine Meilleur, "Ontario's Youth Action Report" (Toronto: August 22, 2012).

Hospital Coalition to Broaden its Focus (*York West Advocate*, November 2006).

Huggins, Kurt, "Marcus Garvey Centre Looks Forward to a New Path" (*York West Advocate*, May 2009).

Hulchanski, J. David, *The three cities within Toronto: income polarization among Toronto's neighbourhoods, 1970–2000* (Toronto: Cities Centre Press, December 2007).

Huntley, Kathy, "Black Expectations Seen Lower by Caribbean Outreach Survey" (*Jane Echo*, June 1981).

Huntley, Kathy, "Tenants Plan to Sue Landlord" (*Jane Echo*, August 1981).

Hynie, Michaela, "The Morning After: Stakeholder Reflections on the Sustainability of the Community-Campus Engagement Centre in the Changing Environment" (Toronto: 2017).

IC Savings Heritage Display, Humber River Hospital (November 1, 2017).

"Interim Report" (North York: San Romanoway Revitalization Association, March 2004).

Jackson, Suzanne F., "Yorkwoods Safe Neighbourhood Project—Interim Evaluation Report", Toronto; December 5, 2000).

Jackson, Suzanne, "The Yorkwoods-Grandravine Neighbourhood in the Broader Jane Finch Community" (Toronto: University of Toronto, Report, late 1990s), 10. .

Jackson, Suzanne, Shelley Cleverly, David Burman, Richard Edwards, Blake Poland and Ann Robertson, *Toward Indicators of Community Capacity: A Study of Four Toronto Communities* (Toronto: Centre for Health Promotion, August 1999).

Jacobs, Jane, *Death and Life of Great American Cities* (New York: Random House, 1961).

James, Carl, *Life at the Intersection: Community, Class and Schooling* (Halifax: Fernwood Publishing, 2012).

James, Royson, "Jane and Finch Dared to Dream—Now Metrolinx Dares to Double-Cross" (*Toronto Star*, July 3, 2020).

"Jane Finch is getting on: What's holding you back?" (Community Forum Report, May 2007).

Jane Finch Task Force, "Community Response to the TSNS 2020: What Neighbourhood Improvement Looks Like from the Perspective of Residents in Jane-Finch" (Toronto: 2015).

"Jane-Finch Launches a New Landmark" (*Jane Finch Caring Community*, November–December 2000).

Jantzi, Dalton, "Chaplaincy in a Highrise Community—One Approach to Urban Ministry" (Toronto: paper, 1982).

JFAAP, *Permanently Temporary: Labour, Precarity and Resistance in Jane-Finch* (Toronto: Jane Finch Action Against Poverty, October 2019).

"Judge Cancels Interview" (*Jane Echo*, March 1981).

Kear, Mark, "A Maker of History in the York West community" (*York West Advocate*, Sep. 2008).

Kear, Sarah, "Africentric Schools, Programs in Toronto" (*York West Advocate*, Dec. 2007).

Khan, Ayesha, "Social Innovation Hub" (*Downsview Advocate*, March 2020).

"Kids Become Partners in Conflict Resolution" (*Jane Finch Caring Community*, June–August 2001).

Klein, Jack and Henry Sears, *A Review of Planning Policies re: Lands Bounded by Finch Ave., Hwy 400, the H.E.P.C. right of way and Jane Street* (North York: North York Planning Board, December 1975).

Kome, Penney, "A High-Rise Isn't a Home for Families and Children" (*Globe and Mail*), November 7, 1973.

LaRose, Winston, telephone conversation with author (2019).

"Lastman 'Gets Even' with OHC" (*Jane Echo*, December 1983).

Letters of Understanding, Community and Neighbourhood Services (City of Toronto, June 24, 2002).

Lewis, Mary, "Case for Community Work" (Toronto: unpublished paper, n.d.).

Lewis, Mary, "Neighbourhoods Under Stress Commentary" (Toronto: unpublished paper, July 2018).

Lewis, Stephen, "Report of the Advisor on Race Relations to the Premier of Ontario" (Toronto: June 9, 1992).

Li Preti, Peter, "Two Year Proposal for Jane Finch to the City of North York" (North York: December 11, 1986).

Li Preti, Peter, Letter to North York Council (North York: December 11, 1986).

Logan, Dave, "Poor Area Planning Troubles in the Schools" (*Jane Corridor*, Dec. 1975).

Lynd, Rev. G. W. and Mrs. Paul Snider, "Elia United Church Centennial—50th Anniversary of the Present Church" (1951).

MacDonald, Michael, "The Beauty within Downsview's History" (*Downsview Advocate*, January 2016).

MacNevin, Wanda, "Summary of Organizations and Services in Jane-Finch/Black Creek Area" (North York: Jane/Finch Community and Family Centre, 2014).

MacNevin, Wanda, "The Historical Highlights of the Jane/Finch Community and Family Centre" (North York: J/FCFC, 2016.

MacNevin, Wanda, "Yorkwoods Safe Neighbourhood Project" (North York: final report, January 16, 2001).

MacNevin, Wanda, *From the Edge: A Woman's Evolution from Abuse to Activism* (Toronto: Picas & Points Publishing, 1999).

MacNevin, Wanda, *If I Only Knew.. Stories of Teen Moms* (Toronto: Black Creek Community Health Centre, 2008).

"Mayor Announces Strategy to Promote a Safer Toronto for Youth" (City of Toronto: media release, May 8, 2002).

McGregor, Heather, "Poverty Reduction Central to Building Back Better" (*Toronto Star*, August 17, 2020).

McLaren, Peter, "My Commitment Deep, Detractors Myopic: Author" (*Jane Echo*, May 1980).

McLaren, Peter, *Cries from the Corridor: The new suburban ghettos* (Toronto: Methuen, 1980).

McLaughlin, Amara, "Cabin Transformed to 'Further Understanding and Reconciliation' for York U Indigenous students" (Toronto: CP24.com, June 21, 2017).

"Meals On Wheels" (*Jane Corridor*, May 1976).

Mendleson, Rachel, "City Turns to Province for Help in Fighting COVID-19 in Hard-Hit Northwest Corner" (*Toronto Star*, July 9, 2020).

Miller, David, "Inaugural Address" (City of Toronto, News Release, December 2, 2003).

Model Schools for Inner City Task Force Report (Toronto District School Board, May 2005).

Monument erected in Jane Finch (*Downsview Post*, June 2002).

Morgan, Tonika and Heather Miller, *From Poverty to Prosperity, Women Moving Forward* (Toronto: Jane/Finch Community and Family Centre, 2011).

Morris, Ruth, "A Short History of Black Creek Focus/PEACH" (North York: November 30, 1998).

Morris, Ruth, "CAN tells the real Jane-Finch story" (*Jane Finch Caring Community*, February–March 2000).

Morris, Ruth, "If Breanna Had Lived" (*Jane Finch Caring Community*, July–August 1999).

Morrison, John (n.d.) in Sandberg, L. Anders, Rene Gualtieri, Jon Johnson, *Re-Connecting with a Historical Site: One Narrative and the Huron-Wendat Ancestral Village at York University* (Toronto: York University, n.d.).

Mothercraft, Early Development Instrument (EDI) Results: 2004–2011 for York West. Toronto Planning, *Report for Action to the Economic and Community Development Committee* (Toronto: February 25, 2020).

MTHA Asked to Cut 'Excessive' Concentration of Subsidized Housing (*Jane Echo*, September 1983).

Muego, Benjamin N., "O'Neill Talks About Ward Problems, Prospects" (*Jane Echo*, February 9, 1979).

Narain, Suzanne and Rajanie Kumar, "Connect the Dots: Best Practices for Jane-Finch and York University Partnerships, Conference Report" (Toronto: December 11, 2013).

Narain, Suzanne, *The Re-Branding Project: The Genealogy of Creating a Neoliberal Jane and Finch* (Toronto, 2012).

Nasser, Shanifa, "TDSB Votes Down Police Presence in High Schools" (Toronto: CBC News, November 2017).

Neighbourhoods Under Stress (Toronto: Joint Task Force on Neighbourhood Support Services, 1983).

Neill, A.S., *Summerhill: A Radical Approach to Child Rearing* (New York: Hart Publishing, 1960).

Newell, Van J., "Rural Roots of Old Jane-Finch" [calendar] (North York: Jackson & Cowan, 1983).

News Release—Ontario Provides Land for a Community Hub and Arts Centre in Toronto (*Toronto Star*, March 11, 2021).

North York Inter-Agency and Community Council, Community Profile of the City of North York (North York Inter-Agency and Community Council, July 1992).

North York Planning Department re: York University Site, Federal-Provincial Housing Lands Jane Street and Steeles Ave. (Reference to ACT for Youth, An Overview of Development in Jane-Finch—1950s to Present), 1960.

Novick, Marvyn, "Metro Suburbs in Transition—Part 1: Evolution and Overview" (Social Planning Council of Metropolitan Toronto, 1979).

Nwosu, Susan, *Evaluation of Northwest Advisory Committee* (North York: October 14, 1988).

O'Neill, Pat, "Consultants Meet the People" (*Jane Corridor*, Dec. 1975).

O'Neill, Pat, "Go Elsewhere Young People to Find Work" (*Jane Echo*, September 1981).

O'Neill, Pat, "I know why daycare is needed" (*Jane Echo*, April 15, 1981).

O'Neill, Pat, "Rally for Just Representation" (*Jane Corridor*, January 19, 1980).

O'Neill, Pat, "Report to the Community Services and Housing Committee" (Borough of North York, September 8, 1982).

O'Neill, Pat, "Youth Hiring Headaches" (*Jane Echo*, May 1982).

OHC, Cadillac plan 1,114 units in North York (*Globe and Mail*, January 23, 1971).

Olimpo, Frances, "Next Stop: Transit City" (*York West Advocate*, Sep. 2008).

Ontario Human Rights Commission, *A Collective Impact: Interim report on the inquiry into racial profiling and racial discrimination of Black persons by the Toronto Police Service* (Toronto: OHRC, December 2018). .

Ontario Human Rights Commission, *A Disparate Impact: Second Interim Report on the Inquiry into Racial Profiling and Racial Discrimination of Black Persons by the Toronto Police Service* (Toronto: OHRC, August 2020) .

Ontario Trillium Foundation news release, 1998.

Pagliaro, Jennifer, "The Lost Decade" (*Toronto Star*, October 13, 2018).

Paradkar, Shree, "The Yonge St. Riot of 1992…or Was It an Uprising?" (*Toronto Star*, update May 8, 2017).

Peace, Tom, "Stops Visited Along the Way" (bus tour narration) (Toronto: York Woods Library, Black Creek Living History Project, 2010).

Pengelly, Irene, "Jane Finch Youth Study" (North York: September 1978).

Peteran, Beth, "Time Marches On in North York" (photocopy—source and date unknown).

Pieti, John, "End Program that Puts Police Officers in Some Toronto Schools" (Toronto: CBC News, November 13, 2017).

Pitt, Steve, "Action Stalls Traffic at Jane-Finch" (*Norwester*, November 2, 1996).

Planning Department, "Jane-Finch Initiative Public Meeting #1" (City of Toronto, November 23, 2020).

"Police Repeat 'Vial of Life' " (*Jane Echo*, May 1984).

Price, Berta and Ed Price, "Oyster Suppers Were a Big Deal Here" (*Jane Echo*, August 27, 1982).

"Project Rebirth, A Community in Action Report: An Assessment of the Needs and Problems of Jane and Finch" (North York: report, March 1990).

Quarter, Jack, Laurie Mook and Betty Jane Richmond, *What Counts: Social Accounting for Non-profits and Cooperatives* (Upper Saddle River New Jersey: Pearson Education, 2003).

"Ratings of Schools in North York" (*Toronto Star*, February 28, 1978).

"Register Now for Jane/Finch Community and Family Centre Seneca College Courses" (*Jane Echo,* January 1977).

"Report for Action from the Jane-Finch Initiative—Community Development Plan and Updated Land Use Planning Framework" (Toronto: February 25, 2020).

"Report on the Outreach Pilot Project" (North York: Mayor's Committee on Community, Race and Ethnic Relations—Appendix F, September 18, 1981).

"Report Seeks Smaller Classes" (*Jane Echo*, March 1981).

"Residents Nix Police Plan" (*Jane Finch Caring Community*, August-September 1999).

Richardson, Chris, "Canada's Toughest Neighbourhood: Surveillance, Myth and Orientalism in Jane Finch" (St. Catharines, Ontario: MA thesis, Brock University, 2008).

Rigakos, George S., Francis Kwashie and Stephen E. Bosanac, "The San Romanoway Community Revitalization Project: Interim Report" (North York: San Romanoway Revitalization Association, March 2004).

Robinson, Mona, letter to the United Community Fund (Toronto: April 19, 1979).

Rochon, Lisa, "Designs for Urban Fear" (*Globe and Mail*, February 2000).

Ros, David, "Jane and Finch to become 'University Heights,' " (North York: *Excalibur*, [York University student newspaper] October 16, 2007).

Ros, David, "York Goes to the Mall. Is This Community U?" (*York West Advocate*, September 2008).

Rothman, Laurel, "Strong Neighbourhoods Task Force: Research Product Two: The Role of Community Infrastructure in Building Strong Neighbourhoods" (Family Services Association of Toronto, 2005).

Sandberg, L. Anders, Rene Gualtieri, Jon Johnson, *Re-Connecting with a Historical Site: One Narrative and the Huron-Wendat Ancestral Village at York University* (Toronto: York University, n.d.).

"Save Our Hospital Protest" (*Downsview Post*, February 2002).

Schultz-Lorentzen, Finn, "Unshaven Tenant Wears Nothing but Underpants" (*Jane Echo*, March 1985).

Sgro, Judy, *Task Force Report on Urban Issues* (North York: 2002).

Shewprasad, Sharmila, "Jane-Finch Women March" (*Jane Finch Caring Community*, November-December 2000).

Social Development, Finance & Administration Division, "The Jane Finch Gang Prevention Project" (Toronto: December 10, 2002).

Social Development, Finance & Administration, *Toronto Strong Neighbourhoods Strategy 2020* (Toronto: 2011).

"Some Class Sizes Here Go Down to 20 Pupils" (*Jane Echo*, June 1981).

Spensieri, Michael, "Movie Flops Miserably as Social Statement" (*Jane Echo*, August 1983).

Spensieri, Michael, "York Finch Updates Equipment" (*Jane Echo*, February 1984).

Spurr, Ben, "In Jane-Finch, Leaders Fume at 'Terrible Betrayal' After Metrolinx Goes Back On Plan to Donate Land For Community Centre" (*Toronto Star*, July 23, 2020).

Stancu, Henry, "Neighbourhood Cringes" (*Toronto Sun*, November 27, 1981, 4), quoted in Peggy Gemmell, "GUNS: No One Here Has Seen Them" (*Jane Echo*, December 1981).

Stein, David Lewis, *Toronto Star*, as quoted in Mark Kear (*York West Advocate*, Sep. 2008).

"Strong neighbourhoods: A call to action" (United Way of Greater Toronto, 2004).

Syed, Fatima, "Here's Everything the Doug Ford Government Cut in Its First Year in Office" (National Observer, June 7, 2019).

Tasko, Patti, "Christmas Concert Was the Big Deal", *Jane Echo*, December 17, 1982; *Henry Snider: His Ancestors and Descendants* (Snider Genealogical and Historical Research Group, 1976).

TDHC, "Review of Humber River Regional Hospital's Redevelopment Proposal: Final Report" (Toronto District Health Council, July 2001).

Tecle, Sam, Abena Offeh-Gyimah, Talisha Ramsaroop, Lorna Schwartzentruber, "Jane Finch Community Research Partnership, Symposium Report" (North York: November 29, 2016).

"The Globe Sends a Reporter Among Us" (*York West Advocate*, May 3, 2006).

"The Teachers Bring School to Parents" (*Jane Echo*, December 1980).

"Three Democratic Heated Debates On the Future of Our Schools" (*York West Advocate*, April 2010).

"Three New Programs for Our Area" (*Jane Echo*, Sept 1980).

Toronto City Summit Alliance, "Enough Talk: An Action Plan for the Toronto Region" (Toronto: 2003).

Toronto Public Health, "Ward Health Profile, Ward 8 York West, Part 1: Health Status and Public Health Services" (Toronto: June 2013).

"Towards An Engaged University: President's Task Force Report on Community Engagement, Final Report and Recommendations" (Toronto: York University, February 5, 2010).

United Way of Greater Toronto and the Canadian Council on Social Development, *Poverty By Postal Code: The Geography of Neighbourhood Poverty, 1981–2001* (Toronto: April 2004).

Van Amelsfort, Lorna, "Raised 5 Sons, Now 'Ma' to Hundreds" (*Jane Echo*, May 28, 1983).

Venesha, Fatema, "Reclaiming What Education Means to Youth: Findings from Participatory Action Research for the Jane/Finch Collaborative on Education to Employment—People for Education Conference" (Toronto: Skills for Change, November 2, 2019).

Verster, Phil letter to Councillor Perruzza (August 6, 2020).

Vyhnak, Carola, "The 1992 Riot that Served as a Wake-Up Call for Police" (*Toronto Star*, May 19, 2017).

Welsh, Moira, " 'Working Poor' Stage Protest" (*Toronto Star*, June 13, 1993).

"What a Way to Live Happily" (*Jane Echo*, May 15, 1980).

Winsa, Patty and Jim Rankin, "TAVIS Police Unit in Eye of the Storm" (*Toronto Star*, September 27, 2013).

Yang, J., K. Allen, R. Mendleson and A. Bailey, "Toronto's COVID-19 Divide: The City's Northwest Corner Has Been 'Failed by the System', " (*Toronto Star*, June 28, 2020).

Yip, Timothy B. and Lena Pizzardi, *DWAC Statistics, A Student Community Service Program* (Toronto: Downsview-Weston Action Community, 1975).

"York Finch Hospital Welcomes New Administrator" (*Jane Echo*, Sep. 1982).